DEMOCRACY IN AMERICA.

BY

ALEXIS DE TOCQUEVILLE.

TRANSLATED BY

HENRY REEVE, Esq.

EDITED, WITH NOTES,

THE TRANSLATION REVISED AND IN GREAT PART REWRITTEN, AND THE ADDITIONS MADE TO THE RECENT PARIS EDITIONS NOW FIRST TRANSLATED,

By FRANCIS BOWEN,

ALFORD PROFESSOR OF MORAL PHILOSOPHY IN HARVARD UNIVERSITY.

VOL. II.

FOURTH EDITION.

CAMBRIDGE:
SEVER AND FRANCIS.
1864.

UNIVERSITY PRESS:
WELCH, BIGELOW, AND COMPANY,
CAMBRIDGE.

ADVERTISEMENT

TO THE SECOND PART.

THE Americans have a democratic state of society, which has naturally suggested to them certain laws and certain political manners. It has also created in their minds many feelings and opinions which were unknown in the old aristocratic societies of Europe. It has destroyed or modified the old relations of men to each other, and has established new ones. The aspect of civil society has been as much altered as the face of the political world.

I have treated of the former subject in the work which I published, five years ago, upon American Democracy; the latter is the object of the present book. These two Parts complete each other, and form but a single work.

But I must warn the reader immediately against an error which would be very prejudicial to me. Because I attribute so many different effects to the principle of equality, it might be inferred that I consider this principle as the only cause of everything that takes place in our day. This would be attributing to me a very narrow view of things.

A multitude of the opinions, sentiments, and instincts which belong to our times owe their origin to circumstances which have nothing to do with the principle of equality, or are even hostile to it. Thus, taking the United States for example, I could easily prove that the nature of the country, the origin of its inhabitants, the religion of the early settlers, their acquired knowledge, their previous habits, have exercised, and still do exercise, independently of democracy, an immense influence upon their modes of thought and feeling. Other causes, equally independent of the principle of equality, would be found in Europe, and would explain much of what is passing there.

I recognize the existence and the efficiency of all these various causes; but my subject does not lead me to speak of them. I have not undertaken to point out the origin and nature of all our inclinations and all our ideas; I have only endeavored to show how far both of them are affected by the equality of men's conditions.

As I am firmly convinced that the democratic revolution which we are now beholding is an irresistible fact, against which it would be neither desirable nor prudent to contend, some persons perhaps may be surprised that, in the course of this book, I have often applied language of strong censure to the democratic communities which this revolution has created. The simple reason is, that precisely because I was not an opponent of democracy, I wished to speak of it with all sincerity. Men will not receive the truth from their enemies, and it is very seldom offered to them by their friends; on this very account, I have frankly uttered it. I believed that many persons would take it upon themselves to inform men of the benefits which they might hope to receive from the establishment of equality, whilst very few would venture to point out from afar the dangers with which it would be attended. It is principally towards these dangers, therefore, that I directed my gaze; and, believing that I had clearly discerned what they are, it would have been cowardice to say nothing about them.

I hope the same impartiality will be found in this second work which people seemed to observe in its predecessor. Placed between the conflicting opinions which divide my countrymen, I have endeavored for the time to stifle in my own bosom the sympathy or the aversion that I felt for either. If the readers of my book find in it a single phrase intended to flatter either of the great parties which have agitated our country, or any one of the petty factions which in our day harass and weaken it, let them raise their voices and accuse me.

The subject which I wished to cover by my investigations is immense; for it includes most of the feelings and opinions produced by the new condition of the world's affairs. Such a subject certainly exceeds my strength, and in the treatment of it I have not been able to satisfy myself. But though I could not reach the object at which I aimed, my readers will at least do me the justice to believe, that I conceived and followed out the undertaking in a spirit which rendered me worthy of success.

CONTENTS OF VOL. II.

FIRST BOOK.

INFLUENCE OF DEMOCRACY UPON THE ACTION OF INTELLECT IN THE UNITED STATES.

CHAPTER XX.

CHAPTER XXI.

SECOND BOOK.

INFLUENCE OF DEMOCRACY ON THE FEELINGS OF THE AMERICANS.

CHAPTER I.

CHAPTER II.

CHAPTER III.

CHAPTER IV.

CHAPTER V.

CHAPTER VI.

CHAPTER VII.

CHAPTER VIII.

THIRD BOOK.

INFLUENCE OF DEMOCRACY ON MANNERS PROPERLY SO CALLED.

CHAPTER IX.

CHAPTER X.

CHAPTER XI.

CHAPTER XII.

CHAPTER XIII.

CHAPTER XIV.

CHAPTER XV.

CHAPTER XVI.

CHAPTER XVII.

CHAPTER XVIII.

CHAPTER XIX.

CHAPTER XX.

CHAPTER XXI.

CHAPTER XXII.

CHAPTER XXIII.

CHAPTER XXIV.

CHAPTER XXV.

CHAPTER XXVI.

FOURTH BOOK.

INFLUENCE OF DEMOCRATIC IDEAS AND FEELINGS ON POLITICAL SOCIETY.

CHAPTER I.

CHAPTER II.

CHAPTER III.

CHAPTER IV.

CHAPTER V.

CHAPTER VI.

CHAPTER VII.

CHAPTER VIII.

DEMOCRACY IN AMERICA.

SECOND PART.

FIRST BOOK.

INFLUENCE OF DEMOCRACY UPON THE ACTION OF INTELLECT IN THE UNITED STATES.

CHAPTER I.

PHILOSOPHICAL METHOD OF THE AMERICANS.

I THINK that in no country in the civilized world is less attention paid to philosophy than in the United States. The Americans have no philosophical school of their own; and they care but little for all the schools into which Europe is divided, the very names of which are scarcely known to them.

Yet it is easy to perceive that almost all the inhabitants of the United States conduct their understanding in the same manner, and govern it by the same rules; that is to say, without ever having taken the trouble to define the rules, they have a philosophical method common to the whole people.

To evade the bondage of system and habit, of family-maxims, class-opinions, and, in some degree, of national prejudices; to accept tradition only as a means of information, and existing facts only as a lesson to be used in doing otherwise and doing better; to seek the reason of things for one's self, and in one's self alone; to tend to results without being bound to means, and to aim at the substance through the form; — such are the principal characteristics of what I shall call the philosophical method of the Americans.

But if I go further, and seek amongst these characteristics the principal one which includes almost all the rest, I discover that, in most of the operations of mind, each American appeals only to the individual effort of his own understanding.

America is therefore one of the countries where the precepts of Descartes are least studied, and are best applied. Nor is this surprising. The Americans do not read the works of Descartes, because their social condition deters them from speculative studies; but they follow his maxims, because this same social condition naturally disposes their minds to adopt them.

In the midst of the continual movement which agitates a democratic community, the tie which unites one generation to another is relaxed or broken; every man there readily loses all trace of the ideas of his forefathers, or takes no care about them.

Men living in this state of society cannot derive their belief from the opinions of the class to which they belong; for, so to speak, there are no longer any classes, or those which still exist are composed of such mobile elements, that the body can never exercise any real control over its members.

As to the influence which the intellect of one man may have on that of another, it must necessarily be very limited in a country where the citizens, placed on an equal footing, are all closely seen by each other; and where, as no signs of incontestable greatness or superiority are perceived in any one of them, they are constantly brought back to their own reason as the most obvious and proximate source of truth. It is not only confidence in this or that man which is destroyed, but the disposition for trusting the authority of any man whatsoever. Every one shuts himself up in his own breast, and affects from that point to judge the world.

The practice which obtains amongst the Americans, of fixing the standard of their judgment in themselves alone, leads them to other habits of mind. As they perceive that they succeed in resolving without assistance all the little difficulties which their practical life presents, they readily conclude that everything in the world may be explained, and that nothing in it transcends the limits of the understanding. Thus they fall to denying what they cannot comprehend; which leaves them but little faith for whatever is extraordinary, and an almost insurmountable distaste for whatever is supernatural. As it is on their own testimony that they are accustomed to rely, they like to discern the object which engages their attention with extreme clearness; they therefore strip off as much as possible all that covers it, they rid themselves of whatever separates them from it, they remove whatever conceals it from sight, in order to view it more closely and in the broad light of day. This disposition of mind soon leads them to contemn forms, which they regard as useless and inconvenient veils placed between them and the truth.

The Americans, then, have not required to extract their philosophical method from books; they have found it in themselves. The same thing may be remarked in what has taken place in Europe. This same method has only been established and made popular in Europe in proportion as the condition of society has become more equal, and men have grown more like each other. Let us consider for a moment the connection of the periods in which this change may be traced.

In the sixteenth century, the Reformers subjected some of the dogmas of the ancient faith to the scrutiny of private judgment; but they still withheld from it the discussion of all the rest. In the seventeenth century, Bacon in the natural sciences, and Descartes in philosophy properly so called, abolished received formulas, destroyed the empire of tradition, and overthrew the authority of the schools. The philosophers of the eighteenth century, generalizing at length the same principle, undertook to submit to the private judgment of each man all the objects of his belief.

Who does not perceive that Luther, Descartes, and Voltaire employed the same method, and that they differed only in the greater or less use which they professed should be made of it? Why did the Reformers confine themselves so closely within the circle of religious ideas? Why did Descartes, choosing only to apply his method to certain matters, though he had made it fit to be applied to all, declare that men might judge for themselves in matters philosophical, but not in matters political? How happened it that, in the eighteenth century, those general applications were all at once drawn from this same method, which Descartes and his predecessors had either not perceived or had rejected? To what, lastly, is the fact to be attributed, that at this period the method we are speaking of suddenly emerged from the schools, to penetrate into society and become the common standard of intelligence; and that, after it had become popular among the French, it has been ostensibly adopted or secretly followed by all the nations of Europe?

The philosophical method here designated may have been born in the sixteenth century, — it may have been more accurately defined and more extensively applied in the seventeenth; but neither in the one nor in the other could it be commonly adopted. Political laws, the condition of society, and the habits of mind which are derived from these causes, were as yet opposed to it.

It was discovered at a time when men were beginning to equalize and assimilate their conditions. It could only be generally followed in ages when those conditions had at length become nearly equal, and men nearly alike.

The philosophical method of the eighteenth century is, then, not only French, but it is democratic; and this explains why it was so readily admitted throughout Europe, where it has contributed so powerfully to change the face of society. It is not because the French have changed their former opinions, and altered their former manners, that they have convulsed the world; but because they were the first to generalize and bring to light a philosophical method, by the aid of which it became easy to attack all that was old, and to open a path to all that was new.

If it be asked why, at the present day, this same method is more rigorously followed and more frequently applied by the French than by the Americans, although the principle of equality is no less complete and of more ancient date amongst the latter people, the fact may be attributed to two circumstances, which it is first essential to have clearly understood.

It must never be forgotten that religion gave birth to Anglo-American society. In the United States, religion is therefore mingled with all the habits of the nation and all the feelings of patriotism, whence it derives a peculiar force. To this reason another of no less power may be added: in America, religion has, as it were, laid down its own limits. Religious institutions have remained wholly distinct from political institutions, so that former laws have been easily changed whilst former belief has remained unshaken. Christianity has therefore retained a strong hold on the public mind in America; and I would more particularly remark, that its sway is not only that of a philosophical doctrine which has been adopted upon inquiry, but of a religion which is believed without discussion. In the United States, Christian sects are infinitely diversified and perpetually modified; but Christianity itself is an established and irresistible fact, which no one undertakes either to attack or to defend. The Americans, having admitted the principal doctrines of the Christian religion without inquiry, are obliged to accept in like manner a great number of moral truths originating in it and connected with it. Hence the activity of individual analysis is restrained within narrow limits, and many of the most important of human opinions are removed from its influence.

The second circumstance to which I have alluded is, that the social condition and the constitution of the Americans are democratic, but they have not had a democratic revolution. They arrived upon the soil they occupy in nearly the condition in which we see them at the present day; and this is of considerable importance.

There are no revolutions which do not shake existing belief, enervate authority, and throw doubts over commonly received ideas. The effect of all revolutions is, therefore, more or less, to surrender men to their own guidance, and to open to the mind of every man a void and almost unlimited range of speculation. When equality of conditions succeeds a protracted conflict between the different classes of which the elder society was composed, envy, hatred, and uncharitableness, pride and exaggerated self-confidence, seize upon the human heart, and plant their sway in it for a time. This, independently of equality itself, tends powerfully to divide men, — to lead them to mistrust the judgment of each other, and to seek the light of truth nowhere but in themselves. Every one then attempts to be his own sufficient guide, and makes it his boast to form his own opinions on all subjects. Men are no longer bound together by ideas, but by interests; and it would seem as if human opinions were reduced to a sort of intellectual dust, scattered on every side, unable to collect, unable to cohere.

Thus, that independence of mind which equality supposes to exist is never so great, never appears so excessive, as at the time when equality is beginning to establish itself, and in the course of that painful labor by which it is established. That sort of intellectual freedom which equality may give ought, therefore, to be very carefully distinguished from the anarchy which revolution brings. Each of these two things must be separately considered, in order not to conceive exaggerated hopes or fears of the future.

I believe that the men who will live under the new forms of society will make frequent use of their private judgment, but I am far from thinking that they will often abuse it. This is attributable to a cause of more general application to all democratic countries, and which, in the long run, must needs restrain in them the independence of individual speculation within fixed, and sometimes narrow, limits.

I shall proceed to point out this cause in the next chapter.

CHAPTER II.

OF THE PRINCIPAL SOURCE OF BELIEF AMONG DEMOCRATIC NATIONS.

AT different periods, dogmatical belief is more or less common. It arises in different ways, and it may change its object and its form; but under no circumstances will dogmatical belief cease to exist, or, in other words, men will never cease to entertain some opinions on trust, and without discussion. If every one undertook to form all his own opinions, and to seek for truth by isolated paths struck out by himself alone, it would follow that no considerable number of men would ever unite in any common belief.

But obviously without such common belief no society can prosper, — say, rather, no society can exist; for without ideas held in common, there is no common action, and without common action there may still be men, but there is no social body. In order that society should exist, and, *a fortiori*, that a society should prosper, it is required that all the minds of the citizens should be rallied and held together by certain predominant ideas; and this cannot be the case unless each of them sometimes draws his opinions from the common source, and consents to accept certain matters of belief already formed.

If I now consider man in his isolated capacity, I find that dogmatical belief is not less indispensable to him in order to live alone, than it is to enable him to co-operate with his fellows. If man were forced to demonstrate for himself all the truths of which he makes daily use, his task would never end. He would exhaust his strength in preparatory demonstrations, without ever advancing beyond them. As, from the shortness of his life, he has not the time, nor, from the limits of his intelligence, the capacity, to accomplish this, he is reduced to take upon trust a number of facts and opinions which he has not had either the time or the power to verify for himself, but which men of greater ability have sought out, or which the world adopts. On this groundwork he raises for himself the structure of his own thoughts; he is not led to proceed in this manner by choice, but is constrained by the inflexible law of his condition. There is no philosopher of so great parts in the world, but that he believes a million of things on the faith of other people, and supposes a great many more truths than he demonstrates.

This is not only necessary, but desirable. A man who should undertake to inquire into everything for himself, could devote to each thing but little time and attention. His task would keep his mind in perpetual unrest, which would prevent him from penetrating to the depth of any truth, or of grappling his mind firmly to any conviction. His intellect would be at once independent and powerless. He must therefore make his choice from amongst the various objects of human belief, and adopt many opinions without discussion, in order to search the better into that smaller number which he sets apart for investigation. It is true, that whoever receives an opinion on the word of another, does so far enslave his mind; but it is a salutary servitude which allows him to make a good use of freedom.

A principle of authority must then always occur, under all circumstances, in some part or other of the moral and intellectual world. Its place is variable, but a place it necessarily has. The independence of individual minds may be greater, or it may be less: unbounded it cannot be. Thus the question is, not to know whether any intellectual authority exists in the ages of democracy, but simply where it resides and by what standard it is to be measured.

I have shown in the preceding chapter how the equality of conditions leads men to entertain a sort of instinctive incredulity of the supernatural, and a very lofty and often exaggerated opinion of the human understanding. The men who live at a period of social equality are not therefore easily led to place that intellectual authority to which they bow either beyond or above humanity. They commonly seek for the sources of truth in themselves, or in those who are like themselves. This would be enough to prove that, at such periods, no new religion could be established, and that all schemes for such a purpose would be not only impious, but absurd and irrational. It may be foreseen that a democratic people will not easily give credence to divine missions; that they will laugh at modern prophets; and that they will seek to discover the chief arbiter of their belief within, and not beyond, the limits of their kind.

When the ranks of society are unequal, and men unlike each other in condition, there are some individuals wielding the power of superior intelligence, learning, and enlightenment, whilst the multitude are sunk in ignorance and prejudice. Men living at these aristocratic periods are therefore naturally induced to shape their opinions by the standard of a superior person, or superior class of persons, whilst they are averse to recognize the infallibility of the mass of the people.

The contrary takes place in ages of equality. The nearer the people are drawn to the common level of an equal and similar condition, the less prone does each man become to place implicit faith in a certain man or a certain class of men. But his readiness to believe the multitude increases, and opinion is more than ever mistress of the world. Not only is common opinion the only guide which private judgment retains amongst a democratic people, but amongst such a people it possesses a power infinitely beyond what it has elsewhere. At periods of equality, men have no faith in one another, by reason of their common resemblance; but this very resemblance gives them almost unbounded confidence in the judgment of the public; for it would not seem probable, as they are all endowed with equal means of judging, but that the greater truth should go with the greater number.

When the inhabitant of a democratic country compares himself individually with all those about him, he feels with pride that he is the equal of any one of them; but when he comes to survey the totality of his fellows, and to place himself in contrast with so huge a body, he is instantly overwhelmed by the sense of his own insignificance and weakness. The same equality which renders him independent of each of his fellow-citizens, taken severally, exposes him alone and unprotected to the influence of the greater number. The public has therefore, among a democratic people, a singular power, which aristocratic nations cannot conceive of; for it does not persuade to certain opinions, but it enforces them, and infuses them into the intellect by a sort of enormous pressure of the minds of all upon the reason of each.

In the United States, the majority undertakes to supply a multitude of ready-made opinions for the use of individuals, who are thus relieved from the necessity of forming opinions of their own. Everybody there adopts great numbers of theories, on philosophy, morals, and politics, without inquiry, upon public trust; and if we look to it very narrowly, it will be perceived that religion herself holds sway there much less as a doctrine of revelation than as a commonly received opinion.

The fact that the political laws of the Americans are such that the majority rules the community with sovereign sway, materially increases the power which that majority naturally exercises over the mind. For nothing is more customary in man than to recognize superior wisdom in the person of his oppressor. This political omnipotence of the majority in the United States doubtless augments the influence which public opinion would obtain without it over the minds of each member of the community; but the foundations of that influence do not rest upon it. They must be sought for in the principle of equality itself, not in the more or less popular institutions which men living under that condition may give themselves. The intellectual dominion of the greater number would probably be less absolute amongst a democratic people governed by a king, than in the sphere of a pure democracy, but it will always be extremely absolute; and by whatever political laws men are governed in the ages of equality, it may be foreseen that faith in public opinion will become a species of religion there, and the majority its ministering prophet.

Thus intellectual authority will be different, but it will not be diminished; and far from thinking that it will disappear, I augur that it may readily acquire too much preponderance, and confine the action of private judgment within narrower limits than are suited either to the greatness or the happiness of the human race. In the principle of equality I very clearly discern two tendencies; the one leading the mind of every man to untried thoughts, the other which would prohibit him from thinking at all. And I perceive how, under the dominion of certain laws, democracy would extinguish that liberty of the mind to which a democratic social condition is favorable; so that, after having broken all the bondage once imposed on it by ranks or by men, the human mind would be closely fettered to the general will of the greatest number.

If the absolute power of a majority were to be substituted, by democratic nations, for all the different powers which checked or retarded overmuch the energy of individual minds, the evil would only have changed character. Men would not have found the means of independent life; they would simply have discovered (no easy task) a new physiognomy of servitude. There is, — and I cannot repeat it too often, — there is here matter for profound reflection to those who look on freedom of thought as a holy thing, and who hate not only the despot, but despotism. For myself, when I feel the hand of power lie heavy on my brow, I care but little to know who oppresses me; and I am not the more disposed to pass beneath the yoke because it is held out to me by the arms of a million of men.

CHAPTER III.

WHY THE AMERICANS SHOW MORE APTITUDE AND TASTE FOR GENERAL IDEAS THAN THEIR FOREFATHERS, THE ENGLISH.

THE Deity does not regard the human race collectively. He surveys at one glance and severally all the beings of whom mankind is composed; and he discerns in each man the resemblances which assimilate him to all his fellows, and the differences which distinguish him from them. God, therefore, stands in no need of general ideas; that is to say, he never feels the necessity of collecting a considerable number of analogous objects under the same form for greater convenience in thinking.

Such is, however, not the case with man. If the human mind were to attempt to examine and pass a judgment on all the individual cases before it, the immensity of detail would soon lead it astray, and it would no longer see anything: in this strait, man has recourse to an imperfect but necessary expedient, which at once assists and demonstrates his weakness.

Having superficially considered a certain number of objects, and remarked their resemblance, he assigns to them a common name, sets them apart, and proceeds onwards.

General ideas are no proof of the strength, but rather of the insufficiency, of the human intellect; for there are in nature no beings exactly alike, no things precisely identical, nor any rules indiscriminately and alike applicable to several objects at once. The chief merit of general ideas is, that they enable the human mind to pass a rapid judgment on a great many objects at once; but, on the other hand, the notions they convey are never otherwise than incomplete, and they always cause the mind to lose as much in accuracy as it gains in comprehensiveness.

As social bodies advance in civilization, they acquire the knowledge of new facts, and they daily lay hold almost unconsciously of some particular truths. The more truths of this kind a man apprehends, the more general ideas is he naturally led to conceive. A multitude of particular facts cannot be seen separately without at last discovering the common tie which connects them. Several individuals lead to the notion of the species, several species to that of the genus. Hence the habit and the taste for general ideas will always be greatest amongst a people of ancient cultivation and extensive knowledge.

But there are other reasons which impel men to generalize their ideas, or which restrain them from it.

The Americans are much more addicted to the use of general ideas than the English, and entertain a much greater relish for them: this appears very singular at first, when it is remembered that the two nations have the same origin, that they lived for centuries under the same laws, and that they still incessantly interchange their opinions and their manners. This contrast becomes much more striking still, if we fix our eyes on our own part of the world, and compare together the two most enlightened nations which inhabit it. It would seem as if the mind of the English could only tear itself reluctantly and painfully away from the observation of particular facts, to rise from them to their causes, and that it only generalizes in spite of itself. Amongst the French, on the contrary, the taste for general ideas would seem to have grown to so ardent a passion that it must be satisfied on every occasion. I am informed every morning when I wake, that some general and eternal law has just been discovered which I never heard mentioned before. There is not a mediocre scribbler who does not try his hand at discovering truths applicable to a great kingdom, and who is not very ill pleased with himself if he does not succeed in compressing the human race into the compass of an article.

So great a dissimilarity between two very enlightened nations surprises me. If I again turn my attention to England, and observe the events which have occurred there in the last half-century, I think I may affirm that a taste for general ideas increases in that country in proportion as its ancient constitution is weakened.

The state of civilization is therefore insufficient by itself to explain what suggests to the human mind the love of general ideas, or diverts it from them.

When the conditions of men are very unequal, and the inequalities are permanent, individual men gradually become so dissimilar, that each class assumes the aspect of a distinct race: only one of these classes is ever in view at the same instant; and, losing sight of that general tie which binds them all within the vast bosom of mankind, the observation invariably rests, not on man, but on certain men. Those who live in this aristocratic state of society never, therefore, conceive very general ideas respecting themselves; and that is enough to imbue them with an habitual distrust of such ideas, and an instinctive aversion for them.

He, on the contrary, who inhabits a democratic country sees around him, on every hand, men differing but little from each other; he cannot turn his mind to any one portion of mankind, without expanding and dilating his thought till it embrace the whole. All the truths which are applicable to himself appear to him equally and similarly applicable to each of his fellow-citizens and fellow-men. Having contracted the habit of generalizing his ideas in the study which engages him most and interests him most, he transfers the same habit to all his pursuits;

and thus it is that the craving to discover general laws in everything, to include a great number of objects under the same formula, and to explain a mass of facts by a single cause, becomes an ardent, and sometimes an undiscerning, passion in the human mind.

Nothing shows the truth of this proposition more clearly than the opinions of the ancients respecting their slaves. The most profound and capacious minds of Rome and Greece were never able to reach the idea, at once so general and so simple, of the common likeness of men, and of the common birthright of each to freedom: they strove to prove that slavery was in the order of nature, and that it would always exist. Nay, more, everything shows that those of the ancients who had been slaves before they became free, many of whom have left us excellent writings, did themselves regard servitude in no other light.

All the great writers of antiquity belonged to the aristocracy of masters, or, at least, they saw that aristocracy established and uncontested before their eyes. Their mind, after it had expanded itself in several directions, was barred from further progress in this one; and the advent of Jesus Christ upon earth was required to teach that all the members of the human race are by nature equal and alike.

In the ages of equality, all men are independent of each other, isolated, and weak. The movements of the multitude are not permanently guided by the will of any individuals: at such times, humanity seems always to advance of itself. In order, therefore, to explain what is passing in the world, man is driven to seek for some great causes, which, acting in the same manner on all our fellow-creatures, thus induce them all voluntarily to pursue the same track. This again naturally leads the human mind to conceive general ideas, and superinduces a taste for them.

I have already shown in what way the equality of conditions leads every man to investigate truth for himself. It may readily be perceived that a method of this kind must insensibly beget a tendency to general ideas in the human mind. When I repudiate the traditions of rank, professions, and birth, when I escape from the authority of example, to seek out, by the single effort of my reason, the path to be followed, I am inclined to derive the motives of my opinions from human nature itself, which leads me necessarily, and almost unconsciously, to adopt a great number of very general notions.

All that I have here said explains why the English display much less aptitude and taste for the generalization of ideas than their American progeny, and still less again than their neighbors the French; and likewise why the English of the present day display more than their forefathers did.

The English have long been a very enlightened and a very aristocratic nation; their enlightened condition urged them constantly to generalize, and their aristocratic habits confined them to the particular. Hence arose that philosophy, at once bold and timid, broad and narrow, which has hitherto prevailed in England, and which still obstructs and stagnates so many minds in that country.

Independently of the causes I have pointed out in what goes before, others may be discerned less apparent, but no less efficacious, which produce amongst almost every democratic people a taste, and frequently a passion, for general ideas. A distinction must be taken between ideas of this kind. Some of them are the result of slow, minute, and conscientious labor of the mind, and these extend the sphere of human knowledge; others spring up at once from the first rapid exercise of the wits, and beget none but very superficial and uncertain notions.

Men who live in ages of equality have a great deal of curiosity and little leisure; their life is so practical, so confused, so excited, so active, that but little time remains to them for thought. Such men are prone to general ideas, because they spare them the trouble of studying particulars; they contain, if I may so speak, a great deal in a little compass, and give, in a little time, a great return. If, then, upon a brief and inattentive investigation, they think they discern a common relation between certain objects, inquiry is not pushed any further; and without examining in detail how far these several objects agree or differ, they are hastily arranged under one formulary, in order to pass to another subject.

One of the distinguishing characteristics of a democratic period is the taste which all men then have for easy success and present enjoyment. This occurs in the pursuits of the intellect as well as in all others. Most of those who live at a time of equality are full of an ambition at once aspiring and relaxed: they would fain succeed brilliantly and at once, but they would be dispensed from great efforts to obtain success. These conflicting tendencies lead straight to the research of general ideas, by aid of which they flatter themselves that they can delineate vast objects with little pains, and draw the attention of the public without much trouble.

And I know not that they are wrong in thinking thus. For their readers are as much averse to investigating anything to the bottom as they are; and what is generally sought in the productions of mind is easy pleasure and information without labor.

If aristocratic nations do not make sufficient use of general ideas, and frequently treat them with inconsiderate disdain, it is true, on the other hand, that a democratic people is ever ready to carry ideas of this kind to excess, and to espouse them with injudicious warmth.

CHAPTER IV.

WHY THE AMERICANS HAVE NEVER BEEN SO EAGER AS THE FRENCH FOR GENERAL IDEAS IN POLITICAL AFFAIRS.

I HAVE observed that the Americans show a less decided taste for general ideas than the French. This is more especially true in politics.

Although the Americans infuse into their legislation far more general ideas than the English, and although they strive more than the latter to adjust the practice of affairs to theory, no political bodies in the United States have ever shown so much love for general ideas as the Constituent Assembly and the Convention in France. At no time has the American people laid hold on ideas of this kind with the passionate energy of the French people in the eighteenth century, or displayed the same blind confidence in the value and absolute truth of any theory.

This difference between the Americans and the French originates in several causes, but principally in the following one. The Americans form a democratic people, who have always directed public affairs themselves. The French are a democratic people, who, for a long time, could only speculate on the best manner of conducting them. The social condition of the French led them to conceive very general ideas on the subject of government, whilst their political constitution prevented them from correcting those ideas by experiment, and from gradually detecting their insufficiency; whereas, in America, the two things constantly balance and correct each other.

It may seem, at first sight, that this is very much opposed to what I have said before, that democratic nations derive their love of theory from the very excitement of their active life. A more attentive examination will show that there is nothing contradictory in the proposition.

Men living in democratic countries eagerly lay hold of general ideas, because they have but little leisure, and because these ideas spare them the trouble of studying particulars. This is true; but it is only to be understood of those matters which are not the necessary and habitual subjects of their thoughts. Mercantile men will take up very eagerly, and without any close scrutiny, all the general ideas on philosophy, politics, science, or the arts, which may be presented to them; but for such as relate to commerce, they will not receive them without inquiry, or adopt them without reserve. The same thing applies to statesmen with regard to general ideas in politics.

If, then, there be a subject upon which a democratic people is peculiarly liable to abandon itself, blindly and extravagantly, to general ideas, the best corrective that can be used will be to make that subject a part of their daily practical occupation. They will then be compelled to enter upon details, and the details will teach them the weak points of the theory. This remedy may frequently be a painful one, but its effect is certain.

Thus it happens, that the democratic institutions which compel every citizen to take a practical part in the government moderate that excessive taste for general theories in politics which the principle of equality suggests.

CHAPTER V.

HOW RELIGION IN THE UNITED STATES AVAILS ITSELF OF DEMOCRATIC TENDENCIES.

I HAVE shown, in a preceding chapter, that men cannot do without dogmatical belief; and even that it is much to be desired that such belief should exist amongst them. I now add, that, of all the kinds of dogmatical belief, the most desirable appears to me to be dogmatical belief in matters of religion; and this is a clear inference, even from no higher consideration than the interests of this world.

There is hardly any human action, however particular it may be, which does not originate in some very general idea men have conceived of the Deity, of his relation to mankind, of the nature of their own souls, and of their duties to their fellow-creatures. Nor can anything prevent these ideas from being the common spring whence all the rest emanates.

Men are therefore immeasurably interested in acquiring fixed ideas of God, of the soul, and of their general duties to their Creator and their fellow-men; for doubt on these first principles would abandon all their actions to chance, and would condemn them in some way to disorder and impotence.

This is, then, the subject on which it is most important for each of us to have fixed ideas; and unhappily it is also the subject on which it is most difficult for each of us, left to himself, to settle his opinions by the sole force of his reason. None but minds singularly free from the ordinary cares of life — minds at once penetrating, subtile, and trained by thinking — can, even with much time and care, sound the depths of these so necessary truths. And, indeed, we see that philosophers are themselves almost always surrounded with uncertainties; that at every step the natural light which illuminates their path grows dimmer and less secure; and that, in spite of all their efforts, they have as yet only discovered a few conflicting notions, on which the mind of man has been tossed about for thousands of years, without ever firmly grasping the truth, or finding novelty even in its errors. Studies of this nature are far above the average capacity of men; and, even if the majority of mankind were capable of such pursuits, it is evident that leisure to cultivate them would still be wanting.

Fixed ideas about God and human nature are indispensable to the daily practice of men's lives; but the practice of their lives prevents them from acquiring such ideas.

The difficulty appears to be without a parallel. Amongst the sciences, there are some which are useful to the mass of mankind, and are within its reach; others can be approached only by the few, and are not cultivated by the many, who require nothing beyond their more remote applications: but the daily practice of the science I speak of is indispensable to all, although the study of it is inaccessible to the greater number.

General ideas respecting God and human nature are therefore the ideas above all others which it is most suitable to withdraw from the habitual action of private judgment, and in which there is most to gain and least to lose by recognizing a principle of authority.

The first object, and one of the principal advantages, of religion is to furnish to each of these fundamental questions a solution which is at once clear, precise, intelligible to the mass of mankind, and lasting. There are religions which are false and very absurd; but it may be affirmed that any religion which remains within the circle I have just traced, without pretending to go beyond it, (as many religions have attempted to do, for the purpose of restraining on every side the free movement of the human mind,) imposes a salutary restraint on the intellect; and it must be admitted that, if it do not save men in another world, it is at least very conducive to their happiness and their greatness in this.

This is more especially true of men living in free countries. When the religion of a people is destroyed, doubt gets hold of the higher powers of the intellect, and half paralyzes all the others. Every man accustoms himself to have only confused and changing notions on the subjects most interesting to his fellow-creatures and himself. His opinions are ill-defended and easily abandoned; and, in despair of ever resolving by himself the hard problems respecting the destiny of man, he ignobly submits to think no more about them.

Such a condition cannot but enervate the soul, relax the springs of the will, and prepare a people for servitude. Not only does it happen, in such a case, that they allow their freedom to be taken from them; they frequently themselves surrender it. When there is no longer any principle of authority in religion, any more than in politics, men are speedily frightened at the aspect of this unbounded independence. The constant agitation of all surrounding things alarms and exhausts them. As everything is at sea in the sphere of the mind, they determine at least that the mechanism of society shall be firm and fixed; and, as they cannot resume their ancient belief, they assume a master.

For my own part, I doubt whether man can ever support at the same time complete religious independence and entire political freedom. And I am inclined to think that, if faith be wanting in him, he must be subject; and if he be free, he must believe.

Perhaps, however, this great utility of religions is still

more obvious amongst nations where equality of conditions prevails, than amongst others. It must be acknowledged that equality, which brings great benefits into the world, nevertheless suggests to men (as will be shown hereafter) some very dangerous propensities. It tends to isolate them from each other, to concentrate every man's attention upon himself; and it lays open the soul to an inordinate love of material gratification.

The greatest advantage of religion is to inspire diametrically contrary principles. There is no religion which does not place the object of man's desires above and beyond the treasures of earth, and which does not naturally raise his soul to regions far above those of the senses. Nor is there any which does not impose on man some duties toward his kind, and thus draw him at times from the contemplation of himself. This occurs in religions the most false and dangerous.

Religious nations are therefore naturally strong on the very point on which democratic nations are weak, which shows of what importance it is for men to preserve their religion as their conditions become more equal.

I have neither the right nor the intention of examining the supernatural means which God employs to infuse religious belief into the heart of man. I am at this moment considering religions in a purely human point of view; my object is to inquire by what means they may most easily retain their sway in the democratic ages upon which we are entering.

It has been shown that, at times of general cultivation and equality, the human mind consents only with reluctance to adopt dogmatical opinions, and feels their necessity acutely only in spiritual matters. This proves, in the first place, that, at such times, religions ought, more cautiously than at any other, to confine themselves within their own precincts; for in seeking to extend their power beyond religious matters, they incur a risk of not being believed at all. The circle within which they seek to restrict the human intellect ought therefore to be carefully traced, and, beyond its verge, the mind should be left entirely free to its own guidance.

Mohammed professed to derive from Heaven, and has inserted in the Koran, not only religious doctrines, but political maxims, civil and criminal laws, and theories of science. The Gospel, on the contrary, only speaks of the general relations of men to God and to each other, beyond which it inculcates and imposes no point of faith. This alone, besides a thousand other reasons, would suffice to prove that the former of these religions will never long predominate in a cultivated and democratic age, whilst the latter is destined to retain its sway at these as at all other periods.

In continuation of this same inquiry, I find that, for religions to maintain their authority, humanly speaking, in democratic ages, not only must they confine themselves strictly within the circle of spiritual matters, but their power also will depend very much on the nature of the belief they inculcate, on the external forms they assume, and on the obligations they impose.

The preceding observation, that equality leads men to very general and very vast ideas, is principally to be understood in respect to religion. Men who are similar and equal in the world readily conceive the idea of the one God, governing every man by the same laws, and granting to every man future happiness on the same conditions. The idea of the unity of mankind constantly leads them back to the idea of the unity of the Creator; whilst, on the contrary, in a state of society where men are broken up into very unequal ranks, they are apt to devise as many deities as there are nations, castes, classes, or families, and to trace a thousand private roads to Heaven.

It cannot be denied that Christianity itself has felt, to

some extent, the influence which social and political conditions exercise on religious opinions.

When the Christian religion first appeared upon earth, Providence, by whom the world was doubtless prepared for its coming, had gathered a large portion of the human race, like an immense flock, under the sceptre of the Cæsars. The men of whom this multitude was composed were distinguished by numerous differences; but they had thus much in common, that they all obeyed the same laws, and that every subject was so weak and insignificant in respect to the Emperor, that all appeared equal when their condition was contrasted with his. This novel and peculiar state of mankind necessarily predisposed men to listen to the general truths which Christianity teaches, and may serve to explain the facility and rapidity with which they then penetrated into the human mind.

The counterpart of this state of things was exhibited after the destruction of the Empire. The Roman World, being then, as it were, shattered into a thousand fragments, each nation resumed its former individuality. A scale of ranks soon grew up in the bosom of these nations; the different races were more sharply defined, and each nation was divided by castes into several peoples. In the midst of this common effort, which seemed to be dividing human society into as many fragments as possible, Christianity did not lose sight of the leading general ideas which it had brought into the world. But it appeared, nevertheless, to lend itself as much as possible to the new tendencies created by this distribution of mankind into fractions. Men continue to worship one God, the Creator and Preserver of all things; but every people, every city, and, so to speak, every man, thought to obtain some distinct privilege, and win the favor of an especial protector near the throne of Grace. Unable to subdivide the Deity, they multiplied and unduly enhanced the importance of his agents. The homage due to saints and angels became an almost idolatrous worship for most Christians; and it might be feared for a moment that the religion of Christ would retrograde towards the superstitions which it had overcome.

It seems evident, that, the more the barriers are removed which separate one nation from another and one citizen from another, the stronger is the bent of the human mind, as if by its own impulse, towards the idea of a single and all-powerful Being, dispensing equal laws in the same manner to every man. In democratic ages, then, it is more particularly important not to allow the homage paid to secondary agents to be confounded with the worship due to the Creator alone.

Another truth is no less clear, — that religions ought to have fewer external observances in democratic periods than at any others.

In speaking of philosophical method among the Americans, I have shown that nothing is more repugnant to the human mind, in an age of equality, than the idea of subjection to forms. Men living at such times are impatient of figures; to their eyes, symbols appear to be puerile artifices used to conceal or to set off truths which should more naturally be bared to the light of day: they are unmoved by ceremonial observances, and are disposed to attach only a secondary importance to the details of public worship.

Those who have to regulate the external forms of religion in a democratic age should pay a close attention to these natural propensities of the human mind, in order not to run counter to them unnecessarily.

I firmly believe in the necessity of forms, which fix the human mind in the contemplation of abstract truths, and aid it in embracing them warmly and holding them with firmness. Nor do I suppose that it is possible to maintain a religion without external observances; but, on the other hand, I am persuaded that, in the ages upon which we are entering, it would be peculiarly dangerous to multiply them beyond measure; and that they ought rather to be limited to as much as is absolutely necessary to perpetuate the doctrine itself, which is the substance of religion, of which the ritual is only the form.* A religion which should become more minute, more peremptory, and more charged with small observances, at a time when men are becoming more equal, would soon find itself reduced to a band of fanatical zealots in the midst of an infidel people.

I anticipate the objection that, as all religions have general and eternal truths for their object, they cannot thus shape themselves to the shifting inclinations of every age, without forfeiting their claim to certainty in the eyes of mankind. To this I reply again, that the principal opinions which constitute a creed, and which theologians call articles of faith, must be very carefully distinguished from the accessories connected with them. Religions are obliged to hold fast to the former, whatever be the peculiar spirit of the age; but they should take good care not to bind themselves in the same manner to the latter, at a time when everything is in transition, and when the mind, accustomed to the moving pageant of human affairs, reluctantly allows itself to be fixed on any point. The fixity of eternal and secondary things can afford a chance of duration only when civil society is itself fixed; under any other circumstances, I hold it to be perilous.

We shall see that, of all the passions which originate in or are fostered by equality, there is one which it renders peculiarly intense, and which it also infuses into the heart

* In all religions, there are some ceremonies which are inherent in the substance of the faith itself, and in these nothing should on any account be changed. This is especially the case with Roman Catholicism, in which the doctrine and the form are frequently so closely united as to form but one point of belief.

of every man, — I mean the love of well-being. The taste for well-being is the prominent and indelible feature of democratic times.

It may be believed that a religion which should undertake to destroy so deep-seated a passion, would in the end be destroyed by it; and if it attempted to wean men entirely from the contemplation of the good things of this world, in order to devote their faculties exclusively to the thought of another, it may be foreseen that the minds of men would at length escape its grasp, to plunge into the exclusive enjoyment of present and material pleasures.

The chief concern of religion is to purify, to regulate, and to restrain the excessive and exclusive taste for well-being which men feel at periods of equality; but it would be an error to attempt to overcome it completely, or to eradicate it. Men cannot be cured of the love of riches; but they may be persuaded to enrich themselves by none but honest means.

This brings me to a final consideration, which comprises, as it were, all the others. The more the conditions of men are equalized and assimilated to each other, the more important is it for religion; whilst it carefully abstains from the daily turmoil of secular affairs, not needlessly to run counter to the ideas which generally prevail, or to the permanent interests which exist in the mass of the people. For, as public opinion grows to be more and more the first and most irresistible of existing powers, the religious principle has no external support strong enough to enable it long to resist its attacks. This is not less true of a democratic people ruled by a despot, than of a republic. In ages of equality kings may often command obedience, but the majority always commands belief: to the majority, therefore, deference is to be paid in whatsoever is not contrary to the faith.

I showed in my former volume how the American clergy

stand aloof from secular affairs. This is the most obvious, but not the only, example of their self-restraint. In America, religion is a distinct sphere, in which the priest is sovereign, but out of which he takes care never to go. Within its limits, he is master of the mind; beyond them, he leaves men to themselves, and surrenders them to the independence and instability which belong to their nature and their age. I have seen no country in which Christianity is clothed with fewer forms, figures, and observances than in the United States; or where it presents more distinct, simple, and general notions to the mind. Although the Christians of America are divided into a multitude of sects, they all look upon their religion in the same light. This applies to Roman Catholicism as well as to the other forms of belief. There are no Romish priests who show less taste for the minute individual observances, for extraordinary or peculiar means of salvation, or who cling more to the spirit, and less to the letter, of the law, than the Roman Catholic priests of the United States. Nowhere is that doctrine of the Church which prohibits the worship reserved to God alone from being offered to the saints, more clearly inculcated or more generally followed. Yet the Roman Catholics of America are very submissive and very sincere.

Another remark is applicable to the clergy of every communion. The American ministers of the Gospel do not attempt to draw or to fix all the thoughts of man upon the life to come; they are willing to surrender a portion of his heart to the cares of the present; seeming to consider the goods of this world as important, though secondary, objects. If they take no part themselves in productive labor, they are at least interested in its progress, and they applaud its results; and whilst they never cease to point to the other world as the great object of the hopes and fears of the believer, they do not forbid him honestly to court prosperity in this. Far from attempting to show that these things are distinct and contrary to one another, they study rather to find out on what point they are most nearly and closely connected.

All the American clergy know and respect the intellectual supremacy exercised by the majority: they never sustain any but necessary conflicts with it. They take no share in the altercations of parties, but they readily adopt the general opinions of their country and their age: and they allow themselves to be borne away without opposition in the current of feeling and opinion by which everything around them is carried along. They endeavor to amend their contemporaries, but they do not quit fellowship with them. Public opinion is therefore never hostile to them: it rather supports and protects them; and their belief owes its authority at the same time to the strength which is its own, and to that which it borrows from the opinions of the majority.

Thus it is, that, by respecting all democratic tendencies not absolutely contrary to herself, and by making use of several of them for her own purposes, Religion sustains a successful struggle with that spirit of individual independence which is her most dangerous opponent.

CHAPTER VI.

THE PROGRESS OF ROMAN CATHOLICISM IN THE UNITED STATES.

AMERICA is the most democratic country in the world, and it is at the same time (according to reports worthy of belief) the country in which the Roman Catholic religion makes most progress. At first sight, this is surprising.

Two things must here be accurately distinguished: equality inclines men to wish to form their own opinions; but, on the other hand, it imbues them with the taste and the idea of unity, simplicity, and impartiality in the power which governs society. Men living in democratic times are therefore very prone to shake off all religious authority; but if they consent to subject themselves to any authority of this kind, they choose at least that it should be single and uniform. Religious powers not radiating from a common centre are naturally repugnant to their minds; and they almost as readily conceive that there should be no religion, as that there should be several.

At the present time, more than in any preceding age, Roman Catholics are seen to lapse into infidelity, and Protestants to be converted to Roman Catholicism. If the Roman Catholic faith be considered within the pale of the Church, it would seem to be losing ground; without that pale, to be gaining it. Nor is this difficult of explanation. The men of our days are naturally little disposed to believe; but, as soon as they have any religion, they immediately find in themselves a latent instinct which urges them unconsciously towards Catholicism. Many of the doctrines and practices of the Romish Church astonish them; but they feel a secret admiration for its discipline, and its great unity attracts them. If Catholicism could at length withdraw itself from the political animosities to which it has given rise, I have hardly any doubt but that the same spirit of the age which appears to be so opposed to it would become so favorable as to admit of its great and sudden advancement.

One of the most ordinary weaknesses of the human intellect is to seek to reconcile contrary principles, and to purchase peace at the expense of logic. Thus there have ever been, and will ever be, men who, after having submitted some portion of their religious belief to the principle of authority, will seek to exempt several other parts of their faith from it, and to keep their minds floating at random between liberty and obedience. But I am inclined to believe that the number of these thinkers will be less in democratic than in other ages; and that our posterity will tend more and more to a division into only two parts, — some relinquishing Christianity entirely, and others returning to the Church of Rome.

CHAPTER VII.

WHAT CAUSES DEMOCRATIC NATIONS TO INCLINE TOWARDS PANTHEISM.

I SHALL show hereafter how the preponderating taste of a democratic people for very general ideas manifests itself in politics; but I wish to point out, at present, its principal effect on philosophy.

It cannot be denied that pantheism has made great progress in our age. The writings of a part of Europe bear visible marks of it: the Germans introduce it into philosophy, and the French into literature. Most of the works of imagination published in France contain some opinions or some tinge caught from pantheistical doctrines, or they disclose some tendency to such doctrines in their authors. This appears to me not to proceed only from an accidental, but from a permanent cause.

When the conditions of society are becoming more equal, and each individual man becomes more like all the rest, more weak and insignificant, a habit grows up of ceasing to notice the citizens, and considering only the people, — of overlooking individuals, to think only of their kind. At such times, the human mind seeks to embrace a multitude of different objects at once; and it constantly strives to connect a variety of consequences with a single cause. The idea of unity so possesses man, and is sought by him so generally, that, if he thinks he has found it, he readily yields himself to repose in that belief. Not content with the discovery that there is nothing in the world but a creation and a Creator, he is still embarrassed by this primary division of things, and seeks to expand and simplify his conception by including God and the Universe in one great Whole.

If there be a philosophical system which teaches that all things material and immaterial, visible and invisible, which the world contains, are to be considered only as the several parts of an immense Being, who alone remains eternal amidst the continual change and ceaseless transformation of all that constitutes him, we may readily infer that such a system, although it destroy the individuality of man, — nay, rather because it destroys that individuality, — will have secret charms for men living in democracies. All their habits of thought prepare them to conceive it, and predispose them to adopt it. It naturally attracts and fixes their imagination ; it fosters the pride, whilst it soothes the indolence, of their minds.

Amongst the different systems by whose aid Philosophy endeavors to explain the Universe, I believe pantheism to be one of those most fitted to seduce the human mind in democratic times. Against it, all who abide in their attachment to the true greatness of man should combine and struggle.

CHAPTER VIII.

HOW EQUALITY SUGGESTS TO THE AMERICANS THE IDEA OF THE INDEFINITE PERFECTIBILITY OF MAN.

EQUALITY suggests to the human mind several ideas which would not have originated from any other source, and it modifies almost all those previously entertained. I take as an example the idea of human perfectibility, because it is one of the principal notions that the intellect can conceive, and because it constitutes of itself a great philosophical theory, which is everywhere to be traced by its consequences in the conduct of human affairs.

Although man has many points of resemblance with the brutes, one trait is peculiar to himself, — he improves: they are incapable of improvement. Mankind could not fail to discover this difference from the beginning. The idea of perfectibility is therefore as old as the world; equality did not give birth to it, but has imparted to it a new character.

When the citizens of a community are classed according to rank, profession, or birth, and when all men are constrained to follow the career which chance has opened before them, every one thinks that the utmost limits of human power are to be discerned in proximity to himself, and no one seeks any longer to resist the inevitable law of his destiny. Not, indeed, that an aristocratic people absolutely deny man's faculty of self-improvement, but they do not hold it to be indefinite; they can conceive amelioration, but not change: they imagine that the future condition of society may be better, but not essentially different; and, whilst they admit that humanity has made progress, and may still have some to make, they assign to it beforehand certain impassable limits.

Thus, they do not presume that they have arrived at the supreme good or at absolute truth, (what people or what man was ever wild enough to imagine it?) but they cherish a persuasion that they have pretty nearly reached that degree of greatness and knowledge which our imperfect nature admits of; and, as nothing moves about them, they are willing to fancy that everything is in its fit place. Then it is that the legislator affects to lay down eternal laws; that kings and nations will raise none but imperishable monuments; and that the present generation undertakes to spare generations to come the care of regulating their destinies.

In proportion as castes disappear and the classes of society approximate, — as manners, customs, and laws vary, from the tumultuous intercourse of men, — as new facts arise, — as new truths are brought to light, — as ancient opinions are dissipated, and others take their place, — the image of an ideal but always fugitive perfection presents itself to the human mind. Continual changes are then every instant occurring under the observation of every man: the position of some is rendered worse; and he learns but too well that no people and no individual, how enlightened soever they may be, can lay claim to infallibility: the condition of others is improved; whence he infers that man is endowed with an indefinite faculty of improvement. His reverses teach him that none have discovered absolute good, — his success stimulates him to the never-ending pursuit of it. Thus, forever seeking, forever falling to rise again, — often disappointed, but not discouraged, — he tends unceasingly towards that unmeasured greatness so indistinctly visible at the end of the long track which humanity has yet to tread.

It can hardly be believed how many facts naturally flow

from the philosophical theory of the indefinite perfectibility of man, or how strong an influence it exercises even on those who, living entirely for the purposes of action and not of thought, seem to conform their actions to it, without knowing anything about it.

I accost an American sailor, and inquire why the ships of his country are built so as to last but for a short time; he answers without hesitation, that the art of navigation is every day making such rapid progress, that the finest vessel would become almost useless if it lasted beyond a few years. In these words, which fell accidentally, and on a particular subject, from an uninstructed man, I recognize the general and systematic idea upon which a great people direct all their concerns.

Aristocratic nations are naturally too apt to narrow the scope of human perfectibility; democratic nations, to expand it beyond reason.

CHAPTER IX.

THE EXAMPLE OF THE AMERICANS DOES NOT PROVE THAT A DEMOCRATIC PEOPLE CAN HAVE NO APTITUDE AND NO TASTE FOR SCIENCE, LITERATURE, OR ART.

IT must be acknowledged that in few of the civilized nations of our time have the higher sciences made less progress than in the United States; and in few have great artists, distinguished poets, or celebrated writers, been more rare.* Many Europeans, struck by this fact, have looked upon it as a natural and inevitable result of equality; and they have thought that, if a democratic state of society and democratic institutions were ever to prevail over the whole earth, the human mind would gradually find its beacon-lights grow dim, and men would relapse into a period of darkness.

To reason thus is, I think, to confound several ideas which it is important to divide and examine separately: it is to mingle, unintentionally, what is democratic with what is only American.

The religion professed by the first emigrants, and bequeathed by them to their descendants, — simple in its forms, austere and almost harsh in its principles, and hostile to external symbols and to ceremonial pomp, — is naturally unfavorable to the fine arts, and only yields reluctantly to the pleasures of literature. The Americans are a very old and a very enlightened people, who have fallen upon a new and unbounded country, where they may extend themselves at pleasure, and which they may fertilize without difficulty.

* See notes to Vol. I. pp. 403, 404. — AM. ED.

This state of things is without a parallel in the history of the world. In America, every one finds facilities unknown elsewhere for making or increasing his fortune. The spirit of gain is always on the stretch, and the human mind, constantly diverted from the pleasures of imagination and the labors of the intellect, is there swayed by no impulse but the pursuit of wealth. Not only are manufacturing and commercial classes to be found in the United States, as they are in all other countries; but, what never occurred elsewhere, the whole community are simultaneously engaged in productive industry and commerce.

But I am convinced that, if the Americans had been alone in the world, with the freedom and the knowledge acquired by their forefathers, and the passions which are their own, they would not have been slow to discover that progress cannot long be made in the application of the sciences without cultivating the theory of them; that all the arts are perfected by one another: and, however absorbed they might have been by the pursuit of the principal object of their desires, they would speedily have admitted that it is necessary to turn aside from it occasionally, in order the better to attain it in the end.

The taste for the pleasures of mind is moreover so natural to the heart of civilized man, that amongst the polite nations, which are least disposed to give themselves up to these pursuits, a certain number of persons are always to be found who take part in them. This intellectual craving, once felt, would very soon have been satisfied.

But at the very time when the Americans were naturally inclined to require nothing of science but its special applications to the useful arts and the means of rendering life comfortable, learned and literary Europe was engaged in exploring the common sources of truth, and in improving at the same time all that can minister to the pleasures or satisfy the wants of man.

At the head of the enlightened nations of the Old World the inhabitants of the United States more particularly distinguished one, to which they were closely united by a common origin and by kindred habits. Amongst this people they found distinguished men of science, able artists, writers of eminence, and they were enabled to enjoy the treasures of the intellect without laboring to amass them. In spite of the ocean which intervenes, I cannot consent to separate America from Europe. I consider the people of the United States as that portion of the English people who are commissioned to explore the forests of the New World; whilst the rest of the nation, enjoying more leisure and less harassed by the drudgery of life, may devote their energies to thought, and enlarge in all directions the empire of mind.

The position of the Americans is therefore quite exceptional, and it may be believed that no democratic people will ever be placed in a similar one. Their strictly Puritanical origin, — their exclusively commercial habits, — even the country they inhabit, which seems to divert their minds from the pursuit of science, literature, and the arts, — the proximity of Europe, which allows them to neglect these pursuits without relapsing into barbarism, — a thousand special causes, of which I have only been able to point out the most important, — have singularly concurred to fix the mind of the American upon purely practical objects. His passions, his wants, his education, and everything about him, seem to unite in drawing the native of the United States earthward: his religion alone bids him turn, from time to time, a transient and distracted glance to heaven. Let us cease, then, to view all democratic nations under the example of the American people, and attempt to survey them at length with their own features.

It is possible to conceive a people not subdivided into any castes or scale of ranks; among whom the law, recognizing no privileges, should divide inherited property into equal shares; but which, at the same time, should be without knowledge and without freedom. Nor is this an empty hypothesis: a despot may find that it is his interest to render his subjects equal and to leave them ignorant, in order more easily to keep them slaves. Not only would a democratic people of this kind show neither aptitude nor taste for science, literature, or art, but it would probably never arrive at the possession of them. The law of descent would of itself provide for the destruction of large fortunes at each succeeding generation; and no new fortunes would be acquired. The poor man, without either knowledge or freedom, would not so much as conceive the idea of raising himself to wealth; and the rich man would allow himself to be degraded to poverty, without a notion of self-defence. Between these two members of the community complete and invincible equality would soon be established. No one would then have time or taste to devote himself to the pursuits or pleasures of the intellect; but all men would remain paralyzed in a state of common ignorance and equal servitude.

When I conceive a democratic society of this kind, I fancy myself in one of those low, close, and gloomy abodes, where the light which breaks in from without soon faints and fades away. A sudden heaviness overpowers me, and I grope through the surrounding darkness, to find an opening which will restore me to the air and the light of day. But all this is not applicable to men already enlightened who retain their freedom, after having abolished those peculiar and hereditary rights which perpetuated the tenure of property in the hands of certain individuals or certain classes.

When men living in a democratic state of society are enlightened, they readily discover that they are not confined and fixed by any limits which constrain them to take up with their present fortune. They all, therefore, conceive the idea of increasing it, — if they are free, they all attempt it; but all do not succeed in the same manner. The legislature, it is true, no longer grants privileges, but nature grants them. As natural inequality is very great, fortunes become unequal as soon as every man exerts all his faculties to get rich.

The law of descent prevents the establishment of wealthy families, but it does not prevent the existence of wealthy individuals. It constantly brings back the members of the community to a common level, from which they as constantly escape; and the inequality of fortunes augments in proportion as their knowledge is diffused and their liberty increased.

A sect which arose in our time, and was celebrated for its talents and its extravagance, proposed to concentrate all property in the hands of a central power, whose function it should afterwards be to parcel it out to individuals, according to their merits. This would have been a method of escaping from that complete and eternal equality which seems to threaten democratic society. But it would be a simpler and less dangerous remedy to grant no privilege to any, giving to all equal cultivation and equal independence, and leaving every one to determine his own position. Natural inequality will soon make way for itself, and wealth will spontaneously pass into the hands of the most capable.

Free and democratic communities, then, will always contain a multitude of people enjoying opulence or a competency. The wealthy will not be so closely linked to each other as the members of the former aristocratic class of society; their inclinations will be different, and they will scarcely ever enjoy leisure as secure or complete; but they will be far more numerous than those who belonged to that class of society could ever be. These persons will not be strictly confined to the cares of practical life; and they will still be able, though in different degrees, to indulge in the pursuits and pleasures of the intellect. In those pleasures they will indulge; for, if it be true that the human mind leans on one side to the limited, the material, and the useful, it naturally rises on the other to the infinite, the spiritual, and the beautiful. Physical wants confine it to the earth; but, as soon as the tie is loosened, it will rise of itself.

Not only will the number of those who can take an interest in the productions of mind be greater, but the taste for intellectual enjoyment will descend, step by step, even to those who, in aristocratic societies, seem to have neither time nor ability to indulge in them. When hereditary wealth, the privileges of rank, and the prerogatives of birth have ceased to be, and when every man derives his strength from himself alone, it becomes evident that the chief cause of disparity between the fortunes of men is the mind. Whatever tends to invigorate, to extend, or to adorn the mind, instantly rises to a high value. The utility of knowledge becomes singularly conspicuous even to the eyes of the multitude: those who have no taste for its charms set store upon its results, and make some efforts to acquire it.

In free and enlightened democratic times there is nothing to separate men from each other, or to retain them in their place: they rise or sink with extreme rapidity. All classes live in continual intercourse, from their great proximity to each other. They communicate and intermingle every day; they imitate and emulate one another: this suggests to the people many ideas, notions, and desires which they would never have entertained if the distinctions of rank had been fixed, and society at rest. In such nations, the servant never considers himself as an entire stranger to the pleasures and toils of his master, nor the poor man to those of the rich; the rural population assimilates itself to that of the towns, and the provinces to the capital. No one easily allows himself to be reduced to the mere material cares of life; and the humblest artisan casts at times an eager and a furtive glance into the higher regions of the intellect. People do not read with the same notions or in the same manner as they do in aristocratic communities; but the circle of readers is unceasingly expanded, till it includes all the people.

As soon as the multitude begin to take an interest in the labors of the mind, it finds out that to excel in some of them is a powerful means of acquiring fame, power, or wealth. The restless ambition which equality begets instantly takes this direction, as it does all others. The number of those who cultivate science, letters, and the arts, becomes immense. The intellectual world starts into prodigious activity: every one endeavors to open for himself a path there, and to draw the eyes of the public after him. Something analogous occurs to what happens in society in the United States politically considered. What is done is often imperfect, but the attempts are innumerable; and, although the results of individual effort are commonly very small, the total amount is always very large.

It is therefore not true to assert, that men living in democratic times are naturally indifferent to science, literature, and the arts: only it must be acknowledged that they cultivate them after their own fashion, and bring to the task their own peculiar qualifications and deficiencies.

CHAPTER X.

WHY THE AMERICANS ARE MORE ADDICTED TO PRACTICAL THAN TO THEORETICAL SCIENCE.

IF a democratic state of society and democratic institutions do not retard the onward course of the human mind, they incontestably guide it in one direction in preference to another. Their efforts, thus circumscribed, are still exceedingly great; and I may be pardoned if I pause for a moment to contemplate them.

We had occasion, in speaking of the philosophical method of the American people, to make several remarks, which must here be turned to account.

Equality begets in man the desire of judging of everything for himself: it gives him, in all things, a taste for the tangible and the real, a contempt for tradition and for forms. These general tendencies are principally discernible in the peculiar subject of this chapter.

Those who cultivate the sciences amongst a democratic people are always afraid of losing their way in visionary speculation. They mistrust systems; they adhere closely to facts, and study facts with their own senses. As they do not easily defer to the mere name of any fellow-man, they are never inclined to rest upon any man's authority; but, on the contrary, they are unremitting in their efforts to find out the weaker points of their neighbors' doctrine. Scientific precedents have little weight with them; they are never long detained by the subtilty of the schools, nor ready to accept big words for sterling coin; they penetrate, as far as they can, into the principal parts of the subject which occupies them, and they like to expound them in the vulgar tongue. Scientific pursuits then follow a freer and safer course, but a less lofty one.

The mind may, as it appears to me, divide science into three parts.

The first comprises the most theoretical principles, and those more abstract notions, whose application is either unknown or very remote.

The second is composed of those general truths which still belong to pure theory, but lead nevertheless by a straight and short road to practical results.

Methods of application and means of execution make up the third.

Each of these different portions of science may be separately cultivated, although reason and experience prove that neither of them can prosper long, if it be absolutely cut off from the two others.

In America, the purely practical part of science is admirably understood, and careful attention is paid to the theoretical portion, which is immediately requisite to application. On this head, the Americans always display a clear, free, original, and inventive power of mind. But hardly any one in the United States devotes himself to the essentially theoretical and abstract portion of human knowledge. In this respect, the Americans carry to excess a tendency which is, I think, discernible, though in a less degree, amongst all democratic nations.

Nothing is more necessary to the culture of the higher sciences, or of the more elevated departments of science, than meditation; and nothing is less suited to meditation than the structure of democratic society. We do not find there, as amongst an aristocratic people, one class which keeps in repose because it is well off; and another, which does not venture to stir because it despairs of improving its condition. Every one is in motion: some in quest of power, others of gain. In the midst of this universal tumult, — this incessant conflict of jarring interests, — this continual striving of men after fortune, — where is that calm to be found which is necessary for the deeper combinations of the intellect? How can the mind dwell upon any single point, when everything whirls around it, and man himself is swept and beaten onwards by the heady current which rolls all things in its course?

But the permanent agitation which subsists in the bosom of a peaceable and established democracy must be distinguished from the tumultuous and revolutionary movements which almost always attend the birth and growth of democratic society. When a violent revolution occurs amongst a highly-civilized people, it cannot fail to give a sudden impulse to their feelings and ideas. This is more particularly true of democratic revolutions, which stir up at once all the classes of which a people is composed, and beget at the same time inordinate ambition in the breast of every member of the community. The French made surprising advances in the exact sciences at the very time at which they were finishing the destruction of the remains of their former feudal society; yet this sudden fecundity is not to be attributed to democracy, but to the unexampled revolution which attended its growth. What happened at that period was a special incident, and it would be unwise to regard it as the test of a general principle.

Great revolutions are not more common amongst democratic than amongst other nations: I am even inclined to believe that they are less so. But there prevails amongst those populations a small, distressing motion, a sort of incessant jostling of men, which annoys and disturbs the mind without exciting or elevating it.

Men who live in democratic communities not only seldom indulge in meditation, but they naturally entertain very little esteem for it. A democratic state of society and democratic institutions keep the greater part of men in constant activity; and the habits of mind which are suited to an active life are not always suited to a contemplative one. The man of action is frequently obliged to content himself with the best he can get, because he would never accomplish his purpose if he chose to carry every detail to perfection. He has perpetually occasion to rely on ideas which he has not had leisure to search to the bottom; for he is much more frequently aided by the seasonableness of an idea than by its strict accuracy; and, in the long run, he risks less in making use of some false principles, than in spending his time in establishing all his principles, on the basis of truth. The world is not led by long or learned demonstrations: a rapid glance at particular incidents, the daily study of the fleeting passions of the multitude, the accidents of the moment and the art of turning them to account, decide all its affairs.

In the ages in which active life is the condition of almost every one, men are therefore generally led to attach an excessive value to the rapid bursts and superficial conceptions of the intellect; and, on the other hand, to depreciate unduly its slower and deeper labors. This opinion of the public influences the judgment of the men who cultivate the sciences; they are persuaded that they may succeed in those pursuits without meditation, or are deterred from such pursuits as demand it.

There are several methods of studying the sciences. Amongst a multitude of men you will find a selfish, mercantile, and trading taste for the discoveries of the mind, which must not be confounded with that disinterested passion which is kindled in the heart of a few. A desire to utilize knowledge is one thing; the pure desire to know is another. I do not doubt that in a few minds, and at long intervals, an ardent, inexhaustible love of truth springs up, self-supported, and living in ceaseless fruition, without ever attaining full satisfaction. This ardent love it is — this proud, disinterested love of what is true — which raises men to the abstract sources of truth, to draw their mother knowledge thence.

If Pascal had had nothing in view but some large gain, or even if he had been stimulated by the love of fame alone, I cannot conceive that he would ever have been able to rally all the powers of his mind, as he did, for the better discovery of the most hidden things of the Creator. When I see him, as it were, tear his soul from all the cares of life to devote it wholly to these researches, and, prematurely snapping the links which bind the frame to life, die of old age before forty, I stand amazed, and perceive that no ordinary cause is at work to produce efforts so extraordinary.

The future will prove whether these passions, at once so rare and so productive, come into being and into growth as easily in the midst of democratic as in aristocratic communities. For myself, I confess that I am slow to believe it.

In aristocratic societies, the class which gives the tone to opinion, and has the guidance of affairs, being permanently and hereditarily placed above the multitude, naturally conceives a lofty idea of itself and of man. It loves to invent for him noble pleasures, to carve out splendid objects for his ambition. Aristocracies often commit very tyrannical and inhuman actions, but they rarely entertain grovelling thoughts; and they show a kind of haughty contempt of little pleasures, even whilst they indulge in them. The effect is greatly to raise the general pitch of society. In aristocratic ages, vast ideas are commonly entertained of the dignity, the power, and the greatness of man. These opinions exert their influence on those who cultivate the sciences, as well as on the rest of the community. They facilitate the natural impulse of the mind to the highest regions of thought; and they naturally prepare it to conceive a sublime, almost a divine, love of truth.

Men of science at such periods are consequently carried away towards theory; and it even happens that they frequently conceive an inconsiderate contempt for practice. "Archimedes," says Plutarch, "was of so lofty a spirit, that he never condescended to write any treatise on the manner of constructing all these engines of war. And as he held this science of inventing and putting together engines, and all arts generally speaking which tended to any useful end in practice, to be vile, low, and mercenary, he spent his talents and his studious hours in writing of those things only whose beauty and subtilty had in them no admixture of necessity." Such is the aristocratic aim of science: it cannot be the same in democratic nations.

The greater part of the men who constitute these nations are extremely eager in the pursuit of actual and physical gratification. As they are always dissatisfied with the position which they occupy, and are always free to leave it, they think of nothing but the means of changing their fortune, or increasing it. To minds thus predisposed, every new method which leads by a shorter road to wealth, every machine which spares labor, every instrument which diminishes the cost of production, every discovery which facilitates pleasures or augments them, seems to be the grandest effort of the human intellect. It is chiefly from these motives that a democratic people addicts itself to scientific pursuits, — that it understands and respects them. In aristocratic ages, science is more particularly called upon to furnish gratification to the mind; in democracies, to the body.

You may be sure that the more a nation is democratic, enlightened, and free, the greater will be the number of these interested promoters of scientific genius, and the more will discoveries immediately applicable to productive industry confer gain, fame, and even power, on their authors. For in democracies, the working class take a part in public affairs; and public honors, as well as pecuniary remuneration, may be awarded to those who deserve them.

In a community thus organized, it may easily be conceived that the human mind may be led insensibly to the neglect of theory; and that it is urged, on the contrary, with unparalleled energy, to the applications of science, or at least to that portion of theoretical science which is necessary to those who make such applications. In vain will some instinctive inclination raise the mind towards the loftier spheres of the intellect; interest draws it down to the middle zone. There it may develop all its energy and restless activity, and bring forth wonders. These very Americans, who have not discovered one of the general laws of mechanics, have introduced into navigation an engine which changes the aspect of the world.

Assuredly I do not contend that the democratic nations of our time are destined to witness the extinction of the great luminaries of man's intelligence, or even that they will never bring new lights into existence. At the age at which the world has now arrived, and amongst so many cultivated nations perpetually excited by the fever of productive industry, the bonds which connect the different parts of science cannot fail to strike the observer; and the taste for practical science itself, if it be enlightened, ought to lead men not to neglect theory. In the midst of so many attempted applications of so many experiments, repeated every day, it is almost impossible that general laws should not frequently be brought to light; so that great discoveries would be frequent, though great inventors may be few.

I believe, moreover, in high scientific vocations. If the democratic principle does not, on the one hand, induce men to cultivate science for its own sake, on the other, it enormously increases the number of those who do cultivate it. Nor is it credible that, amid so great a multitude, a speculative genius should not from time to time arise inflamed by the love of truth alone. Such an one, we may be sure, would dive into the deepest mysteries of nature, whatever be the spirit of his country and his age. He requires no assistance in his course, — it is enough that he is not checked in it. All that I mean to say is this: permanent inequality of conditions leads men to confine themselves to the arrogant and sterile research of abstract truths, whilst the social condition and the institutions of democracy prepare them to seek the immediate and useful practical results of the sciences. This tendency is natural and inevitable: it is curious to be acquainted with it, and it may be necessary to point it out.

If those who are called upon to guide the nations of our time clearly discerned from afar off these new tendencies, which will soon be irresistible, they would understand that, possessing education and freedom, men living in democratic ages cannot fail to improve the industrial part of science; and that henceforward all the efforts of the constituted authorities ought to be directed to support the highest branches of learning, and to foster the nobler passion for science itself. In the present age, the human mind must be coerced into theoretical studies; it runs of its own accord to practical applications; and, instead of perpetually referring it to the minute examination of secondary effects, it is well to divert it from them sometimes, in order to raise it up to the contemplation of primary causes.

Because the civilization of ancient Rome perished in consequence of the invasion of the Barbarians, we are perhaps too apt to think that civilization cannot perish in any other manner. If the light by which we are guided is ever extinguished, it will dwindle by degrees, and expire of itself. By dint of close adherence to mere applications, principles would be lost sight of; and when the principles were wholly forgotten, the methods derived from them would be ill pursued. New methods could no longer be invented, and men would continue to apply, without intelligence and without art, scientific processes no longer understood.

When Europeans first arrived in China, three hundred years ago, they found that almost all the arts had reached a certain degree of perfection there; and they were surprised that a people which had attained this point should not have gone beyond it. At a later period, they discovered traces of some higher branches of science which had been lost. The nation was absorbed in productive industry; the greater part of its scientific processes had been preserved, but science itself no longer existed there. This served to explain the strange immobility in which they found the minds of this people. The Chinese, in following the track of their forefathers, had forgotten the reasons by which the latter had been guided. They still used the formula, without asking for its meaning; they retained the instrument, but they no longer possessed the art of altering or renewing it. The Chinese, then, had lost the power of change; for them, improvement was impossible. They were compelled, at all times and in all points, to imitate their predecessors, lest they should stray into utter darkness by deviating for an instant from the path already laid down for them. The source of human knowledge was all but dry; and though the stream still ran on, it could neither swell its waters, nor alter its course.

Notwithstanding this, China had subsisted peaceably for centuries. The invaders who had conquered the country assumed the manners of the inhabitants, and order prevailed there. A sort of physical prosperity was everywhere discernible: revolutions were rare, and war was, so to speak, unknown.

It is then a fallacy to flatter ourselves with the reflection that the Barbarians are still far from us; for if there be some nations which allow civilization to be torn from their grasp, there are others who trample it themselves under their feet.

CHAPTER XI.

IN WHAT SPIRIT THE AMERICANS CULTIVATE THE ARTS.

IT would be to waste the time of my readers and my own, if I strove to demonstrate how the general mediocrity of fortunes, the absence of superfluous wealth, the universal desire of comfort, and the constant efforts by which every one attempts to procure it, make the taste for the useful predominate over the love of the beautiful in the heart of man. Democratic nations, amongst whom all these things exist, will therefore cultivate the arts which serve to render life easy, in preference to those whose object is to adorn it. They will habitually prefer the useful to the beautiful, and they will require that the beautiful should be useful.

But I propose to go further; and, after having pointed out this first feature, to sketch several others.

It commonly happens that, in the ages of privilege, the practice of almost all the arts becomes a privilege; and that every profession is a separate walk, upon which it is not allowable for every one to enter. Even when productive industry is free, the fixed character which belongs to aristocratic nations gradually segregates all the persons who practise the same art, till they form a distinct class, always composed of the same families, whose members are all known to each other, and amongst whom a public opinion of their own, and a species of corporate pride, soon spring up. In a class or guild of this kind, each artisan has not only his fortune to make, but his reputation to preserve. He is not exclusively swayed by his own interest, or even by that of his customer, but by that of the body to which he belongs; and the interest of that body is, that each artisan should produce the best possible workmanship. In aristocratic ages, the object of the arts is therefore to manufacture as well as possible, — not with the greatest despatch, or at the lowest rate.

When, on the contrary, every profession is open to all, — when a multitude of persons are constantly embracing and abandoning it, — and when its several members are strangers, indifferent to, and from their numbers hardly seen by, each other, — the social tie is destroyed, and each workman, standing alone, endeavors simply to gain the most money at the least cost. The will of the customer is then his only limit. But at the same time, a corresponding change takes place in the customer also. In countries in which riches, as well as power, are concentrated and retained in the hands of a few, the use of the greater part of this world's goods belongs to a small number of individuals, who are always the same. Necessity, public opinion, or moderate desires, exclude all others from the enjoyment of them. As this aristocratic class remains fixed at the pinnacle of greatness on which it stands, without diminution or increase, it is always acted upon by the same wants, and affected by them in the same manner. The men of whom it is composed naturally derive from their superior and hereditary position a taste for what is extremely well made and lasting. This affects the general way of thinking of the nation in relation to the arts. It often occurs, among such a people, that even the peasant will rather go without the objects he covets, than procure them in a state of imperfection. In aristocracies, then, the handicraftsmen work for only a limited number of fastidious customers: the profit they hope to make depends principally on the perfection of their workmanship.

Such is no longer the case when, all privileges being

abolished, ranks are intermingled, and men are forever rising or sinking upon the social scale. Amongst a democratic people, a number of citizens always exist whose patrimony is divided and decreasing. They have contracted, under more prosperous circumstances, certain wants, which remain after the means of satisfying such wants are gone; and they are anxiously looking out for some surreptitious method of providing for them. On the other hand, there are always in democracies a large number of men whose fortune is upon the increase, but whose desires grow much faster than their fortunes: and who gloat upon the gifts of wealth in anticipation, long before they have means to command them. Such men are eager to find some short cut to these gratifications, already almost within their reach. From the combination of these two causes the result is, that in democracies there is always a multitude of persons whose wants are above their means, and who are very willing to take up with imperfect satisfaction, rather than abandon the object of their desires altogether.

The artisan readily understands these passions, for he himself partakes in them: in an aristocracy, he would seek to sell his workmanship at a high price to the few; he now conceives that the more expeditious way of getting rich is to sell them at a low price to all. But there are only two ways of lowering the price of commodities. The first is to discover some better, shorter, and more ingenious method of producing them: the second is to manufacture a larger quantity of goods, nearly similar, but of less value. Amongst a democratic population, all the intellectual faculties of the workman are directed to these two objects: he strives to invent methods which may enable him not only to work better, but quicker and cheaper; or, if he cannot succeed in that, to diminish the intrinsic quality of the thing he makes, without rendering it wholly unfit for the use for which it is intended. When none but the wealthy had watches, they were almost all very good ones: few are now made which are worth much, but everybody has one in his pocket. Thus the democratic principle not only tends to direct the human mind to the useful arts, but it induces the artisan to produce with great rapidity many imperfect commodities, and the consumer to content himself with these commodities.

Not that, in democracies, the arts are incapable, in case of need, of producing wonders. This may occasionally be the case, if customers appear who are ready to pay for time and trouble. In this rivalry of every kind of industry, in the midst of this immense competition and these countless experiments, some excellent workmen are formed, who reach the utmost limits of their craft. But they have rarely an opportunity of showing what they can do; they are scrupulously sparing of their powers; they remain in a state of accomplished mediocrity, which judges itself, and, though well able to shoot beyond the mark before it, aims only at what it hits. In aristocracies, on the contrary, workmen always do all they can; and when they stop, it is because they have reached the limit of their art.

When I arrive in a country where I find some of the finest productions of the arts, I learn from this fact nothing of the social condition or of the political constitution of the country. But if I perceive that the productions of the arts are generally of an inferior quality, very abundant and very cheap, I am convinced that, amongst the people where this occurs, privilege is on the decline, and that ranks are beginning to intermingle, and will soon be confounded together.

The handicraftsmen of democratic ages endeavor not only to bring their useful productions within the reach of the whole community, but they strive to give to all their commodities attractive qualities which they do not in reality possess. In the confusion of all ranks, every one hopes to appear what he is not, and makes great exertions to succeed in this object. This sentiment, indeed, which is but too natural to the heart of man, does not originate in the democratic principle; but that principle applies it to material objects. The hypocrisy of virtue is of every age, but the hypocrisy of luxury belongs more particularly to the ages of democracy.

To satisfy these new cravings of human vanity, the arts have recourse to every species of imposture; and these devices sometimes go so far as to defeat their own purpose. Imitation diamonds are now made which may be easily mistaken for real ones; as soon as the art of fabricating false diamonds shall become so perfect that they cannot be distinguished from real ones, it is probable that both will be abandoned, and become mere pebbles again.

This leads me to speak of those arts which are called, by way of distinction, the fine arts. I do not believe that it is a necessary effect of a democratic social condition and of democratic institutions to diminish the number of those who cultivate the fine arts; but these causes exert a powerful influence on the manner in which these arts are cultivated. Many of those who had already contracted a taste for the fine arts are impoverished: on the other hand, many of those who are not yet rich begin to conceive that taste, at least by imitation; the number of consumers increases, but opulent and fastidious consumers become more scarce. Something analogous to what I have already pointed out in the useful arts then takes place in the fine arts; the productions of artists are more numerous, but the merit of each production is diminished. No longer able to soar to what is great, they cultivate what is pretty and elegant; and appearance is more attended to than reality.

In aristocracies, a few great pictures are produced; in democratic countries, a vast number of insignificant ones.

In the former, statues are raised of bronze; in the latter, they are modelled in plaster.

When I arrived for the first time at New York, by that part of the Atlantic Ocean which is called the East River, I was surprised to perceive along the shore, at some distance from the city, a number of little palaces of white marble, several of which were of ancient architecture. When I went the next day to inspect more closely one which had particularly attracted my notice, I found that its walls were of whitewashed brick, and its columns of painted wood. All the edifices which I had admired the night before were of the same kind.

The social condition and the institutions of democracy impart, moreover, certain peculiar tendencies to all the imitative arts, which it is easy to point out. They frequently withdraw them from the delineation of the soul, to fix them exclusively on that of the body; and they substitute the representation of motion and sensation for that of sentiment and thought: in a word, they put the Real in the place of the Ideal.

I doubt whether Raphael studied the minute intricacies of the mechanism of the human body as thoroughly as the draughtsmen of our own time. He did not attach the same importance as they do to rigorous accuracy on this point, because he aspired to surpass nature. He sought to make of man something which should be superior to man, and to embellish beauty itself. David and his scholars were, on the contrary, as good anatomists as they were painters. They wonderfully depicted the models which they had before their eyes, but they rarely imagined anything beyond them: they followed nature with fidelity, whilst Raphael sought for something better than nature. They have left us an exact portraiture of man; but he discloses in his works a glimpse of the Divinity.

This remark as to the manner of treating a subject is no

less applicable to the choice of it. The painters of the Renaissance generally sought far above themselves, and away from their own time, for mighty subjects, which left to their imagination an unbounded range. Our painters often employ their talents in the exact imitation of the details of private life, which they have always before their eyes; and they are forever copying trivial objects, the originals of which are only too abundant in nature.

CHAPTER XII.

WHY THE AMERICANS RAISE SOME INSIGNIFICANT MONUMENTS, AND OTHERS THAT ARE VERY GRAND.

I HAVE just observed, that, in democratic ages, monuments of the arts tend to become more numerous and less important. I now hasten to point out the exception to this rule.

In a democratic community, individuals are very weak; but the state, which represents them all, and contains them all in its grasp, is very powerful. Nowhere do citizens appear so insignificant as in a democratic nation; nowhere does the nation itself appear greater, or does the mind more easily take in a wide survey of it. In democratic communities, the imagination is compressed when men consider themselves; it expands indefinitely when they think of the state. Hence it is that the same men who live on a small scale in narrow dwellings, frequently aspire to gigantic splendor in the erection of their public monuments.

The Americans have traced out the circuit of an immense city on the site which they intended to make their capital, but which, up to the present time, is hardly more densely peopled than Pontoise, though, according to them, it will one day contain a million of inhabitants. They have already rooted up trees for ten miles round, lest they should interfere with the future citizens of this imaginary metropolis. They have erected a magnificent palace for Congress in the centre of the city, and have given it the pompous name of the Capitol.

The several States of the Union are every day planning

and erecting for themselves prodigious undertakings, which would astonish the engineers of the great European nations.

Thus democracy not only leads men to a vast number of inconsiderable productions; it also leads them to raise some monuments on the largest scale: but between these two extremes there is a blank. A few scattered specimens of enormous buildings can therefore teach us nothing of the social condition and the institutions of the people by whom they were raised. I may add, though the remark is out of my subject, that they do not make us better acquainted with its greatness, its civilization, and its real prosperity. Whenever a power of any kind shall be able to make a whole people co-operate in a single undertaking, that power, with a little knowledge and a great deal of time, will succeed in obtaining something enormous from efforts so multiplied. But this does not lead to the conclusion that the people are very happy, very enlightened, or even very strong.

The Spaniards found the city of Mexico full of magnificent temples and vast palaces; but that did not prevent Cortes from conquering the Mexican empire with six hundred foot-soldiers and sixteen horses.

If the Romans had been better acquainted with the laws of hydraulics, they would not have constructed all the aqueducts which surround the ruins of their cities, — they would have made a better use of their power and their wealth. If they had invented the steam-engine, perhaps they would not have extended to the extremities of their empire those long artificial ways which are called Roman Roads. These things are the splendid memorials at once of their ignorance and of their greatness.

A people which should leave no other vestige of its track than a few leaden pipes in the earth, and a few iron rods upon its surface, might have been more the master of Nature than the Romans.

CHAPTER XIII.

LITERARY CHARACTERISTICS OF DEMOCRATIC TIMES.

WHEN a traveller goes into a bookseller's shop in the United States, and examines the American books upon the shelves, the number of works appears very great; whilst that of known authors seems, on the contrary, extremely small. He will first find a multitude of elementary treatises, destined to teach the rudiments of human knowledge. Most of these books are written in Europe; * the Americans reprint them, adapting them to their own use. Next comes an enormous quantity of religious works, Bibles, sermons, edifying anecdotes, controversial divinity, and reports of charitable societies; lastly appears the long catalogue of political pamphlets. In America, parties do not write books to combat each other's opinions, but pamphlets, which are circulated for a day with incredible rapidity, and then expire.†

In the midst of all these obscure productions of the human brain appear the more remarkable works of a small number of authors, whose names are, or ought to be, known to Europeans.

Although America is perhaps in our days the civilized

* On the contrary, many elementary text-books written in America are republished in England; the reverse is true only in comparatively few cases. It is notorious that better school-books, dictionaries, &c. are written in the United States than in England. — AM. ED.

† This may have been true when M. de Tocqueville wrote; but now-a-days political pamphlets are comparatively obsolete, having been superseded by the newspapers, which reach a vastly larger audience than can be obtained by the ablest pamphlet. — AM. ED.

country in which literature is least attended to, still a large number of persons there take an interest in the productions of mind, and make them, if not the study of their lives, at least the charm of their leisure hours. But England supplies these readers with most of the books which they require. Almost all important English books are republished in the United States. The literary genius of Great Britain still darts its rays into the recesses of the forests of the New World. There is hardly a pioneer's hut which does not contain a few odd volumes of Shakespeare. I remember that I read the feudal drama of Henry V. for the first time in a log-house.

Not only do the Americans constantly draw upon the treasures of English literature, but it may be said with truth that they find the literature of England growing on their own soil. The larger part of that small number of men in the United States who are engaged in the composition of literary works are English in substance, and still more so in form. Thus they transport into the midst of democracy the ideas and literary fashions which are current amongst the aristocratic nation they have taken for their model. They paint with colors borrowed from foreign manners; and as they hardly ever represent the country they were born in as it really is, they are seldom popular there.

The citizens of the United States are themselves so convinced that it is not for them that books are published, that, before they can make up their minds upon the merit of one of their authors, they generally wait till his fame has been ratified in England; just as, in pictures, the author of an original is held entitled to judge of the merit of a copy.

The inhabitants of the United States have then, at present, properly speaking, no literature. The only authors whom I acknowledge as American are the journalists. They indeed are not great writers, but they speak the language of their country, and make themselves heard. Other authors are aliens; they are to the Americans what the imitators of the Greeks and Romans were to us at the revival of learning, — an object of curiosity, not of general sympathy. They amuse the mind, but they do not act upon the manners of the people.*

I have already said that this state of things is far from originating in democracy alone, and that the causes of it must be sought for in several peculiar circumstances independent of the democratic principle. If the Americans, retaining the same laws and social condition, had had a different origin, and had been transported into another country, I do not question that they would have had a literature. Even as they are, I am convinced that they will ultimately have one; but its character will be different from that which marks the American literary productions of our time, and that character will be peculiarly its own. Nor is it impossible to trace this character beforehand.

I suppose an aristocratic people amongst whom letters are cultivated; the labors of the mind, as well as the affairs of state, are conducted there by a ruling class in society. The literary as well as the political career is almost entirely confined to this class, or to those nearest to it in rank. These premises suffice for a key to all the rest.

When a small number of the same men are engaged at the same time upon the same objects, they easily concert with one another, and agree upon certain leading rules which are to govern them each and all. If the object which attracts the attention of these men is literature, the productions of the mind will soon be subjected by them to precise canons, from which it will no longer be allowable to depart. If these men occupy an hereditary position in the country, they will be naturally inclined, not only to

* All this is curiously untrue at the present day; but I need only to refer again to the notes on pp. 403, 404, of Vol. I. — AM. ED.

adopt a certain number of fixed rules for themselves, but to follow those which their forefathers laid down for their own guidance; their code will be at once strict and traditional. As they are not necessarily engrossed by the cares of daily life, — as they have never been so, any more than their fathers were before them, — they have learned to take an interest, for several generations back, in the labors of mind. They have learned to understand literature as an art, to love it in the end for its own sake, and to feel a scholar-like satisfaction in seeing men conform to its rules. Nor is this all: the men of whom I speak began and will end their lives in easy or affluent circumstances; hence they have naturally conceived a taste for choice gratifications, and a love of refined and delicate pleasures. Nay, more: a kind of softness of mind and heart, which they frequently contract in the midst of this long and peaceful enjoyment of so much welfare, leads them to put aside, even from their pleasures, whatever might be too startling or too acute. They had rather be amused than intensely excited; they wish to be interested, but not to be carried away.

Now let us fancy a great number of literary performances executed by the men, or for the men, whom I have just described, and we shall readily conceive a style of literature in which everything will be regular and prearranged. The slightest work will be carefully touched in its least details; art and labor will be conspicuous in everything; each kind of writing will have rules of its own, from which it will not be allowed to swerve, and which distinguish it from all others. Style will be thought of almost as much importance as thought, and the form will be no less considered than the matter; the diction will be polished, measured, and uniform. The tone of the mind will be always dignified, seldom very animated; and writers will care more to perfect what they produce, than to multiply their productions. It will sometimes happen that the members of the literary class, always living amongst themselves, and writing for themselves alone, will entirely lose sight of the rest of the world, which will infect them with a false and labored style; they will lay down minute literary rules for their exclusive use, which will insensibly lead them to deviate from common sense, and finally to transgress the bounds of nature. By dint of striving after a mode of parlance different from the vulgar, they will arrive at a sort of aristocratic jargon, which is hardly less remote from pure language than is the coarse dialect of the people. Such are the natural perils of literature amongst aristocracies. Every aristocracy which keeps itself entirely aloof from the people becomes impotent, — a fact which is as true in literature as it is in politics.*

Let us now turn the picture, and consider the other side of it: let us transport ourselves into the midst of a democracy not unprepared by ancient traditions and present culture to partake in the pleasures of mind. Ranks are there intermingled and confounded; knowledge and power are both infinitely subdivided, and, if I may use the expression, scattered on every side. Here, then, is a motley multitude whose intellectual wants are to be supplied. These new votaries of the pleasures of mind have not all received the same education; they do not resemble their fathers, — nay, they perpetually differ from themselves, for they live in a state of incessant change of place, feelings, and fortunes. The mind of each is therefore unattached to that of his

* All this is especially true of the aristocratic countries which have been long and peacefully subject to a monarchical government. When liberty prevails in an aristocracy, the higher ranks are constantly obliged to make use of the lower classes; and when they use, they approach them. This frequently introduces something of a democratic spirit into an aristocratic community. There springs up, moreover, in a governing privileged body, an energy and habitually bold policy, a taste for stir and excitement, which must infallibly affect all literary performances.

fellows by tradition or common habits; and they have never had the power, the inclination, or the time to concert together. It is, however, from the bosom of this heterogeneous and agitated mass that authors spring; and from the same source their profits and their fame are distributed.

I can without difficulty understand that, under these circumstances, I must expect to meet in the literature of such a people with but few of those strict conventional rules which are admitted by readers and writers in aristocratic times. If it should happen that the men of some one period were agreed upon any such rules, that would prove nothing for the following period; for, amongst democratic nations, each new generation is a new people. Amongst such nations, then, literature will not easily be subjected to strict rules, and it is impossible that any such rules should ever be permanent.

In democracies, it is by no means the case that all who cultivate literature have received a literary education; and most of those who have some tinge of belles-lettres are either engaged in politics or in a profession which only allows them to taste occasionally and by stealth the pleasures of mind. These pleasures, therefore, do not constitute the principal charm of their lives; but they are considered as a transient and necessary recreation amidst the serious labors of life. Such men can never acquire a sufficiently intimate knowledge of the art of literature to appreciate its more delicate beauties; and the minor shades of expression must escape them. As the time they can devote to letters is very short, they seek to make the best use of the whole of it. They prefer books which may be easily procured, quickly read, and which require no learned researches to be understood. They ask for beauties self-proffered, and easily enjoyed; above all, they must have what is unexpected and new. Accustomed to the struggle, the crosses, and the monotony of practical life, they require strong and rapid emotions, startling passages, — truths or errors brilliant enough to rouse them up, and to plunge them at once, as if by violence, into the midst of the subject.

Why should I say more? or who does not understand what is about to follow, before I have expressed it? Taken as a whole, literature in democratic ages can never present, as it does in the periods of aristocracy, an aspect of order, regularity, science, and art; its form will, on the contrary, ordinarily be slighted, sometimes despised. Style will frequently be fantastic, incorrect, overburdened, and loose, — almost always vehement and bold. Authors will aim at rapidity of execution, more than at perfection of detail. Small productions will be more common than bulky books: there will be more wit than erudition, more imagination than profundity; and literary performances will bear marks of an untutored and rude vigor of thought, — frequently of great variety and singular fecundity. The object of authors will be to astonish rather than to please, and to stir the passions more than to charm the taste.

Here and there, indeed, writers will doubtless occur who will choose a different track, and who will, if they are gifted with superior abilities, succeed in finding readers, in spite of their defects or their better qualities; but these exceptions will be rare; and even the authors who shall so depart from the received practice in the main subject of their works, will always relapse into it in some lesser details.

I have just depicted two extreme conditions: the transition by which a nation passes from the former to the latter is not sudden, but gradual, and marked with shades of very various intensity. In the passage which conducts a lettered people from the one to the other, there is almost always a moment at which the literary genius of democratic nations has its confluence with that of aristocracies, and both seek to establish their joint sway over the human mind. Such epochs are transient, but very brilliant: they are fertile without exuberance, and animated without confusion. The French literature of the eighteenth century may serve as an example.

I should say more than I mean, if I were to assert that the literature of a nation is always subordinate to its social state and its political constitution. I am aware that, independently of these causes, there are several others which confer certain characteristics on literary productions; but these appear to me to be the chief. The relations which exist between the social and political condition of a people and the genius of its authors are always numerous: whoever knows the one, is never completely ignorant of the other.

CHAPTER XIV.

THE TRADE OF LITERATURE.

DEMOCRACY not only infuses a taste for letters among the trading classes, but introduces a trading spirit into literature.

In aristocracies, readers are fastidious and few in number; in democracies, they are far more numerous and far less difficult to please. The consequence is, that among aristocratic nations no one can hope to succeed without great exertion, and this exertion may earn great fame, but can never procure much money; whilst among democratic nations a writer may flatter himself that he will obtain at a cheap rate a moderate reputation and a large fortune. For this purpose he need not be admired, it is enough that he is liked.

The ever-increasing crowd of readers, and their continual craving for something new, insures the sale of books which nobody much esteems.

In democratic times, the public frequently treat authors as kings do their courtiers; they enrich and despise them. What more is needed by the venal souls who are born in courts, or are worthy to live there?

Democratic literature is always infested with a tribe of writers who look upon letters as a mere trade; and for some few great authors who adorn it, you may reckon thousands of idea-mongers.

CHAPTER XV.

THE STUDY OF GREEK AND LATIN LITERATURE IS PECULIARLY USEFUL IN DEMOCRATIC COMMUNITIES.

WHAT was called the People in the most democratic republics of antiquity was very unlike what we designate by that term. In Athens, all the citizens took part in public affairs; but there were only twenty thousand citizens to more than three hundred and fifty thousand inhabitants. All the rest were slaves, and discharged the greater part of those duties which belong at the present day to the lower, or even to the middle classes. Athens then, with her universal suffrage, was, after all, merely an aristocratic republic, in which all the nobles had an equal right to the government.

The struggle between the patricians and plebeians of Rome must be considered in the same light: it was simply an intestine feud between the elder and younger branches of the same family. All the citizens belonged, in fact, to the aristocracy, and partook of its character.

It is to be remarked, moreover, that, amongst the ancients, books were always scarce and dear; and that very great difficulties impeded their publication and circulation. These circumstances concentrated literary tastes and habits amongst a small number of men, who formed a small literary aristocracy out of the choicer spirits of the great political aristocracy. Accordingly, nothing goes to prove that literature was ever treated as a trade amongst the Greeks and Romans.

These communities, which were not only aristocracies,

but very polished and free nations, of course imparted to their literary productions the special defects and merits which characterize the literature of aristocratic times. And indeed a very superficial survey of the works of ancient authors will suffice to convince us, that, if those writers were sometimes deficient in variety and fertility in their subjects, or in boldness, vivacity, and power of generalization in their thoughts, they always displayed exquisite care and skill in their details. Nothing in their works seems to be done hastily, or at random: every line is written for the eye of the connoisseur, and is shaped after some conception of ideal beauty. No literature places those fine qualities in which the writers of democracies are naturally deficient in bolder relief than that of the ancients: no literature, therefore, ought to be more studied in democratic times. This study is better suited than any other to combat the literary defects inherent in those times: as for their natural literary qualities, these will spring up of their own accord, without its being necessary to learn to acquire them.

It is important that this point should be clearly understood. A particular study may be useful to the literature of a people, without being appropriate to its social and political wants. If men were to persist in teaching nothing but the literature of the dead languages in a community where every one is habitually led to make vehement exertions to augment or to maintain his fortune, the result would be a very polished, but a very dangerous, set of citizens. For as their social and political condition would give them every day a sense of wants, which their education would never teach them to supply, they would perturb the state, in the name of the Greeks and Romans, instead of enriching it by their productive industry.

It is evident, that, in democratic communities, the interest of individuals, as well as the security of the commonwealth, demands that the education of the greater number should be scientific, commercial, and industrial, rather than literary. Greek and Latin should not be taught in all the schools; but it is important that those who, by their natural disposition or their fortune, are destined to cultivate letters or prepared to relish them, should find schools where a complete knowledge of ancient literature may be acquired, and where the true scholar may be formed. A few excellent universities would do more towards the attainment of this object than a multitude of bad grammar-schools, where superfluous matters, badly learned, stand in the way of sound instruction in necessary studies.

All who aspire to literary excellence in democratic nations ought frequently to refresh themselves at the springs of ancient literature: there is no more wholesome medicine for the mind. Not that I hold the literary productions of the ancients to be irreproachable; but I think that they have some special merits, admirably calculated to counterbalance our peculiar defects. They are a prop on the side on which we are in most danger of falling.

CHAPTER XVI.

HOW THE AMERICAN DEMOCRACY HAS MODIFIED THE ENGLISH LANGUAGE.

IF the reader has rightly understood what I have already said on the subject of literature in general, he will have no difficulty in understanding that species of influence which a democratic social condition and democratic institutions may exercise over language itself, which is the chief instrument of thought.

American authors may truly be said to live rather in England than in their own country; since they constantly study the English writers, and take them every day for their models. But it is not so with the bulk of the population, which is more immediately subjected to the peculiar causes acting upon the United States. It is not then to the written, but to the spoken language, that attention must be paid, if we would detect the changes which the idiom of an aristocratic people may undergo when it becomes the language of a democracy.

Englishmen of education, and more competent judges than I can be of the nicer shades of expression, have frequently assured me that the language of the educated classes in the United States is notably different from that of the educated classes in Great Britain. They complain, not only that the Americans have brought into use a number of new words, — the difference and the distance between the two countries might suffice to explain that much, — but that these new words are more especially taken from the jargon of parties, the mechanical arts, or the language of trade.* They assert, in addition to this, that old English words are often used by the Americans in new acceptations; and lastly, that the inhabitants of the United States frequently intermingle phraseology in the strangest manner, and sometimes place words together which are always kept apart in the language of the mother country. These remarks, which were made to me at various times by persons who appeared to be worthy of credit, led me to reflect upon the subject; and my reflections brought me, by theoretical reasoning, to the same point at which my informants had arrived by practical observation.

In aristocracies, language must naturally partake of that state of repose in which everything remains. Few new words are coined, because few new things are made; and, even if new things were made, they would be designated by known words, whose meaning had been determined by tradition. If it happens that the human mind bestirs itself at length, or is roused by light breaking in from without, the novel expressions which are introduced have a learned, intellectual, and philosophical character, which shows that they do not originate in a democracy. After the fall of Constantinople had turned the tide of science and letters towards the west, the French language was almost immedi-

* More new words and phrases, by which I mean words and phrases unknown to the standard English authors of the last century, can be found in ten pages of a popular English writer of the present day, than in a hundred of one of his American contemporaries. And the reason is obvious. The Americans, like the Scotch, having the dread of provincialism before their eyes, write with a timid regard to purity, which amounts almost to affectation; whilst the English often abuse their mother tongue on the ground of their original and exclusive right to it, — that is, on the principle that a man may do what he likes with his own. Hume, Robertson, and Dugald Stewart, three Scotchmen, wrote purer English than Gibbon, Johnson, or Jeremy Bentham; and for a similar reason, in our own times, such writers as Carlyle and Grote corrupt and debase our noble mother tongue, while such as Irving and Prescott contribute to refine and purify it. — Am. Ed.

ately invaded by a multitude of new words, which all had Greek or Latin roots. An erudite neologism then sprang up in France, which was confined to the educated classes, and which produced no sensible effect, or at least a very gradual one, upon the people.

All the nations of Europe successively exhibited the same change. Milton alone introduced more than six hundred words into the English language, almost all derived from the Latin, the Greek, or the Hebrew. The constant agitation which prevails in a democratic community tends unceasingly, on the contrary, to change the character of the language, as it does the aspect of affairs. In the midst of this general stir and competition of minds, a great number of new ideas are formed, old ideas are lost, or reappear, or are subdivided into an infinite variety of minor shades. The consequence is, that many words must fall into desuetude, and others must be brought into use.

Besides, democratic nations love change for its own sake; and this is seen in their language as much as in their politics. Even when they have no need to change words, they sometimes have the desire.

The genius of a democratic people is not only shown by the great number of words they bring into use, but also by the nature of the ideas these new words represent. Amongst such a people, the majority lays down the law in language, as well as in everything else; its prevailing spirit is as manifest in this as in other respects. But the majority is more engaged in business than in study; in political and commercial interests, than in philosophical speculation or literary pursuits. Most of the words coined or adopted for its use will bear the mark of these habits; they will mainly serve to express the wants of business, the passions of party, or the details of the public administration. In these departments, the language will constantly grow, whilst it will gradually lose ground in metaphysics and theology.

As to the source whence democratic nations are wont to derive their new expressions, and the manner in which they coin them, both may easily be described. Men living in democratic countries know but little of the language which was spoken at Athens or at Rome, and they do not care to dive into the lore of antiquity to find the expression which they want. If they have sometimes recourse to learned etymologies, vanity will induce them to search for roots from the dead languages; but erudition does not naturally furnish them its resources. The most ignorant, it sometimes happens, will use them most. The eminently democratic desire to get above their own sphere will often lead them to seek to dignify a vulgar profession by a Greek or Latin name. The lower the calling is, and the more remote from learning, the more pompous and erudite is its appellation. Thus, the French rope-dancers have transformed themselves into "Acrobates" and "Funambules."

Having little knowledge of the dead languages, democratic nations are apt to borrow words from living tongues; for they have constant mutual intercourse, and the inhabitants of different countries imitate each other the more readily as they grow more like each other every day.

But it is principally upon their own languages that democratic nations attempt to make innovations. From time to time they resume and restore to use forgotten expressions in their vocabulary, or they borrow from some particular class of the community a term peculiar to it, which they introduce with a figurative meaning into the language of daily life. Many expressions which originally belonged to the technical language of a profession or a party, are thus drawn into general circulation.

The most common expedient employed by democratic nations to make an innovation in language consists in giving an unwonted meaning to an expression already in use. This method is very simple, prompt, and convenient; no learning is required to use it aright, and ignorance itself rather facilitates the practice; but that practice is most dangerous to the language. When a democratic people double the meaning of a word in this way, they sometimes render the signification which it retains as ambiguous as that which it acquires. An author begins by a slight deflection of a known expression from its primitive meaning, and, thus modified, he adapts it as well as he can to his subject. A second writer twists the sense of the expression in another way; a third takes possession of it for another purpose; and as there is no common appeal to the sentence of a permanent tribunal which may definitively settle the signification of the word, it remains in an ambulatory condition. The consequence is, that writers hardly ever appear to dwell upon a single thought, but they always seem to aim at a group of ideas, leaving the reader to judge which of them has been hit.

This is a deplorable consequence of democracy. I had rather that the language should be made hideous with words imported from the Chinese, the Tartars, or the Hurons, than that the meaning of a word in our own language should become indeterminate. Harmony and uniformity are only secondary beauties in composition: many of these things are conventional, and, strictly speaking, it is possible to do without them; but without clear phraseology there is no good language.

The principle of equality necessarily introduces several other changes into language.

In aristocratic ages, when each nation tends to stand aloof from all others, and likes to have a physiognomy of its own, it often happens that several communities which have a common origin become nevertheless strangers to each other; so that, without ceasing to understand the same language, they no longer all speak it in the same manner. In these ages, each nation is divided into a certain number of classes, which see but little of each other, and do not intermingle. Each of these classes contracts, and invariably retains, habits of mind peculiar to itself, and adopts by choice certain words and certain terms, which afterwards pass from generation to generation, like their estates. The same idiom then comprises a language of the poor and a language of the rich, — a language of the commoner and a language of the nobility, — a learned language and a vulgar one. The deeper the divisions, and the more impassable the barriers of society become, the more must this be the case. I would lay a wager that amongst the castes of India there are amazing variations of language, and that there is almost as much difference between the language of a Pariah and that of a Brahmin, as there is in their dress.

When, on the contrary, men, being no longer restrained by ranks, meet on terms of constant intercourse, — when castes are destroyed, and the classes of society are recruited from and intermixed with each other, all the words of a language are mingled. Those which are unsuitable to the greater number perish: the remainder form a common store, whence every one chooses pretty nearly at random. Almost all the different dialects which divided the idioms of European nations are manifestly declining: there is no *patois* in the New World, and it is disappearing every day from the old countries.

The influence of this revolution in social condition is as much felt in style as it is in language. Not only does every one use the same words, but a habit springs up of using them without discrimination. The rules which style had set up are almost abolished: the line ceases to be drawn between expressions which seem by their very nature vulgar, and others which appear to be refined. Persons springing from different ranks of society carry the terms and expressions they are accustomed to use with them, into whatever circumstances they may pass; thus the origin of words is lost like the origin of individuals, and there is as much confusion in language as there is in society.

I am aware that, in the classification of words, there are rules which do not belong to one form of society any more than to another, but which are derived from the nature of things. Some expressions and phrases are vulgar, because the ideas they are meant to express are low in themselves; others are of a higher character, because the objects they are intended to designate are naturally lofty. No intermixture of ranks will ever efface these differences. But the principle of equality cannot fail to root out whatever is merely conventional and arbitrary in the forms of thought. Perhaps the necessary classification which I have just pointed out will always be less respected by a democratic people than by any other, because, amongst such a people, there are no men who are permanently disposed, by education, culture, and leisure, to study the natural laws of language, and who cause those laws to be respected by their own observance of them.

I shall not quit this topic without touching on a feature of democratic languages, which is, perhaps, more characteristic of them than any other. It has already been shown that democratic nations have a taste, and sometimes a passion, for general ideas, and that this arises from their peculiar merits and defects. This liking for general ideas is displayed in democratic languages by the continual use of generic terms or abstract expressions, and by the manner in which they are employed. This is the great merit and the great imperfection of these languages.

Democratic nations are passionately addicted to generic terms and abstract expressions, because these modes of speech enlarge thought, and assist the operations of the mind by enabling it to include many objects in a small compass. A democratic writer will be apt to speak of *capacities* in the abstract for *men of capacity*, and without specifying the objects to which their capacity is applied: he will talk about *actualities* to designate in one word the things passing before his eyes at the moment; and, in French, he will comprehend under the term *éventualités* whatever may happen in the universe, dating from the moment at which he speaks. Democratic writers are perpetually coining abstract words of this kind, in which they sublimate into further abstraction the abstract terms of the language. Nay, more, to render their mode of speech more succinct, they personify the object of these abstract terms, and make it act like a real person. Thus they would say in French, *La force des choses* veut *que les capacités gouvernent.*

I cannot better illustrate what I mean than by my own example. I have frequently used the word EQUALITY in an absolute sense, — nay, I have personified equality in several places; thus I have said, that equality does such and such things, or refrains from doing others. It may be affirmed that the writers of the age of Louis XIV. would not have spoken in this manner: they would never have thought of using the word *equality* without applying it to some particular thing; and they would rather have renounced the term altogether, than have consented to make it a living personage.

These abstract terms which abound in democratic languages, and which are used on every occasion without attaching them to any particular fact, enlarge and obscure the thoughts they are intended to convey; they render the mode of speech more succinct, and the idea contained in it less clear. But with regard to language, democratic nations prefer obscurity to labor.

I know not, indeed, whether this loose style has not some secret charm for those who speak and write amongst these nations. As the men who live there are frequently left to the efforts of their individual powers of mind, they are almost always a prey to doubt: and as their situation in life is forever changing, they are never held fast to any of their opinions by the immobility of their fortunes. Men living in democratic countries are, then, apt to entertain unsettled ideas, and they require loose expressions to convey them. As they never know whether the idea they express to-day will be appropriate to the new position they may occupy to-morrow, they naturally acquire a liking for abstract terms. An abstract term is like a box with a false bottom; you may put in it what ideas you please, and take them out again without being observed.

Amongst all nations, generic and abstract terms form the basis of language. I do not, therefore, pretend that these terms are found only in democratic languages; I say only, that men have an especial tendency, in the ages of democracy, to multiply words of this kind, — to take them always by themselves in their most abstract acceptation, and to use them on all occasions, even when the nature of the discourse does not require them.

CHAPTER XVII.

OF SOME SOURCES OF POETRY AMONGST DEMOCRATIC NATIONS.

MANY different significations have been given to the word Poetry. It would weary my readers if I were to lead them to discuss which of these definitions ought to be selected: I prefer telling them at once that which I have chosen. In my opinion, Poetry is the search after, and the delineation of, the Ideal.

The Poet is he who, by suppressing a part of what exists, by adding some imaginary touches to the picture, and by combining certain real circumstances which do not in fact happen together, completes and extends the work of nature. Thus, the object of poetry is not to represent what is true, but to adorn it, and to present to the mind some loftier image. Verse, regarded as the ideal beauty of language, may be eminently poetical; but verse does not of itself constitute poetry.

I now proceed to inquire whether, amongst the actions, the sentiments, and the opinions of democratic nations, there are any which lead to a conception of the ideal, and which may for this reason be considered as natural sources of poetry.

It must, in the first place, be acknowledged that the taste for ideal beauty, and the pleasure derived from the expression of it, are never so intense or so diffused amongst a democratic as amongst an aristocratic people. In aristocratic nations, it sometimes happens that the body acts as it were spontaneously, whilst the higher faculties are bound and burdened by repose. Amongst these nations, the people will often display poetic tastes, and their fancy sometimes ranges beyond and above what surrounds them.

But in democracies, the love of physical gratification, the notion of bettering one's condition, the excitement of competition, the charm of anticipated success, are so many spurs to urge men onward in the active professions they have embraced, without allowing them to deviate for an instant from the track. The main stress of the faculties is to this point. The imagination is not extinct; but its chief function is to devise what may be useful, and to represent what is real. The principle of equality not only diverts men from the description of ideal beauty; it also diminishes the number of objects to be described.

Aristocracy, by maintaining society in a fixed position, is favorable to the solidity and duration of positive religions, as well as to the stability of political institutions. It not only keeps the human mind within a certain sphere of belief, but it predisposes the mind to adopt one faith rather than another. An aristocratic people will always be prone to place intermediate powers between God and man. In this respect, it may be said that the aristocratic element is favorable to poetry. When the universe is peopled with supernatural beings, not palpable to sense, but discovered by the mind, the imagination ranges freely; and poets, finding a thousand subjects to delineate, also find a countless audience to take an interest in their productions.

In democratic ages, it sometimes happens, on the contrary, that men are as much afloat in matters of faith as they are in their laws. Scepticism then draws the imagination of poets back to earth, and confines them to the real and visible world. Even when the principle of equality does not disturb religious conviction, it tends to simplify it, and to divert attention from secondary agents, to fix it principally on the Supreme Power.

Aristocracy naturally leads the human mind to the contemplation of the past, and fixes it there. Democracy, on the contrary, gives men a sort of instinctive distaste for what is ancient. In this respect, aristocracy is far more favorable to poetry; for things commonly grow larger and more obscure as they are more remote; and, for this twofold reason, they are better suited to the delineation of the ideal.

After having deprived poetry of the past, the principle of equality robs it in part of the present. Amongst aristocratic nations, there are a certain number of privileged personages, whose situation is, as it were, without and above the condition of man: to these, power, wealth, fame, wit, refinement, and distinction in all things appear peculiarly to belong. The crowd never sees them very closely, or does not watch them in minute details; and little is needed to make the description of such men poetical. On the other hand, amongst the same people, you will meet with classes so ignorant, low, and enslaved, that they are no less fit objects for poetry, from the excess of their rudeness and wretchedness, than the former are from their greatness and refinement. Besides, as the different classes of which an aristocratic community is composed are widely separated, and imperfectly acquainted with each other, the imagination may always represent them with some addition to, or some subtraction from, what they really are.

In democratic communities, where men are all insignificant and very much alike, each man instantly sees all his fellows when he surveys himself. The poets of democratic ages can never, therefore, take any man in particular as the subject of a piece; for an object of slender importance, which is distinctly seen on all sides, will never lend itself to an ideal conception.

Thus the principle of equality, in proportion as it has

established itself in the world, has dried up most of the old springs of poetry. Let us now attempt to show what new ones it may disclose.

When scepticism had depopulated heaven, and the progress of equality had reduced each individual to smaller and better-known proportions, the poets, not yet aware of what they could substitute for the great themes which were departing together with the aristocracy, turned their eyes to inanimate nature. As they lost sight of gods and heroes, they set themselves to describe streams and mountains. Thence originated, in the last century, that kind of poetry which has been called, by way of distinction, *descriptive*. Some have thought that this embellished delineation of all the physical and inanimate objects which cover the earth was the kind of poetry peculiar to democratic ages; but I believe this to be an error, and that it belongs only to a period of transition.

I am persuaded that, in the end, democracy diverts the imagination from all that is external to man, and fixes it on man alone. Democratic nations may amuse themselves for a while with considering the productions of nature; but they are excited in reality only by a survey of themselves. Here, and here alone, the true sources of poetry amongst such nations are to be found; and it may be believed that the poets who shall neglect to draw their inspirations hence, will lose all sway over the minds which they would enchant, and will be left in the end with none but unimpassioned spectators of their transports.

I have shown how the ideas of progression and of the indefinite perfectibility of the human race belong to democratic ages. Democratic nations care but little for what has been, but they are haunted by visions of what will be; in this direction, their unbounded imagination grows and dilates beyond all measure. Here, then, is the widest range open to the genius of poets, which allows them to remove their performances to a sufficient distance from the eye. Democracy, which shuts the past against the poet, opens the future before him.

As all the citizens who compose a democratic community are nearly equal and alike, the poet cannot dwell upon any one of them; but the nation itself invites the exercise of his powers. The general similitude of individuals, which renders any one of them taken separately an improper subject of poetry, allows poets to include them all in the same imagery, and to take a general survey of the people itself. Democratic nations have a clearer perception than any others of their own aspect; and an aspect so imposing is admirably fitted to the delineation of the ideal.

I readily admit that the Americans have no poets; I cannot allow that they have no poetic ideas. In Europe, people talk a great deal of the wilds of America, but the Americans themselves never think about them: they are insensible to the wonders of inanimate nature, and they may be said not to perceive the mighty forests which surround them till they fall beneath the hatchet. Their eyes are fixed upon another sight: the American people views its own march across these wilds, — drying swamps, turning the course of rivers, peopling solitudes, and subduing nature. This magnificent image of themselves does not meet the gaze of the Americans at intervals only; it may be said to haunt every one of them in his least as well as in his most important actions, and to be always flitting before his mind.

Nothing conceivable is so petty, so insipid, so crowded with paltry interests, in one word, so anti-poetic, as the life of a man in the United States. But amongst the thoughts which it suggests, there is always one which is full of poetry, and this is the hidden nerve which gives vigor to the whole frame.

In aristocratic ages, each people, as well as each individual, is prone to stand separate and aloof from all others. In democratic ages, the extreme fluctuations of men, and the impatience of their desires, keep them perpetually on the move; so that the inhabitants of different countries intermingle, see, listen to, and borrow from each other. It is not only, then, the members of the same community who grow more alike; communities themselves are assimilated to one another, and the whole assemblage presents to the eye of the spectator one vast democracy, each citizen of which is a nation. This displays the aspect of mankind for the first time in the broadest light. All that belongs to the existence of the human race taken as a whole, to its vicissitudes and its future, becomes an abundant mine of poetry.

The poets who lived in aristocratic ages have been eminently successful in their delineations of certain incidents in the life of a people or a man; but none of them ever ventured to include within his performances the destinies of mankind, — a task which poets writing in democratic ages may attempt.

At that same time at which every man, raising his eyes above his country, begins at length to discern mankind at large, the Deity is more and more manifest to the human mind in full and entire majesty. If, in democratic ages, faith in positive religion be often shaken, and the belief in intermediate agents, by whatever name they are called, be overcast; on the other hand, men are disposed to conceive a far broader idea of Providence itself, and its interference in human affairs assumes a new and more imposing appearance to their eyes. Looking at the human race as one great whole, they easily conceive that its destinies are regulated by the same design; and in the actions of every individual they are led to acknowledge a trace of that universal and eternal plan on which God rules our race. This consideration may be taken as another prolific source of poetry which is opened in democratic times.

Democratic poets will always appear trivial and frigid if they seek to invest gods, demons, or angels with corporeal forms, and if they attempt to draw them down from heaven to dispute the supremacy of earth. But if they strive to connect the great events they commemorate with the general providential designs which govern the universe, and, without showing the finger of the Supreme Governor, reveal the thoughts of the Supreme Mind, their works will be admired and understood, for the imagination of their contemporaries takes this direction of its own accord.

It may be foreseen in like manner, that poets living in democratic times will prefer the delineation of passions and ideas to that of persons and achievements. The language, the dress, and the daily actions of men in democracies are repugnant to conceptions of the ideal. These things are not poetical in themselves; and if it were otherwise, they would cease to be so, because they are too familiar to all those to whom the poet would speak of them. This forces the poet constantly to search below the external surface which is palpable to the senses, in order to read the inner soul: and nothing lends itself more to the delineation of the ideal, than the scrutiny of the hidden depths in the immaterial nature of man. I need not traverse earth and sky to discover a wondrous object woven of contrasts, of infinite greatness and littleness, of intense gloom and amazing brightness, — capable at once of exciting pity, admiration, terror, contempt. I have only to look at myself. Man springs out of nothing, crosses time, and disappears forever in the bosom of God; he is seen but for a moment, wandering on the verge of the two abysses, and there he is lost.

If man were wholly ignorant of himself, he would have no poetry in him; for it is impossible to describe what the mind does not conceive. If man clearly discerned his own nature, his imagination would remain idle, and would have nothing to add to the picture. But the nature of man is sufficiently disclosed for him to apprehend something of himself, and sufficiently obscure for all the rest to be plunged in thick darkness, in which he gropes forever,—and forever in vain,—to lay hold on some completer notion of his being.

Amongst a democratic people, poetry will not be fed with legends or the memorials of old traditions. The poet will not attempt to people the universe with supernatural beings, in whom his readers and his own fancy have ceased to believe; nor will he coldly personify virtues and vices, which are better received under their own features. All these resources fail him; but Man remains, and the poet needs no more. The destinies of mankind—man himself, taken aloof from his country and his age, and standing in the presence of Nature and of God, with his passions, his doubts, his rare prosperities and inconceivable wretchedness—will become the chief, if not the sole, theme of poetry amongst these nations.

Experience may confirm this assertion, if we consider the productions of the greatest poets who have appeared since the world has been turned to democracy. The authors of our age who have so admirably delineated the features of Faust, Childe Harold, Réné, and Jocelyn, did not seek to record the actions of an individual, but to enlarge and to throw light on some of the obscurer recesses of the human heart.

Such are the poems of democracy. The principle of equality does not then destroy all the subjects of poetry: it renders them less numerous, but more vast.

CHAPTER XVIII.

WHY AMERICAN WRITERS AND ORATORS OFTEN USE AN INFLATED STYLE.

I HAVE frequently remarked that the Americans, who generally treat of business in clear, plain language, devoid of all ornament, and so extremely simple as to be often coarse, are apt to become inflated as soon as they attempt a more poetical diction. They then vent their pomposity from one end of a harangue to the other; and to hear them lavish imagery on every occasion, one might fancy that they never spoke of anything with simplicity.

The English less frequently commit a similar fault. The cause of this may be pointed out without much difficulty. In democratic communities, each citizen is habitually engaged in the contemplation of a very puny object, namely, himself. If he ever raises his looks higher, he perceives only the immense form of society at large, or the still more imposing aspect of mankind. His ideas are all either extremely minute and clear, or extremely general and vague: what lies between is a void. When he has been drawn out of his own sphere, therefore, he always expects that some amazing object will be offered to his attention; and it is on these terms alone that he consents to tear himself for a moment from the petty, complicated cares which form the charm and the excitement of his life.

This appears to me sufficiently to explain why men in democracies, whose concerns are in general so paltry, call upon their poets for conceptions so vast and descriptions so unlimited.

The authors, on their part, do not fail to obey a propensity of which they themselves partake; they perpetually inflate their imaginations, and, expanding them beyond all bounds, they not unfrequently abandon the great in order to reach the gigantic. By these means, they hope to attract the observation of the multitude, and to fix it easily upon themselves: nor are their hopes disappointed; for, as the multitude seeks for nothing in poetry but objects of vast dimensions, it has neither the time to measure with accuracy the proportions of all the objects set before it, nor a taste sufficiently correct to perceive at once in what respect they are out of proportion. The author and the public at once vitiate one another.

We have also seen, that, amongst democratic nations, the sources of poetry are grand, but not abundant. They are soon exhausted: and poets, not finding the elements of the ideal in what is real and true, abandon them entirely and create monsters. I do not fear that the poetry of democratic nations will prove insipid, or that it will fly too near the ground; I rather apprehend that it will be forever losing itself in the clouds, and that it will range at last to purely imaginary regions. I fear that the productions of democratic poets may often be surcharged with immense and incoherent imagery, with exaggerated descriptions and strange creations; and that the fantastic beings of their brain may sometimes make us regret the world of reality.

CHAPTER XIX.

SOME OBSERVATIONS ON THE DRAMA AMONGST DEMOCRATIC NATIONS.

WHEN the revolution which has changed the social and political state of an aristocratic people begins to penetrate into literature, it generally first manifests itself in the drama, and it always remains conspicuous there.

The spectator of a dramatic piece is, to a certain extent, taken by surprise by the impression it conveys. He has no time to refer to his memory, or to consult those more able to judge than himself. It does not occur to him to resist the new literary tendencies which begin to be felt by him; he yields to them before he knows what they are.

Authors are very prompt in discovering which way the taste of the public is thus secretly inclined. They shape their productions accordingly; and the literature of the stage, after having served to indicate the approaching literary revolution, speedily completes it altogether. If you would judge beforehand of the literature of a people which is lapsing into democracy, study its dramatic productions.

The literature of the stage, moreover, even amongst aristocratic nations, constitutes the most democratic part of their literature. No kind of literary gratification is so much within the reach of the multitude as that which is derived from theatrical representations. Neither preparation nor study is required to enjoy them: they lay hold on you in the midst of your prejudices and your ignorance. When the yet untutored love of the pleasures of mind begins to affect a class of the community, it immediately draws them to the stage. The theatres of aristocratic nations have always been filled with spectators not belonging to the aristocracy. At the theatre alone, the higher ranks mix with the middle and the lower classes; there alone do the former consent to listen to the opinion of the latter, or at least to allow them to give an opinion at all. At the theatre, men of cultivation and of literary attainments have always had more difficulty than elsewhere in making their taste prevail over that of the people, and in preventing themselves from being carried away by the latter. The pit has frequently made laws for the boxes.

If it be difficult for an aristocracy to prevent the people from getting the upper hand in the theatre, it will readily be understood that the people will be supreme there when democratic principles have crept into the laws and manners, — when ranks are intermixed, — when minds as well as fortunes are brought more nearly together, — and when the upper class has lost, with its hereditary wealth, its power, its traditions, and its leisure. The tastes and propensities natural to democratic nations, in respect to literature, will therefore first be discernible in the drama, and it may be foreseen that they will break out there with vehemence. In written productions, the literary canons of aristocracy will be gently, gradually, and, so to speak, legally modified; at the theatre, they will be riotously overthrown.

The drama brings out most of the good qualities, and almost all the defects, inherent in democratic literature. Democratic communities hold erudition very cheap, and care but little for what occurred at Rome and Athens; they want to hear something which concerns themselves, and the delineation of the present age is what they demand. When the heroes and the manners of antiquity are frequently brought upon the stage, and dramatic authors faithfully observe the rules of antiquated precedent, that is enough to warrant a conclusion that the democratic classes have not yet got the upper hand in the theatres.

Racine makes a very humble apology in the preface to the Britannicus for having disposed of Junia amongst the Vestals, who, according to Aulus Gellius, he says, "admitted no one below six years of age, nor above ten." We may be sure that he would neither have accused nor defended himself for such an offence, if he had written for our contemporaries.

A fact of this kind not only illustrates the state of literature at the time when it occurred, but also that of society itself. A democratic stage does not prove that the nation is in a state of democracy, for, as we have just seen, it may happen even in aristocracies that democratic tastes affect the drama: but when the spirit of aristocracy reigns exclusively on the stage, the fact irrefragably demonstrates that the whole of society is aristocratic; and it may be boldly inferred that the same lettered and learned class which sways the dramatic writers commands the people and governs the country.

The refined tastes and the arrogant bearing of an aristocracy will rarely fail to lead it, when it manages the stage, to make a kind of selection in human nature. Some of the conditions of society claim its chief interest; and the scenes which delineate their manners are preferred upon the stage. Certain virtues, and even certain vices, are thought more particularly to deserve to figure there; and they are applauded whilst all others are excluded. Upon the stage, as well as elsewhere, an aristocratic audience wishes to meet only persons of quality, and to be moved only by the misfortunes of kings. The same remark applies to style: an aristocracy is apt to impose upon dramatic authors certain modes of expression which give the key in which everything is to be delivered. By these means, the stage frequently comes to delineate only one side of man, or sometimes even to represent what is not to be met with in human nature at all, — to rise above nature, and to go beyond it.

In democratic communities, the spectators have no such preferences, and they rarely display any such antipathies: they like to see upon the stage that medley of conditions, feelings, and opinions which occurs before their eyes. The drama becomes more striking, more vulgar, and more true. Sometimes, however, those who write for the stage in democracies also transgress the bounds of human nature; but it is on a different side from their predecessors. By seeking to represent in minute detail the little singularities of the present moment, and the peculiar characteristics of certain personages, they forget to portray the general features of the race.

When the democratic classes rule the stage, they introduce as much license in the manner of treating subjects as in the choice of them. As the love of the drama is, of all literary tastes, that which is most natural to democratic nations, the number of authors and of spectators, as well as of theatrical representations, is constantly increasing amongst these communities. Such a multitude, composed of elements so different and scattered in so many different places, cannot acknowledge the same rules, or submit to the same laws. No agreement is possible amongst judges so numerous, who know not when they may meet again, and therefore each pronounces his own separate opinion on the piece. If the effect of democracy is generally to question the authority of all literary rules and conventions, on the stage it abolishes them altogether, and puts in their place nothing but the caprice of each author and each public.

The drama also displays in an especial manner the truth of what I have before said in speaking more generally of style and art in democratic literature. In reading the criticisms which were occasioned by the dramatic productions of the age of Louis XIV., one is surprised to remark the great stress which the public laid on the probability of the plot, and the importance which was attached to the perfect consistency of the characters, and to their doing nothing which could not be easily explained and understood. The value which was set upon the forms of language at that period, and the paltry strife about words with which dramatic authors were assailed, are no less surprising. It would seem that the men of the age of Louis XIV. attached very exaggerated importance to those details which may be perceived in the study, but which escape attention on the stage; for, after all, the principal object of a dramatic piece is to be performed, and its chief merit is to affect the audience. But the audience and the readers in that age were the same: on quitting the theatre, they called up the author for judgment to their own firesides.

In democracies, dramatic pieces are listened to, but not read. Most of those who frequent the amusements of the stage do not go there to seek the pleasures of mind, but the keen emotions of the heart. They do not expect to hear a fine literary work, but to see a play; and provided the author writes the language of his country correctly enough to be understood, and that his characters excite curiosity and awaken sympathy, the audience are satisfied. They ask no more of fiction, and immediately return to real life. Accuracy of style is therefore less required, because the attentive observance of its rules is less perceptible on the stage.

As for the probability of the plot, it is incompatible with perpetual novelty, surprise, and rapidity of invention. It is therefore neglected, and the public excuses the neglect. You may be sure that, if you succeed in bringing your audience into the presence of something that affects them, they will not care by what road you brought them there:

and they will never reproach you for having excited their emotions in spite of dramatic rules.

The Americans, when they go to the theatres, very broadly display all the different propensities which I have here described; but it must be acknowledged that, as yet, very few of them go to theatres at all. Although play-goers and plays have prodigiously increased in the United States in the last forty years, the population indulge in this kind of amusement only with the greatest reserve. This is attributable to peculiar causes, which the reader is already acquainted with, and of which a few words will suffice to remind him.

The Puritans who founded the American republics were not only enemies to amusements, but they professed an especial abhorrence for the stage. They considered it as an abominable pastime; and as long as their principles prevailed with undivided sway, scenic performances were wholly unknown amongst them. These opinions of the first fathers of the colony have left very deep traces on the minds of their descendants.

The extreme regularity of habits and the great strictness of morals which are observable in the United States, have as yet been little favorable to the growth of dramatic art. There are no dramatic subjects in a country which has witnessed no great political catastrophes, and in which love invariably leads by a straight and easy road to matrimony. People who spend every day in the week in making money, and the Sunday in going to church, have nothing to invite the Muse of Comedy.

A single fact suffices to show that the stage is not very popular in the United States. The Americans, whose laws allow of the utmost freedom, and even license of language in all other respects, have nevertheless subjected their dramatic authors to a sort of censorship. Theatrical performances can only take place by permission of the municipal authorities.* This may serve to show how much communities are like individuals; they surrender themselves unscrupulously to their ruling passions, and afterwards take the greatest care not to yield too much to the vehemence of tastes which they do not possess.

No portion of literature is connected by closer or more numerous ties with the present condition of society than the drama. The drama of one period can never be suited to the following age, if in the interval an important revolution has affected the manners and laws of the nation.

The great authors of a preceding age may be read; but pieces written for a different public will not attract an audience. The dramatic authors of the past live only in books. The traditional taste of certain individuals, vanity, fashion, or the genius of an actor, may sustain or resuscitate for a time the aristocratic drama amongst a democracy; but it will speedily fall away of itself, — not overthrown, but abandoned.

* This is only a regulation of police, and not a censorship of the plays; its object is to forbid improper popular amusements, such as bull-baiting or gambling. But when a theatre is once licensed, the actors can represent any plays that they choose. — AM. ED.

CHAPTER XX.

SOME CHARACTERISTICS OF HISTORIANS IN DEMOCRATIC TIMES.

HISTORIANS who write in aristocratic ages are wont to refer all occurrences to the particular will and character of certain individuals; and they are apt to attribute the most important revolutions to slight accidents. They trace out the smallest causes with sagacity, and frequently leave the greatest unperceived.

Historians who live in democratic ages exhibit precisely opposite characteristics. Most of them attribute hardly any influence to the individual over the destiny of the race, or to citizens over the fate of a people; but, on the other hand, they assign great general causes to all petty incidents. These contrary tendencies explain each other.

When the historian of aristocratic ages surveys the theatre of the world, he at once perceives a very small number of prominent actors, who manage the whole piece. These great personages, who occupy the front of the stage, arrest attention, and fix it on themselves; and whilst the historian is bent on penetrating the secret motives which make these persons speak and act, the others escape his memory. The importance of the things which some men are seen to do, gives him an exaggerated estimate of the influence which one man may possess; and naturally leads him to think, that, in order to explain the impulses of the multitude, it is necessary to refer them to the particular influence of some one individual.

When, on the contrary, all the citizens are independent

of one another, and each of them is individually weak, no one is seen to exert a great, or still less a lasting, power over the community. At first sight, individuals appear to be absolutely devoid of any influence over it; and society would seem to advance alone by the free and voluntary action of all the men who compose it. This naturally prompts the mind to search for that general reason which operates upon so many men's faculties at once, and turns them simultaneously in the same direction.

I am very well convinced that, even amongst democratic nations, the genius, the vices, or the virtues of certain individuals retard or accelerate the natural current of a people's history; but causes of this secondary and fortuitous nature are infinitely more various, more concealed, more complex, less powerful, and consequently less easy to trace, in periods of equality than in ages of aristocracy, when the task of the historian is simply to detach from the mass of general events the particular influence of one man or of a few men. In the former case, the historian is soon wearied by the toil; his mind loses itself in this labyrinth; and, in his inability clearly to discern or conspicuously to point out the influence of individuals, he denies that they have any. He prefers talking about the characteristics of race, the physical conformation of the country, or the genius of civilization, — which abridges his own labors, and satisfies his reader better at less cost.

M. de Lafayette says somewhere in his Memoirs, that the exaggerated system of general causes affords surprising consolations to second-rate statesmen. I will add, that its effects are not less consolatory to second-rate historians; it can always furnish a few mighty reasons to extricate them from the most difficult part of their work, and it indulges the indolence or incapacity of their minds, whilst it confers upon them the honors of deep thinking.

For myself, I am of opinion that, at all times, one great

portion of the events of this world are attributable to very general facts, and another to special influences. These two kinds of cause are always in operation; their proportion only varies. General facts serve to explain more things in democratic than in aristocratic ages, and fewer things are then assignable to individual influences. During periods of aristocracy, the reverse takes place: special influences are stronger, general causes weaker; unless, indeed, we consider as a general cause the fact itself of the inequality of condition, which allows some individuals to baffle the natural tendencies of all the rest.

The historians who seek to describe what occurs in democratic societies are right, therefore, in assigning much to general causes, and in devoting their chief attention to discover them; but they are wrong in wholly denying the special influence of individuals, because they cannot easily trace or follow it.

The historians who live in democratic ages are not only prone to assign a great cause to every incident, but they are also given to connect incidents together so as to deduce a system from them. In aristocratic ages, as the attention of historians is constantly drawn to individuals, the connection of events escapes them; or, rather, they do not believe in any such connection. To them, the clew of history seems every instant crossed and broken by the step of man. In democratic ages, on the contrary, as the historian sees much more of actions than of actors, he may easily establish some kind of sequence and methodical order amongst the former.

Ancient literature, which is so rich in fine historical compositions, does not contain a single great historical system, whilst the poorest of modern literatures abound with them. It would appear that the ancient historians did not make sufficient use of those general theories which our historical writers are ever ready to carry to excess.

Those who write in democratic ages have another more dangerous tendency. When the traces of individual action upon nations are lost, it often happens that the world goes on to move, though the moving agent is no longer discoverable. As it becomes extremely difficult to discern and analyze the reasons which, acting separately on the will of each member of the community, concur in the end to produce movement in the whole mass, men are led to believe that this movement is involuntary, and that societies unconsciously obey some superior force ruling over them. But even when the general fact which governs the private volition of all individuals is supposed to be discovered upon the earth, the principle of human free-will is not secured. A cause sufficiently extensive to affect millions of men at once, and sufficiently strong to bend them all together in the same direction, may well seem irresistible: having seen that mankind do yield to it, the mind is close upon the inference that mankind cannot resist it.

Historians who live in democratic ages, then, not only deny that the few have any power of acting upon the destiny of a people, but they deprive the people themselves of the power of modifying their own condition, and they subject them either to an inflexible Providence or to some blind necessity. According to them, each nation is indissolubly bound by its position, its origin, its antecedents, and its character, to a certain lot which no efforts can ever change. They involve generation in generation, and thus, going back from age to age, and from necessity to necessity, up to the origin of the world, they forge a close and enormous chain, which girds and binds the human race. To their minds it is not enough to show what events have occurred: they would fain show that events could not have occurred otherwise. They take a nation arrived at a certain stage of its history, and they affirm that it could not but follow the track which brought it thither. It is easier to make such an assertion than to show how the nation might have adopted a better course.

In reading the historians of aristocratic ages, and especially those of antiquity, it would seem that, to be master of his lot and to govern his fellow-creatures, man requires only to be master of himself. In perusing the historical volumes which our age has produced, it would seem that man is utterly powerless over himself and over all around him. The historians of antiquity taught how to command: those of our time teach only how to obey; in their writings the author often appears great, but humanity is always diminutive.

If this doctrine of necessity, which is so attractive to those who write history in democratic ages, passes from authors to their readers, till it infects the whole mass of the community and gets possession of the public mind, it will soon paralyze the activity of modern society, and reduce Christians to the level of the Turks.

I would moreover observe, that such doctrines are peculiarly dangerous at the period at which we are arrived. Our contemporaries are but too prone to doubt of human free-will, because each of them feels himself confined on every side by his own weakness; but they are still willing to acknowledge the strength and independence of men united in society. Let not this principle be lost sight of; for the great object in our time is to raise the faculties of men, not to complete their prostration.

CHAPTER XXI.

OF PARLIAMENTARY ELOQUENCE IN THE UNITED STATES.

AMONGST aristocratic nations, all the members of the community are connected with, and dependent upon, each other; the graduated scale of different ranks acts as a tie, which keeps every one in his proper place, and the whole body in subordination. Something of the same kind always occurs in the political assemblies of these nations. Parties naturally range themselves under certain leaders, whom they obey by a sort of instinct, which is only the result of habits contracted elsewhere. They carry the manners of general society into the lesser assemblage.

In democratic countries, it often happens that a great number of citizens are tending to the same point; but each one only moves thither, or at least flatters himself that he moves, of his own accord. Accustomed to regulate his doings by personal impulse alone, he does not willingly submit to dictation from without. This taste and habit of independence accompany him into the councils of the nation. If he consents to connect himself with other men in the prosecution of the same purpose, at least he chooses to remain free to contribute to the common success after his own fashion. Hence it is that, in democratic countries, parties are so impatient of control, and are never manageable except in moments of great public danger. Even then, the authority of leaders, which under such circumstances may be able to make men act or speak, hardly ever reaches the extent of making them keep silence.

Amongst aristocratic nations, the members of political

assemblies are at the same time members of the aristocracy. Each of them enjoys high established rank in his own right, and the position which he occupies in the assembly is often less important in his eyes than that which he fills in the country. This consoles him for playing no part in the discussion of public affairs, and restrains him from too eagerly attempting to play an insignificant one.

In America, it generally happens that a representative only becomes somebody from his position in the assembly. He is therefore perpetually haunted by a craving to acquire importance there, and he feels a petulant desire to be constantly obtruding his opinions upon his fellow-members. His own vanity is not the only stimulant which urges him on in this course, but that of his constituents, and the continual necessity of propitiating them. Amongst aristocratic nations, a member of the legislature is rarely in strict dependence upon his constituents: he is frequently to them a sort of unavoidable representative; sometimes they are themselves strictly dependent upon him; and if, at length, they reject him, he may easily get elected elsewhere, or, retiring from public life, he may still enjoy the pleasures of splendid idleness. In a democratic country, like the United States, a representative has hardly ever a lasting hold on the minds of his constituents. However small an electoral body may be, the fluctuations of democracy are constantly changing its aspect: it must therefore be courted unceasingly. One is never sure of his supporters, and, if they forsake him, he is left without a resource; for his natural position is not sufficiently elevated for him to be easily known to those not close to him; and, with the complete state of independence prevailing among the people, he cannot hope that his friends or the government will send him down to be returned by an electoral body unacquainted with him. The seeds of his fortune are, therefore, sown in his own neighborhood: from that nook of earth he must start, to raise himself to command the people and to influence the destinies of the world. Thus it is natural that, in democratic countries, the members of political assemblies should think more of their constituents than of their party, whilst, in aristocracies, they think more of their party than of their constituents.

But what ought to be said to gratify constituents is not always what ought to be said in order to serve the party to which representatives profess to belong. The general interest of a party frequently demands that members belonging to it should not speak on great questions which they understand imperfectly; that they should speak but little on those minor questions which impede the great ones; lastly, and for the most part, that they should not speak at all. To keep silence is the most useful service that an indifferent spokesman can render to the commonwealth.

Constituents, however, do not think so. The population of a district send a representative to take a part in the government of a country, because they entertain a very high notion of his merits. As men appear greater in proportion to the littleness of the objects by which they are surrounded, it may be assumed that the opinion entertained of the delegate will be so much the higher, as talents are more rare among his constituents. It will therefore frequently happen, that, the less constituents ought to expect from their representative, the more they will anticipate from him; and, however incompetent he may be, they will not fail to call upon him for signal exertions, corresponding to the rank they have conferred upon him.

Independently of his position as a legislator of the State, electors also regard their representative as the natural patron of the constituency in the legislature; they almost consider him as the proxy of each of his supporters, and they flatter themselves that he will not be less zealous in defence of their private interests than of those of the country. Thus electors are well assured beforehand that the representative of their choice will be an orator; that he will speak often if he can, and that, in case he is forced to refrain, he will strive at any rate to compress into his less frequent orations an inquiry into all the great questions of state, combined with a statement of all the petty grievances they have themselves to complain of; so that, though he be not able to come forward frequently, he should on each occasion prove what he is capable of doing; and that, instead of perpetually lavishing his powers, he should occasionally condense them in a small compass, so as to furnish a sort of complete and brilliant epitome of his constituents and of himself. On these terms, they will vote for him at the next election.

These conditions drive worthy men of humble abilities to despair; who, knowing their own powers, would never voluntarily have come forward. But thus urged on, the representative begins to speak, to the great alarm of his friends; and, rushing imprudently into the midst of the most celebrated orators, he perplexes the debate and wearies the House.

All laws which tend to make the representative more dependent on the elector, not only affect the conduct of the legislators, as I have remarked elsewhere, but also their language. They exercise a simultaneous influence on affairs themselves, and on the manner in which affairs are discussed.

There is hardly a member of Congress who can make up his mind to go home without having despatched at least one speech to his constituents; nor who will endure any interruption until he has introduced into his harangue whatever useful suggestions may be made touching the four and twenty States of which the Union is composed, and especially the district which he represents. He therefore presents to the mind of his auditors a succession of great general truths (which he himself only comprehends, and expresses, confusedly), and of petty minutiæ, which he is but too able to discover and to point out. The consequence is, that the debates of that great assembly are frequently vague and perplexed, and that they seem rather to drag their slow length along, than to advance towards a distinct object. Some such state of things will, I believe, always arise in the public assemblies of democracies.

Propitious circumstances and good laws might succeed in drawing to the legislature of a democratic people men very superior to those who are returned by the Americans to Congress; but nothing will ever prevent the men of slender abilities who sit there from obtruding themselves with complacency, and in all ways, upon the public. The evil does not appear to me to be susceptible of entire cure, because it not only originates in the tactics of that assembly, but in its constitution and in that of the country. The inhabitants of the United States seem themselves to consider the matter in this light; and they show their long experience of parliamentary life, not by abstaining from making bad speeches, but by courageously submitting to hear them made. They are resigned to it, as to an evil which they know to be inevitable.

We have shown the petty side of political debates in democratic assemblies,—let us now exhibit the imposing one. The proceedings within the Parliament of England for the last one hundred and fifty years have never occasioned any great sensation out of that country; the opinions and feelings expressed by the speakers have never awakened much sympathy, even amongst the nations placed nearest to the great arena of British liberty; whereas Europe was excited by the very first debates which took place in the small colonial assemblies of America, at the time of the Revolution.

This was attributable not only to particular and fortuitous circumstances, but to general and lasting causes. I can conceive nothing more admirable or more powerful than a great orator debating great questions of state in a democratic assembly. As no particular class is ever represented there by men commissioned to defend its own interests, it is always to the whole nation, and in the name of the whole nation, that the orator speaks. This expands his thoughts, and heightens his power of language. As precedents have there but little weight, — as there are no longer any privileges attached to certain property, nor any rights inherent in certain individuals, — the mind must have recourse to general truths derived from human nature to resolve the particular question under discussion. Hence the political debates of a democratic people, however small it may be, have a degree of breadth which frequently renders them attractive to mankind. All men are interested by them, because they treat of *man*, who is everywhere the same.

Amongst the greatest aristocratic nations, on the contrary, the most general questions are almost always argued on some special grounds derived from the practice of a particular time or the rights of a particular class, which interest that class alone, or at most the people amongst whom that class happens to exist.

It is owing to this, as much as to the greatness of the French people and the favorable disposition of the nations who listen to them, that the great effect which the French political debates sometimes produce in the world must be attributed. The orators of France frequently speak to mankind, even when they are addressing their countrymen only.

SECOND BOOK.

INFLUENCE OF DEMOCRACY ON THE FEELINGS OF THE AMERICANS.

CHAPTER I.

WHY DEMOCRATIC NATIONS SHOW A MORE ARDENT AND ENDURING LOVE OF EQUALITY THAN OF LIBERTY.

THE first and most intense passion which is produced by equality of condition is, I need hardly say, the love of that equality. My readers will therefore not be surprised that I speak of this feeling before all others.

Everybody has remarked that, in our time, and especially in France, this passion for equality is every day gaining ground in the human heart. It has been said a hundred times, that our contemporaries are far more ardently and tenaciously attached to equality than to freedom; but, as I do not find that the causes of the fact have been sufficiently analyzed, I shall endeavor to point them out.

It is possible to imagine an extreme point at which freedom and equality would meet and be confounded together. Let us suppose that all the people take a part in the government, and that each one of them has an equal right to take a part in it. As no one is different from his fellows, none can exercise a tyrannical power; men will be perfectly free, because they are all entirely equal; and they will all be perfectly equal, because they are entirely free. To this ideal state democratic nations tend. This is the only complete form that equality can assume upon earth; but there are a thousand others which, without being equally perfect, are not less cherished by those nations.

The principle of equality may be established in civil society, without prevailing in the political world. Equal rights may exist of indulging in the same pleasures, of entering the same professions, of frequenting the same places; in a word, of living in the same manner and seeking wealth by the same means, — although all men do not take an equal share in the government. A kind of equality may even be established in the political world, though there should be no political freedom there. A man may be the equal of all his countrymen save one, who is the master of all without distinction, and who selects equally from among them all the agents of his power. Several other combinations might be easily imagined, by which very great equality would be united to institutions more or less free, or even to institutions wholly without freedom.

Although men cannot become absolutely equal unless they are entirely free; and consequently equality, pushed to its furthest extent, may be confounded with freedom, yet there is good reason for distinguishing the one from the other. The taste which men have for liberty, and that which they feel for equality, are, in fact, two different things; and I am not afraid to add, that, amongst democratic nations, they are two unequal things.

Upon close inspection, it will be seen that there is in every age some peculiar and preponderating fact with which all others are connected; this fact almost always gives birth to some pregnant idea or some ruling passion, which attracts to itself and bears away in its course all the feelings and opinions of the time: it is like a great stream, towards which each of the neighboring rivulets seems to flow.

Freedom has appeared in the world at different times

and under various forms; it has not been exclusively bound to any social condition, and it is not confined to democracies. Freedom cannot, therefore, form the distinguishing characteristic of democratic ages. The peculiar and preponderating fact which marks those ages as its own is the equality of condition; the ruling passion of men in those periods is the love of this equality. Ask not what singular charm the men of democratic ages find in being equal, or what special reasons they may have for clinging so tenaciously to equality rather than to the other advantages which society holds out to them: equality is the distinguishing characteristic of the age they live in; that, of itself, is enough to explain that they prefer it to all the rest.

But independently of this reason, there are several others, which will at all times habitually lead men to prefer equality to freedom.

If a people could ever succeed in destroying, or even in diminishing, the equality which prevails in its own body, they could do so only by long and laborious efforts. Their social condition must be modified, their laws abolished, their opinions superseded, their habits changed, their manners corrupted. But political liberty is more easily lost; to neglect to hold it fast, is to allow it to escape. Men therefore cling to equality not only because it is dear to them; they also adhere to it because they think it will last forever.

That political freedom may compromise in its excesses the tranquillity, the property, the lives of individuals, is obvious even to narrow and unthinking minds. On the contrary, none but attentive and clear-sighted men perceive the perils with which equality threatens us, and they commonly avoid pointing them out. They know that the calamities they apprehend are remote, and flatter themselves that they will only fall upon future generations, for which the present generation takes but little thought. The evils which freedom sometimes brings with it are immediate; they are apparent to all, and all are more or less affected by them. The evils which extreme equality may produce are slowly disclosed; they creep gradually into the social frame; they are seen only at intervals; and at the moment at which they become most violent, habit already causes them to be no longer felt.

The advantages which freedom brings are only shown by the lapse of time; and it is always easy to mistake the cause in which they originate. The advantages of equality are immediate, and they may always be traced from their source.

Political liberty bestows exalted pleasures, from time to time, upon a certain number of citizens. Equality every day confers a number of small enjoyments on every man. The charms of equality are every instant felt, and are within the reach of all; the noblest hearts are not insensible to them, and the most vulgar souls exult in them. The passion which equality creates must therefore be at once strong and general. Men cannot enjoy political liberty unpurchased by some sacrifices, and they never obtain it without great exertions. But the pleasures of equality are self-proffered: each of the petty incidents of life seems to occasion them; and in order to taste them, nothing is required but to live.

Democratic nations are at all times fond of equality, but there are certain epochs at which the passion they entertain for it swells to the height of fury. This occurs at the moment when the old social system, long menaced, is overthrown after a severe intestine struggle, and the barriers of rank are at length thrown down. At such times, men pounce upon equality as their booty, and they cling to it as to some precious treasure which they fear to lose. The passion for equality penetrates on every side into men's hearts, expands there, and fills them entirely. Tell them not that, by this blind surrender of themselves to an exclusive passion, they risk their dearest interests: they are deaf.

Show them not freedom escaping from their grasp, whilst they are looking another way: they are blind, or, rather, they can discern but one object to be desired in the universe.

What I have said is applicable to all democratic nations; what I am about to say concerns the French alone. Amongst most modern nations, and especially amongst all those of the continent of Europe, the taste and the idea of freedom only began to exist and to be developed at the time when social conditions were tending to equality, and as a consequence of that very equality. Absolute kings were the most efficient levellers of ranks amongst their subjects. Amongst these nations, equality preceded freedom: equality was therefore a fact of some standing when freedom was still a novelty; the one had already created customs, opinions, and laws belonging to it, when the other, alone and for the first time, came into actual existence. Thus the latter was still only an affair of opinion and of taste, whilst the former had already crept into the habits of the people, possessed itself of their manners, and given a particular turn to the smallest actions in their lives. Can it be wondered at that the men of our own time prefer the one to the other?

I think that democratic communities have a natural taste for freedom: left to themselves, they will seek it, cherish it, and view any privation of it with regret. But for equality, their passion is ardent, insatiable, incessant, invincible: they call for equality in freedom; and if they cannot obtain that, they still call for equality in slavery. They will endure poverty, servitude, barbarism; but they will not endure aristocracy.

This is true at all times, and especially in our own day. All men and all powers seeking to cope with this irresistible passion will be overthrown and destroyed by it. In our age, freedom cannot be established without it, and despotism itself cannot reign without its support.

CHAPTER II.

OF INDIVIDUALISM* IN DEMOCRATIC COUNTRIES.

I HAVE shown how it is that, in ages of equality, every man seeks for his opinions within himself: I am now to show how it is that, in the same ages, all his feelings are turned towards himself alone. *Individualism* is a novel expression, to which a novel idea has given birth. Our fathers were only acquainted with *égoïsme* (selfishness). Selfishness is a passionate and exaggerated love of self, which leads a man to connect everything with himself, and to prefer himself to everything in the world. Individualism is a mature and calm feeling, which disposes each member of the community to sever himself from the mass of his fellows, and to draw apart with his family and his friends; so that, after he has thus formed a little circle of his own, he willingly leaves society at large to itself. Selfishness originates in blind instinct: individualism proceeds from erroneous judgment more than from depraved feelings; it originates as much in deficiencies of mind as in perversity of heart.

Selfishness blights the germ of all virtue: individualism, at first, only saps the virtues of public life; but, in the long run, it attacks and destroys all others, and is at length

* I adopt the expression of the original, however strange it may seem to the English ear, partly because it illustrates the remark on the introduction of general terms into democratic language which was made in a preceding chapter, and partly because I know of no English word exactly equivalent to the expression. The chapter itself defines the meaning attached to it by the author. — *English Translator's Note.*

absorbed in downright selfishness. Selfishness is a vice as old as the world, which does not belong to one form of society more than to another: individualism is of democratic origin, and it threatens to spread in the same ratio as the equality of condition.

Amongst aristocratic nations, as families remain for centuries in the same condition, often on the same spot, all generations become, as it were, contemporaneous. A man almost always knows his forefathers, and respects them: he thinks he already sees his remote descendants, and he loves them. He willingly imposes duties on himself towards the former and the latter; and he will frequently sacrifice his personal gratifications to those who went before and to those who will come after him. Aristocratic institutions have, moreover, the effect of closely binding every man to several of his fellow-citizens. As the classes of an aristocratic people are strongly marked and permanent, each of them is regarded by its own members as a sort of lesser country, more tangible and more cherished than the country at large. As, in aristocratic communities, all the citizens occupy fixed positions, one above the other, the result is, that each of them always sees a man above himself whose patronage is necessary to him, and, below himself, another man whose co-operation he may claim. Men living in aristocratic ages are therefore almost always closely attached to something placed out of their own sphere, and they are often disposed to forget themselves. It is true that, in these ages, the notion of human fellowship is faint, and that men seldom think of sacrificing themselves for mankind; but they often sacrifice themselves for other men. In democratic times, on the contrary, when the duties of each individual to the race are much more clear, devoted service to any one man becomes more rare; the bond of human affection is extended, but it is relaxed.

Amongst democratic nations, new families are constantly

springing up, others are constantly falling away, and all that remain change their condition; the woof of time is every instant broken, and the track of generations effaced. Those who went before are soon forgotten; of those who will come after, no one has any idea: the interest of man is confined to those in close propinquity to himself. As each class approximates to other classes, and intermingles with them, its members become indifferent, and as strangers to one another. Aristocracy had made a chain of all the members of the community, from the peasant to the king: democracy breaks that chain, and severs every link of it.

As social conditions become more equal, the number of persons increases who, although they are neither rich nor powerful enough to exercise any great influence over their fellows, have nevertheless acquired or retained sufficient education and fortune to satisfy their own wants. They owe nothing to any man, they expect nothing from any man; they acquire the habit of always considering themselves as standing alone, and they are apt to imagine that their whole destiny is in their own hands.

Thus, not only does democracy make every man forget his ancestors, but it hides his descendants and separates his contemporaries from him; it throws him back forever upon himself alone, and threatens in the end to confine him entirely within the solitude of his own heart.

CHAPTER III.

INDIVIDUALISM STRONGER AT THE CLOSE OF A DEMOCRATIC REVOLUTION THAN AT OTHER PERIODS.

THE period when the construction of democratic society upon the ruins of an aristocracy has just been completed is especially that at which this isolation of men from one another, and the selfishness resulting from it, most forcibly strike the observation. Democratic communities not only contain a large number of independent citizens, but they are constantly filled with men who, having entered but yesterday upon their independent condition, are intoxicated with their new power. They entertain a presumptuous confidence in their own strength, and, as they do not suppose that they can henceforward ever have occasion to claim the assistance of their fellow-creatures, they do not scruple to show that they care for nobody but themselves.

An aristocracy seldom yields without a protracted struggle, in the course of which implacable animosities are kindled between the different classes of society. These passions survive the victory, and traces of them may be observed in the midst of the democratic confusion which ensues. Those members of the community who were at the top of the late gradations of rank cannot immediately forget their former greatness; they will long regard themselves as aliens in the midst of the newly-composed society. They look upon all those whom this state of society has made their equals as oppressors, whose destiny can excite no sympathy; they have lost sight of their former equals, and feel no longer bound by a common interest to their fate: each of them, standing aloof, thinks that he is reduced to care for himself alone. Those, on the contrary, who were formerly at the foot of the social scale, and who have been brought up to the common level by a sudden revolution, cannot enjoy their newly-acquired independence without secret uneasiness; and if they meet with some of their former superiors on the same footing as themselves, they stand aloof from them with an expression of triumph and fear.

It is, then, commonly at the outset of democratic society that citizens are most disposed to live apart. Democracy leads men not to draw near to their fellow-creatures; but democratic revolutions lead them to shun each other, and perpetuate in a state of equality the animosities which the state of inequality created.

The great advantage of the Americans is, that they have arrived at a state of democracy without having to endure a democratic revolution; and that they are born equal, instead of becoming so.

CHAPTER IV.

THAT THE AMERICANS COMBAT THE EFFECTS OF INDIVIDUALISM BY FREE INSTITUTIONS.

DESPOTISM, which is of a very timorous nature, is never more secure of continuance than when it can keep men asunder; and all its influence is commonly exerted for that purpose. No vice of the human heart is so acceptable to it as selfishness: a despot easily forgives his subjects for not loving him, provided they do not love each other. He does not ask them to assist him in governing the state; it is enough that they do not aspire to govern it themselves. He stigmatizes as turbulent and unruly spirits those who would combine their exertions to promote the prosperity of the community; and, perverting the natural meaning of words, he applauds as good citizens those who have no sympathy for any but themselves.

Thus the vices which despotism produces are precisely those which equality fosters. These two things mutually and perniciously complete and assist each other. Equality places men side by side, unconnected by any common tie; despotism raises barriers to keep them asunder: the former predisposes them not to consider their fellow-creatures, the latter makes general indifference a sort of public virtue.

Despotism, then, which is at all times dangerous, is more particularly to be feared in democratic ages. It is easy to see that in those same ages men stand most in need of freedom. When the members of a community are forced to attend to public affairs, they are necessarily drawn from the circle of their own interests, and snatched at times from self-observation. As soon as a man begins to treat of public affairs in public, he begins to perceive that he is not so independent of his fellow-men as he had at first imagined, and that, in order to obtain their support, he must often lend them his co-operation.

When the public govern, there is no man who does not feel the value of public good-will, or who does not endeavor to court it by drawing to himself the esteem and affection of those amongst whom he is to live. Many of the passions which congeal and keep asunder human hearts, are then obliged to retire and hide below the surface. Pride must be dissembled; disdain dares not break out; selfishness fears its own self. Under a free government, as most public offices are elective, the men whose elevated minds or aspiring hopes are too closely circumscribed in private life constantly feel that they cannot do without the people who surround them. Men learn at such times to think of their fellow-men from ambitious motives; and they frequently find it, in a manner, their interest to forget themselves.

I may here be met by an objection derived from electioneering intrigues, the meanness of candidates, and the calumnies of their opponents. These are occasions of enmity which occur the oftener, the more frequent elections become. Such evils are doubtless great, but they are transient; whereas the benefits which attend them remain. The desire of being elected may lead some men for a time to violent hostility; but this same desire leads all men in the long run mutually to support each other; and, if it happens that an election accidentally severs two friends, the electoral system brings a multitude of citizens permanently together, who would otherwise always have remained unknown to each other. Freedom produces private animosities, but despotism gives birth to general indifference.

The Americans have combated by free institutions the

tendency of equality to keep men asunder, and they have subdued it. The legislators of America did not suppose that a general representation of the whole nation would suffice to ward off a disorder at once so natural to the frame of democratic society, and so fatal: they also thought that it would be well to infuse political life into each portion of the territory, in order to multiply to an infinite extent opportunities of acting in concert for all the members of the community, and to make them constantly feel their mutual dependence on each other. The plan was a wise one. The general affairs of a country only engage the attention of leading politicians, who assemble from time to time in the same places; and, as they often lose sight of each other afterwards, no lasting ties are established between them. But if the object be to have the local affairs of a district conducted by the men who reside there, the same persons are always in contact, and they are, in a manner, forced to be acquainted, and to adapt themselves to one another.

It is difficult to draw a man out of his own circle to interest him in the destiny of the state, because he does not clearly understand what influence the destiny of the state can have upon his own lot. But if it be proposed to make a road cross the end of his estate, he will see at a glance that there is a connection between this small public affair and his greatest private affairs; and he will discover, without its being shown to him, the close tie which unites private to general interest. Thus, far more may be done by intrusting to the citizens the administration of minor affairs than by surrendering to them the control of important ones, towards interesting them in the public welfare, and convincing them that they constantly stand in need one of another in order to provide for it. A brilliant achievement may win for you the favor of a people at one stroke; but to earn the love and respect of the population which surrounds you, a long succession of little services rendered and of obscure good deeds, — a constant habit of kindness, and an established reputation for disinterestedness, — will be required. Local freedom, then, which leads a great number of citizens to value the affection of their neighbors and of their kindred, perpetually brings men together, and forces them to help one another, in spite of the propensities which sever them.

In the United States, the more opulent citizens take great care not to stand aloof from the people; on the contrary, they constantly keep on easy terms with the lower classes: they listen to them, they speak to them every day. They know that the rich in democracies always stand in need of the poor; and that, in democratic times, you attach a poor man to you more by your manner than by benefits conferred. The magnitude of such benefits, which sets off the difference of condition, causes a secret irritation to those who reap advantage from them; but the charm of simplicity of manners is almost irresistible: affability carries men away, and even want of polish is not always displeasing. This truth does not take root at once in the minds of the rich. They generally resist it as long as the democratic revolution lasts, and they do not acknowledge it immediately after that revolution is accomplished. They are very ready to do good to the people, but they still choose to keep them at arm's length; they think that is sufficient, but they are mistaken. They might spend fortunes thus without warming the hearts of the population around them; — that population does not ask them for the sacrifice of their money, but of their pride.

It would seem as if every imagination in the United States were upon the stretch to invent means of increasing the wealth and satisfying the wants of the public. The best-informed inhabitants of each district constantly use their information to discover new truths which may augment the general prosperity; and, if they have made any such discoveries, they eagerly surrender them to the mass of the people.

When the vices and weaknesses frequently exhibited by those who govern in America are closely examined, the prosperity of the people occasions, but improperly occasions, surprise. Elected magistrates do not make the American democracy flourish; it flourishes because the magistrates are elective.

It would be unjust to suppose that the patriotism and the zeal which every American displays for the welfare of his fellow-citizens are wholly insincere. Although private interest directs the greater part of human actions in the United States, as well as elsewhere, it does not regulate them all. I must say that I have often seen Americans make great and real sacrifices to the public welfare; and I have remarked a hundred instances in which they hardly ever failed to lend faithful support to each other. The free institutions which the inhabitants of the United States possess, and the political rights of which they make so much use, remind every citizen, and in a thousand ways, that he lives in society. They every instant impress upon his mind the notion that it is the duty, as well as the interest, of men to make themselves useful to their fellow-creatures; and as he sees no particular ground of animosity to them, since he is never either their master or their slave, his heart readily leans to the side of kindness. Men attend to the interests of the public, first by necessity, afterwards by choice: what was intentional becomes an instinct; and by dint of working for the good of one's fellow-citizens, the habit and the taste for serving them is at length acquired.

Many people in France consider equality of condition as one evil, and political freedom as a second. When they are obliged to yield to the former, they strive at least to escape from the latter. But I contend that, in order to combat the evils which equality may produce, there is only one effectual remedy, — namely, political freedom.

CHAPTER V.

OF THE USE WHICH THE AMERICANS MAKE OF PUBLIC ASSOCIATIONS IN CIVIL LIFE.

I DO not propose to speak of those political associations by the aid of which men endeavor to defend themselves against the despotic action of a majority, or against the aggressions of regal power. That subject I have already treated. If each citizen did not learn, in proportion as he individually becomes more feeble, and consequently more incapable of preserving his freedom single-handed, to combine with his fellow-citizens for the purpose of defending it, it is clear that tyranny would unavoidably increase together with equality.

Those associations only which are formed in civil life, without reference to political objects, are here adverted to. The political associations which exist in the United States are only a single feature in the midst of the immense assemblage of associations in that country. Americans of all ages, all conditions, and all dispositions, constantly form associations. They have not only commercial and manufacturing companies, in which all take part, but associations of a thousand other kinds, — religious, moral, serious, futile, general or restricted, enormous or diminutive. The Americans make associations to give entertainments, to found seminaries, to build inns, to construct churches, to diffuse books, to send missionaries to the antipodes; they found in this manner hospitals, prisons, and schools. If it be proposed to inculcate some truth, or to foster some feeling, by the encouragement of a great example, they form a society. Wherever, at the head of some new undertaking, you see the government in France, or a man of rank in England, in the United States you will be sure to find an association.

I met with several kinds of associations in America of which I confess I had no previous notion; and I have often admired the extreme skill with which the inhabitants of the United States succeed in proposing a common object to the exertions of a great many men, and in inducing them voluntarily to pursue it.

I have since travelled over England, whence the Americans have taken some of their laws and many of their customs; and it seemed to me that the principle of association was by no means so constantly or adroitly used in that country. The English often perform great things singly, whereas the Americans form associations for the smallest undertakings. It is evident that the former people consider association as a powerful means of action, but the latter seem to regard it as the only means they have of acting.

Thus, the most democratic country on the face of the earth is that in which men have, in our time, carried to the highest perfection the art of pursuing in common the object of their common desires, and have applied this new science to the greatest number of purposes. Is this the result of accident? or is there in reality any necessary connection between the principle of association and that of equality?

Aristocratic communities always contain, amongst a multitude of persons who by themselves are powerless, a small number of powerful and wealthy citizens, each of whom can achieve great undertakings single-handed. In aristocratic societies, men do not need to combine in order to act, because they are strongly held together. Every wealthy and powerful citizen constitutes the head of a permanent and compulsory association, composed of all those who are dependent upon him, or whom he makes subservient to the execution of his designs.

Amongst democratic nations, on the contrary, all the citizens are independent and feeble; they can do hardly anything by themselves, and none of them can oblige his fellow-men to lend him their assistance. They all, therefore, become powerless, if they do not learn voluntarily to help each other. If men living in democratic countries had no right and no inclination to associate for political purposes, their independence would be in great jeopardy; but they might long preserve their wealth and their cultivation: whereas, if they never acquired the habit of forming associations in ordinary life, civilization itself would be endangered. A people amongst whom individuals should lose the power of achieving great things single-handed, without acquiring the means of producing them by united exertions, would soon relapse into barbarism.

Unhappily, the same social condition which renders associations so necessary to democratic nations, renders their formation more difficult amongst those nations than amongst all other. When several members of an aristocracy agree to combine, they easily succeed in doing so: as each of them brings great strength to the partnership, the number of its members may be very limited; and when the members of an association are limited in number, they may easily become mutually acquainted, understand each other, and establish fixed regulations. The same opportunities do not occur amongst democratic nations, where the associated members must always be very numerous for their association to have any power.

I am aware that many of my countrymen are not in the least embarrassed by this difficulty. They contend, that, the more enfeebled and incompetent the citizens become, the more able and active the government ought to be rendered, in order that society at large may execute what individuals can no longer accomplish. They believe this answers the whole difficulty, but I think they are mistaken.

A government might perform the part of some of the largest American companies; and several States, members of the Union, have already attempted it; but what political power could ever carry on the vast multitude of lesser undertakings which the American citizens perform every day, with the assistance of the principle of association? It is easy to foresee that the time is drawing near when man will be less and less able to produce, of himself alone, the commonest necessaries of life. The task of the governing power will therefore perpetually increase, and its very efforts will extend it every day. The more it stands in the place of associations, the more will individuals, losing the notion of combining together, require its assistance: these are causes and effects which unceasingly create each other. Will the administration of the country ultimately assume the management of all the manufactures which no single citizen is able to carry on? And if a time at length arrives when, in consequence of the extreme subdivision of landed property, the soil is split into an infinite number of parcels, so that it can only be cultivated by companies of husbandmen, will it be necessary that the head of the government should leave the helm of state to follow the plough? The morals and the intelligence of a democratic people would be as much endangered as its business and manufactures, if the government ever wholly usurped the place of private companies.

Feelings and opinions are recruited, the heart is enlarged, and the human mind is developed, only by the reciprocal influence of men upon each other. I have shown that these influences are almost null in democratic countries; they must therefore be artificially created, and this can only be accomplished by associations.

When the members of an aristocratic community adopt

a new opinion, or conceive a new sentiment, they give it a station, as it were, beside themselves, upon the lofty platform where they stand; and opinions or sentiments so conspicuous to the eyes of the multitude are easily introduced into the minds or hearts of all around. In democratic countries, the governing power alone is naturally in a condition to act in this manner; but it is easy to see that its action is always inadequate, and often dangerous. A government can no more be competent to keep alive and to renew the circulation of opinions and feelings amongst a great people, than to manage all the speculations of productive industry. No sooner does a government attempt to go beyond its political sphere, and to enter upon this new track, than it exercises, even unintentionally, an insupportable tyranny; for a government can only dictate strict rules, the opinions which it favors are rigidly enforced, and it is never easy to discriminate between its advice and its commands. Worse still will be the case, if the government really believes itself interested in preventing all circulation of ideas; it will then stand motionless and oppressed by the heaviness of voluntary torpor. Governments, therefore, should not be the only active powers: associations ought, in democratic nations, to stand in lieu of those powerful private individuals whom the equality of conditions has swept away.

As soon as several of the inhabitants of the United States have taken up an opinion or a feeling which they wish to promote in the world, they look out for mutual assistance; and as soon as they have found each other out, they combine. From that moment they are no longer isolated men, but a power seen from afar, whose actions serve for an example, and whose language is listened to. The first time I heard in the United States that a hundred thousand men had bound themselves publicly to abstain from spirituous liquors, it appeared to me more like a joke than a serious engagement; and I did not at once perceive why these temperate citizens could not content themselves with drinking water by their own firesides. I at last understood that these hundred thousand Americans, alarmed by the progress of drunkenness around them, had made up their minds to patronize temperance. They acted just in the same way as a man of high rank who should dress very plainly, in order to inspire the humbler orders with a contempt of luxury. It is probable that, if these hundred thousand men had lived in France, each of them would singly have memorialized the government to watch the public houses all over the kingdom.

Nothing, in my opinion, is more deserving of our attention than the intellectual and moral associations of America. The political and industrial associations of that country strike us forcibly; but the others elude our observation, or, if we discover them, we understand them imperfectly, because we have hardly ever seen anything of the kind. It must, however, be acknowledged, that they are as necessary to the American people as the former, and perhaps more so. In democratic countries, the science of association is the mother of science; the progress of all the rest depends upon the progress it has made.

Amongst the laws which rule human societies, there is one which seems to be more precise and clear than all others. If men are to remain civilized, or to become so, the art of associating together must grow and improve in the same ratio in which the equality of conditions is increased.

CHAPTER VI.

OF THE RELATION BETWEEN PUBLIC ASSOCIATIONS AND THE NEWSPAPERS.

WHEN men are no longer united amongst themselves by firm and lasting ties, it is impossible to obtain the co-operation of any great number of them, unless you can persuade every man whose help you require that his private interest obliges him voluntarily to unite his exertions to the exertions of all the others. This can be habitually and conveniently effected only by means of a newspaper: nothing but a newspaper can drop the same thought into a thousand minds at the same moment. A newspaper is an adviser who does not require to be sought, but who comes of his own accord, and talks to you briefly every day of the common weal, without distracting you from your private affairs.

Newspapers therefore become more necessary in proportion as men become more equal, and individualism more to be feared. To suppose that they only serve to protect freedom would be to diminish their importance: they maintain civilization. I shall not deny that, in democratic countries, newspapers frequently lead the citizens to launch together into very ill-digested schemes; but if there were no newspapers, there would be no common activity. The evil which they produce is therefore much less than that which they cure.

The effect of a newspaper is not only to suggest the same purpose to a great number of persons, but to furnish means for executing in common the designs which they may have singly conceived. The principal citizens who inhabit an aristocratic country discern each other from afar; and if they wish to unite their forces, they move towards each other, drawing a multitude of men after them. It frequently happens, on the contrary, in democratic countries, that a great number of men who wish or who want to combine cannot accomplish it, because, as they are very insignificant and lost amidst the crowd, they cannot see, and know not where to find, one another. A newspaper then takes up the notion or the feeling which had occurred simultaneously, but singly, to each of them. All are then immediately guided towards this beacon; and these wandering minds, which had long sought each other in darkness, at length meet and unite. The newspaper brought them together, and the newspaper is still necessary to keep them united.

In order that an association amongst a democratic people should have any power, it must be a numerous body. The persons of whom it is composed are therefore scattered over a wide extent, and each of them is detained in the place of his domicile by the narrowness of his income, or by the small unremitting exertions by which he earns it. Means must then be found to converse every day without seeing each other, and to take steps in common without having met. Thus, hardly any democratic association can do without newspapers.

There is, consequently, a necessary connection between public associations and newspapers: newspapers make associations, and associations make newspapers; and if it has been correctly advanced, that associations will increase in number as the conditions of men become more equal, it is not less certain that the number of newspapers increases in proportion to that of associations. Thus it is, in America, that we find at the same time the greatest number of associations and of newspapers.

This connection between the number of newspapers and that of associations leads us to the discovery of a further connection between the state of the periodical press and the form of the administration in a country, and shows that the number of newspapers must diminish or increase amongst a democratic people, in proportion as its administration is more or less centralized. For, amongst democratic nations, the exercise of local powers cannot be intrusted to the principal members of the community, as in aristocracies. Those powers must either be abolished, or placed in the hands of very large numbers of men, who then in fact constitute an association permanently established by law, for the purpose of administering the affairs of a certain extent of territory; and they require a journal, to bring to them every day, in the midst of their own minor concerns, some intelligence of the state of their public weal. The more numerous local powers are, the greater is the number of men in whom they are vested by law; and as this want is hourly felt, the more profusely do newspapers abound.

The extraordinary subdivision of administrative power has much more to do with the enormous number of American newspapers, than the great political freedom of the country and the absolute liberty of the press. If all the inhabitants of the Union had the suffrage, — but a suffrage which should extend only to the choice of their legislators in Congress, — they would require but few newspapers, because they would have to act together only on very important, but very rare, occasions. But within the great national association, lesser associations have been established by law in every county, every city, and indeed in every village, for the purposes of local administration. The laws of the country thus compel every American to co-operate every day of his life with some of his fellow-citizens for a common purpose, and each one of them requires a newspaper to inform him what all the others are doing.

I am of opinion that a democratic people,* without any national representative assemblies, but with a great number of small local powers, would have in the end more newspapers than another people governed by a centralized administration and an elective legislature. What best explains to me the enormous circulation of the daily press in the United States is, that, amongst the Americans, I find the utmost national freedom combined with local freedom of every kind.

There is a prevailing opinion in France and England, that the circulation of newspapers would be indefinitely increased by removing the taxes which have been laid upon the press. This is a very exaggerated estimate of the effects of such a reform. Newspapers increase in numbers, not according to their cheapness, but according to the more or less frequent want which a great number of men may feel for intercommunication and combination.

In like manner, I should attribute the increasing influence of the daily press to causes more general than those by which it is commonly explained. A newspaper can only subsist on the condition of publishing sentiments or principles common to a large number of men. A newspaper, therefore, always represents an association which is composed of its habitual readers. This association may be more or less defined, more or less restricted, more or less numerous; but the fact that the newspaper keeps alive, is a proof that at least the germ of such an association exists in the minds of its readers.

* I say a *democratic people:* the administration of an aristocratic people may be the reverse of centralized, and yet the want of newspapers be little felt, because local powers are then vested in the hands of a very small number of men, who either act apart, or who know each other, and can easily meet and come to an understanding.

This leads me to a last reflection, with which I shall conclude this chapter. The more equal the conditions of men become, and the less strong men individually are, the more easily do they give way to the current of the multitude, and the more difficult is it for them to adhere by themselves to an opinion which the multitude discard. A newspaper represents an association; it may be said to address each of its readers in the name of all the others, and to exert its influence over them in proportion to their individual weakness. The power of the newspaper press must therefore increase as the social conditions of men become more equal.

CHAPTER VII.

RELATION OF CIVIL TO POLITICAL ASSOCIATIONS.

THERE is only one country on the face of the earth where the citizens enjoy unlimited freedom of association for political purposes. This same country is the only one in the world where the continual exercise of the right of association has been introduced into civil life, and where all the advantages which civilization can confer are procured by means of it.

In all the countries where political associations are prohibited, civil associations are rare. It is hardly probable that this is the result of accident; but the inference should rather be, that there is a natural, and perhaps a necessary, connection between these two kinds of associations.

Certain men happen to have a common interest in some concern; either a commercial undertaking is to be managed, or some speculation in manufactures to be tried: they meet, they combine, and thus, by degrees, they become familiar with the principle of association. The greater the multiplicity of small affairs, the more do men, even without knowing it, acquire facility in prosecuting great undertakings in common.

Civil associations, therefore, facilitate political association; but, on the other hand, political association singularly strengthens and improves associations for civil purposes. In civil life, every man may, strictly speaking, fancy that he can provide for his own wants; in politics, he can fancy no such thing. When a people, then, have any knowledge of public life, the notion of association, and the wish to coalesce, present themselves every day to the minds of the whole community: whatever natural repugnance may restrain men from acting in concert, they will always be ready to combine for the sake of a party. Thus political life makes the love and practice of association more general; it imparts a desire of union, and teaches the means of combination to numbers of men who otherwise would have always lived apart.

Politics not only give birth to numerous associations, but to associations of great extent. In civil life, it seldom happens that any one interest draws a very large number of men to act in concert; much skill is required to bring such an interest into existence: but in politics, opportunities present themselves every day. Now it is solely in great associations that the general value of the principle of association is displayed. Citizens who are individually powerless do not very clearly anticipate the strength which they may acquire by uniting together; it must be shown to them in order to be understood. Hence it is often easier to collect a multitude for a public purpose than a few persons; a thousand citizens do not see what interest they have in combining together; ten thousand will be perfectly aware of it. In politics, men combine for great undertakings; and the use they make of the principle of association in important affairs practically teaches them that it is their interest to help each other in those of less moment. A political association draws a number of individuals at the same time out of their own circle; however they may be naturally kept asunder by age, mind, and fortune, it places them nearer together, and brings them into contact. Once met, they can always meet again.

Men can embark in few civil partnerships without risking a portion of their possessions; this is the case with all manufacturing and trading companies. When men are as yet but little versed in the art of association, and are unacquainted with its principal rules, they are afraid, when first they combine in this manner, of buying their experience dear. They therefore prefer depriving themselves of a powerful instrument of success, to running the risks which attend the use of it. They are, however, less reluctant to join political associations, which appear to them to be without danger, because they adventure no money in them. But they cannot belong to these associations for any length of time, without finding out how order is maintained amongst a large number of men, and by what contrivance they are made to advance, harmoniously and methodically, to the same object. Thus they learn to surrender their own will to that of all the rest, and to make their own exertions subordinate to the common impulse, — things which it is not less necessary to know in civil than in political associations. Political associations may therefore be considered as large free schools, where all the members of the community go to learn the general theory of association.

But even if political association did not directly contribute to the progress of civil association, to destroy the former would be to impair the latter. When citizens can only meet in public for certain purposes, they regard such meetings as a strange proceeding of rare occurrence, and they rarely think at all about it. When they are allowed to meet freely for all purposes, they ultimately look upon public association as the universal, or in a manner the sole, means which men can employ to accomplish the different purposes they may have in view. Every new want instantly revives the notion. The art of association then becomes, as I have said before, the mother of action, studied and applied by all.

When some kinds of associations are prohibited and others allowed, it is difficult to distinguish the former from the latter beforehand. In this state of doubt, men abstain from them altogether, and a sort of public opinion passes current, which tends to cause any association whatsoever to be regarded as a bold, and almost an illicit enterprise.*

It is therefore chimerical to suppose that the spirit of association, when it is repressed on some one point, will nevertheless display the same vigor on all others; and that, if men be allowed to prosecute certain undertakings in common, that is quite enough for them eagerly to set about them. When the members of a community are allowed and accustomed to combine for all purposes, they will combine as readily for the lesser as for the more important ones; but if they are only allowed to combine for small affairs, they will be neither inclined nor able to effect it. It is in vain that you will leave them entirely free to prosecute their business on joint-stock account: they will hardly care to avail themselves of the rights you have granted to them; and, after having exhausted your strength in vain efforts to put down prohibited associations, you will be surprised that you cannot persuade men to form the associations you encourage.

* This is more especially true when the executive government has a discretionary power of allowing or prohibiting associations. When certain associations are simply prohibited by law, and the courts of justice have to punish infringements of that law, the evil is far less considerable. Then, every citizen knows beforehand pretty nearly what he has to expect. He judges himself before he is judged by the law, and, abstaining from prohibited associations, he embarks in those which are legally sanctioned. It is by these restrictions that all free nations have always admitted that the right of association might be limited. But if the legislature should invest a man with a power of ascertaining beforehand which associations are dangerous and which are useful, and should authorize him to destroy all associations in the bud, or to allow them to be formed, as nobody would be able to foresee in what cases associations might be established, and in what cases they would be put down, the spirit of association would be entirely paralyzed. The former of these laws would only assail certain associations; the latter would apply to society itself, and inflict an injury upon it. I can conceive that a regular government may have recourse to the former, but I do not concede that any government has the right of enacting the latter.

I do not say that there can be no civil associations in a country where political association is prohibited; for men can never live in society without embarking in some common undertakings: but I maintain that, in such a country, civil associations will always be few in number, feebly planned, unskilfully managed, that they will never form any vast designs, or that they will fail in the execution of them.

This naturally leads me to think that freedom of association in political matters is not so dangerous to public tranquillity as is supposed; and that possibly, after having agitated society for some time, it may strengthen the state in the end. In democratic countries, political associations are, so to speak, the only powerful persons who aspire to rule the state. Accordingly, the governments of our time look upon associations of this kind just as sovereigns in the Middle Ages regarded the great vassals of the crown: they entertain a sort of instinctive abhorrence of them, and combat them on all occasions. They bear, on the contrary, a natural good-will to civil associations, because they readily discover that, instead of directing the minds of the community to public affairs, these institutions serve to divert them from such reflections; and that, by engaging them more and more in the pursuit of objects which cannot be attained without public tranquillity, they deter them from revolutions. But these governments do not attend to the fact, that political associations tend amazingly to multiply and facilitate those of a civil character, and that, in avoiding a dangerous evil, they deprive themselves of an efficacious remedy.

When you see the Americans freely and constantly forming associations for the purpose of promoting some political principle, of raising one man to the head of affairs, or of wresting power from another, you have some difficulty in understanding how men so independent do not constantly fall into the abuse of freedom. If, on the other hand, you survey the infinite number of trading companies which are in operation in the United States, and perceive that the Americans are on every side unceasingly engaged in the execution of important and difficult plans, which the slightest revolution would throw into confusion, you will readily comprehend why people so well employed are by no means tempted to perturb the state, nor to destroy that public tranquillity by which they all profit.

Is it enough to observe these things separately, or should we not discover the hidden tie which connects them? In their political associations, the Americans, of all conditions, minds, and ages, daily acquire a general taste for association, and grow accustomed to the use of it. There they meet together in large numbers, — they converse, they listen to each other, and they are mutually stimulated to all sorts of undertakings. They afterwards transfer to civil life the notions they have thus acquired, and make them subservient to a thousand purposes. Thus it is by the enjoyment of a dangerous freedom that the Americans learn the art of rendering the dangers of freedom less formidable.

If a certain moment in the existence of a nation be selected, it is easy to prove that political associations perturb the state and paralyze productive industry; but take the whole life of a people, and it may perhaps be easy to demonstrate, that freedom of association in political matters is favorable to the prosperity, and even to the tranquillity, of the community.

I said in the former part of this work: "The unrestrained liberty of political association cannot be entirely assimilated to the liberty of the press. The one is at the same time less necessary and more dangerous than the other. A nation may confine it within certain limits, without ceasing to be mistress of itself; and it may sometimes be obliged to do so, in order to maintain its own authority." And, further on, I added: "It cannot be denied that the unrestrained liberty of association for political purposes is the last degree of liberty which a people is fit for. If it does not throw them into anarchy, it perpetually brings them, as it were, to the verge of it." Thus, I do not think that a nation is always at liberty to invest its citizens with an absolute right of association for political purposes; and I doubt whether, in any country or in any age, it be wise to set no limits to freedom of association.

A certain nation, it is said, could not maintain tranquillity in the community, cause the laws to be respected, or establish a lasting government, if the right of association were not confined within narrow limits. These blessings are doubtless invaluable; and I can imagine that, to acquire or to preserve them, a nation may impose upon itself severe temporary restrictions: but still it is well that the nation should know at what price these blessings are purchased. I can understand that it may be advisable to cut off a man's arm in order to save his life; but it would be ridiculous to assert that he will be as dexterous as he was before he lost it.

CHAPTER VIII.

HOW THE AMERICANS COMBAT INDIVIDUALISM BY THE PRINCIPLE OF INTEREST RIGHTLY UNDERSTOOD.

WHEN the world was managed by a few rich and powerful individuals, these persons loved to entertain a lofty idea of the duties of man. They were fond of professing that it is praiseworthy to forget one's self, and that good should be done without hope of reward, as it is by the Deity himself. Such were the standard opinions of that time in morals.

I doubt whether men were more virtuous in aristocratic ages than in others; but they were incessantly talking of the beauties of virtue, and its utility was only studied in secret. But since the imagination takes less lofty flights, and every man's thoughts are centred in himself, moralists are alarmed by this idea of self-sacrifice, and they no longer venture to present it to the human mind. They therefore content themselves with inquiring, whether the personal advantage of each member of the community does not consist in working for the good of all; and when they have hit upon some point on which private interest and public interest meet and amalgamate, they are eager to bring it into notice. Observations of this kind are gradually multiplied: what was only a single remark becomes a general principle; and it is held as a truth, that man serves himself in serving his fellow-creatures, and that his private interest is to do good.

I have already shown, in several parts of this work, by what means the inhabitants of the United States almost always manage to combine their own advantage with that of their fellow-citizens: my present purpose is to point out the general rule which enables them to do so. In the United States, hardly anybody talks of the beauty of virtue; but they maintain that virtue is useful, and prove it every day. The American moralists do not profess that men ought to sacrifice themselves for their fellow-creatures *because* it is noble to make such sacrifices; but they boldly aver that such sacrifices are as necessary to him who imposes them upon himself, as to him for whose sake they are made.

They have found out that, in their country and their age, man is brought home to himself by an irresistible force; and, losing all hope of stopping that force, they turn all their thoughts to the direction of it. They therefore do not deny that every man may follow his own interest; but they endeavor to prove that it is the interest of every man to be virtuous. I shall not here enter into the reasons they allege, which would divert me from my subject: suffice it to say, that they have convinced their fellow-countrymen.

Montaigne said long ago, "Were I not to follow the straight road for its straightness, I should follow it for having found by experience that, in the end, it is commonly the happiest and most useful track." The doctrine of interest rightly understood is not then new, but amongst the Americans of our time it finds universal acceptance: it has become popular there; you may trace it at the bottom of all their actions, you will remark it in all they say. It is as often asserted by the poor man as by the rich. In Europe, the principle of interest is much grosser than it is in America, but it is also less common, and especially it is less avowed; amongst us, men still constantly feign great abnegation which they no longer feel.

The Americans, on the contrary, are fond of explaining almost all the actions of their lives by the principle of interest rightly understood; they show with complacency how an enlightened regard for themselves constantly prompts them to assist each other, and inclines them willingly to sacrifice a portion of their time and property to the welfare of the state. In this respect, I think they frequently fail to do themselves justice; for, in the United States, as well as elsewhere, people are sometimes seen to give way to those disinterested and spontaneous impulses which are natural to man: but the Americans seldom allow that they yield to emotions of this kind; they are more anxious to do honor to their philosophy than to themselves.

I might here pause, without attempting to pass a judgment on what I have described. The extreme difficulty of the subject would be my excuse, but I shall not avail myself of it; and I had rather that my readers, clearly perceiving my object, should refuse to follow me, than that I should leave them in suspense.

The principle of interest rightly understood is not a lofty one, but it is clear and sure. It does not aim at mighty objects, but it attains without excessive exertion all those at which it aims. As it lies within the reach of all capacities, every one can without difficulty apprehend and retain it. By its admirable conformity to human weaknesses, it easily obtains great dominion; nor is that dominion precarious, since the principle checks one personal interest by another, and uses, to direct the passions, the very same instrument which excites them.

The principle of interest rightly understood produces no great acts of self-sacrifice, but it suggests daily small acts of self-denial. By itself, it cannot suffice to make a man virtuous; but it disciplines a number of persons in habits of regularity, temperance, moderation, foresight, self-command; and, if it does not lead men straight to virtue by the will, it gradually draws them in that direction by their habits. If the principle of interest rightly understood were to sway the whole moral world, extraordinary virtues would doubtless be more rare; but I think that gross depravity would then also be less common. The principle of interest rightly understood perhaps prevents men from rising far above the level of mankind; but a great number of other men, who were falling far below it, are caught and restrained by it. Observe some few individuals, they are lowered by it; survey mankind, they are raised.

I am not afraid to say, that the principle of interest rightly understood appears to me the best suited of all philosophical theories to the wants of the men of our time, and that I regard it as their chief remaining security against themselves. Towards it, therefore, the minds of the moralists of our age should turn; even should they judge it to be incomplete, it must nevertheless be adopted as necessary.

I do not think, upon the whole, that there is more selfishness amongst us than in America; the only difference is, that there it is enlightened, here it is not. Every American will sacrifice a portion of his private interests to preserve the rest; we would fain preserve the whole, and oftentimes the whole is lost. Everybody I see about me seems bent on teaching his contemporaries, by precept and example, that what is useful is never wrong. Will nobody undertake to make them understand how what is right may be useful?

No power upon earth can prevent the increasing equality of conditions from inclining the human mind to seek out what is useful, or from leading every member of the community to be wrapped up in himself. It must therefore be expected that personal interest will become more than ever the principal, if not the sole, spring of men's actions; but it remains to be seen how each man will understand his personal interest. If the members of a community, as they become more equal, become more ignorant and coarse, it is difficult to foresee to what pitch of stupid excesses their selfishness may lead them; and no one can foretell into what disgrace and wretchedness they would plunge themselves, lest they should have to sacrifice something of their own well-being to the prosperity of their fellow-creatures.

I do not think that the system of interest, as it is professed in America, is, in all its parts, self-evident; but it contains a great number of truths so evident, that men, if they are but educated, cannot fail to see them. Educate, then, at any rate; for the age of implicit self-sacrifice and instinctive virtues is already flitting far away from us, and the time is fast approaching when freedom, public peace, and social order itself will not be able to exist without education.

CHAPTER IX.

THAT THE AMERICANS APPLY THE PRINCIPLE OF INTEREST RIGHTLY UNDERSTOOD TO RELIGIOUS MATTERS.

IF the principle of interest rightly understood had nothing but the present world in view, it would be very insufficient, for there are many sacrifices which can only find their recompense in another; and whatever ingenuity may be put forth to demonstrate the utility of virtue, it will never be an easy task to make that man live aright who has no thought of dying.

It is therefore necessary to ascertain whether the principle of interest rightly understood can be easily reconciled with religious belief. The philosophers who inculcate this system of morals tell men that, to be happy in this life, they must watch their own passions, and steadily control their excess; that lasting happiness can be secured only by renouncing a thousand transient gratifications; and that a man must perpetually triumph over himself in order to secure his own advantage. The founders of almost all religions have held the same language. The track they point out to man is the same, only the goal is more remote; instead of placing in this world the reward of the sacrifices they impose, they transport it to another.

Nevertheless, I cannot believe that all those who practise virtue from religious motives are actuated only by the hope of a recompense. I have known zealous Christians who constantly forgot themselves, to work with greater ardor for the happiness of their fellow-men; and I have heard them declare that all they did was only to earn the blessings of a future state. I cannot but think that they deceive themselves: I respect them too much to believe them.

Christianity, indeed, teaches that a man must prefer his neighbor to himself, in order to gain eternal life; but Christianity also teaches that men ought to benefit their fellow-creatures for the love of God. A sublime expression! Man searches by his intellect into the Divine conception, and sees that order is the purpose of God; he freely gives his own efforts to aid in prosecuting this great design, and, whilst he sacrifices his personal interests to this consummate order of all created things, expects no other recompense than the pleasure of contemplating it.

I do not believe that interest is the sole motive of religious men: but I believe that interest is the principal means which religions themselves employ to govern men, and I do not question that in this way they strike the multitude and become popular. I do not see clearly why the principle of interest rightly understood should undermine the religious opinions of men; it seems to me more easy to show why it should strengthen them. Let it be supposed that, in order to attain happiness in this world, a man combats his instincts on all occasions, and deliberately calculates every action of his life; that, instead of yielding blindly to the impetuosity of first desires, he has learned the art of resisting them, and that he has accustomed himself to sacrifice without an effort the pleasure of a moment to the lasting interest of his whole life. If such a man believes in the religion which he professes, it will cost him but little to submit to the restrictions it may impose. Reason herself counsels him to obey, and habit has prepared him to endure these limitations. If he should have conceived any doubts as to the object of his hopes, still he will not easily allow himself to be stopped by them; and he will decide that it is wise to risk some of the advantages of this world, in order to preserve his rights to the great inheritance promised him in another. "To be mistaken in believing that the Christian religion is true," says Pascal, "is no great loss to any one; but how dreadful to be mistaken in believing it to be false!"

The Americans do not affect a brutal indifference to a future state; they affect no puerile pride in despising perils which they hope to escape from. They therefore profess their religion without shame and without weakness; but there generally is, even in their zeal, something so indescribably tranquil, methodical, and deliberate, that it would seem as if the head, far more than the heart, brought them to the foot of the altar.

The Americans not only follow their religion from interest, but they often place in this world the interest which makes them follow it. In the Middle Ages, the clergy spoke of nothing but a future state; they hardly cared to prove that a sincere Christian may be a happy man here below. But the American preachers are constantly referring to the earth; and it is only with great difficulty that they can divert their attention from it. To touch their congregations, they always show them how favorable religious opinions are to freedom and public tranquillity; and it is often difficult to ascertain from their discourses whether the principal object of religion is to procure eternal felicity in the other world, or prosperity in this.

CHAPTER X.

OF THE TASTE FOR PHYSICAL WELL-BEING IN AMERICA.

IN America, the passion for physical well-being is not always exclusive, but it is general; and if all do not feel it in the same manner, yet it is felt by all. Carefully to satisfy even the least wants of the body, and to provide the little conveniences of life, is uppermost in every mind. Something of an analogous character is more and more apparent in Europe. Amongst the causes which produce these similar consequences in both hemispheres, several are so connected with my subject as to deserve notice.

When riches are hereditarily fixed in families, a great number of men enjoy the comforts of life without feeling an exclusive taste for those comforts. The heart of man is not so much caught by the undisturbed possession of anything valuable, as by the desire, as yet imperfectly satisfied, of possessing it, and by the incessant dread of losing it. In aristocratic communities, the wealthy, never having experienced a condition different from their own, entertain no fear of changing it; the existence of such conditions hardly occurs to them. The comforts of life are not to them the end of life, but simply a way of living; they regard them as existence itself, — enjoyed, but scarcely thought of. As the natural and instinctive taste which all men feel for being well off is thus satisfied without trouble and without apprehension, their faculties are turned elsewhere, and applied to more arduous and lofty undertakings, which excite and engross their minds.

Hence it is that, in the very midst of physical gratifications, the members of an aristocracy often display a haughty contempt of these very enjoyments, and exhibit singular powers of endurance under the privation of them. All the revolutions which have ever shaken or destroyed aristocracies have shown how easily men accustomed to superfluous luxuries can do without the necessaries of life; whereas men who have toiled to acquire a competency can hardly live after they have lost it.

If I turn my observation from the upper to the lower classes, I find analogous effects produced by opposite causes. Amongst a nation where aristocracy predominates in society, and keeps it stationary, the people in the end get as much accustomed to poverty as the rich to their opulence. The latter bestow no anxiety on their physical comforts, because they enjoy them without an effort; the former do not think of things which they despair of obtaining, and which they hardly know enough of to desire them. In communities of this kind, the imagination of the poor is driven to seek another world; the miseries of real life enclose it around, but it escapes from their control, and flies to seek its pleasures far beyond.

When, on the contrary, the distinctions of ranks are confounded together and privileges are destroyed, — when hereditary property is subdivided, and education and freedom widely diffused, the desire of acquiring the comforts of the world haunts the imagination of the poor, and the dread of losing them that of the rich. Many scanty fortunes spring up; those who possess them have a sufficient share of physical gratifications to conceive a taste for these pleasures, — not enough to satisfy it. They never procure them without exertion, and they never indulge in them without apprehension. They are therefore always straining to pursue or to retain gratifications so delightful, so imperfect, so fugitive.

If I were to inquire what passion is most natural to men

who are stimulated and circumscribed by the obscurity of their birth or the mediocrity of their fortune, I could discover none more peculiarly appropriate to their condition than this love of physical prosperity. The passion for physical comforts is essentially a passion of the middle classes: with those classes it grows and spreads, with them it preponderates. From them it mounts into the higher orders of society, and descends into the mass of the people.

I never met in America with any citizen so poor as not to cast a glance of hope and envy on the enjoyments of the rich, or whose imagination did not possess itself by anticipation of those good things which fate still obstinately withheld from him.

On the other hand, I never perceived amongst the wealthier inhabitants of the United States that proud contempt of physical gratifications which is sometimes to be met with even in the most opulent and dissolute aristocracies. Most of these wealthy persons were once poor: they have felt the sting of want; they were long a prey to adverse fortunes; and now that the victory is won, the passions which accompanied the contest have survived it: their minds are, as it were, intoxicated by the small enjoyments which they have pursued for forty years.

Not but that in the United States, as elsewhere, there are a certain number of wealthy persons, who, having come into their property by inheritance, possess without exertion an opulence they have not earned. But even these men are not less devotedly attached to the pleasures of material life. The love of well-being is now become the predominant taste of the nation; the great current of human passions runs in that channel, and sweeps everything along in its course.

CHAPTER XI.

PECULIAR EFFECTS OF THE LOVE OF PHYSICAL GRATIFICATIONS IN DEMOCRATIC TIMES.

IT may be supposed, from what has just been said, that the love of physical gratifications must constantly urge the Americans to irregularities in morals, disturb the peace of families, and threaten the security of society at large. But it is not so: the passion for physical gratifications produces in democracies effects very different from those which it occasions in aristocratic nations.

It sometimes happens that, wearied with public affairs and sated with opulence, amidst the ruin of religious belief and the decline of the state, the heart of an aristocracy may by degrees be seduced to the pursuit of sensual enjoyments alone. At other times, the power of the monarch or the weakness of the people, without stripping the nobility of their fortune, compels them to stand aloof from the administration of affairs, and, whilst the road to mighty enterprise is closed, abandons them to the inquietude of their own desires; they then fall back heavily upon themselves, and seek in the pleasures of the body oblivion of their former greatness.

When the members of an aristocratic body are thus exclusively devoted to the pursuit of physical gratifications, they commonly turn in that direction all the energy which they derive from their long experience of power. Such men are not satisfied with the pursuit of comfort; they require sumptuous depravity and splendid corruption. The worship they pay the senses is a gorgeous one; and they seem to vie with each other in the art of degrading their own natures. The stronger, the more famous, and the more free an aristocracy has been, the more depraved will it then become; and, however brilliant may have been the lustre of its virtues, I dare predict that they will always be surpassed by the splendor of its vices.

The taste for physical gratifications leads a democratic people into no such excesses. The love of well-being is there displayed as a tenacious, exclusive, universal passion; but its range is confined. To build enormous palaces, to conquer or to mimic nature, to ransack the world in order to gratify the passions of a man, is not thought of: but to add a few roods of land to your field, to plant an orchard, to enlarge a dwelling, to be always making life more comfortable and convenient, to avoid trouble, and to satisfy the smallest wants without effort and almost without cost. These are small objects, but the soul clings to them; it dwells upon them closely and day by day, till they at last shut out the rest of the world, and sometimes intervene between itself and Heaven.

This, it may be said, can only be applicable to those members of the community who are in humble circumstances; wealthier individuals will display tastes akin to those which belonged to them in aristocratic ages. I contest the proposition: in point of physical gratifications, the most opulent members of a democracy will not display tastes very different from those of the people; whether it be that, springing from the people, they really share those tastes, or that they esteem it a duty to submit to them. In democratic society, the sensuality of the public has taken a moderate and tranquil course, to which all are bound to conform: it is as difficult to depart from the common rule by one's vices as by one's virtues. Rich men who live amidst democratic nations are therefore more intent on providing for their smallest wants, than for their extraordinary enjoyments; they gratify a number of petty desires, without indulging in any great irregularities of passion: thus, they are more apt to become enervated than debauched.

The special taste which the men of democratic times entertain for physical enjoyments is not naturally opposed to the principles of public order; nay, it often stands in need of order, that it may be gratified. Nor is it adverse to regularity of morals, for good morals contribute to public tranquillity and are favorable to industry. It may even be frequently combined with a species of religious morality: men wish to be as well off as they can in this world, without foregoing their chance of another. Some physical gratifications cannot be indulged in without crime; from such they strictly abstain. The enjoyment of others is sanctioned by religion and morality; to these the heart, the imagination, and life itself, are unreservedly given up; till, in snatching at these lesser gifts, men lose sight of those more precious possessions which constitute the glory and the greatness of mankind.

The reproach I address to the principle of equality is not that it leads men away in the pursuit of forbidden enjoyments, but that it absorbs them wholly in quest of those which are allowed. By these means, a kind of virtuous materialism may ultimately be established in the world, which would not corrupt, but enervate, the soul, and noiselessly unbend its springs of action.

CHAPTER XII.

WHY SOME AMERICANS MANIFEST A SORT OF FANATICAL SPIRITUALISM.

ALTHOUGH the desire of acquiring the good things of this world is the prevailing passion of the American people, certain momentary outbreaks occur, when their souls seem suddenly to burst the bonds of matter by which they are restrained, and to soar impetuously towards Heaven. In all the States of the Union, but especially in the half-peopled country of the Far West, itinerant preachers may be met with, who hawk about the word of God from place to place. Whole families, old men, women, and children, cross rough passes and untrodden wilds, coming from a great distance, to join a camp-meeting, where they totally forget, for several days and nights, in listening to these discourses, the cares of business and even the most urgent wants of the body.

Here and there, in the midst of American society, you meet with men full of a fanatical and almost wild spiritualism, which hardly exists in Europe. From time to time, strange sects arise, which endeavor to strike out extraordinary paths to eternal happiness. Religious insanity is very common in the United States.

Nor ought these facts to surprise us. It was not man who implanted in himself the taste for what is infinite, and the love of what is immortal: these lofty instincts are not the offspring of his capricious will; their steadfast foundation is fixed in human nature, and they exist in spite of his efforts. He may cross and distort them; destroy them he cannot.

The soul has wants which must be satisfied; and whatever pains be taken to divert it from itself, it soon grows weary, restless, and disquieted amidst the enjoyments of sense. If ever the faculties of the great majority of mankind were exclusively bent upon the pursuit of material objects, it might be anticipated that an amazing reaction would take place in the souls of some men. They would drift at large in the world of spirits, for fear of remaining shackled by the close bondage of the body.

It is not, then, wonderful, if, in the midst of a community whose thoughts tend earthward, a small number of individuals are to be found who turn their looks to Heaven. I should be surprised if mysticism did not soon make some advance amongst a people solely engaged in promoting their own worldly welfare.

It is said that the deserts of the Thebaid were peopled by the persecutions of the Emperors and the massacres of the Circus; I should rather say, that it was by the luxuries of Rome and the Epicurean philosophy of Greece.

If their social condition, their present circumstances, and their laws did not confine the minds of the Americans so closely to the pursuit of worldly welfare, it is probable that they would display more reserve and more experience whenever their attention is turned to things immaterial, and that they would check themselves without difficulty. But they feel imprisoned within bounds, which they will apparently never be allowed to pass. As soon as they have passed these bounds, their minds know not where to fix themselves, and they often rush unrestrained beyond the range of common sense.

CHAPTER XIII.

WHY THE AMERICANS ARE SO RESTLESS IN THE MIDST OF THEIR PROSPERITY.

IN certain remote corners of the Old World, you may still sometimes stumble upon a small district which seems to have been forgotten amidst the general tumult, and to have remained stationary whilst everything around it was in motion. The inhabitants are, for the most part, extremely ignorant and poor; they take no part in the business of the country, and are frequently oppressed by the government; yet their countenances are generally placid, and their spirits light.

In America, I saw the freest and most enlightened men placed in the happiest circumstances which the world affords: it seemed to me as if a cloud habitually hung upon their brow, and I thought them serious, and almost sad, even in their pleasures.

The chief reason of this contrast is, that the former do not think of the ills they endure, while the latter are forever brooding over advantages they do not possess. It is strange to see with what feverish ardor the Americans pursue their own welfare; and to watch the vague dread that constantly torments them, lest they should not have chosen the shortest path which may lead to it.

A native of the United States clings to this world's goods as if he were certain never to die; and he is so hasty in grasping at all within his reach, that one would suppose he was constantly afraid of not living long enough to enjoy them. He clutches everything, he holds nothing fast, but soon loosens his grasp to pursue fresh gratifications.

In the United States, a man builds a house in which to spend his old age, and he sells it before the roof is on; he plants a garden, and lets it just as the trees are coming into bearing; he brings a field into tillage, and leaves other men to gather the crops; he embraces a profession, and gives it up; he settles in a place, which he soon afterwards leaves, to carry his changeable longings elsewhere. If his private affairs leave him any leisure, he instantly plunges into the vortex of politics; and if, at the end of a year of unremitting labor, he finds he has a few days' vacation, his eager curiosity whirls him over the vast extent of the United States, and he will travel fifteen hundred miles in a few days, to shake off his happiness. Death at length overtakes him, but it is before he is weary of his bootless chase of that complete felicity which forever escapes him.

At first sight, there is something surprising in this strange unrest of so many happy men, restless in the midst of abundance. The spectacle itself is, however, as old as the world; the novelty is, to see a whole people furnish an exemplification of it.

Their taste for physical gratifications must be regarded as the original source of that secret inquietude which the actions of the Americans betray, and of that inconstancy of which they daily afford fresh examples. He who has set his heart exclusively upon the pursuit of worldly welfare is always in a hurry, for he has but a limited time at his disposal to reach, to grasp, and to enjoy it. The recollection of the shortness of life is a constant spur to him. Besides the good things which he possesses, he every instant fancies a thousand others, which death will prevent him from trying if he does not try them soon. This thought fills him with anxiety, fear, and regret, and keeps his mind in ceaseless trepidation, which leads him perpetually to change his plans and his abode.

If, in addition to the taste for physical well-being, a social condition be superadded, in which neither laws nor customs retain any person in his place, there is a great additional stimulant to this restlessness of temper. Men will then be seen continually to change their track, for fear of missing the shortest cut to happiness.

It may readily be conceived, that, if men, passionately bent upon physical gratifications, desire eagerly, they are also easily discouraged: as their ultimate object is to enjoy, the means to reach that object must be prompt and easy, or the trouble of acquiring the gratification would be greater than the gratification itself. Their prevailing frame of mind, then, is at once ardent and relaxed, violent and enervated. Death is often less dreaded by them than perseverance in continuous efforts to one end.

The equality of conditions leads by a still straighter road to several of the effects which I have here described. When all the privileges of birth and fortune are abolished, when all professions are accessible to all, and a man's own energies may place him at the top of any one of them, an easy and unbounded career seems open to his ambition, and he will readily persuade himself that he is born to no vulgar destinies. But this is an erroneous notion, which is corrected by daily experience. The same equality which allows every citizen to conceive these lofty hopes, renders all the citizens less able to realize them: it circumscribes their powers on every side, whilst it gives freer scope to their desires. Not only are they themselves powerless, but they are met at every step by immense obstacles, which they did not at first perceive. They have swept away the privileges of some of their fellow-creatures which stood in their way, but they have opened the door to universal competition; the barrier has changed its shape rather than its position. When men are nearly alike, and all follow the same track, it is very difficult for any one individual to walk quick and cleave a way through the dense throng which surrounds and presses him. This constant strife between the inclinations springing from the equality of condition and the means it supplies to satisfy them, harasses and wearies the mind.

It is possible to conceive men arrived at a degree of freedom which should completely content them; they would then enjoy their independence without anxiety and without impatience. But men will never establish any equality with which they can be contented. Whatever efforts a people may make, they will never succeed in reducing all the conditions of society to a perfect level; and even if they unhappily attained that absolute and complete equality of position, the inequality of minds would still remain, which, coming directly from the hand of God, will forever escape the laws of man. However democratic, then, the social state and the political constitution of a people may be, it is certain that every member of the community will always find out several points about him which overlook his own position; and we may foresee that his looks will be doggedly fixed in that direction. When inequality of conditions is the common law of society, the most marked inequalities do not strike the eye: when everything is nearly on the same level, the slightest are marked enough to hurt it. Hence, the desire of equality always becomes more insatiable in proportion as equality is more complete.

Amongst democratic nations, men easily attain a certain equality of condition; but they can never attain as much as they desire. It perpetually retires from before them, yet without hiding itself from their sight, and in retiring draws them on. At every moment they think they are about to grasp it; it escapes at every moment from their hold. They are near enough to see its charms, but too far off to enjoy them; and before they have fully tasted its delights, they die.

To these causes must be attributed that strange melancholy which oftentimes haunts the inhabitants of democratic countries in the midst of their abundance, and that disgust at life which sometimes seizes upon them in the midst of calm and easy circumstances. Complaints are made in France that the number of suicides increases; in America suicide is rare, but insanity is said to be more common there than anywhere else. These are all different symptoms of the same disease. The Americans do not put an end to their lives, however disquieted they may be, because their religion forbids it; and amongst them materialism may be said hardly to exist, notwithstanding the general passion for physical gratification. The will resists, but reason frequently gives way.

In democratic times, enjoyments are more intense than in the ages of aristocracy, and the number of those who partake in them is vastly larger: but, on the other hand, it must be admitted that man's hopes and desires are oftener blasted, the soul is more stricken and perturbed, and care itself more keen.

CHAPTER XIV.

HOW THE TASTE FOR PHYSICAL GRATIFICATIONS IS UNITED IN AMERICA TO LOVE OF FREEDOM AND ATTENTION TO PUBLIC AFFAIRS.

WHEN a democratic state turns to absolute monarchy, the activity which was before directed to public and to private affairs is all at once centred upon the latter: the immediate consequence is, for some time, great physical prosperity; but this impulse soon slackens, and the amount of productive industry is checked. I know not if a single trading or manufacturing people can be cited, from the Tyrians down to the Florentines and the English, who were not a free people also. There is therefore a close bond and necessary relation between these two elements, — freedom and productive industry.

This proposition is generally true of all nations, but especially of democratic nations. I have already shown that men who live in ages of equality continually require to form associations in order to procure the things they covet; and, on the other hand, I have shown how great political freedom improves and diffuses the art of association. Freedom in these ages is therefore especially favorable to the production of wealth; nor is it difficult to perceive, that despotism is especially adverse to the same result.

The nature of despotic power in democratic ages is not to be fierce or cruel, but minute and meddling. Despotism of this kind, though it does not trample on humanity, is directly opposed to the genius of commerce and the pursuits of industry.

Thus, the men of democratic times require to be free in order more readily to procure those physical enjoyments for which they are always longing. It sometimes happens, however, that the excessive taste they conceive for these same enjoyments makes them surrender to the first master who appears. The passion for worldly welfare then defeats itself, and, without their perceiving it, throws the object of their desires to a greater distance.

There is, indeed, a most dangerous passage in the history of a democratic people. When the taste for physical gratifications amongst them has grown more rapidly than their education and their experience of free institutions, the time will come when men are carried away, and lose all self-restraint, at the sight of the new possessions they are about to obtain. In their intense and exclusive anxiety to make a fortune, they lose sight of the close connection which exists between the private fortune of each and the prosperity of all. It is not necessary to do violence to such a people in order to strip them of the rights they enjoy; they themselves willingly loosen their hold. The discharge of political duties appears to them to be a troublesome impediment, which diverts them from their occupations and business. If they be required to elect representatives, to support the government by personal service, to meet on public business, they think they have no time, — they cannot waste their precious hours in useless engagements: such idle amusements are unsuited to serious men, who are engaged with the more important interests of life. These people think they are following the principle of self-interest, but the idea they entertain of that principle is a very rude one; and the better to look after what they call their own business, they neglect their chief business, which is to remain their own masters.

As the citizens who labor do not care to attend to public affairs, and as the class which might devote its leisure to these duties has ceased to exist, the place of the government is, as it were, unfilled. If, at that critical moment, some able and ambitious man grasps the supreme power, he will find the road to every kind of usurpation open before him. If he does but attend for some time to the material prosperity of the country, no more will be demanded of him. Above all, he must insure public tranquillity: men who are possessed by the passion for physical gratification generally find out that the turmoil of freedom disturbs their welfare, before they discover how freedom itself serves to promote it. If the slightest rumor of public commotion intrudes into the petty pleasures of private life, they are aroused and alarmed by it. The fear of anarchy perpetually haunts them, and they are always ready to fling away their freedom at the first disturbance.

I readily admit that public tranquillity is a great good; but at the same time, I cannot forget that all nations have been enslaved by being kept in good order. Certainly, it is not to be inferred that nations ought to despise public tranquillity; but that state ought not to content them. A nation which asks nothing of its government but the maintenance of order is already a slave at heart, — the slave of its own well-being, awaiting but the hand that will bind it.

By such a nation, the despotism of faction is not less to be dreaded than the despotism of an individual. When the bulk of the community are engrossed by private concerns, the smallest parties need not despair of getting the upper hand in public affairs. At such times, it is not rare to see upon the great stage of the world, as we see at our theatres, a multitude represented by a few players, who alone speak in the name of an absent or inattentive crowd: they alone are in action, whilst all others are stationary; they regulate everything by their own caprice; they change the laws, and tyrannize at will over the manners of the country; and then men wonder to see into how small a number of weak and worthless hands a great people may fall.

Hitherto, the Americans have fortunately escaped all the perils which I have just pointed out; and in this respect they are really deserving of admiration. Perhaps there is no country in the world where fewer idle men are to be met with than in America, or where all who work are more eager to promote their own welfare. But if the passion of the Americans for physical gratifications is vehement, at least it is not indiscriminate; and reason, though unable to restrain it, still directs its course.

An American attends to his private concerns as if he were alone in the world, and the next minute he gives himself up to the common weal as if he had forgotten them. At one time, he seems animated by the most selfish cupidity; at another, by the most lively patriotism. The human heart cannot be thus divided. The inhabitants of the United States alternately display so strong and so similar a passion for their own welfare and for their freedom, that it may be supposed that these passions are united and mingled in some part of their character. And indeed, the Americans believe their freedom to be the best instrument and surest safeguard of their welfare: they are attached to the one by the other. They by no means think that they are not called upon to take a part in public affairs; they believe, on the contrary, that their chief business is to secure for themselves a government which will allow them to acquire the things they covet, and which will not debar them from the peaceful enjoyment of those possessions which they have already acquired.

CHAPTER XV.

HOW RELIGIOUS BELIEF SOMETIMES TURNS THE THOUGHTS OF THE AMERICANS TO IMMATERIAL PLEASURES.

IN the United States, on the seventh day of every week, the trading and working life of the nation seems suspended; all noises cease; a deep tranquillity, say rather the solemn calm of meditation, succeeds the turmoil of the week, and the soul resumes possession and contemplation of itself. Upon this day, the marts of traffic are deserted; every member of the community, accompanied by his children, goes to church, where he listens to strange language, which would seem unsuited to his ear. He is told of the countless evils caused by pride and covetousness; he is reminded of the necessity of checking his desires, of the finer pleasures which belong to virtue alone, and of the true happiness which attends it. On his return home, he does not turn to the ledgers of his business, but he opens the book of Holy Scripture; there he meets with sublime and affecting descriptions of the greatness and goodness of the Creator, of the infinite magnificence of the handiwork of God, and of the lofty destinies of man, his duties, and his immortal privileges.

Thus it is, that the American at times steals an hour from himself; and, laying aside for a while the petty passions which agitate his life, and the ephemeral interests which engross it, he strays at once into an ideal world, where all is great, eternal, and pure.

I have endeavored to point out, in another part of this work, the causes to which the maintenance of the political institutions of the Americans is attributable, and religion appeared to be one of the most prominent amongst them. I am now treating of the Americans in an individual capacity, and I again observe, that religion is not less useful to each citizen than to the whole state. The Americans show, by their practice, that they feel the high necessity of imparting morality to democratic communities by means of religion. What they think of themselves in this respect is a truth of which every democratic nation ought to be thoroughly persuaded.

I do not doubt that the social and political constitution of a people predisposes them to adopt certain doctrines and tastes, which afterwards flourish without difficulty amongst them; whilst the same causes may divert them from certain other opinions and propensities, without any voluntary effort, and, as it were, without any distinct consciousness, on their part. The whole art of the legislator is correctly to discern beforehand these natural inclinations of communities of men, in order to know whether they should be fostered, or whether it may not be necessary to check them. For the duties incumbent on the legislator differ at different times; only the goal towards which the human race ought ever to be tending is stationary: the means of reaching it are perpetually varied.

If I had been born in an aristocratic age, in the midst of a nation where the hereditary wealth of some, and the irremediable penury of others, equally diverted men from the idea of bettering their condition, and held the soul, as it were, in a state of torpor, fixed on the contemplation of another world, I should then wish that it were possible for me to rouse that people to a sense of their wants; I should seek to discover more rapid and easy means for satisfying the fresh desires which I might have awakened; and, directing the most strenuous efforts of the citizens to physical pursuits, I should endeavor to stimulate them to promote their own well-being. If it happened that some men were thus immoderately incited to the pursuit of riches, and caused to display an excessive liking for physical gratifications, I should not be alarmed; these peculiar cases would soon disappear in the general aspect of the whole community.

The attention of the legislators of democracies is called to other cares. Give democratic nations education and freedom, and leave them alone. They will soon learn to draw from this world all the benefits which it can afford; they will improve each of the useful arts, and will day by day render life more comfortable, more convenient, and more easy. Their social condition naturally urges them in this direction; I do not fear that they will slacken their course.

But whilst man takes delight in this honest and lawful pursuit of his own well-being, it is to be apprehended that he may, in the end, lose the use of his sublimest faculties; and that, whilst he is busied in improving all around him, he may at length degrade himself. Here, and here only, does the peril lie. It should therefore be the unceasing object of the legislators of democracies, and of all the virtuous and enlightened men who live there, to raise the souls of their fellow-citizens, and keep them lifted up towards Heaven. It is necessary that all who feel an interest in the future destinies of democratic society should unite, and that all should make joint and continual efforts to diffuse the love of the infinite, lofty aspirations, and a love of pleasures not of earth. If, amongst the opinions of a democratic people, any of those pernicious theories exist which tend to inculcate that all perishes with the body, let men by whom such theories are professed be marked as the natural foes of the whole people.

The materialists are offensive to me in many respects; their doctrines I hold to be pernicious, and I am disgusted at their arrogance. If their system could be of any utility to man, it would seem to be by giving him a modest opinion of himself: but these reasoners show that it is not so; and when they think they have said enough to prove that they are brutes, they appear as proud as if they had demonstrated that they are gods.

Materialism is, amongst all nations, a dangerous disease of the human mind; but it is more especially to be dreaded amongst a democratic people, because it readily amalgamates with that vice which is most familiar to the heart under such circumstances. Democracy encourages a taste for physical gratification: this taste, if it become excessive, soon disposes men to believe that all is matter only; and materialism, in its turn, hurries them on with mad impatience to these same delights: such is the fatal circle within which democratic nations are driven round. It were well that they should see the danger, and hold back.

Most religions are only general, simple, and practical means of teaching men the doctrine of the immortality of the soul. That is the greatest benefit which a democratic people derives from its belief, and hence belief is more necessary to such a people than to all others. When, therefore, any religion has struck its roots deep into a democracy, beware that you do not disturb it; but rather watch it carefully, as the most precious bequest of aristocratic ages. Seek not to supersede the old religious opinions of men by new ones, lest in the passage from one faith to another, the soul being left for a while stripped of all belief the love of physical gratifications should grow upon it, and fill it wholly.

The doctrine of metempsychosis is assuredly not more rational than that of materialism; nevertheless, if it were absolutely necessary that a democracy should choose one of the two, I should not hesitate to decide that the community would run less risk of being brutalized by believing that the soul of man will pass into the carcass of a hog, than by believing that the soul of man is nothing at all.

The belief in a supersensual and immortal principle, united for a time to matter, is so indispensable to man's greatness, that its effects are striking, even when it is not united to the doctrine of future reward and punishment, or even when it teaches no more than that, after death, the divine principle contained in man is absorbed in the Deity, or transferred to animate the frame of some other creature. Men holding so imperfect a belief will still consider the body as the secondary and inferior portion of their nature, and will despise it even whilst they yield to its influence; whereas they have a natural esteem and secret admiration for the immaterial part of man, even though they sometimes refuse to submit to its authority. That is enough to give a lofty cast to their opinions and their tastes, and to bid them tend, with no interested motive, and as it were by impulse, to pure feelings and elevated thoughts.

It is not certain that Socrates and his followers had any fixed opinions as to what would befall man hereafter; but the sole point of belief which they did firmly maintain — that the soul has nothing in common with the body, and survives it — was enough to give the Platonic philosophy that sublime aspiration by which it is distinguished.

It is clear, from the works of Plato, that many philosophical writers, his predecessors or contemporaries, professed materialism. These writers have not reached us, or have reached us in mere fragments. The same thing has happened in almost all ages; the greater part of the most famous minds in literature adhere to the doctrines of a spiritual philosophy. The instinct and the taste of the human race maintain those doctrines; they save them oftentimes in spite of men themselves, and raise the names of their defenders above the tide of time. It must not, then, be supposed that, at any period, or under any political condition, the passion for physical gratifications, and the opinions which are superinduced by that passion, can ever content a whole people. The heart of man is of a larger mould; it can at once comprise a taste for the possessions of earth, and the love of those of Heaven: at times, it may seem to cling devotedly to the one, but it will never be long without thinking of the other.

If it be easy to see that it is more particularly important in democratic ages that spiritual opinions should prevail, it is not easy to say by what means those who govern democratic nations may make them predominate. I am no believer in the prosperity, any more than in the durability, of official philosophies; and as to state religions, I have always held that, if they be sometimes of momentary service to the interests of political power, they always, sooner or later, become fatal to the Church. Nor do I agree with those who think that, to raise religion in the eyes of the people, and to make them do honor to her spiritual doctrines, it is desirable indirectly to give her ministers a political influence which the laws deny them. I am so much alive to the almost inevitable dangers which beset religious belief whenever the clergy take part in public affairs, and I am so convinced that Christianity must be maintained at any cost in the bosom of modern democracies, that I had rather shut up the priesthood within the sanctuary, than allow them to step beyond it.

What means then remain in the hands of constituted authorities to bring men back to spiritual opinions, or to hold them fast to the religion by which those opinions are suggested?

My answer will do me harm in the eyes of politicians. I believe that the sole effectual means which governments can employ, in order to have the doctrine of the immortality of the soul duly respected, is ever to act as if they believed in it themselves; and I think that it is only by scrupulous conformity to religious morality in great affairs, that they can hope to teach the community at large to know, to love, and to observe it in the lesser concerns of life.

CHAPTER XVI.

HOW EXCESSIVE CARE FOR WORLDLY WELFARE MAY IMPAIR THAT WELFARE.

THERE is a closer tie than is commonly supposed between the improvement of the soul and the amelioration of what belongs to the body. Man may leave these two things apart, and consider each of them alternately; but he cannot sever them entirely without at last losing sight of both.

The beasts have the same senses as ourselves, and very nearly the same appetites. We have no sensual passions which are not common to our race and theirs, and which are not to be found, at least in the germ, in a dog as well as in a man. Whence is it, then, that the animals can only provide for their first and lowest wants, whereas we can infinitely vary and endlessly increase our enjoyments?

We are superior to the beasts in this, that we use our souls to find out those material benefits to which they are only led by instinct. In man, the angel teaches the brute the art of satisfying its desires. It is because man is capable of rising above the things of the body, and of contemning life itself, of which the beasts have not the least notion, that he can multiply these same goods of the body to a degree which the inferior races cannot conceive of.

Whatever elevates, enlarges, and expands the soul, renders it more capable of succeeding in those very undertakings which concern it not. Whatever, on the other hand, enervates or lowers it, weakens it for all purposes, the chief as well as the least, and threatens to render it almost equally impotent for both. Hence the soul must remain great and strong, though it were only to devote its strength and greatness from time to time to the service of the body. If men were ever to content themselves with material objects, it is probable that they would lose by degrees the art of producing them; and they would enjoy them in the end, like the brutes, without discernment and without improvement.

CHAPTER XVII.

HOW, WHEN CONDITIONS ARE EQUAL AND SCEPTICISM IS RIFE, IT IS IMPORTANT TO DIRECT HUMAN ACTIONS TO DISTANT OBJECTS.

IN ages of faith, the final aim of life is placed beyond life. The men of those ages, therefore, naturally and almost involuntarily, accustom themselves to fix their gaze for many years on some immovable object, towards which they are constantly tending; and they learn by insensible degrees to repress a multitude of petty passing desires, in order to be the better able to content that great and lasting desire which possesses them. When these same men engage in the affairs of this world, the same habits may be traced in their conduct. They are apt to set up some general and certain aim and end to their actions here below, towards which all their efforts are directed: they do not turn from day to day to chase some novel object of desire, but they have settled designs which they are never weary of pursuing.

This explains why religious nations have so often achieved such lasting results: for whilst they were thinking only of the other world, they had found out the great secret of success in this. Religions give men a general habit of conducting themselves with a view to futurity: in this respect, they are not less useful to happiness in this life than to felicity hereafter; and this is one of their chief political characteristics.

But in proportion as the light of faith grows dim, the range of man's sight is circumscribed, as if the end and aim of human actions appeared every day to be more within his reach. When men have once allowed themselves to think no more of what is to befall them after life, they readily lapse into that complete and brutal indifference to futurity which is but too conformable to some propensities of mankind. As soon as they have lost the habit of placing their chief hopes upon remote events, they naturally seek to gratify without delay their smallest desires; and no sooner do they despair of living forever, than they are disposed to act as if they were to exist but for a single day. In sceptical ages, it is always therefore to be feared, that men may perpetually give way to their daily casual desires; and that, wholly renouncing whatever cannot be acquired without protracted effort, they may establish nothing great, permanent, and calm.

If the social condition of a people, under these circumstances, becomes democratic, the danger which I here point out is thereby increased. When every one is constantly striving to change his position; when an immense field for competition is thrown open to all; when wealth is amassed or dissipated in the shortest possible space of time amidst the turmoil of democracy, — visions of sudden and easy fortunes, of great possessions easily won and lost, of chance under all its forms, haunt the mind. The instability of society itself fosters the natural instability of man's desires. In the midst of these perpetual fluctuations of his lot, the present grows upon his mind, until it conceals futurity from his sight, and his looks go no further than the morrow.

In those countries in which, unhappily, irreligion and democracy coexist, philosophers and those in power ought to be always striving to place the objects of human actions far beyond man's immediate range. Adapting himself to the spirit of his country and his age, the moralist must learn to vindicate his principles in that position. He must constantly endeavor to show his contemporaries, that, even in the midst of the perpetual commotion around them, it is easier than they think to conceive and to execute protracted undertakings. He must teach them that, although the aspect of mankind may have changed, the methods by which men may provide for their prosperity in this world are still the same; and that, amongst democratic nations, as well as elsewhere, it is only by resisting a thousand petty selfish passions of the hour, that the general and unquenchable passion for happiness can be satisfied.

The task of those in power is not less clearly marked out. At all times it is important that those who govern nations should act with a view to the future: but this is even more necessary in democratic and sceptical ages than in any others. By acting thus, the leading men of democracies not only make public affairs prosperous, but they also teach private individuals, by their example, the art of managing their private concerns.

Above all, they must strive as much as possible to banish chance from the sphere of politics. The sudden and undeserved promotion of a courtier produces only a transient impression in an aristocratic country, because the aggregate institutions and opinions of the nation habitually compel men to advance slowly in tracks which they cannot get out of. But nothing is more pernicious than similar instances of favor exhibited to a democratic people: they give the last impulse to the public mind in a direction where everything hurries it onwards. At times of scepticism and equality more especially, the favor of the people or of the prince, which chance may confer or chance withhold, ought never to stand in lieu of attainments or services. It is desirable that every advancement should there appear to be the result of some effort; so that no greatness should be of too easy acquirement, and that ambition should be obliged to fix its gaze long upon an object before it is gratified.

Governments must apply themselves to restore to men

that love of the future with which religion and the state of society no longer inspire them ; and, without saying so, they must practically teach the community day by day that wealth, fame, and power are the rewards of labor ; that great success stands at the utmost range of long desires, and that there is nothing lasting but what is obtained by toil.

When men have accustomed themselves to foresee from afar what is likely to befall them in the world, and to feed upon hopes, they can hardly confine their minds within the precise limits of life, and they are ready to break the boundary, and cast their looks beyond. I do not doubt that, by training the members of a community to think of their future condition in this world, they would be gradually and unconsciously brought nearer to religious convictions. Thus, the means which allow men, up to a certain point, to go without religion, are perhaps, after all, the only means we still possess for bringing mankind back, by a long and roundabout path, to a state of faith.

CHAPTER XVIII.

WHY AMONGST THE AMERICANS ALL HONEST CALLINGS ARE CONSIDERED HONORABLE.

AMONGST a democratic people, where there is no hereditary wealth, every man works to earn a living, or has worked, or is born of parents who have worked. The notion of labor is therefore presented to the mind, on every side, as the necessary, natural, and honest condition of human existence. Not only is labor not dishonorable amongst such a people, but it is held in honor: the prejudice is not against it, but in its favor. In the United States, a wealthy man thinks that he owes it to public opinion to devote his leisure to some kind of industrial or commercial pursuit, or to public business. He would think himself in bad repute if he employed his life solely in living. It is for the purpose of escaping this obligation to work, that so many rich Americans come to Europe, where they find some scattered remains of aristocratic society, amongst whom idleness is still held in honor.

Equality of conditions not only ennobles the notion of labor, but it raises the notion of labor as a source of profit.

In aristocracies, it is not exactly labor that is despised, but labor with a view to profit. Labor is honorable in itself, when it is undertaken at the bidding of ambition or virtue. Yet, in aristocratic society, it constantly happens that he who works for honor is not insensible to the attractions of profit. But these two desires only intermingle in the depths of his soul: he carefully hides from every eye the point at which they join; he would fain conceal it from himself. In aristocratic countries there are few public officers who do not affect to serve their country without interested motives. Their salary is an incident of which they think but little, and of which they always affect not to think at all. Thus the notion of profit is kept distinct from that of labor; however they may be united in point of fact, they are not thought of together.

In democratic communities these two notions are, on the contrary, always palpably united. As the desire of well-being is universal, as fortunes are slender or fluctuating, as every one wants either to increase his own resources or to provide fresh ones for his progeny, men clearly see that it is profit which, if not wholly, at least partially, leads them to work. Even those who are principally actuated by the love of fame are necessarily made familiar with the thought that they are not exclusively actuated by that motive; and they discover that the desire of getting a living is mingled in their minds with the desire of making life illustrious.

As soon as, on the one hand, labor is held by the whole community to be an honorable necessity of man's condition, — and, on the other, as soon as labor is always ostensibly performed, wholly or in part, for the purpose of earning remuneration, — the immense interval which separated different callings in aristocratic societies disappears. If all are not alike, all at least have one feature in common. No profession exists in which men do not work for money; and the remuneration which is common to them all gives them all an air of resemblance.

This serves to explain the opinions which the Americans entertain with respect to different callings. In America, no one is degraded because he works, for every one about him works also; nor is any one humiliated by the notion of receiving pay, for the President of the United States also works for pay. He is paid for commanding, other men for obeying orders. In the United States, professions are more or less laborious, more or less profitable; but they are never either high or low: every honest calling is honorable.

CHAPTER XIX.

WHAT CAUSES ALMOST ALL AMERICANS TO FOLLOW INDUSTRIAL CALLINGS.

AGRICULTURE is, perhaps, of all the useful arts that which improves most slowly amongst democratic nations. Frequently, indeed, it would seem to be stationary, because other arts are making rapid strides towards perfection. On the other hand, almost all the tastes and habits which the equality of condition produces naturally lead men to commercial and industrial occupations.

Suppose an active, enlightened, and free man, enjoying a competency, but full of desires: he is too poor to live in idleness; he is rich enough to feel himself protected from the immediate fear of want, and he thinks how he can better his condition. This man has conceived a taste for physical gratifications, which thousands of his fellow-men indulge in around him; he has himself begun to enjoy these pleasures, and he is eager to increase his means of satisfying these tastes more completely. But life is slipping away, time is urgent; — to what is he to turn? The cultivation of the ground promises an almost certain result to his exertions, but a slow one; men are not enriched by it without patience and toil. Agriculture is therefore only suited to those who have already large superfluous wealth, or to those whose penury bids them only seek a bare subsistence. The choice of such a man as we have supposed is soon made; he sells his plot of ground, leaves his dwelling, and embarks in some hazardous but lucrative calling.

Democratic communities abound in men of this kind;

and, in proportion as the equality of conditions becomes greater, their multitude increases. Thus, democracy not only swells the number of working-men, but it leads men to prefer one kind of labor to another; and, whilst it diverts them from agriculture, it encourages their taste for commerce and manufactures.*

This spirit may be observed even amongst the richest members of the community. In democratic countries, however opulent a man is supposed to be, he is almost always discontented with his fortune, because he finds that he is less rich than his father was, and he fears that his sons will be less rich than himself. Most rich men in democracies are therefore constantly haunted by the desire of obtaining wealth, and they naturally turn their attention to trade and manufactures, which appear to offer the readiest and most efficient means of success. In this respect, they share the instincts of the poor without feeling the same necessities; say, rather, they feel the most imperious of all necessities, that of not sinking in the world.

In aristocracies, the rich are at the same time the governing power. The attention which they unceasingly devote to important public affairs diverts them from the lesser cares

* It has often been remarked, that manufacturers and mercantile men are inordinately addicted to physical gratifications, and this has been attributed to commerce and manufactures; but that is, I apprehend, to take the effect for the cause. The taste for physical gratifications is not imparted to men by commerce or manufactures, but it is rather this taste which leads men to embark in commerce and manufactures, as a means by which they hope to satisfy themselves more promptly and more completely. If commerce and manufactures increase the desire of well-being, it is because every passion gathers strength in proportion as it is cultivated, and is increased by all the efforts made to satiate it. All the causes which make the love of worldly welfare predominate in the heart of man, are favorable to the growth of commerce and manufactures. Equality of conditions is one of those causes; it encourages trade, not directly, by giving men a taste for business, but indirectly, by strengthening and expanding in their minds a taste for prosperity.

which trade and manufactures demand. But if an individual happens to turn his attention to business, the will of the body to which he belongs will immediately prevent him from pursuing it; for, however men may declaim against the rule of numbers, they cannot wholly escape it; and even amongst those aristocratic bodies which most obstinately refuse to acknowledge the rights of the national majority, a private majority is formed which governs the rest.*

In democratic countries, where money does not lead those who possess it to political power, but often removes

* Some aristocracies, however, have devoted themselves eagerly to commerce, and have cultivated manufactures with success. The history of the world furnishes several conspicuous examples. But, generally speaking, the aristocratic principle is not favorable to the growth of trade and manufactures. Moneyed aristocracies are the only exception to the rule. Amongst such aristocracies, there are hardly any desires which do not require wealth to satisfy them; the love of riches becomes, so to speak, the high road of human passions, which is crossed by or connected with all lesser tracks. The love of money and the thirst for that distinction which attaches to power, are then so closely intermixed in the same souls, that it becomes difficult to discover whether men grow covetous from ambition, or whether they are ambitious from covetousness. This is the case in England, where men seek to get rich in order to arrive at distinction, and seek distinctions as a manifestation of their wealth. The mind is then seized by both ends, and hurried into trade and manufactures, which are the shortest roads that lead to opulence.

This, however, strikes me as an exceptional and transitory circumstance. When wealth is become the only symbol of aristocracy, it is very difficult for the wealthy to maintain sole possession of political power, to the exclusion of all other men. The aristocracy of birth and pure democracy are the two extremes of the social and political state of nations: between them moneyed aristocracy finds its place. The latter approximates to the aristocracy of birth by conferring great privileges on a small number of persons; it so far belongs to the democratic element, that these privileges may be successively acquired by all. It frequently forms a natural transition between these two conditions of society, and it is difficult to say whether it closes the reign of aristocratic institutions, or whether it already opens the new era of democracy.

them from it, the rich do not know how to spend their leisure. They are driven into active life by the inquietude and the greatness of their desires, by the extent of their resources, and by the taste for what is extraordinary, which is almost always felt by those who rise, by whatsoever means, above the crowd. Trade is the only road open to them. In democracies, nothing is more great or more brilliant than commerce: it attracts the attention of the public, and fills the imagination of the multitude; all energetic passions are directed towards it. Neither their own prejudices nor those of anybody else can prevent the rich from devoting themselves to it. The wealthy members of democracies never form a body which has manners and regulations of its own; the opinions peculiar to their class do not restrain them, and the common opinions of their country urge them on. Moreover, as all the large fortunes which are found in a democratic community are of commercial growth, many generations must succeed each other before their possessors can have entirely laid aside their habits of business.

Circumscribed within the narrow space which politics leave them, rich men in democracies eagerly embark in commercial enterprise: there they can extend and employ their natural advantages; and indeed, it is even by the boldness and the magnitude of their industrial speculations that we may measure the slight esteem in which productive industry would have been held by them, if they had been born amidst an aristocracy.

A similar observation is likewise applicable to all men living in democracies, whether they be poor or rich. Those who live in the midst of democratic fluctuations have always before their eyes the image of chance; and they end by liking all undertakings in which chance plays a part. They are therefore all led to engage in commerce, not only for the sake of the profit it holds out to them, but for the love of the constant excitement occasioned by that pursuit.

The United States of America have only been emancipated for half a century from the state of colonial dependence in which they stood to Great Britain: the number of large fortunes there is small, and capital is still scarce. Yet no people in the world have made such rapid progress in trade and manufactures as the Americans: they constitute at the present day the second maritime nation in the world; and although their manufactures have to struggle with almost insurmountable natural impediments, they are not prevented from making great and daily advances.

In the United States, the greatest undertakings and speculations are executed without difficulty, because the whole population are engaged in productive industry, and because the poorest as well as the most opulent members of the commonwealth are ready to combine their efforts for these purposes. The consequence is, that a stranger is constantly amazed by the immense public works executed by a nation which contains, so to speak, no rich men. The Americans arrived but as yesterday on the territory which they inhabit, and they have already changed the whole order of nature for their own advantage. They have joined the Hudson to the Mississippi, and made the Atlantic Ocean communicate with the Gulf of Mexico, across a continent of more than five hundred leagues in extent which separates the two seas. The longest railroads which have been constructed, up to the present time, are in America.

But what most astonishes me in the United States is not so much the marvellous grandeur of some undertakings, as the innumerable multitude of small ones. Almost all the farmers of the United States combine some trade with agriculture; most of them make agriculture itself a trade. It seldom happens that an American farmer settles for good upon the land which he occupies: especially in the districts of the Far West, he brings land into tillage in order to sell it again, and not to farm it: he builds a farm-house on the speculation, that, as the state of the country will soon be changed by the increase of population, a good price may be obtained for it.

Every year, a swarm of people from the North arrive in the Southern States, and settle in the parts where the cotton-plant and the sugar-cane grow. These men cultivate the soil in order to make it produce in a few years enough to enrich them; and they already look forward to the time when they may return home to enjoy the competency thus acquired. Thus the Americans carry their business-like qualities into agriculture; and their trading passions are displayed in that, as in their other pursuits.

The Americans make immense progress in productive industry, because they all devote themselves to it at once; and for this same reason, they are exposed to unexpected and formidable embarrassments. As they are all engaged in commerce, their commercial affairs are affected by such various and complex causes, that it is impossible to foresee what difficulties may arise. As they are all more or less engaged in productive industry, at the least shock given to business, all private fortunes are put in jeopardy at the same time, and the state is shaken. I believe that the return of these commercial panics is an endemic disease of the democratic nations of our age. It may be rendered less dangerous, but it cannot be cured; because it does not originate in accidental circumstances, but in the temperament of these nations.

CHAPTER XX.

HOW AN ARISTOCRACY MAY BE CREATED BY MANUFACTURES.

I HAVE shown how democracy favors the growth of manufactures, and increases without limit the numbers of the manufacturing classes: we shall now see by what side-road manufacturers may possibly, in their turn, bring men back to aristocracy.

It is acknowledged, that, when a workman is engaged every day upon the same details, the whole commodity is produced with greater ease, promptitude, and economy. It is likewise acknowledged, that the cost of production of manufactured goods is diminished by the extent of the establishment in which they are made, and by the amount of capital employed or of credit. These truths had long been imperfectly discerned, but in our time they have been demonstrated. They have been already applied to many very important kinds of manufactures, and the humblest will gradually be governed by them. I know of nothing in politics which deserves to fix the attention of the legislator more closely than these two new axioms of the science of manufactures.

When a workman is unceasingly and exclusively engaged in the fabrication of one thing, he ultimately does his work with singular dexterity; but, at the same time, he loses the general faculty of applying his mind to the direction of the work. He every day becomes more adroit and less industrious; so that it may be said of him, that, in proportion as the workman improves, the man is degraded. What can be expected of a man who has spent twenty years of his life in making heads for pins? and to what can that mighty human intelligence, which has so often stirred the world, be applied in him, except it be to investigate the best method of making pins' heads? When a workman has spent a considerable portion of his existence in this manner, his thoughts are forever set upon the object of his daily toil; his body has contracted certain fixed habits, which it can never shake off: in a word, he no longer belongs to himself, but to the calling which he has chosen. It is in vain that laws and manners have been at pains to level all the barriers round such a man, and to open to him on every side a thousand different paths to fortune; a theory of manufactures more powerful than manners and laws binds him to a craft, and frequently to a spot, which he cannot leave: it assigns to him a certain place in society, beyond which he cannot go: in the midst of universal movement, it has rendered him stationary.

In proportion as the principle of the division of labor is more extensively applied, the workman becomes more weak, more narrow-minded, and more dependent. The art advances, the artisan recedes. On the other hand, in proportion as it becomes more manifest that the productions of manufactures are by so much the cheaper and better as the manufacture is larger, and the amount of capital employed more considerable, wealthy and educated men come forward to embark in manufactures, which were heretofore abandoned to poor or ignorant handicraftsmen. The magnitude of the efforts required, and the importance of the results to be obtained, attract them. Thus, at the very time at which the science of manufactures lowers the class of workmen, it raises the class of masters.

While the workman concentrates his faculties more and more upon the study of a single detail, the master surveys an extensive whole, and the mind of the latter is enlarged in proportion as that of the former is narrowed. In a short time, the one will require nothing but physical strength without intelligence; the other stands in need of science, and almost of genius, to insure success. This man resembles more and more the administrator of a vast empire, — that man, a brute.

The master and the workman have then here no similarity, and their differences increase every day. They are only connected as the two rings at the extremities of a long chain. Each of them fills the station which is made for him, and which he does not leave: the one is continually, closely, and necessarily dependent upon the other, and seems as much born to obey, as that other is to command. What is this but aristocracy?

As the conditions of men constituting the nation become more and more equal, the demand for manufactured commodities becomes more general and extensive; and the cheapness which places these objects within the reach of slender fortunes becomes a great element of success. Hence, there are every day more men of great opulence and education who devote their wealth and knowledge to manufactures; and who seek, by opening large establishments, and by a strict division of labor, to meet the fresh demands which are made on all sides. Thus, in proportion as the mass of the nation turns to democracy, that particular class which is engaged in manufactures becomes more aristocratic. Men grow more alike in the one, more different in the other; and inequality increases in the less numerous class, in the same ratio in which it decreases in the community. Hence it would appear, on searching to the bottom, that aristocracy should naturally spring out of the bosom of democracy.

But this kind of aristocracy by no means resembles those kinds which preceded it. It will be observed at once, that, as it applies exclusively to manufactures and to some manufacturing callings, it is a monstrous exception in the general aspect of society. The small aristocratic societies, which are formed by some manufacturers in the midst of the immense democracy of our age, contain, like the great aristocratic societies of former ages, some men who are very opulent, and a multitude who are wretchedly poor. The poor have few means of escaping from their condition and becoming rich; but the rich are constantly becoming poor, or they give up business when they have realized a fortune. Thus the elements of which the class of the poor is composed are fixed; but the elements of which the class of the rich is composed are not so. To say the truth, though there are rich men, the class of rich men does not exist; for these rich individuals have no feelings or purposes in common, no mutual traditions or mutual hopes; there are individuals, therefore, but no definite class.

Not only are the rich not compactly united amongst themselves, but there is no real bond between them and the poor. Their relative position is not a permanent one; they are constantly drawn together or separated by their interests. The workman is generally dependent on the master, but not on any particular master: these two men meet in the factory, but know not each other elsewhere; and whilst they come into contact on one point, they stand very wide apart on all others. The manufacturer asks nothing of the workman but his labor; the workman expects nothing from him but his wages. The one contracts no obligation to protect, nor the other to defend; and they are not permanently connected either by habit or duty. The aristocracy created by business rarely settles in the midst of the manufacturing population which it directs: the object is not to govern that population, but to use it. An aristocracy thus constituted can have no great hold upon those whom it employs; and, even if it succeed in retaining them at one moment, they escape the next: it knows not how to will, and it cannot act.

The territorial aristocracy of former ages was either bound by law, or thought itself bound by usage, to come to the relief of its serving-men, and to succor their distresses. But the manufacturing aristocracy of our age first impoverishes and debases the men who serve it, and then abandons them to be supported by the charity of the public. This is a natural consequence of what has been said before. Between the workman and the master there are frequent relations, but no real association.

I am of opinion, upon the whole, that the manufacturing aristocracy which is growing up under our eyes is one of the harshest which ever existed in the world; but, at the same time, it is one of the most confined and least dangerous. Nevertheless, the friends of democracy should keep their eyes anxiously fixed in this direction; for if ever a permanent inequality of conditions and aristocracy again penetrate into the world, it may be predicted that this is the gate by which they will enter.

THIRD BOOK.

INFLUENCE OF DEMOCRACY ON MANNERS PROPERLY SO CALLED.

CHAPTER I.

HOW MANNERS ARE SOFTENED AS SOCIAL CONDITIONS BECOME MORE EQUAL.

WE perceive that, for several centuries, social conditions have tended to equality, and we discover that at the same time the manners of society have been softened. Are these two things merely contemporaneous, or does any secret link exist between them, so that the one cannot advance without the other? Several causes may concur to render the manners of a people less rude; but, of all these causes, the most powerful appears to me to be the equality of conditions. Equality of conditions and greater mildness in manners are then, in my eyes, not only contemporaneous occurrences, but correlative facts.

When the fabulists seek to interest us in the actions of beasts, they invest them with human notions and passions; the poets who sing of spirits and angels do the same: there is no wretchedness so deep, nor any happiness so pure, as to fill the human mind and touch the heart, unless we are ourselves held up to our own eyes under other features.

This is strictly applicable to our present subject. When all men are irrevocably marshalled in an aristocratic community, according to their professions, their property, and their birth, the members of each class, considering themselves as children of the same family, cherish a constant and lively sympathy towards each other, which can never be felt in an equal degree by the citizens of a democracy. But the same feeling does not exist between the several classes towards each other.

Amongst an aristocratic people, each caste has its own opinions, feelings, rights, manners, and modes of living. Thus, the men who compose it do not resemble the mass of their fellow-citizens; they do not think or feel in the same manner, and they scarcely believe that they belong to the same race. They cannot therefore thoroughly understand what others feel, nor judge of others by themselves. Yet they are sometimes eager to lend each other aid; but this is not contrary to my previous observation.

These aristocratic institutions, which made the beings of one and the same race so different, nevertheless bound them to each other by close political ties. Although the serf had no natural interest in the fate of the nobles, he did not the less think himself obliged to devote his person to the service of that noble who happened to be his lord: and although the noble held himself to be of a different nature from that of his serfs, he nevertheless held that his duty and his honor constrained him to defend, at the risk of his own life, those who dwelt upon his domains.

It is evident that these mutual obligations did not originate in the law of nature, but in the law of society; and that the claim of social duty was more stringent than that of mere humanity. These services were not supposed to be due from man to man, but to the vassal or to the lord. Feudal institutions awakened a lively sympathy for the sufferings of certain men, but none at all for the miseries of mankind. They infused generosity rather than mildness into the manners of the time; and although they prompted men to great acts of self-devotion, they created no real sympathies, for real sympathies can only exist between those who are alike; and, in aristocratic ages, men acknowledge none but the members of their own caste to be like themselves.

When the chroniclers of the Middle Ages, who all belonged to the aristocracy by birth or education, relate the tragical end of a noble, their grief flows apace; whereas they tell you at a breath, and without wincing, of massacres and tortures inflicted on the common sort of people. Not that these writers felt habitual hatred or systematic disdain for the people; war between the several classes of the community was not yet declared. They were impelled by an instinct rather than by a passion; as they had formed no clear notion of a poor man's sufferings, they cared but little for his fate.

The same feelings animated the lower orders whenever the feudal tie was broken. The same ages which witnessed so many heroic acts of self-devotion on the part of vassals for their lords, were stained with atrocious barbarities practised from time to time by the lower classes on the higher.

It must not be supposed that this mutual insensibility arose solely from the absence of public order and education, for traces of it are to be found in the following centuries, which became tranquil and enlightened whilst they remained aristocratic.

In 1675 the lower classes in Brittany revolted at the imposition of a new tax. These disturbances were put down with unexampled severity. Observe the language in which Madame de Sévigné, a witness of these horrors, relates them to her daughter: —

"Aux Rochers, October 30, 1675.

"Your letter from Aix, my daughter, is droll enough. At least, read your letters over again before sending them; allow yourself to be surprised by the pretty things that you have put into them, and console yourself by this pleasure for the trouble you have had in writing so many. Then you have kissed all the people of Provence,* have you? There would be no satisfaction in kissing all Brittany, unless one liked to smell of wine. . . . . . Do you wish to hear the news from Rennes? A tax of a hundred thousand crowns has been imposed upon the citizens; and if this sum is not produced within four and twenty hours, it is to be doubled, and collected by the soldiers. They have cleared the houses and sent away the occupants of one of the great streets, and forbidden anybody to receive them on pain of death; so that the poor wretches — old men, women near their confinement, and children included — may be seen wandering round and crying on their departure from this city, without knowing where to go, and without food or a place to lie in. Day before yesterday, a fiddler was broken on the wheel for getting up a dance and stealing some stamped paper. He was quartered after death, and his limbs exposed at the four corners of the city. Sixty citizens have been thrown into prison, and the business of punishing them is to begin to-morrow. This province sets a fine example to the others, teaching them above all things to respect their governors and *gouvernantes*, and not to throw any more stones into their garden.

"Yesterday, a delightful day, Madame de Tarente visited these wilds; there is no question about preparing a chamber or a collation; she comes by the barrier, and returns the same way. . . . . ."

In another letter she adds: —

"You talk very pleasantly about our miseries; but we are no longer so jaded with capital punishments; only one a week now, just to keep up appearances. It is true that

* Madame de Grignan was *Gouvernante* of Provence, and her mother is here joking with her about the official civilities which she was obliged to practise towards the people who were under her charge.

hanging now seems to me quite a cooling entertainment. I have got a wholly new idea of justice since I have been in this region. Your galley-slaves seem to me a society of good people who have retired from the world in order to lead a quiet life."

It would be a mistake to suppose that Madame de Sévigné, who wrote these lines, was a selfish or cruel person; she was passionately attached to her children, and very ready to sympathize in the sorrows of her friends; nay, her letters show that she treated her vassals and servants with kindness and indulgence. But Madame de Sévigné had no clear notion of suffering in any one who was not a person of quality.

In our time, the harshest man, writing to the most insensible person of his acquaintance, would not venture to indulge in the cruel jocularity which I have quoted; and even if his own manners allowed him to do so, the manners of society at large would forbid it. Whence does this arise? Have we more sensibility than our fathers? I do not know that we have; but I am sure that our sensibility is extended to many more objects.

When all the ranks of a community are nearly equal, as all men think and feel in nearly the same manner, each of them may judge in a moment of the sensations of all the others: he casts a rapid glance upon himself, and that is enough. There is no wretchedness into which he cannot readily enter, and a secret instinct reveals to him its extent. It signifies not that strangers or foes be the sufferers; imagination puts him in their place: something like a personal feeling is mingled with his pity, and makes himself suffer whilst the body of his fellow-creature is in torture.

In democratic ages, men rarely sacrifice themselves for one another; but they display general compassion for the members of the human race. They inflict no useless ills;

and they are happy to relieve the griefs of others, when they can do so without much hurting themselves; they are not disinterested, but they are humane.

Although the Americans have in a manner reduced selfishness to a social and philosophical theory, they are nevertheless extremely open to compassion. In no country is criminal justice administered with more mildness than in the United States. Whilst the English seem disposed carefully to retain the bloody traces of the Middle Ages in their penal legislation, the Americans have almost expunged capital punishment from their codes. North America is, I think, the only country upon earth in which the life of no one citizen has been taken for a political offence in the course of the last fifty years.

The circumstance which conclusively shows that this singular mildness of the Americans arises chiefly from their social condition, is the manner in which they treat their slaves. Perhaps there is not, upon the whole, a single European colony in the New World, in which the physical condition of the blacks is less severe than in the United States; yet the slaves still endure frightful misery there, and are constantly exposed to very cruel punishments. It is easy to perceive that the lot of these unhappy beings inspires their masters with but little compassion, and that they look upon slavery not only as an institution which is profitable to them, but as an evil which does not affect them. Thus, the same man who is full of humanity towards his fellow-creatures, when they are at the same time his equals, becomes insensible to their afflictions as soon as that equality ceases. His mildness should therefore be attributed to the equality of conditions, rather than to civilization and education.

What I have here remarked of individuals is to a certain extent applicable to nations. When each nation has its distinct opinions, belief, laws, and customs, it looks upon itself as the whole of mankind, and is moved by no sorrows but its own. Should war break out between two nations animated by this feeling, it is sure to be waged with great cruelty.

At the time of their highest culture, the Romans slaughtered the generals of their enemies, after having dragged them in triumph behind a car; and they flung their prisoners to the beasts of the Circus for the amusement of the people. Cicero, who declaimed so vehemently at the notion of crucifying a Roman citizen, had not a word to say against these horrible abuses of victory. It is evident that, in his eyes, a barbarian did not belong to the same human race as a Roman.

On the contrary, in proportion as nations become more like each other, they become reciprocally more compassionate, and the law of nations is mitigated.

CHAPTER II.

HOW DEMOCRACY RENDERS THE HABITUAL INTERCOURSE OF THE AMERICANS SIMPLE AND EASY.

DEMOCRACY does not attach men strongly to each other; but it places their habitual intercourse upon an easier footing.

If two Englishmen chance to meet at the Antipodes, where they are surrounded by strangers whose language and manners are almost unknown to them, they will first stare at each other with much curiosity, and a kind of secret uneasiness; they will then turn away, or, if one accosts the other, they will take care only to converse with a constrained and absent air, upon very unimportant subjects. Yet there is no enmity between these men; they have never seen each other before, and each believes the other to be a respectable person. Why then should they stand so cautiously apart? We must go back to England to learn the reason.

When it is birth alone, independent of wealth, which classes men in society, every one knows exactly what his own position is upon the social scale; he does not seek to rise, he does not fear to sink. In a community thus organized, men of different castes communicate very little with each other; but if accident brings them together, they are ready to converse without hoping or fearing to lose their own position. Their intercourse is not upon a footing of equality, but it is not constrained.

When a moneyed aristocracy succeeds to an aristocracy of birth, the case is altered. The privileges of some are still extremely great, but the possibility of acquiring those privileges is open to all: whence it follows, that those who possess them are constantly haunted by the apprehension of losing them, or of other men's sharing them; those who do not yet enjoy them long to possess them at any cost, or, if they fail, to appear at least to possess them, — which is not impossible. As the social importance of men is no longer ostensibly and permanently fixed by blood, and is infinitely varied by wealth, ranks still exist, but it is not easy clearly to distinguish at a glance those who respectively belong to them. Secret hostilities then arise in the community; one set of men endeavor by innumerable artifices to penetrate, or to appear to penetrate, amongst those who are above them; another set are constantly in arms against these usurpers of their rights; or, rather, the same individual does both at once, and whilst he seeks to raise himself into a higher circle, he is always on the defensive against the intrusion of those below him.

Such is the condition of England at the present time; and I am of opinion that the peculiarity just adverted to must be attributed principally to this cause. As aristocratic pride is still extremely great amongst the English, and as the limits of aristocracy are ill-defined, everybody lives in constant dread lest advantage should be taken of his familiarity. Unable to judge at once of the social position of those he meets, an Englishman prudently avoids all contact with them. Men are afraid lest some slight service rendered should draw them into an unsuitable acquaintance; they dread civilities, and they avoid the obtrusive gratitude of a stranger quite as much as his hatred.

Many people attribute these singular anti-social propensities, and the reserved and taciturn bearing of the English, to purely physical causes. I may admit that there is something of it in their race, but much more of it is attributable to their social condition, as is proved by the contrast of the Americans.

In America, where the privileges of birth never existed, and where riches confer no peculiar rights on their possessors, men unacquainted with each other are very ready to frequent the same places, and find neither peril nor advantage in the free interchange of their thoughts. If they meet by accident, they neither seek nor avoid intercourse; their manner is therefore natural, frank, and open: it is easy to see that they hardly expect or apprehend anything from each other, and that they do not care to display, any more than to conceal, their position in the world. If their demeanor is often cold and serious, it is never haughty or constrained; and if they do not converse, it is because they are not in a humor to talk, not because they think it their interest to be silent.

In a foreign country two Americans are at once friends, simply because they are Americans. They are repulsed by no prejudice; they are attracted by their common country. For two Englishmen, the same blood is not enough; they must be brought together by the same rank. The Americans remark this unsociable mood of the English as much as the French do, and are not less astonished by it. Yet the Americans are connected with England by their origin, their religion, their language, and partially by their manners: they only differ in their social condition. It may therefore be inferred, that the reserve of the English proceeds from the constitution of their country, much more than from that of its inhabitants.

CHAPTER III.

WHY THE AMERICANS SHOW SO LITTLE SENSITIVENESS IN THEIR OWN COUNTRY, AND ARE SO SENSITIVE IN EUROPE.

THE temper of the Americans is vindictive, like that of all serious and reflecting nations. They hardly ever forget an offence, but it is not easy to offend them; and their resentment is as slow to kindle as it is to abate.

In aristocratic communities, where a small number of persons manage everything, the outward intercourse of men is subject to settled conventional rules. Every one then thinks he knows exactly what marks of respect or of condescension he ought to display, and none are presumed to be ignorant of the science of etiquette. These usages of the first class in society afterwards serve as a model to all the others; besides which, each of the latter lays down a code of its own, to which all its members are bound to conform. Thus the rules of politeness form a complex system of legislation, which it is difficult to be perfectly master of, but from which it is dangerous for any one to deviate; so that men are constantly exposed involuntarily to inflict or to receive bitter affronts.

But as the distinctions of rank are obliterated, as men differing in education and in birth meet and mingle in the same places of resort, it is almost impossible to agree upon the rules of good breeding. As its laws are uncertain, to disobey them is not a crime, even in the eyes of those who know what they are: men attach more importance to intentions than to forms, and they grow less civil, but at the same time less quarrelsome.

There are many little attentions which an American does not care about; he thinks they are not due to him, or he presumes that they are not known to be due: he therefore either does not perceive a rudeness, or he forgives it; his manners become less courteous, and his character more plain and masculine.

The mutual indulgence which the Americans display, and the manly confidence with which they treat each other, also result from another deeper and more general cause, which I have already adverted to in the preceding chapter. In the United States, the distinctions of rank in civil society are slight, in political society they are null; an American, therefore, does not think himself bound to pay particular attentions to any of his fellow-citizens, nor does he require such attentions from them towards himself. As he does not see that it is his interest eagerly to seek the company of any of his countrymen, he is slow to fancy that his own company is declined: despising no one on account of his station, he does not imagine that any one can despise him for that cause; and until he has clearly perceived an insult, he does not suppose that an affront was intended. The social condition of the Americans naturally accustoms them not to take offence in small matters; and, on the other hand, the democratic freedom which they enjoy transfuses this same mildness of temper into the character of the nation.

The political institutions of the United States constantly bring citizens of all ranks into contact, and compel them to pursue great undertakings in concert. People thus engaged have scarcely time to attend to the details of etiquette, and they are besides too strongly interested in living harmoniously for them to stick at such things. They therefore soon acquire a habit of considering the feelings and opinions of those whom they meet more than their manners, and they do not allow themselves to be annoyed by trifles.

I have often remarked, in the United States, that it is not easy to make a man understand that his presence may be dispensed with; hints will not always suffice to shake him off. I contradict an American at every word he says, to show him that his conversation bores me; he instantly labors with fresh pertinacity to convince me: I preserve a dogged silence, and he thinks I am meditating deeply on the truths which he is uttering: at last, I rush from his company, and he supposes that some urgent business hurries me elsewhere. This man will never understand that he wearies me to death, unless I tell him so; and the only way to get rid of him is to make him my enemy for life.

It appears surprising, at first sight, that the same man, transported to Europe, suddenly becomes so sensitive and captious, that I often find it as difficult to avoid offending him here, as it was there to put him out of countenance. These two opposite effects proceed from the same cause. Democratic institutions generally give men a lofty notion of their country and of themselves. An American leaves his country with a heart swollen with pride: on arriving in Europe, he at once finds out that we are not so engrossed by the United States and the great people who inhabit them as he had supposed; and this begins to annoy him. He has been informed that the conditions of society are not equal in our part of the globe; and he observes that, among the nations of Europe, the traces of rank are not wholly obliterated, — that wealth and birth still retain some indeterminate privileges, which force themselves upon his notice whilst they elude definition. He is therefore profoundly ignorant of the place which he ought to occupy in this half-ruined scale of classes, which are sufficiently distinct to hate and despise each other, yet sufficiently alike for him to be always confounding them. He is afraid of ranging himself too high, still more is he afraid of being ranged too low: this twofold peril keeps his mind constantly on the stretch, and embarrasses all he says and does.

He learns from tradition that in Europe ceremonial observances were infinitely varied according to different ranks; this recollection of former times completes his perplexity, and he is the more afraid of not obtaining those marks of respect which are due to him, as he does not exactly know in what they consist. He is like a man surrounded by traps: society is not a recreation for him, but a serious toil: he weighs your least actions, interrogates your looks, and scrutinizes all you say, lest there should be some hidden allusion to affront him. I doubt whether there was ever a provincial man of quality so punctilious in breeding as he is: he endeavors to attend to the slightest rules of etiquette, and does not allow one of them to be waived towards himself: he is full of scruples, and at the same time of pretensions; he wishes to do enough, but fears to do too much; and as he does not very well know the limits of the one or of the other, he keeps up a haughty and embarrassed air of reserve.

But this is not all: here is yet another double of the human heart. An American is forever talking of the admirable equality which prevails in the United States: aloud, he makes it the boast of his country, but in secret, he deplores it for himself; and he aspires to show that, for his part, he is an exception to the general state of things which he vaunts. There is hardly an American to be met with who does not claim some remote kindred with the first founders of the Colonies; and as for the scions of the noble families of England, America seemed to me to be covered with them. When an opulent American arrives in Europe, his first care is to surround himself with all the luxuries of wealth: he is so afraid of being taken for the plain citizen of a democracy, that he adopts a hundred distorted ways of bringing some new instance of his wealth before you every day. His house will be in the most fashionable part of the town: he will always be surrounded by a host of servants. I have heard an American complain that, in the best houses of Paris, the society was rather mixed; the taste which prevails there was not pure enough for him; and he ventured to hint that, in his opinion, there was a want of elegance of manner; he could not accustom himself to see wit concealed under such unpretending forms.

These contrasts ought not to surprise us. If the vestiges of former aristocratic distinctions were not so completely effaced in the United States, the Americans would be less simple and less tolerant in their own country; they would require less, and be less fond of borrowed manners, in ours.

CHAPTER IV.

CONSEQUENCES OF THE THREE PRECEDING CHAPTERS.

WHEN men feel a natural compassion for the sufferings of each other, — when they are brought together by easy and frequent intercourse, and no sensitive feelings keep them asunder, — it may readily be supposed that they will lend assistance to one another whenever it is needed. When an American asks for the co-operation of his fellow-citizens, it is seldom refused; and I have often seen it afforded spontaneously, and with great good-will. If an accident happens on the highway, everybody hastens to help the sufferer; if some great and sudden calamity befalls a family, the purses of a thousand strangers are at once willingly opened, and small but numerous donations pour in to relieve their distress.

It often happens, amongst the most civilized nations of the globe, that a poor wretch is as friendless in the midst of a crowd as the savage in his wilds: this is hardly ever the case in the United States. The Americans, who are always cold and often coarse in their manners, seldom show insensibility; and if they do not proffer services eagerly, yet they do not refuse to render them.

All this is not in contradiction to what I have said before on the subject of individualism. The two things are so far from combating each other, that I can see how they agree. Equality of conditions, whilst it makes men feel their independence, shows them their own weakness: they are free, but exposed to a thousand accidents; and experience soon teaches them that, although they do not habitually require the assistance of others, a time almost always comes when they cannot do without it.

We constantly see, in Europe, that men of the same profession are ever ready to assist each other; they are all exposed to the same ills, and that is enough to teach them to seek mutual preservatives, however hard-hearted and selfish they may otherwise be. When one of them falls into danger, from which the others may save him by a slight transient sacrifice or a sudden effort, they do not fail to make the attempt. Not that they are deeply interested in his fate, — for if, by chance, their exertions are unavailing, they immediately forget the object of them, and return to their own business, — but a sort of tacit and almost involuntary agreement has been passed between them, by which each one owes to the others a temporary support, which he may claim for himself in turn.

Extend to a people the remark here applied to a class, and you will understand my meaning. A similar covenant exists, in fact, between all the citizens of a democracy: they all feel themselves subject to the same weakness and the same dangers; and their interest, as well as their sympathy, makes it a rule with them to lend each other mutual assistance when required. The more equal social conditions become, the more do men display this reciprocal disposition to oblige each other. In democracies, no great benefits are conferred, but good offices are constantly rendered; a man seldom displays self-devotion, but all men are ready to be of service to one another.

CHAPTER V.

HOW DEMOCRACY AFFECTS THE RELATIONS OF MASTERS AND SERVANTS.

AN American who had travelled for a long time in Europe once said to me: "The English treat their servants with a stiffness and imperiousness of manner which surprise us; but, on the other hand, the French sometimes treat their attendants with a degree of familiarity or of politeness which we cannot understand. It looks as if they were afraid to give orders; the posture of the superior and the inferior is ill maintained." The remark was a just one, and I have often made it myself. I have always considered England as the country of all the world where, in our time, the bond of domestic service is drawn most tightly, and France as the country where it is most relaxed. Nowhere have I seen masters stand so high or so low as in these two countries. Between these two extremes the Americans are to be placed. Such is the fact, as it appears upon the surface of things: to discover the causes of that fact, it is necessary to search the matter thoroughly.

No communities have ever yet existed in which social conditions have been so equal that there were neither rich nor poor, and, consequently, neither masters nor servants. Democracy does not prevent the existence of these two classes, but it changes their dispositions, and modifies their mutual relations.

Amongst aristocratic nations, servants form a distinct class, not more variously composed than that of their masters. A settled order is soon established; in the former as well as in the latter class a scale is formed, with numerous distinctions or marked gradations of rank, and generations succeed each other thus, without any change of position. These two communities are superposed one above the other, always distinct, but regulated by analogous principles. This aristocratic constitution does not exert a less powerful influence on the notions and manners of servants than on those of masters; and, although the effects are different, the same cause may easily be traced.

Both classes constitute small communities in the heart of the nation, and certain permanent notions of right and wrong are ultimately established amongst them. The different acts of human life are viewed by one peculiar and unchanging light. In the society of servants, as in that of masters, men exercise a great influence over each other: they acknowledge settled rules, and, in the absence of law, they are guided by a sort of public opinion; their habits are settled, and their conduct is placed under a certain control.

These men, whose destiny it is to obey, certainly do not understand fame, virtue, honesty, and honor in the same manner as their masters; but they have a pride, a virtue, and an honesty pertaining to their condition; and they have a notion, if I may use the expression, of a sort of servile honor.* Because a class is mean, it must not be supposed that all who belong to it are mean-hearted; to think so would be a great mistake. However lowly it may be, he who is foremost there, and who has no notion of quit-

* If the principal opinions by which men are guided are examined closely and in detail, the analogy appears still more striking, and one is surprised to find amongst them, just as much as amongst the haughtiest scions of a feudal race, pride of birth, respect for their ancestry and their descendants, disdain of their inferiors, a dread of contact, and a taste for etiquette, precedents, and antiquity.

ting it, occupies an aristocratic position which inspires him with lofty feelings, pride, and self-respect, that fit him for the higher virtues, and for actions above the common.

Amongst aristocratic nations, it was by no means rare to find men of noble and vigorous minds in the service of the great, who felt not the servitude they bore, and who submitted to the will of their masters without any fear of their displeasure.

But this was hardly ever the case amongst the inferior ranks of domestic servants. It may be imagined, that he who occupies the lowest stage of the order of menials stands very low indeed. The French created a word on purpose to designate the servants of the aristocracy, — they called them "lackeys." This word *lackey* served as the strongest expression, when all others were exhausted, to designate human meanness. Under the old French monarchy, to denote by a single expression a low-spirited contemptible fellow, it was usual to say that he had the *soul of a lackey;* the term was enough to convey all that was intended.

The permanent inequality of conditions not only gives servants certain peculiar virtues and vices, but it places them in a peculiar relation with respect to their masters. Amongst aristocratic nations, the poor man is familiarized from his childhood with the notion of being commanded; to whichever side he turns his eyes, the graduated structure of society and the aspect of obedience meet his view. Hence, in those countries, the master readily obtains prompt, complete, respectful, and easy obedience from his servants, because they revere in him, not only their master, but the class of masters. He weighs down their will by the whole weight of the aristocracy. He orders their actions; to a certain extent, he even directs their thoughts. In aristocracies, the master often exercises, even without being aware of it, an amazing sway over the opinions, the habits, and the manners of those who obey him, and his influence extends even further than his authority.

In aristocratic communities, there are not only hereditary families of servants as well as of masters, but the same families of servants adhere for several generations to the same families of masters (like two parallel lines which neither meet nor separate); and this considerably modifies the mutual relations of these two classes of persons. Thus, although in aristocratic society the master and servant have no natural resemblance, — although, on the contrary, they are placed at an immense distance on the scale of human beings by their fortune, education, and opinions, — yet time ultimately binds them together. They are connected by a long series of common reminiscences, and however different they may be, they grow alike; whilst in democracies, where they are naturally almost alike, they always remain strangers to each other. Amongst an aristocratic people, the master gets to look upon his servants as an inferior and secondary part of himself, and he often takes an interest in their lot by a last stretch of selfishness.

Servants, on their part, are not averse to regard themselves in the same light; and they sometimes identify themselves with the person of the master, so that they become an appendage to him in their own eyes as well as in his. In aristocracies, a servant fills a subordinate position which he cannot get out of; above him is another man, holding a superior rank, which he cannot lose. On one side, are obscurity, poverty, obedience for life; on the other, and also for life, fame, wealth, and command. The two conditions are always distinct and always in propinquity; the tie that connects them is as lasting as they are themselves.

In this predicament, the servant ultimately detaches his notion of interest from his own person; he deserts himself as it were, or rather he transports himself into the character of his master, and thus assumes an imaginary personality. He complacently invests himself with the wealth of those who command him; he shares their fame, exalts himself by their rank, and feeds his mind with borrowed greatness, to which he attaches more importance than those who fully and really possess it. There is something touching, and at the same time ridiculous, in this strange confusion of two different states of being. These passions of masters, when they pass into the souls of menials, assume the natural dimensions of the place they occupy; they are contracted and lowered. What was pride in the former becomes puerile vanity and paltry ostentation in the latter. The servants of a great man are commonly most punctilious as to the marks of respect due to him, and they attach more importance to his slightest privileges than he does himself. In France, a few of these old servants of the aristocracy are still to be met with, here and there; they have survived their race, which will soon disappear with them altogether.

In the United States, I never saw any one at all like them. The Americans are not only unacquainted with the kind of man, but it is hardly possible to make them understand that such ever existed. It is scarcely less difficult for them to conceive it, than for us to form a correct notion of what a slave was amongst the Romans, or a serf in the Middle Ages. All these men were, in fact, though in different degrees, results of the same cause: they are all retiring from our sight, and disappearing in the obscurity of the past, together with the social condition to which they owed their origin.

Equality of conditions turns servants and masters into new beings, and places them in new relative positions. When social conditions are nearly equal, men are constantly changing their situations in life: there is still a class of menials and a class of masters, but these classes are not always composed of the same individuals, still less of the same families; and those who command are not more secure of perpetuity than those who obey. As servants do not form a separate people, they have no habits, prejudices, or manners peculiar to themselves: they are not remarkable for any particular turn of mind or moods of feeling. They know no vices or virtues of their condition, but they partake of the education, the opinions, the feelings, the virtues and the vices of their contemporaries; and they are honest men or scoundrels in the same way as their masters are.

The conditions of servants are not less equal than those of masters. As no marked ranks or fixed subordination are to be found amongst them, they will not display either the meanness or the greatness which characterize the aristocracy of menials, as well as all other aristocracies. I never saw a man in the United States who reminded me of that class of confidential servants of which we still retain a reminiscence in Europe, neither did I ever meet with such a thing as a *lackey:* all traces of the one and the other have disappeared.

In democracies, servants are not only equal amongst themselves, but it may be said that they are, in some sort, the equals of their masters. This requires explanation in order to be rightly understood. At any moment, a servant may become a master, and he aspires to rise to that condition: the servant is therefore not a different man from the master. Why then has the former a right to command, and what compels the latter to obey? — the free and temporary consent of both their wills. Neither of them is, by nature, inferior to the other; they only become so for a time, by covenant. Within the terms of this covenant, the one is a servant, the other a master; beyond it, they are two citizens of the commonwealth, — two men.

I beg the reader particularly to observe, that this is not only the notion which servants themselves entertain of their own condition; domestic service is looked upon by masters in the same light; and the precise limits of authority and obedience are as clearly settled in the mind of the one as in that of the other.

When the greater part of the community have long attained a condition nearly alike, and when equality is an old and acknowledged fact, the public mind, which is never affected by exceptions, assigns certain general limits to the value of man, above or below which no man can long remain placed. It is in vain that wealth and poverty, authority and obedience, accidentally interpose great distances between two men; public opinion, founded upon the usual order of things, draws them to a common level, and creates a species of imaginary equality between them, in spite of the real inequality of their conditions. This all-powerful opinion penetrates at length even into the hearts of those whose interest might arm them to resist it; it affects their judgment, whilst it subdues their will.

In their inmost convictions the master and the servant no longer perceive any deep-seated difference between them, and they neither hope nor fear to meet with any such at any time. They are therefore neither subject to disdain nor to anger, and they discern in each other neither humility nor pride. The master holds the contract of service to be the only source of his power, and the servant regards it as the only cause of his obedience. They do not quarrel about their reciprocal situations, but each knows his own and keeps it.

In the French army, the common soldier is taken from nearly the same class as the officer, and may hold the same commissions: out of the ranks, he considers himself entirely equal to his military superiors, and, in point of fact, he is so; but when under arms, he does not hesitate to obey, and his obedience is not the less prompt, precise, and ready, for being voluntary and defined. This example may give a notion of what takes place between masters and servants in democratic communities.

It would be preposterous to suppose that those warm and deep-seated affections which are sometimes kindled in the domestic service of aristocracy will ever spring up between these two men, or that they will exhibit strong instances of self-sacrifice. In aristocracies, masters and servants live apart, and frequently their only intercourse is through a third person; yet they commonly stand firmly by one another. In democratic countries, the master and the servant are close together: they are in daily personal contact, but their minds do not intermingle; they have common occupations, hardly ever common interests.

Amongst such a people, the servant always considers himself as a sojourner in the dwelling of his masters. He knew nothing of their forefathers; he will see nothing of their descendants; he has nothing lasting to expect from them. Why, then, should he confound his life with theirs, and whence should so strange a surrender of himself proceed? The reciprocal position of the two men is changed; their mutual relations must be so, too.

I would fain illustrate all these reflections by the example of the Americans; but, for this purpose, the distinctions of persons and places must be accurately traced. In the South of the Union, slavery exists; all that I have just said is consequently inapplicable there. In the North, the majority of servants are either freedmen, or the children of freedmen: * these persons occupy a contested position in the public estimation; by the laws, they are brought up to

* This is a natural mistake for a stranger to make. In hotels, and other large public establishments, it may be true that a majority of the servants are free blacks; but very few such persons are employed as servants in private families at the North. — AM. ED.

the level of their masters; by the manners of the country, they are obstinately detruded from it. They do not themselves clearly know their proper place, and are almost always either insolent or craven.

But in the Northern States, especially in New England, there are a certain number of whites who agree, for wages, to yield a temporary obedience to the will of their fellow-citizens. I have heard that these servants commonly perform the duties of their situations with punctuality and intelligence; and that, without thinking themselves naturally inferior to the person who orders them, they submit without reluctance to obey him. They appeared to me to carry into service some of those manly habits which independence and equality create. Having once selected a hard way of life, they do not seek to escape from it by indirect means; and they have sufficient respect for themselves not to refuse to their masters that obedience which they have freely promised. On their part, masters require nothing of their servants but the faithful and rigorous performance of the covenant: they do not ask for marks of respect, they do not claim their love, or devoted attachment; it is enough that, as servants, they are exact and honest.

It would not, then, be true to assert that, in democratic society, the relation of servants and masters is disorganized: it is organized on another footing; the rule is different, but there is a rule.

It is not my purpose to inquire whether the new state of things which I have just described is inferior to that which preceded it, or simply different. Enough for me that it is fixed and determined; for what is most important to meet with among men is not any given ordering, but order.

But what shall I say of those sad and troubled times at which equality is established in the midst of the tumult of revolution, — when democracy, after having been introduced into the state of society, still struggles with difficulty against the prejudices and manners of the country? The laws, and partially public opinion, already declare that no natural or permanent inferiority exists between the servant and the master. But this new belief has not yet reached the innermost convictions of the latter, or rather his heart rejects it: in the secret persuasion of his mind, the master thinks that he belongs to a peculiar and superior race; he dares not say so, but he shudders at allowing himself to be dragged to the same level. His authority over his servants becomes timid, and at the same time harsh; he has already ceased to entertain for them the feelings of patronizing kindness which long uncontested power always produces, and he is surprised that, being changed himself, his servant changes also. He wants his attendants to form regular and permanent habits, in a condition of domestic service which is only temporary; he requires that they should appear contented with and proud of a servile condition, which they will one day shake off, — that they should sacrifice themselves to a man who can neither protect nor ruin them; and, in short, that they should contract an indissoluble engagement to a being like themselves, and one who will last no longer than they will.

Amongst aristocratic nations, it often happens that the condition of domestic service does not degrade the character of those who enter upon it, because they neither know nor imagine any other; and the amazing inequality which is manifest between them and their master appears to be the necessary and unavoidable consequence of some hidden law of Providence.

In democracies, the condition of domestic service does not degrade the character of those who enter upon it, because it is freely chosen, and adopted for a time only, — because it is not stigmatized by public opinion, and creates no permanent inequality between the servant and the master.

But whilst the transition from one social condition to another is going on, there is almost always a time when men's minds fluctuate between the aristocratic notion of subjection and the democratic notion of obedience. Obedience then loses its moral importance in the eyes of him who obeys; he no longer considers it as a species of divine obligation, and he does not yet view it under its purely human aspect; it has to him no character of sanctity or of justice, and he submits to it as to a degrading but profitable condition.

At that period, a confused and imperfect phantom of equality haunts the minds of servants; they do not at once perceive whether the equality to which they are entitled is to be found within or without the pale of domestic service; and they rebel in their hearts against a subordination to which they have subjected themselves, and from which they derive actual profit. They consent to serve, and they blush to obey: they like the advantages of service, but not the master; or, rather, they are not sure that they ought not themselves to be masters, and they are inclined to consider him who orders them as an unjust usurper of their own rights.

Then it is that the dwelling of every citizen offers a spectacle somewhat analogous to the gloomy aspect of political society. A secret and intestine warfare is going on there between powers ever rivals and suspicious of one another: the master is ill-natured and weak, the servant ill-natured and intractable; the one constantly attempts to evade by unfair restrictions his obligation to protect and to remunerate, — the other, his obligation to obey. The reins of domestic government dangle between them, to be snatched at by one or the other. The lines which divide authority from oppression, liberty from license, and right from might, are to their eyes so jumbled together and confused, that no one knows exactly what he is, or what he may be, or what he ought to be. Such a condition is not democracy, but revolution.

CHAPTER VI.

HOW DEMOCRATIC INSTITUTIONS AND MANNERS TEND TO RAISE RENTS AND SHORTEN THE TERMS OF LEASES.

WHAT has been said of servants and masters is applicable, to a certain extent, to land-owners and farming tenants; but this subject deserves to be considered by itself.

In America there are, properly speaking, no farming tenants; every man owns the ground he tills. It must be admitted that democratic laws tend greatly to increase the number of land-owners, and to diminish that of farming tenants. Yet what takes place in the United States is much less attributable to the institutions of the country, than to the country itself. In America land is cheap, and any one may easily become a land-owner; its returns are small, and its produce cannot well be divided between a land-owner and a farmer. America therefore stands alone in this respect, as well as in many others, and it would be a mistake to take it as an example.

I believe that, in democratic as well as in aristocratic countries, there will be land-owners and tenants, but the connection existing between them will be of a different kind. In aristocracies, the hire of a farm is paid to the landlord, not only in rent, but in respect, regard, and duty; in democracies, the whole is paid in cash. When estates are divided and passed from hand to hand, and the permanent connection which existed between families and the soil is dissolved, the land-owner and the tenant are only casually brought into contact. They meet for a moment to settle the conditions of the agreement, and then lose sight of each other; they are two strangers brought together by a common interest, and who keenly talk over a matter of business, the sole object of which is to make money.

In proportion as property is subdivided and wealth distributed over the country, the community is filled with people whose former opulence is declining, and with others whose fortunes are of recent growth, and whose wants increase more rapidly than their resources. For all such persons the smallest pecuniary profit is a matter of importance, and none of them feel disposed to waive any of their claims, or to lose any portion of their income.

As ranks are intermingled, and as very large as well as very scanty fortunes become more rare, every day brings the social condition of the land-owner nearer to that of the farmer: the one has not naturally any uncontested superiority over the other; between two men who are equal, and not at ease in their circumstances, the contract of hire is exclusively an affair of money.

A man whose estate extends over a whole district, and who owns a hundred farms, is well aware of the importance of gaining at the same time the affections of some thousands of men; this object appears to call for his exertions, and to attain it he will readily make considerable sacrifices. But he who owns a hundred acres is insensible to similar considerations, and cares but little to win the private regard of his tenant.

An aristocracy does not expire, like a man, in a single day; the aristocratic principle is slowly undermined in men's opinion, before it is attacked in their laws. Long before open war is declared against it, the tie which had hitherto united the higher classes to the lower may be seen to be gradually relaxed. Indifference and contempt are betrayed by one class, jealousy and hatred by the others: the intercourse between rich and poor becomes less frequent and less kind, and rents are raised. This is not the consequence of a democratic revolution, but its certain harbinger: for an aristocracy which has lost the affections of the people, once and forever, is like a tree dead at the root, which is the more easily torn up by the winds the higher its branches have spread.

In the course of the last fifty years the rents of farms have amazingly increased, not only in France, but throughout the greater part of Europe. The remarkable improvements which have taken place in agriculture and manufactures within the same period do not suffice, in my opinion, to explain this fact: recourse must be had to another cause, more powerful and more concealed. I believe that cause is to be found in the democratic institutions which several European nations have adopted, and in the democratic passions which more or less agitate all the rest.

I have frequently heard great English land-owners congratulate themselves that, at the present day, they derive a much larger income from their estates than their fathers did. They have perhaps good reason to be glad; but most assuredly they know not what they are glad of. They think they are making a clear gain, when it is in reality only an exchange: their influence is what they are parting with for cash; and what they gain in money will erelong be lost in power.

There is yet another sign by which it is easy to know that a great democratic revolution is going on or approaching. In the Middle Ages, almost all lands were leased for lives, or for very long terms: the domestic economy of that period shows that leases for ninety-nine years were more frequent then than leases for twelve years are now. Men then believed that families were immortal; men's conditions seemed settled forever, and the whole of society appeared to be so fixed, that it was not supposed anything would ever be stirred or shaken in its structure. In ages of equality, the human mind takes a different bent: the prevailing notion is that nothing abides, and man is haunted by the thought of mutability. Under this impression, the land-owner and the tenant himself are instinctively averse to protracted terms of obligation: they are afraid of being tied up to-morrow by the contract which benefits them to-day. They have vague anticipations of some sudden and unforeseen change in their conditions; they mistrust themselves; they fear lest their taste should change, and lest they should lament that they cannot rid themselves of what they coveted. Nor are such fears unfounded; for, in democratic times, that which is most fluctuating amidst the fluctuation of all around is the heart of man.

CHAPTER VII.

INFLUENCE OF DEMOCRACY ON WAGES.

MOST of the remarks which I have already made in speaking of masters and servants may be applied to masters and workmen. As the gradations of the social scale come to be less observed, whilst the great sink and the humble rise, and poverty as well as opulence ceases to be hereditary, the distance, both in reality and in opinion, which heretofore separated the workman from the master, is lessened every day. The workman conceives a more lofty opinion of his rights, of his future, of himself; he is filled with new ambition and new desires, he is harassed by new wants. Every instant he views with longing eyes the profits of his employer; and in order to share them, he strives to dispose of his labor at a higher rate, and he generally succeeds at length in the attempt.

In democratic countries, as well as elsewhere, most of the branches of productive industry are carried on at a small cost, by men little removed by their wealth or education above the level of those whom they employ. These manufacturing speculators are extremely numerous; their interests differ; they cannot therefore easily concert or combine their exertions. On the other hand, the workmen have always some sure resources, which enable them to refuse to work when they cannot get what they conceive to be the fair price of their labor. In the constant struggle for wages which is going on between these two classes, their strength is divided, and success alternates from one to the other.

It is even probable that, in the end, the interest of the working class will prevail; for the high wages which they have already obtained make them every day less dependent on their masters; and as they grow more independent, they have greater facilities for obtaining a further increase of wages.

I shall take for example that branch of productive industry which is still, at the present day, the most generally followed in France, and in almost all the countries of the world;—I mean the cultivation of the soil. In France, most of those who labor for hire in agriculture are themselves owners of certain plots of ground, which just enable them to subsist without working for any one else. When these laborers come to offer their services to a neighboring land-owner or farmer, if he refuses them a certain rate of wages, they retire to their own small property and await another opportunity.

I think that, upon the whole, it may be asserted that a slow and gradual rise of wages is one of the general laws of democratic communities. In proportion as social conditions become more equal, wages rise; and as wages are higher, social conditions become more equal.

But a great and gloomy exception occurs in our own time. I have shown, in a preceding chapter, that aristocracy, expelled from political society, has taken refuge in certain departments of productive industry, and has established its sway there under another form; this powerfully affects the rate of wages.

As a large capital is required to embark in the great manufacturing speculations to which I allude, the number of persons who enter upon them is exceedingly limited: as their number is small, they can easily concert together, and fix the rate of wages as they please.

Their workmen, on the contrary, are exceedingly numerous, and the number of them is always increasing; for, from time to time, an extraordinary run of business takes place, during which wages are inordinately high, and they attract the surrounding population to the factories. But, when men have once embraced that line of life, we have already seen that they cannot quit it again, because they soon contract habits of body and mind which unfit them for any other sort of toil. These men have generally but little education and industry, with but few resources; they stand, therefore, almost at the mercy of the master.

When competition, or other fortuitous circumstances, lessen his profits, he can reduce the wages of his workmen almost at pleasure, and make from them what he loses by the chances of business. Should the workmen strike, the master, who is a rich man, can very well wait, without being ruined, until necessity brings them back to him; but they must work day by day or they die, for their only property is in their hands. They have long been impoverished by oppression, and the poorer they become, the more easily may they be oppressed: they can never escape from this fatal circle of cause and consequence.

It is not surprising then that wages, after having sometimes suddenly risen, are permanently lowered in this branch of industry; whereas, in other callings, the price of labor, which generally increases but little, is nevertheless constantly augmented.

This state of dependence and wretchedness, in which a part of the manufacturing population of our time live, forms an exception to the general rule, contrary to the state of all the rest of the community; but, for this very reason, no circumstance is more important or more deserving of the especial consideration of the legislator; for when the whole of society is in motion, it is difficult to keep any one class stationary; and when the greater number of men are opening new paths to fortune, it is no less difficult to make the few support in peace their wants and their desires.

CHAPTER VIII.

INFLUENCE OF DEMOCRACY ON THE FAMILY.

I HAVE just examined the changes which the equality of conditions produces in the mutual relations of the several members of the community amongst democratic nations, and amongst the Americans in particular. I would now go deeper, and inquire into the closer ties of family: my object here is not to seek for new truths, but to show in what manner facts already known are connected with my subject.

It has been universally remarked, that, in our time, the several members of a family stand upon an entirely new footing towards each other; that the distance which formerly separated a father from his sons has been lessened; and that paternal authority, if not destroyed, is at least impaired.

Something analogous to this, but even more striking, may be observed in the United States. In America, the family, in the Roman and aristocratic signification of the word, does not exist. All that remains of it are a few vestiges in the first years of childhood, when the father exercises, without opposition, that absolute domestic authority which the feebleness of his children renders necessary, and which their interest, as well as his own incontestable superiority, warrants. But as soon as the young American approaches manhood, the ties of filial obedience are relaxed day by day: master of his thoughts, he is soon master of his conduct. In America, there is, strictly speaking, no adolescence: at the close of boyhood, the man appears, and begins to trace out his own path.

It would be an error to suppose that this is preceded by a domestic struggle, in which the son has obtained by a sort of moral violence the liberty that his father refused him. The same habits, the same principles, which impel the one to assert his independence, predispose the other to consider the use of that independence as an incontestable right. The former does not exhibit any of those rancorous or irregular passions which disturb men long after they have shaken off an established authority; the latter feels none of that bitter and angry regret which is apt to survive a by-gone power. The father foresees the limits of his authority long beforehand, and when the time arrives, he surrenders it without a struggle: the son looks forward to the exact period at which he will be his own master; and he enters upon his freedom without precipitation and without effort, as a possession which is his own, and which no one seeks to wrest from him.*

It may, perhaps, be useful to show how these changes

* The Americans, however, have not yet thought fit to strip the parent, as has been done in France, of one of the chief elements of parental authority, by depriving him of the power of disposing of his property at his death. In the United States, there are no restrictions on the powers of a testator.

In this respect, as in almost all others, it is easy to perceive that, if the political legislation of the Americans is much more democratic than that of the French, the civil legislation of the latter is infinitely more democratic than that of the former. This may easily be accounted for. The civil legislation of France was the work of a man who saw that it was his interest to satisfy the democratic passions of his contemporaries in all that was not directly and immediately hostile to his own power. He was willing to allow some popular principles to regulate the distribution of property and the government of families, provided they were not to be introduced into the administration of public affairs. Whilst the torrent of democracy overwhelmed the civil laws of the country, he hoped to find an easy shelter behind its political institutions. This policy was at once both adroit and selfish: but a compromise of this kind could not last; for in the end, political institutions never fail to become the image and expression of civil society; and in this sense it may be said, that nothing is more political in a nation than its civil legislation.

which take place in family relations are closely connected with the social and political revolution which is approaching its consummation under our own eyes.

There are certain great social principles which a people either introduces everywhere or tolerates nowhere. In countries which are aristocratically constituted with all the gradations of rank, the government never makes a direct appeal to the mass of the governed: as men are united together, it is enough to lead the foremost; the rest will follow. This is applicable to the family, as well as to all aristocracies which have a head. Amongst aristocratic nations, social institutions recognize, in truth, no one in the family but the father; children are received by society at his hands; society governs him, he governs them. Thus, the parent has not only a natural right, but he acquires a political right, to command them: he is the author and the support of his family; but he is also its constituted ruler.

In democracies, where the government picks out every individual singly from the mass to make him subservient to the general laws of the community, no such intermediate person is required: a father is there, in the eye of the law, only a member of the community, older and richer than his sons.

When most of the conditions of life are extremely unequal, and the inequality of these conditions is permanent, the notion of a superior grows upon the imaginations of men: if the law invested him with no privileges, custom and public opinion would concede them. When, on the contrary, men differ but little from each other, and do not always remain in dissimilar conditions of life, the general notion of a superior becomes weaker and less distinct: it is vain for legislation to strive to place him who obeys very much beneath him who commands; the manners of the time bring the two men nearer to one another, and draw them daily towards the same level.

Although the legislation of an aristocratic people should grant no peculiar privileges to the heads of families, I shall not be the less convinced that their power is more respected and more extensive than in a democracy; for I know that, whatsoever the laws may be, superiors always appear higher, and inferiors lower, in aristocracies than amongst democratic nations.

When men live more for the remembrance of what has been than for the care of what is, and when they are more given to attend to what their ancestors thought than to think themselves, the father is the natural and necessary tie between the past and the present, — the link by which the ends of these two chains are connected. In aristocracies, then, the father is not only the civil head of the family, but the organ of its traditions, the expounder of its customs, the arbiter of its manners. He is listened to with deference, he is addressed with respect, and the love which is felt for him is always tempered with fear.

When the condition of society becomes democratic, and men adopt as their general principle that it is good and lawful to judge of all things for one's self, using former points of belief not as a rule of faith, but simply as a means of information, the power which the opinions of a father exercise over those of his sons diminishes, as well as his legal power.

Perhaps the subdivision of estates which democracy brings about contributes more than anything else to change the relations existing between a father and his children. When the property of the father of a family is scanty, his son and himself constantly live in the same place, and share the same occupations: habit and necessity bring them together, and force them to hold constant communication: the inevitable consequence is a sort of familiar intimacy, which renders authority less absolute, and which can ill be reconciled with the external forms of respect.

Now, in democratic countries, the class of those who are possessed of small fortunes is precisely that which gives strength to the notions and a particular direction to the manners of the community. That class makes its opinions preponderate as universally as its will; and even those who are most inclined to resist its commands are carried away in the end by its example. I have known eager opponents of democracy, who allowed their children to address them with perfect colloquial equality.

Thus, at the same time that the power of aristocracy is declining, the austere, the conventional, and the legal part of parental authority vanishes, and a species of equality prevails around the domestic hearth. I know not, upon the whole, whether society loses by the change, but I am inclined to believe that man individually is a gainer by it. I think that, in proportion as manners and laws become more democratic, the relation of father and son becomes more intimate and more affectionate; rules and authority are less talked of, confidence and tenderness are oftentimes increased, and it would seem that the natural bond is drawn closer in proportion as the social bond is loosened.

In a democratic family, the father exercises no other power than that which is granted to the affection and the experience of age; his orders would perhaps be disobeyed, but his advice is for the most part authoritative. Though he be not hedged in with ceremonial respect, his sons at least accost him with confidence; they have no settled form of addressing him, but they speak to him constantly, and are ready to consult him every day: the master and the constituted ruler have vanished; the father remains.

Nothing more is needed in order to judge of the difference between the two states of society in this respect, than to peruse the family correspondence of aristocratic ages. The style is always correct, ceremonious, stiff, and so cold that the natural warmth of the heart can hardly be felt in the language. In democratic countries, on the contrary, the language addressed by a son to his father is always marked by mingled freedom, familiarity, and affection, which at once show that new relations have sprung up in the bosom of the family.

A similar revolution takes place in the mutual relations of children. In aristocratic families, as well as in aristocratic society, every place is marked out beforehand. Not only does the father occupy a separate rank, in which he enjoys extensive privileges, but even the children are not equal amongst themselves. The age and sex of each irrevocably determine his rank, and secure to him certain privileges: most of these distinctions are abolished or diminished by democracy.

In aristocratic families, the eldest son, inheriting the greater part of the property, and almost all the rights of the family, becomes the chief, and, to a certain extent, the master, of his brothers. Greatness and power are for him; for them, mediocrity and dependence. But it would be wrong to suppose that, amongst aristocratic nations, the privileges of the eldest son are advantageous to himself alone, or that they excite nothing but envy and hatred around him. The eldest son commonly endeavors to procure wealth and power for his brothers, because the general splendor of the house is reflected back on him who represents it; the younger sons seek to back the elder brother in all his undertakings, because the greatness and power of the head of the family better enable him to provide for all its branches. The different members of an aristocratic family are therefore very closely bound together; their interests are connected, their minds agree, but their hearts are seldom in harmony.

Democracy also binds brothers to each other, but by very different means. Under democratic laws, all the children are perfectly equal, and consequently independent: noth ing brings them forcibly together, but nothing keeps them apart; and as they have the same origin, as they are trained under the same roof, as they are treated with the same care, and as no peculiar privilege distinguishes or divides them, the affectionate and frank intimacy of early years easily springs up between them. Scarcely anything can occur to break the tie thus formed at the outset of life, for brotherhood brings them daily together, without embarrassing them. It is not then by interest, but by common associations and by the free sympathy of opinion and of taste, that democracy unites brothers to each other. It divides their inheritance, but allows their hearts and minds to unite.

Such is the charm of these democratic manners, that even the partisans of aristocracy are attracted by it; and after having experienced it for some time, they are by no means tempted to revert to the respectful and frigid observances of aristocratic families. They would be glad to retain the domestic habits of democracy, if they might throw off its social conditions and its laws; but these elements are indissolubly united, and it is impossible to enjoy the former without enduring the latter.

The remarks I have made on filial love and fraternal affection are applicable to all the passions which emanate spontaneously from human nature itself.

If a certain mode of thought or feeling is the result of some peculiar condition of life, when that condition is altered nothing whatever remains of the thought or feeling. Thus, a law may bind two members of the community very closely to one another; but that law being abolished, they stand asunder. Nothing was more strict than the tie which united the vassal to the lord under the feudal system: at the present day, the two men know not each other; the fear, the gratitude, and the affection which formerly connected them have vanished, and not a vestige of the tie remains.

Such, however, is not the case with those feelings which are natural to mankind. Whenever a law attempts to tutor these feelings in any particular manner, it seldom fails to weaken them ; by attempting to add to their intensity, it robs them of some of their elements, for they are never stronger than when left to themselves.

Democracy, which destroys or obscures almost all the old conventional rules of society, and which prevents men from readily assenting to new ones, entirely effaces most of the feelings to which these conventional rules have given rise; but it only modifies some others, and frequently imparts to them a degree of energy and sweetness unknown before.

Perhaps it is not impossible to condense into a single proposition the whole purport of this chapter, and of several others that preceded it. Democracy loosens social ties, but tightens natural ones ; it brings kindred more closely together, whilst it throws citizens more apart.

CHAPTER IX.

EDUCATION OF YOUNG WOMEN IN THE UNITED STATES.

NO free communities ever existed without morals; and, as I observed in the former part of this work, morals are the work of woman. Consequently, whatever affects the condition of women, their habits and their opinions, has great political importance in my eyes.

Amongst almost all Protestant nations, young women are far more the mistresses of their own actions than they are in Catholic countries. This independence is still greater in Protestant countries like England, which have retained or acquired the right of self-government; freedom is then infused into the domestic circle by political habits and by religious opinions. In the United States, the doctrines of Protestantism are combined with great political liberty and a most democratic state of society; and nowhere are young women surrendered so early or so completely to their own guidance.

Long before an American girl arrives at the marriageable age, her emancipation from maternal control begins: she has scarcely ceased to be a child, when she already thinks for herself, speaks with freedom, and acts on her own impulse. The great scene of the world is constantly open to her view: far from seeking to conceal it from her, it is every day disclosed more completely, and she is taught to survey it with a firm and calm gaze. Thus the vices and dangers of society are early revealed to her; as she sees them clearly, she views them without illusion, and braves them without fear; for she is full of reliance on her own strength, and her confidence seems to be shared by all around her.

An American girl scarcely ever displays that virginal softness in the midst of young desires, or that innocent and ingenuous grace, which usually attend the European woman in the transition from girlhood to youth. It is rare that an American woman, at any age, displays childish timidity or ignorance. Like the young women of Europe, she seeks to please, but she knows precisely the cost of pleasing. If she does not abandon herself to evil, at least she knows that it exists; and she is remarkable rather for purity of manners than for chastity of mind.

I have been frequently surprised, and almost frightened, at the singular address and happy boldness with which young women in America contrive to manage their thoughts and their language, amidst all the difficulties of free conversation; a philosopher would have stumbled at every step along the narrow path which they trod without accident and without effort. It is easy, indeed, to perceive that, even amidst the independence of early youth, an American woman is always mistress of herself: she indulges in all permitted pleasures, without yielding herself up to any of them; and her reason never allows the reins of self-guidance to drop, though it often seems to hold them loosely.

In France, where traditions of every age are still so strangely mingled in the opinions and tastes of the people, women commonly receive a reserved, retired, and almost conventual education, as they did in aristocratic times; and then they are suddenly abandoned, without a guide and without assistance, in the midst of all the irregularities inseparable from democratic society.

The Americans are more consistent. They have found out that, in a democracy, the independence of individuals cannot fail to be very great, youth premature, tastes ill-restrained, customs fleeting, public opinion often unsettled and powerless, paternal authority weak, and marital authority contested. Under these circumstances, believing that they had little chance of repressing in woman the most vehement passions of the human heart, they held that the surer way was to teach her the art of combating those passions for herself. As they could not prevent her virtue from being exposed to frequent danger, they determined that she should know how best to defend it; and more reliance was placed on the free vigor of her will than on safeguards which have been shaken or overthrown. Instead then of inculcating mistrust of herself, they constantly seek to enhance her confidence in her own strength of character. As it is neither possible nor desirable to keep a young woman in perpetual and complete ignorance, they hasten to give her a precocious knowledge on all subjects. Far from hiding the corruptions of the world from her, they prefer that she should see them at once, and train herself to shun them; and they hold it of more importance to protect her conduct, than to be over-scrupulous of the innocence of her thoughts.

Although the Americans are a very religious people, they do not rely on religion alone to defend the virtue of woman; they seek to arm her reason also. In this respect they have followed the same method as in several others: they first make vigorous efforts to cause individual independence to control itself, and they do not call in the aid of religion until they have reached the utmost limits of human strength.

I am aware that an education of this kind is not without danger; I am sensible that it tends to invigorate the judgment at the expense of the imagination, and to make cold and virtuous women instead of affectionate wives and agreeable companions to man. Society may be more tranquil and better regulated, but domestic life has often fewer charms. These, however, are secondary evils, which may be braved for the sake of higher interests. At the stage at which we are now arrived, the choice is no longer left to us; a democratic education is indispensable to protect women from the dangers with which democratic institutions and manners surround them.

CHAPTER X.

THE YOUNG WOMAN IN THE CHARACTER OF A WIFE.

IN America, the independence of woman is irrecoverably lost in the bonds of matrimony. If an unmarried woman is less constrained there than elsewhere, a wife is subjected to stricter obligations. The former makes her father's house an abode of freedom and of pleasure; the latter lives in the home of her husband as if it were a cloister. Yet these two different conditions of life are perhaps not so contrary as may be supposed, and it is natural that the American women should pass through the one to arrive at the other.

Religious communities and trading nations entertain peculiarly serious notions of marriage: the former consider the regularity of woman's life as the best pledge and most certain sign of the purity of her morals; the latter regard it as the highest security for the order and prosperity of the household. The Americans are, at the same time, a puritanical people and a commercial nation; their religious opinions, as well as their trading habits, consequently lead them to require much abnegation on the part of women, and a constant sacrifice of her pleasures to her duties, which is seldom demanded of her in Europe. Thus, in the United States, the inexorable opinion of the public carefully circumscribes woman within the narrow circle of domestic interests and duties, and forbids her to step beyond it.

Upon her entrance into the world, a young American woman finds these notions firmly established; she sees the rules which are derived from them; she is not slow to perceive that she cannot depart for an instant from the established usages of her contemporaries, without putting in jeopardy her peace of mind, her honor, nay, even her social existence; and she finds the energy required for such an act of submission in the firmness of her understanding, and in the virile habits which her education has given her. It may be said that she has learned, by the use of her independence, to surrender it without a struggle and without a murmur when the time comes for making the sacrifice.

But no American woman falls into the toils of matrimony as into a snare held out to her simplicity and ignorance. She has been taught beforehand what is expected of her, and voluntarily and freely enters upon this engagement. She supports her new condition with courage, because she chose it. As, in America, paternal discipline is very relaxed and the conjugal tie very strict, a young woman does not contract the latter without considerable circumspection and apprehension. Precocious marriages are rare. American women do not marry until their understandings are exercised and ripened; whereas, in other countries, most women generally only begin to exercise and ripen their understandings after marriage.

I by no means suppose, however, that the great change which takes place in all the habits of women in the United States, as soon as they are married, ought solely to be attributed to the constraint of public opinion; it is frequently imposed upon themselves by the sole effort of their own will. When the time for choosing a husband is arrived, that cold and stern reasoning power which has been educated and invigorated by the free observation of the world teaches an American woman that a spirit of levity and independence in the bonds of marriage is a constant subject of annoyance, not of pleasure; it tells her that the amusements of the girl cannot become the recreations of the wife, and that the sources of a married woman's happiness are in the home of her husband. As she clearly discerns beforehand the only road which can lead to domestic happiness, she enters upon it at once, and follows it to the end without seeking to turn back.

The same strength of purpose which the young wives of America display, in bending themselves at once and without repining to the austere duties of their new condition, is no less manifest in all the great trials of their lives. In no country in the world are private fortunes more precarious than in the United States. It is not uncommon for the same man, in the course of his life, to rise and sink again through all the grades which lead from opulence to poverty. American women support these vicissitudes with calm and unquenchable energy: it would seem that their desires contract as easily as they expand with their fortunes.

The greater part of the adventurers who migrate every year to people the Western wilds belong, as I observed in the former part of this work, to the old Anglo-American race of the Northern States. Many of these men, who rush so boldly onwards in pursuit of wealth, were already in the enjoyment of a competency in their own part of the country. They take their wives along with them, and make them share the countless perils and privations which always attend the commencement of these expeditions. I have often met, even on the verge of the wilderness, with young women who, after having been brought up amidst all the comforts of the large towns of New England, had passed, almost without any intermediate stage, from the wealthy abode of their parents to a comfortless hovel in a forest. Fever, solitude, and a tedious life had not broken the springs of their courage. Their features were impaired and faded, but their looks were firm; they appeared to be at once sad and resolute.* I do not doubt that these young American women had amassed, in the education of their early years, that inward strength which they displayed under these circumstances. The early culture of the girl may still, therefore, be traced, in the United States, under the aspect of marriage; her part is changed, her habits are different, but her character is the same.

* See Appendix S.

CHAPTER XI.

HOW EQUALITY OF CONDITION CONTRIBUTES TO MAINTAIN GOOD MORALS IN AMERICA.

SOME philosophers and historians have said or hinted that the strictness of female morality was increased or diminished simply by the distance of a country from the equator. This solution of the difficulty was an easy one; and nothing was required but a globe and a pair of compasses to settle in an instant one of the most difficult problems in the condition of mankind. But I am not sure that this principle of the materialists is supported by facts. The same nations have been chaste or dissolute, at different periods of their history; the strictness or the laxity of their morals depended, therefore, on some variable cause, and not alone on the natural qualities of their country, which were invariable. I do not deny that, in certain climates, the passions which are occasioned by the mutual attraction of the sexes are peculiarly intense; but I believe that this natural intensity may always be excited or restrained by the condition of society, and by political institutions.

Although the travellers who have visited North America differ on many points, they all agree in remarking that morals are far more strict there than elsewhere. It is evident that, on this point, the Americans are very superior to their progenitors, the English. A superficial glance at the two nations will establish the fact.

In England, as in all other countries of Europe, public malice is constantly attacking the frailties of women. Philosophers and statesmen are heard to deplore that morals are not sufficiently strict, and the literary productions of the country constantly lead one to suppose so. In America, all books, novels not excepted, suppose women to be chaste, and no one thinks of relating affairs of gallantry.

No doubt, this great regularity of American morals is due in part to qualities of country, race, and religion; but all these causes, which operate elsewhere, do not suffice to account for it: recourse must be had to some special reason. This reason appears to me to be the principle of equality, and the institutions derived from it. Equality of condition does not of itself produce regularity of morals, but it unquestionably facilitates and increases it.*

Amongst aristocratic nations, birth and fortune frequently make two such different beings of man and woman, that they can never be united to each other. Their passions draw them together, but the condition of society, and the notions suggested by it, prevent them from contracting a permanent and ostensible tie. The necessary consequence is a great number of transient and clandestine connections. Nature secretly avenges herself for the constraint imposed upon her by the laws of man.

This is not so much the case when the equality of conditions has swept away all the imaginary or the real barriers which separated man from woman. No girl then believes that she cannot become the wife of the man who loves her; and this renders all breaches of morality before marriage very uncommon: for, whatever be the credulity of the passions, a woman will hardly be able to persuade herself that

* It is not the equality of condition which makes men immoral and irreligious; but when men, being equal, are also immoral and irreligious, the effects of immorality and irreligion more easily manifest themselves, because men have but little influence over each other, and no class exists which can undertake to keep society in order. Equality of condition never creates profligacy of morals, but it sometimes allows that profligacy to show itself.

she is beloved, when her lover is perfectly free to marry her and does not.

The same cause operates, though more indirectly, on married life. Nothing better serves to justify an illicit passion, either to the minds of those who have conceived it or to the world which looks on, than marriages made by compulsion or chance.*

In a country in which a woman is always free to exercise her choice, and where education has prepared her to choose rightly, public opinion is inexorable to her faults. The rigor of the Americans arises in part from this cause. They consider marriages as a covenant which is often onerous, but every condition of which the parties are strictly bound to fulfil, because they knew all those conditions beforehand, and were perfectly free not to have contracted them.

The very circumstances which render matrimonial fidelity more obligatory, also render it more easy.

In aristocratic countries, the object of marriage is rather to unite property than persons; hence the husband is sometimes at school and the wife at nurse when they are betrothed. It cannot be wondered at if the conjugal tie which holds the fortunes of the pair united allows their

* The literature of Europe sufficiently corroborates this remark. When a European author wishes to depict in a work of fiction any of those great catastrophes in matrimony which so frequently occur amongst us, he takes care to bespeak the compassion of the reader by bringing before him ill-assorted or compulsory marriages. Although habitual tolerance has long since relaxed our morals, an author could hardly succeed in interesting us in the misfortunes of his characters, if he did not first palliate their faults. This artifice seldom fails: the daily scenes we witness prepare us beforehand to be indulgent. But American writers could never render these palliations probable to their readers; their customs and laws are opposed to it; and as they despair of rendering levity of conduct pleasing, they cease to depict it. This is one of the causes to which must be attributed the small number of novels published in the United States.

hearts to rove ; this is the result of the nature of the contract. When, on the contrary, a man always chooses a wife for himself, without any exernal coercion, or even guidance, it is generally a conformity of tastes and opinions which brings a man and a woman together, and this same conformity keeps and fixes them in close habits of intimacy.

Our forefathers had conceived a strange opinion on the subject of marriage ; as they had remarked that the small number of love-matches which occurred in their time almost always turned out ill, they resolutely inferred that it was dangerous to listen to the dictates of the heart on the subject. Accident appeared to them a better guide than choice.

Yet it was not difficult to perceive that the examples which they witnessed in fact proved nothing at all. For, in the first place, if democratic nations leave a woman at liberty to choose her husband, they take care to give her mind sufficient knowledge, and her will sufficient strength, to make so important a choice ; whereas the young women who, amongst aristocratic nations, furtively elope from the authority of their parents to throw themselves of their own accord into the arms of men whom they have had neither time to know, nor ability to judge of, are totally without those securities. It is not surprising that they make a bad use of their freedom of action the first time they avail themselves of it ; nor that they fall into such cruel mistakes when, not having received a democratic education, they choose to marry in conformity to democratic customs. But this is not all. When a man and woman are bent upon marriage in spite of the differences of an aristocratic state of society, the difficulties to be overcome are enormous. Having broken or relaxed the bonds of filial obedience, they have then to emancipate themselves by a final effort from the sway of custom and the tyranny of opinion ;

and when at length they have succeeded in this arduous task, they stand estranged from their natural friends and kinsmen: the prejudice they have crossed separates them from all, and places them in a situation which soon breaks their courage and sours their hearts.

If, then, a couple married in this manner are first unhappy and afterwards criminal, it ought not to be attributed to the freedom of their choice, but rather to their living in a community in which this freedom of choice is not admitted.

Moreover, it should not be forgotten that the same effort which makes a man violently shake off a prevailing error, commonly impels him beyond the bounds of reason; that, to dare to declare war, in however just a cause, against the opinion of one's age and country, a violent and adventurous spirit is required, and that men of this character seldom arrive at happiness or virtue, whatever be the path they follow. And this, it may be observed by the way, is the reason why, in the most necessary and righteous revolutions, it is so rare to meet with virtuous or moderate revolutionary characters. There is, then, no just ground for surprise if a man who, in an age of aristocracy, chooses to consult nothing but his own opinion and his own taste in the choice of a wife, soon finds that infractions of morality and domestic wretchedness invade his household; but when this same line of action is in the natural and ordinary course of things, — when it is sanctioned by parental authority, and backed by public opinion, — it cannot be doubted that the internal peace of families will be increased by it, and conjugal fidelity more rigidly observed.

Almost all men in democracies are engaged in public or professional life; and on the other hand, the limited income obliges a wife to confine herself to the house, in order to watch in person, and very closely, over the details of domestic economy. All these distinct and compulsory occupations are so many natural barriers, which, by keeping the two sexes asunder, render the solicitations of the one less frequent and less ardent, the resistance of the other more easy.

The equality of conditions cannot, it is true, ever succeed in making men chaste, but it may impart a less dangerous character to their breaches of morality. As no one has then either sufficient time or opportunity to assail a virtue armed in self-defence, there will be at the same time a great number of courtesans and a great number of virtuous women. This state of things causes lamentable cases of individual hardship, but it does not prevent the body of society from being strong and alert: it does not destroy family ties, or enervate the morals of the nation. Society is endangered, not by the great profligacy of a few, but by laxity of morals amongst all. In the eyes of a legislator, prostitution is less to be dreaded than intrigue.

The tumultuous and constantly harassed life which equality makes men lead, not only distracts them from the passion of love, by denying them time to indulge it, but it diverts them from it by another more secret but more certain road. All men who live in democratic times more or less contract the ways of thinking of the manufacturing and trading classes; their minds take a serious, deliberate, and positive turn; they are apt to relinquish the ideal, in order to pursue some visible and proximate object, which appears to be the natural and necessary aim of their desires. Thus, the principle of equality does not destroy the imagination, but lowers its flight to the level of the earth.

No men are less addicted to reverie than the citizens of a democracy; and few of them are ever known to give way to those idle and solitary meditations which commonly precede and produce the great emotions of the heart. It is true they attach great importance to procuring for themselves that sort of deep, regular, and quiet affection, which constitutes the charm and safeguard of life; but they are not apt to run after those violent and capricious sources of excitement which disturb and abridge it.

I am aware that all this is applicable in its full extent only to America, and cannot at present be extended to Europe. In the course of the last half-century, whilst laws and customs have impelled several European nations with unexampled force towards democracy, we have not had occasion to observe that the relations of man and woman have become more orderly or more chaste. In some places, the very reverse may be detected: some classes are more strict, the general morality of the people appears to be more lax. I do not hesitate to make the remark, for I am as little disposed to flatter my contemporaries as to malign them.

This fact must distress, but it ought not to surprise us. The propitious influence which a democratic state of society may exercise upon orderly habits is one of those tendencies which can only be discovered after a time. If equality of condition is favorable to purity of morals, the social commotion by which conditions are rendered equal is adverse to it. In the last fifty years, during which France has been undergoing this transformation, it has rarely had freedom, always disturbance. Amidst this universal confusion of notions and this general stir of opinions, — amidst this incoherent mixture of the just and the unjust, of truth and falsehood, of right and might, — public virtue has become doubtful, and private morality wavering. But all revolutions, whatever may have been their object or their agents, have at first produced similar consequences; even those which have in the end drawn tighter the bonds of morality, began by loosening them. The violations of morality which the French frequently witness do not appear to me to have a permanent character; and this is already betokened by some curious signs of the times.

Nothing is more wretchedly corrupt than an aristocracy which retains its wealth when it has lost its power, and which still enjoys a vast deal of leisure after it is reduced to mere vulgar pastimes. The energetic passions and great conceptions which animated it heretofore leave it then; and nothing remains to it but a host of petty consuming vices, which cling about it like worms upon a carcass.

No one denies that the French aristocracy of the last century was extremely dissolute; yet established habits and ancient belief still preserved some respect for morality amongst the other classes of society. Nor will it be denied that, at the present day, the remnants of that same aristocracy exhibit a certain severity of morals; whilst laxity of morals appears to have spread amongst the middle and lower ranks. Thus the same families which were most profligate fifty years ago are now-a-days the most exemplary, and democracy seems only to have strengthened the morality of the aristocratic classes. The French Revolution, by dividing the fortunes of the nobility, by forcing them to attend assiduously to their affairs and to their families, by making them live under the same roof with their children, and, in short, by giving a more rational and serious turn to their minds, has imparted to them, almost without their being aware of it, a reverence for religious belief, a love of order, of tranquil pleasures, of domestic endearments, and of comfort; whereas the rest of the nation, which had naturally these same tastes, was carried away into excesses by the effort which was required to overthrow the laws and political habits of the country.

The old French aristocracy has undergone the consequences of the revolution, but it neither felt the revolutionary passions, nor shared the anarchical excitement which produced it; it may easily be conceived that this aristocracy feels the salutary influence of the revolution on its manners, before those who achieved it. It may therefore be said, though at first it seems paradoxical, that, at the present day, the most anti-democratic classes of the nation principally exhibit the kind of morality which may reasonably be anticipated from democracy. I cannot but think that, when we shall have obtained all the effects of this democratic revolution, after having got rid of the tumult it has caused, the observations which are now only applicable to the few will gradually become true of the whole community.

CHAPTER XII.

HOW THE AMERICANS UNDERSTAND THE EQUALITY OF THE SEXES.

I HAVE shown how democracy destroys or modifies the different inequalities which originate in society; but is this all? or does it not ultimately affect that great inequality of man and woman which has seemed, up to the present day, to be eternally based in human nature? I believe that the social changes which bring nearer to the same level the father and son, the master and servant, and, in general, superiors and inferiors, will raise woman, and make her more and more the equal of man. But here, more than ever, I feel the necessity of making myself clearly understood; for there is no subject on which the coarse and lawless fancies of our age have taken a freer range.

There are people in Europe who, confounding together the different characteristics of the sexes, would make man and woman into beings not only equal, but alike. They would give to both the same functions, impose on both the same duties, and grant to both the same rights; they would mix them in all things,—their occupations, their pleasures, their business. It may readily be conceived, that, by thus attempting to make one sex equal to the other, both are degraded; and from so preposterous a medley of the works of nature, nothing could ever result but weak men and disorderly women.

It is not thus that the Americans understand that species of democratic equality which may be established between the sexes. They admit that, as nature has appointed such wide differences between the physical and moral constitution of man and woman, her manifest design was to give a distinct employment to their various faculties; and they hold that improvement does not consist in making beings so dissimilar do pretty nearly the same things, but in causing each of them to fulfil their respective tasks in the best possible manner. The Americans have applied to the sexes the great principle of political economy which governs the manufactures of our age, by carefully dividing the duties of man from those of woman, in order that the great work of society may be the better carried on.

In no country has such constant care been taken as in America to trace two clearly distinct lines of action for the two sexes, and to make them keep pace one with the other, but in two pathways which are always different. American women never manage the outward concerns of the family, or conduct a business, or take a part in political life; nor are they, on the other hand, ever compelled to perform the rough labor of the fields, or to make any of those laborious exertions which demand the exertion of physical strength. No families are so poor as to form an exception to this rule. If, on the one hand, an American woman cannot escape from the quiet circle of domestic employments, she is never forced, on the other, to go beyond it. Hence it is, that the women of America, who often exhibit a masculine strength of understanding and a manly energy, generally preserve great delicacy of personal appearance, and always retain the manners of women, although they sometimes show that they have the hearts and minds of men.

Nor have the Americans ever supposed that one consequence of democratic principles is the subversion of marital power, or the confusion of the natural authorities in families. They hold that every association must have a head in order to accomplish its object, and that the natural head of the conjugal association is man. They do not therefore deny him the right of directing his partner; and they maintain that, in the smaller association of husband and wife, as well as in the great social community, the object of democracy is to regulate and legalize the powers which are necessary, and not to subvert all power.

This opinion is not peculiar to one sex, and contested by the other: I never observed that the women of America consider conjugal authority as a fortunate usurpation of their rights, nor that they thought themselves degraded by submitting to it. It appeared to me, on the contrary, that they attach a sort of pride to the voluntary surrender of their own will, and make it their boast to bend themselves to the yoke, — not to shake it off. Such, at least, is the feeling expressed by the most virtuous of their sex; the others are silent; and, in the United States, it is not the practice for a guilty wife to clamor for the rights of women, whilst she is trampling on her own holiest duties.

It has often been remarked, that in Europe a certain degree of contempt lurks even in the flattery which men lavish upon women: although a European frequently affects to be the slave of woman, it may be seen that he never sincerely thinks her his equal. In the United States, men seldom compliment women, but they daily show how much they esteem them. They constantly display an entire confidence in the understanding of a wife, and a profound respect for her freedom; they have decided that her mind is just as fitted as that of a man to discover the plain truth, and her heart as firm to embrace it; and they have never sought to place her virtue, any more than his, under the shelter of prejudice, ignorance, and fear.

It would seem that, in Europe, where man so easily submits to the despotic sway of women, they are nevertheless deprived of some of the greatest attributes of the human species, and considered as seductive but imperfect beings;

and (what may well provoke astonishment) women ultimately look upon themselves in the same light, and almost consider it as a privilege that they are entitled to show themselves futile, feeble, and timid. The women of America claim no such privileges.

Again, it may be said that in our morals we have reserved strange immunities to man; so that there is, as it were, one virtue for his use, and another for the guidance of his partner; and that, according to the opinion of the public, the very same act may be punished alternately as a crime, or only as a fault. The Americans know not this iniquitous division of duties and rights; amongst them, the seducer is as much dishonored as his victim.

It is true that the Americans rarely lavish upon women those eager attentions which are commonly paid them in Europe; but their conduct to women always implies that they suppose them to be virtuous and refined; and such is the respect entertained for the moral freedom of the sex, that in the presence of a woman the most guarded language is used, lest her ear should be offended by an expression. In America, a young unmarried woman may, alone and without fear, undertake a long journey.

The legislators of the United States, who have mitigated almost all the penalties of criminal law, still make rape a capital offence, and no crime is visited with more inexorable severity by public opinion. This may be accounted for; as the Americans can conceive nothing more precious than a woman's honor, and nothing which ought so much to be respected as her independence, they hold that no punishment is too severe for the man who deprives her of them against her will. In France, where the same offence is visited with far milder penalties, it is frequently difficult to get a verdict from a jury against the prisoner. Is this a consequence of contempt of decency, or contempt of women? I cannot but believe that it is a contempt of both.

Thus, the Americans do not think that man and woman have either the duty or the right to perform the same offices, but they show an equal regard for both their respective parts; and though their lot is different, they consider both of them as beings of equal value. They do not give to the courage of woman the same form or the same direction as to that of man; but they never doubt her courage: and if they hold that man and his partner ought not always to exercise their intellect and understanding in the same manner, they at least believe the understanding of the one to be as sound as that of the other, and her intellect to be as clear. Thus, then, whilst they have allowed the social inferiority of woman to subsist, they have done all they could to raise her morally and intellectually to the level of man; and in this respect they appear to me to have excellently understood the true principle of democratic improvement.

As for myself, I do not hesitate to avow, that, although the women of the United States are confined within the narrow circle of domestic life, and their situation is, in some respects, one of extreme dependence, I have nowhere seen woman occupying a loftier position; and if I were asked, now that I am drawing to the close of this work, in which I have spoken of so many important things done by the Americans, to what the singular prosperity and growing strength of that people ought mainly to be attributed, I should reply, To the superiority of their women.

CHAPTER XIII.

HOW THE PRINCIPLE OF EQUALITY NATURALLY DIVIDES THE AMERICANS INTO A MULTITUDE OF SMALL PRIVATE CIRCLES.

IT might be supposed that the final and necessary effect of democratic institutions would be to confound together all the members of the community in private as well as in public life, and to compel them all to live alike; but this would be to ascribe a very coarse and oppressive form to the equality which originates in democracy. No state of society or laws can render men so much alike, but that education, fortune, and tastes will interpose some differences between them; and, though different men may sometimes find it their interest to combine for the same purposes, they will never make it their pleasure. They will therefore always tend to evade the provisions of law, whatever they may be; and, escaping in some respect from the circle in which the legislator sought to confine them, they will set up, close by the great political community, small private societies, united together by similitude of conditions, habits, and manners.

In the United States, the citizens have no sort of preeminence over each other; they owe each other no mutual obedience or respect; they all meet for the administration of justice, for the government of the state, and, in general, to treat of the affairs which concern their common welfare; but I never heard that attempts have been made to bring them all to follow the same diversions, or to amuse themselves promiscuously in the same places of recreation.

The Americans, who mingle so readily in their political

assemblies and courts of justice, are wont carefully to separate into small distinct circles, in order to indulge by themselves in the enjoyments of private life. Each of them willingly acknowledges all his fellow-citizens as his equals, but will only receive a very limited number of them as his friends or his guests. This appears to me to be very natural. In proportion as the circle of public society is extended, it may be anticipated that the sphere of private intercourse will be contracted; far from supposing that the members of modern society will ultimately live in common, I am afraid they will end by forming only small coteries.

Amongst aristocratic nations, the different classes are like vast enclosures, out of which it is impossible to get, into which it is impossible to enter. These classes have no communication with each other, but within them men necessarily live in daily contact; even though they would not naturally suit, the general conformity of a similar condition brings them near together.

But when neither law nor custom professes to establish frequent and habitual relations between certain men, their intercourse originates in the accidental similarity of opinions and tastes; hence private society is infinitely varied. In democracies, where the members of the community never differ much from each other, and naturally stand so near that they may all at any time be confounded in one general mass, numerous artificial and arbitrary distinctions spring up, by means of which every man hopes to keep himself aloof, lest he should be carried away against his will in the crowd.

This can never fail to be the case; for human institutions can be changed, but man cannot: whatever may be the general endeavor of a community to render its members equal and alike, the personal pride of individuals will always seek to rise above the line, and to form somewhere an inequality to their own advantage.

In aristocracies, men are separated from each other by lofty stationary barriers: in democracies, they are divided by many small and almost invisible threads, which are constantly broken or moved from place to place. Thus, whatever may be the progress of equality, in democratic nations a great number of small private associations will always be formed within the general pale of political society; but none of them will bear any resemblance in its manners to the higher class in aristocracies.

CHAPTER XIV.

SOME REFLECTIONS ON AMERICAN MANNERS.

NOTHING seems at first sight less important than the outward form of human actions, yet there is nothing upon which men set more store: they grow used to everything except to living in a society which has not their own manners. The influence of the social and political state of a country upon manners is therefore deserving of serious examination.

Manners are generally the product of the very basis of character, but they are also sometimes the result of an arbitrary convention between certain men; thus they are at once natural and acquired.

When some men perceive that they are the foremost persons in society, without contest and without effort, — when they are constantly engaged on large objects, leaving the more minute details to others, — and when they live in the enjoyment of wealth which they did not amass and do not fear to lose, — it may be supposed that they feel a kind of haughty disdain of the petty interests and practical cares of life, and that their thoughts assume a natural greatness, which their language and their manners denote. In democratic countries, manners are generally devoid of dignity, because private life is there extremely petty in its character; and they are frequently low, because the mind has few opportunities of rising above the engrossing cares of domestic interests.

True dignity in manners consists in always taking one's proper station, neither too high nor too low; and this is as much within the reach of a peasant as of a prince. In democracies, all stations appear doubtful; hence it is that the manners of democracies, though often full of arrogance, are commonly wanting in dignity, and, moreover, they are never either well-trained or accomplished.

The men who live in democracies are too fluctuating for a certain number of them ever to succeed in laying down a code of good breeding, and in forcing people to follow it. Every man therefore behaves after his own fashion, and there is always a certain incoherence in the manners of such times, because they are moulded upon the feelings and notions of each individual, rather than upon an ideal model proposed for general imitation. This, however, is much more perceptible when an aristocracy has just been overthrown, than after it has long been destroyed. New political institutions and new social elements then bring to the same places of resort, and frequently compel to live in common, men whose education and habits are still amazingly dissimilar, and this renders the motley composition of society peculiarly visible. The existence of a former strict code of good breeding is still remembered, but what it contained, or where it is to be found, is already forgotten. Men have lost the common law of manners, and they have not yet made up their minds to do without it; but every one endeavors to make to himself some sort of arbitrary and variable rule, from the remnant of former usages; so that manners have neither the regularity and the dignity which they often display amongst aristocratic nations, nor the simplicity and freedom which they sometimes assume in democracies; they are at once constrained and without constraint.

This, however, is not the normal state of things. When the equality of conditions is long established and complete, as all men entertain nearly the same notions and do nearly the same things, they do not require to agree, or to copy from one another, in order to speak or act in the same manner; their manners are constantly characterized by a number of lesser diversities, but not by any great differences. They are never perfectly alike, because they do not copy from the same pattern; they are never very unlike, because their social condition is the same. At first sight, a traveller would say that the manners of all Americans are exactly similar; it is only upon close examination that the peculiarities in which they differ may be detected.

The English make game of the manners of the Americans; but it is singular that most of the writers who have drawn these ludicrous delineations belonged themselves to the middle classes in England, to whom the same delineations are exceedingly applicable; so that these pitiless censors furnish, for the most part, an example of the very thing they blame in the United States: they do not perceive that they are deriding themselves, to the great amusement of the aristocracy of their own country.

Nothing is more prejudicial to democracy than its outward forms of behavior; many men would willingly endure its vices, who cannot support its manners. I cannot, however, admit that there is nothing commendable in the manners of a democratic people.

Amongst aristocratic nations, all who live within reach of the first class in society commonly strain to be like it, which gives rise to ridiculous and insipid imitations. As a democratic people do not possess any models of high breeding, at least they escape the daily necessity of seeing wretched copies of them. In democracies, manners are never so refined as amongst aristocratic nations, but, on the other hand, they are never so coarse. Neither the coarse oaths of the populace, nor the elegant and choice expressions of the nobility, are to be heard there: the manners of such a people are often vulgar, but they are neither brutal nor mean.

I have already observed that, in democracies, no such thing as a regular code of good breeding can be laid down; this has some inconveniences and some advantages. In aristocracies, the rules of propriety impose the same demeanor on every one; they make all the members of the same class appear alike, in spite of their private inclinations; they adorn and they conceal the natural man. Amongst a democratic people, manners are neither so tutored nor so uniform, but they are frequently more sincere. They form, as it were, a light and loosely-woven veil, through which the real feelings and private opinions of each individual are easily discernible. The form and the substance of human actions, therefore, often stand there in closer relation; and if the great picture of human life be less embellished, it is more true. Thus it may be said, in one sense, that the effect of democracy is not exactly to give men any particular manners, but to prevent them from having manners at all.

The feelings, the passions, the virtues, and the vices of an aristocracy may sometimes reappear in a democracy, but not its manners; they are lost, and vanish forever, as soon as the democratic revolution is completed. It would seem that nothing is more lasting than the manners of an aristocratic class, for they are preserved by that class for some time after it has lost its wealth and its power, — nor so fleeting, for no sooner have they disappeared, than not a trace of them is to be found; and it is scarcely possible to say what they have been, as soon as they have ceased to be. A change in the state of society works this miracle, and a few generations suffice to consummate it. The principal characteristics of aristocracy are handed down by history after an aristocracy is destroyed; but the light and exquisite touches of manners are effaced from men's memories almost immediately after its fall. Men can no longer conceive what these manners were, when they have ceased to witness them; they are gone, and their departure was unseen, unfelt; for in order to feel that refined enjoyment which is derived from choice and distinguished manners, habit and education must have prepared the heart, and the taste for them is lost almost as easily as the practice of them. Thus, not only a democratic people cannot have aristocratic manners, but they neither comprehend nor desire them; and as they never have thought of them, it is to their minds as if such things had never been. Too much importance should not be attached to this loss, but it may well be regretted.

I am aware that it has not unfrequently happened that the same men have had very high-bred manners and very low-born feelings: the interior of courts has sufficiently shown what imposing externals may conceal the meanest hearts. But though the manners of aristocracy do not constitute virtue, they sometimes embellish virtue itself. It was no ordinary sight to see a numerous and powerful class of men, whose every outward action seemed constantly to be dictated by a natural elevation of thought and feeling, by delicacy and regularity of taste, and by urbanity of manners. Those manners threw a pleasing illusory charm over human nature; and though the picture was often a false one, it could not be viewed without a noble satisfaction.

CHAPTER XV.

OF THE GRAVITY OF THE AMERICANS, AND WHY IT DOES NOT PREVENT THEM FROM OFTEN DOING INCONSIDERATE THINGS.

MEN who live in democratic countries do not value the simple, turbulent, or coarse diversions in which the people in aristocratic communities indulge: such diversions are thought by them to be puerile or insipid. Nor have they a greater inclination for the intellectual and refined amusements of the aristocratic classes. They want something productive and substantial in their pleasures; they want to mix actual fruition with their joy.

In aristocratic communities, the people readily give themselves up to bursts of tumultuous and boisterous gayety, which shake off at once the recollection of their privations: the inhabitants of democracies are not fond of being thus violently broken in upon, and they never lose sight of themselves without regret. Instead of these frivolous delights, they prefer those more serious and silent amusements which are like business, and which do not drive business wholly out of their minds.

An American, instead of going in a leisure hour to dance merrily at some place of public resort, as the fellows of his class continue to do throughout the greater part of Europe, shuts himself up at home to drink. He thus enjoys two pleasures; he can go on thinking of his business, and can get drunk decently by his own fireside.

I thought that the English constituted the most serious nation on the face of the earth; but I have since seen the

Americans and have changed my opinion. I do not mean to say that temperament has not a great deal to do with the character of the inhabitants of the United States, but I think that their political institutions are a still more influ ential cause.

I believe the seriousness of the Americans arises partly from their pride. In democratic countries, even poor men entertain a lofty notion of their personal importance: they look upon themselves with complacency, and are apt to suppose that others are looking at them too. With this disposition, they watch their language and their actions with care, and do not lay themselves open so as to betray their deficiencies; to preserve their dignity, they think it necessary to retain their gravity.

But I detect another more deep-seated and powerful cause, which instinctively produces amongst the Americans this astonishing gravity. Under a despotism, communities give way at times to bursts of vehement joy; but they are generally gloomy and moody, because they are afraid. Under absolute monarchies tempered by the customs and manners of the country, their spirits are often cheerful and even, because, as they have some freedom and a good deal of security, they are exempted from the most important cares of life; but all free nations are serious, because their minds are habitually absorbed by the contemplation of some dangerous or difficult purpose. This is more especially the case amongst those free nations which form democratic communities. Then there are, in all classes, a large number of men constantly occupied with the serious affairs of the government; and those whose thoughts are not engaged in the matters of the commonwealth, are wholly engrossed by the acquisition of a private fortune. Amongst such a people, a serious demeanor ceases to be peculiar to certain men, and becomes a habit of the nation.

We are told of small democracies in the days of antiquity, in which the citizens met upon the public places with garlands of roses, and spent almost all their time in dancing and theatrical amusements. I do not believe in such republics, any more than in that of Plato; or, if the things we read of really happened, I do not hesitate to affirm that these supposed democracies were composed of very different elements from ours, and that they had nothing in common with the latter except their name.

But it must not be supposed that, in the midst of all their toils, the people who live in democracies think themselves to be pitied; the contrary is remarked to be the case. No men are fonder of their own condition. Life would have no relish for them, if they were delivered from the anxieties which harass them, and they show more attachment to their cares than aristocratic nations to their pleasures.

I am next led to inquire how it is that these same democratic nations which are so serious, sometimes act in so inconsiderate a manner. The Americans, who almost always preserve a staid demeanor and a frigid air, nevertheless frequently allow themselves to be borne away, far beyond the bounds of reason, by a sudden passion or a hasty opinion, and sometimes gravely commit strange absurdities.

This contrast ought not to surprise us. There is one sort of ignorance which originates in extreme publicity. In despotic states, men know not how to act, because they are told nothing: in democratic nations, they often act at random, because nothing is to be left untold. The former do not know, the latter forget; and the chief features of each picture are lost to them in a bewilderment of details.

It is astonishing what imprudent language a public man may sometimes use in free countries, and especially in democratic states, without being compromised; whereas, in absolute monarchies, a few words dropped by accident are enough to unmask him forever, and ruin him without hope of redemption. This is explained by what goes before. When a man speaks in the midst of a great crowd, many of his words are not heard, or are forthwith obliterated from the memories of those who hear them; but amidst the silence of a mute and motionless throng, the slightest whisper strikes the ear.

In democracies men are never stationary; a thousand chances waft them to and fro, and their life is always the sport of unforeseen or (so to speak) extemporaneous circumstances. Thus, they are often obliged to do things which they have imperfectly learned, to say things which they imperfectly understand, and to devote themselves to work for which they are unprepared by long apprenticeship. In aristocracies, every man has one sole object, which he unceasingly pursues; but amongst democratic nations the existence of man is more complex; the same mind will almost always embrace several objects at once, and these objects are frequently wholly foreign to each other: as it cannot know them all well, the mind is readily satisfied with imperfect notions of each.

When the inhabitant of a democracy is not urged by his wants, he is so at least by his desires; for of all the possessions which he sees around him, none are wholly beyond his reach. He therefore does everything in a hurry, he is always satisfied with "pretty well," and never pauses more than an instant to consider what he has been doing. His curiosity is at once insatiable and cheaply satisfied; for he cares more to know a great deal quickly, than to know anything well: he has no time and but little taste to search things to the bottom.

Thus, then, a democratic people are grave, because their social and political condition constantly leads them to engage in serious occupations; and they act inconsiderately, because they give but little time and attention to each of these occupations. The habit of inattention must be considered as the greatest defect of the democratic character.

CHAPTER XVI.

WHY THE NATIONAL VANITY OF THE AMERICANS IS MORE RESTLESS AND CAPTIOUS THAN THAT OF THE ENGLISH.

ALL free nations are vainglorious, but national pride is not displayed by all in the same manner. The Americans, in their intercourse with strangers, appear impatient of the smallest censure, and insatiable of praise. The most slender eulogium is acceptable to them, the most exalted seldom contents them; they unceasingly harass you to extort praise, and if you resist their entreaties, they fall to praising themselves. It would seem as if, doubting their own merit, they wished to have it constantly exhibited before their eyes. Their vanity is not only greedy, but restless and jealous; it will grant nothing, whilst it demands everything, but is ready to beg and to quarrel at the same time.

If I say to an American that the country he lives in is a fine one, "Ay," he replies, "there is not its equal in the world." If I applaud the freedom which its inhabitants enjoy, he answers, "Freedom is a fine thing, but few nations are worthy to enjoy it." If I remark the purity of morals which distinguishes the United States, "I can imagine," says he, "that a stranger, who has witnessed the corruption that prevails in other nations, should be astonished at the difference." At length, I leave him to the contemplation of himself; but he returns to the charge, and does not desist till he has got me to repeat all I had just been saying. It is impossible to conceive a more troublesome or more garrulous patriotism; it wearies even those who are disposed to respect it.*

Such is not the case with the English. An Englishman calmly enjoys the real or imaginary advantages which, in his opinion, his country possesses. If he grants nothing to other nations, neither does he solicit anything for his own. The censure of foreigners does not affect him, and their praise hardly flatters him; his position with regard to the rest of the world is one of disdainful and ignorant reserve: his pride requires no sustenance, — it nourishes itself. It is remarkable that two nations, so recently sprung from the same stock, should be so opposite to one another in their manner of feeling and conversing.

In aristocratic countries the great possess immense privileges, upon which their pride rests, without seeking to rely upon the lesser advantages which accrue to them. As these privileges came to them by inheritance, they regard them in some sort as a portion of themselves, or at least as a natural right inherent in their own persons. They therefore entertain a calm sense of their own superiority; they do not dream of vaunting privileges which every one perceives and no one contests, and these things are not sufficiently new to be made topics of conversation. They stand unmoved in their solitary greatness, well assured that they are seen of all the world without any effort to show themselves off, and that no one will attempt to drive them from that position. When an aristocracy carries on the public affairs, its national pride naturally assumes this reserved, indifferent, and haughty form, which is imitated by all the other classes of the nation.

When, on the contrary, social conditions differ but little, the slightest privileges are of some importance; as every man sees around himself a million of people enjoying precisely similar or analogous advantages, his pride becomes

* See Appendix T.

craving and jealous, he clings to mere trifles, and doggedly defends them. In democracies, as the conditions of life are very fluctuating, men have almost always recently acquired the advantages which they possess ; the consequence is, that they feel extreme pleasure in exhibiting them, to show others and convince themselves that they really enjoy them. As at any instant these same advantages may be lost, their possessors are constantly on the alert, and make a point of showing that they still retain them. Men living in democracies love their country just as they love themselves, and they transfer the habits of their private vanity to their vanity as a nation.

The restless and insatiable vanity of a democratic people originates so entirely in the equality and precariousness of their social condition, that the members of the haughtiest nobility display the very same passion in those lesser portions of their existence in which there is anything fluctuating or contested. An aristocratic class always differs greatly from the other classes of the nation, by the extent and perpetuity of its privileges ; but it often happens that the only differences between the members who belong to it consist in small, transient advantages, which may any day be lost or acquired. The members of a powerful aristocracy, collected in a capital or a court, have been known to contest with virulence those frivolous privileges which depend on the caprice of fashion or the will of their master. These persons then displayed towards each other precisely the same puerile jealousies which animate the men of democracies, the same eagerness to snatch the smallest advantages which their equals contested, and the same desire to parade ostentatiously those of which they were in possession.

If national pride ever entered into the minds of courtiers, I do not question that they would display it in the same manner as the members of a democratic community.

CHAPTER XVII.

HOW THE ASPECT OF SOCIETY IN THE UNITED STATES IS AT ONCE EXCITED AND MONOTONOUS.

IT would seem that nothing could be more adapted to stimulate and to feed curiosity than the aspect of the United States. Fortunes, opinions, and laws are there in ceaseless variation: it is as if immutable Nature herself were mutable, such are the changes worked upon her by the hand of man. Yet, in the end, the spectacle of this excited community becomes monotonous, and, after having watched the moving pageant for a time, the spectator is tired of it.

Amongst aristocratic nations, every man is pretty nearly stationary in his own sphere; but men are astonishingly unlike each other, — their passions, their notions, their habits, and their tastes are essentially different: nothing changes, but everything differs. In democracies, on the contrary, all men are alike, and do things pretty nearly alike. It is true that they are subject to great and frequent vicissitudes; but as the same events of good or adverse fortune are continually recurring, the name of the actors only is changed, the piece is always the same. The aspect of American society is animated, because men and things are always changing; but it is monotonous, because all these changes are alike.

Men living in democratic times have many passions, but most of their passions either end in the love of riches, or proceed from it. The cause of this is, not that their souls are narrower, but that the importance of money is really greater at such times. When all the members of a community are independent of or indifferent to each other, the co-operation of each of them can be obtained only by paying for it: this infinitely multiplies the purposes to which wealth may be applied, and increases its value. When the reverence which belonged to what is old has vanished, birth, condition, and profession no longer distinguish men, or scarcely distinguish them: hardly anything but money remains to create strongly marked differences between them, and to raise some of them above the common level. The distinction originating in wealth is increased by the disappearance or diminution of all other distinctions. Amongst aristocratic nations, money reaches only to a few points on the vast circle of man's desires: in democracies, it seems to lead to all.

The love of wealth is therefore to be traced, either as a principal or an accessory motive, at the bottom of all that the Americans do: this gives to all their passions a sort of family likeness, and soon renders the survey of them exceedingly wearisome. This perpetual recurrence of the same passion is monotonous; the peculiar methods by which this passion seeks its own gratification are no less so.

In an orderly and peaceable democracy like the United States, where men cannot enrich themselves by war, by public office, or by political confiscation, the love of wealth mainly drives them into business and manufactures. Although these pursuits often bring about great commotions and disasters, they cannot prosper without strictly regular habits and a long routine of petty uniform acts. The stronger the passion is, the more regular are these habits, and the more uniform are these acts. It may be said that it is the vehemence of their desires which makes the Americans so methodical; it perturbs their minds, but it disciplines their lives.

The remark I here apply to America may indeed be

addressed to almost all our contemporaries. Variety is disappearing from the human race; the same ways of acting, thinking, and feeling are to be met with all over the world. This is not only because nations work more upon each other, and copy each other more faithfully; but as the men of each country relinquish more and more the peculiar opinions and feelings of a caste, a profession, or a family, they simultaneously arrive at something nearer to the constitution of man, which is everywhere the same. Thus they become more alike, even without having imitated each other. Like travellers scattered about some large wood, intersected by paths converging to one point, if all of them keep their eyes fixed upon that point, and advance towards it, they insensibly draw nearer together, — though they seek not, though they see not and know not each other; and they will be surprised at length to find themselves all collected on the same spot. All the nations which take, not any particular man, but Man himself, as the object of their researches and their imitations, are tending in the end to a similar state of society, like these travellers converging to the central plot of the forest.

CHAPTER XVIII.

OF HONOR* IN THE UNITED STATES AND IN DEMOCRATIC COMMUNITIES.

IT would seem that men employ two very distinct methods in the judgment which they pass upon the actions of their fellow-men; at one time, they judge them by those simple notions of right and wrong which are diffused all over the world; at another, they appreciate them by a few very special rules which belong exclusively to some particular age and country. It often happens that these two standards differ; they sometimes conflict: but they are never either entirely identified or entirely annulled by one another.

Honor, at the periods of its greatest power, sways the will more than the belief of men; and even whilst they yield without hesitation and without a murmur to its dictates, they feel notwithstanding, by a dim but mighty instinct, the existence of a more general, more ancient, and more holy law, which they sometimes disobey, although they cease not to acknowledge it. Some actions have been held to be at the same time virtuous and dishonorable; — a refusal to fight a duel is an instance.

* The word Honor is not always used in the same sense either in French or English. 1. It first signifies the esteem, glory, or reverence which a man receives from his kind; and in this sense, a man is said *to acquire honor*. 2. Honor signifies the aggregate of those rules by the aid of which this esteem, glory, or reverence is obtained. Thus we say that *a man has always strictly obeyed the laws of honor*; or *a man has violated his honor*. In this chapter, the word is always used in the latter sense.

I think these peculiarities may be otherwise explained than by the mere caprices of certain individuals and nations, as has hitherto been customary. Mankind are subject to general and permanent wants that have created moral laws, to the neglect of which men have ever and in all places attached the notion of censure and shame: to infringe them was *to do ill*, — *to do well* was to conform to them.

Within this vast association of the human race, lesser associations have been formed, which are called nations; and amidst these nations, further subdivisions have assumed the names of classes or castes. Each of these associations forms, as it were, a separate species of the human race; and though it has no essential difference from the mass of mankind, to a certain extent it stands apart, and has certain wants peculiar to itself. To these special wants must be attributed the modifications which affect, in various degrees and in different countries, the mode of considering human actions, and the estimate which is formed of them. It is the general and permanent interest of mankind that men should not kill each other; but it may happen to be the peculiar and temporary interest of a people or a class to justify, or even to honor, homicide.

Honor is simply that peculiar rule founded upon a peculiar state of society, by the application of which a people or a class allot praise or blame. Nothing is more unproductive to the mind than an abstract idea; I therefore hasten to call in the aid of facts and examples to illustrate my meaning.

I select the most extraordinary kind of honor which has ever been known in the world, and that which we are best acquainted with, — viz. aristocratic honor springing out of feudal society. I shall explain it by means of the principle already laid down, and explain the principle by means of this illustration.

I am not here led to inquire when and how the aristocracy of the Middle Ages came into existence, why it was so deeply severed from the remainder of the nation, or what founded and consolidated its power. I take its existence as an established fact, and I am endeavoring to account for the peculiar view which it took of the greater part of human actions.

The first thing that strikes me is, that, in the feudal world, actions were not always praised or blamed with reference to their intrinsic worth, but were sometimes appreciated exclusively with reference to the person who was the actor or the object of them, which is repugnant to the general conscience of mankind. Thus, some of the actions which were indifferent on the part of a man in humble life, dishonored a noble; others changed their whole character according as the person aggrieved by them belonged, or did not belong, to the aristocracy.

When these different notions first arose, the nobility formed a distinct body amidst the people, which it commanded from the inaccessible heights where it was ensconced. To maintain this peculiar position, which constituted its strength, it not only required political privileges, but it required a standard of right and wrong for its own special use.

That some particular virtue or vice belonged to the nobility rather than to the humble classes, — that certain actions were guiltless when they affected the villain, which were criminal when they touched the noble, — these were often arbitrary matters; but that honor or shame should be attached to a man's actions according to his condition, was a result of the internal constitution of an aristocratic community. This has been actually the case in all the countries which have had an aristocracy; as long as a trace of the principle remains, these peculiarities will still exist: to debauch a woman of color scarcely injures the reputation of an American, — to marry her dishonors him.

In some cases, feudal honor enjoined revenge, and stigmatized the forgiveness of insults; in others, it imperiously commanded men to conquer their own passions, and required forgetfulness of self. It did not make humanity or kindness its law, but it extolled generosity; it set more store on liberality than on benevolence; it allowed men to enrich themselves by gambling or by war, but not by labor; it preferred great crimes to small earnings; cupidity was less distasteful to it than avarice; violence it often sanctioned, but cunning and treachery it invariably reprobated as contemptible.

These fantastical notions did not proceed exclusively from the caprice of those who entertained them. A class which has succeeded in placing itself above all others, and which makes perpetual exertions to maintain this lofty position, must especially honor those virtues which are conspicuous for their dignity and splendor, and which may be easily combined with pride and the love of power. Such men would not hesitate to invert the natural order of conscience in order to give these virtues precedence over all others. It may even be conceived that some of the more bold and brilliant vices would readily be set above the quiet, unpretending virtues. The very existence of such a class in society renders these things unavoidable.

The nobles of the Middle Ages placed military courage foremost amongst virtues, and in lieu of many of them. This, again, was a peculiar opinion, which arose necessarily from the peculiar state of society. Feudal aristocracy existed by war and for war; its power had been founded by arms, and by arms that power was maintained: it therefore required nothing more than military courage, and that quality was naturally exalted above all others; whatever denoted it, even at the expense of reason and humanity, was therefore approved and frequently enjoined by the manners of the time. Such was the main principle; the caprice of man was to be traced only in minuter details. That a man should regard a tap on the cheek as an unbearable insult, and should be obliged to kill in single combat the person who struck him thus lightly, is an arbitrary rule; but that a noble could not tranquilly receive an insult, and was dishonored if he allowed himself to take a blow without fighting, were direct consequences of the fundamental principles and the wants of a military aristocracy.

Thus it was true, to a certain extent, that the laws of honor were capricious; but these caprices of honor were always confined within certain necessary limits. The peculiar rule which was called honor by our forefathers is so far from being an arbitrary law in my eyes, that I would readily engage to ascribe its most incoherent and fantastical injunctions to a small number of fixed and invariable wants inherent in feudal society.

If I were to trace the notion of feudal honor into the domain of politics, I should not find it more difficult to explain its dictates. The state of society and the political institutions of the Middle Ages were such, that the supreme power of the nation never governed the community directly. That power did not exist in the eyes of the people: every man looked up to a certain individual whom he was bound to obey; by that intermediate personage he was connected with all the others. Thus, in feudal society, the whole system of the commonwealth rested upon the sentiment of fidelity to the person of the lord; to destroy that sentiment was to fall into anarchy. Fidelity to a political superior was, moreover, a sentiment of which all the members of the aristocracy had constant opportunities of estimating the importance; for every one of them was a vassal as well as a lord, and had to command as well as to obey. To remain faithful to the lord, to sacrifice one's self for him if called upon, to share his good or evil fortunes, to stand by him in his undertakings whatever they might be, — such were the first injunctions of feudal honor in relation to the political institutions of those times. The treachery of a vassal was branded with extraordinary severity by public opinion, and a name of peculiar infamy was invented for the offence; it was called *felony*.

On the contrary, few traces are to be found in the Middle Ages of the passion which constituted the life of the nations of antiquity, — I mean patriotism; the word itself is not of very ancient date in the language.* Feudal institutions concealed the country at large from men's sight, and rendered the love of it less necessary. The nation was forgotten in the passions which attached men to persons. Hence it was no part of the strict law of feudal honor to remain faithful to one's country. Not indeed that the love of their country did not exist in the hearts of our forefathers; but it constituted a dim and feeble instinct, which has grown more clear and strong in proportion as aristocratic classes have been abolished, and the supreme power of the nation centralized.

This may be clearly seen from the contrary judgments which European nations have passed upon the various events of their histories, according to the generations by which such judgments were formed. The circumstance which most dishonored the Constable de Bourbon in the eyes of his contemporaries was, that he bore arms against his king: that which most dishonors him in our eyes is, that he made war against his country. We brand him as deeply as our forefathers did, but for different reasons.

I have chosen the honor of feudal times by way of illustration of my meaning, because its characteristics are more distinctly marked and more familiar to us than those of any other period; but I might have taken an example else-

* Even the word *patrie* was not used by the French writers until the sixteenth century.

where, and I should have reached the same conclusion by a different road.

Although we are less perfectly acquainted with the Romans than with our own ancestors, yet we know that certain peculiar notions of glory and disgrace obtained amongst them, which were not derived solely from the general principles of right and wrong. Many human actions were judged differently, according as they affected a Roman citizen or a stranger, a freeman or a slave; certain vices were blazoned abroad, certain virtues were extolled above all others. "In that age," says Plutarch, in the Life of Coriolanus, "martial prowess was more honored and prized in Rome than all the other virtues, insomuch that it was called *virtus*, the name of virtue itself, by applying the name of the kind to this particular species; so that *virtue* in Latin was as much as to say *valor*." Can any one fail to recognize the peculiar want of that singular community which was formed for the conquest of the world?

Any nation would furnish us with similar grounds of observation; for, as I have already remarked, whenever men collect together as a distinct community, the notion of honor instantly grows up amongst them; that is to say, a system of opinions peculiar to themselves as to what is blamable or commendable; and these peculiar rules always originate in the special habits and special interests of the community.

This is applicable to a certain extent to democratic communities as well as to others, as we shall now proceed to prove by the example of the Americans.*

Some loose notions of the old aristocratic honor of Europe are still to be found scattered amongst the opinions of the Americans; but these traditional opinions are few in

* I speak here of the Americans inhabiting those States where slavery does not exist; they alone can be said to present a complete picture of democratic society.

number, they have but little root in the country, and but little power. They are like a religion which has still some temples left standing, though men have ceased to believe in it. But amidst these half-obliterated notions of exotic honor some new opinions have sprung up, which constitute what may be termed in our days American honor.

I have shown how the Americans are constantly driven to engage in commerce and industry. Their origin, their social condition, their political institutions, and even the region they inhabit, urge them irresistibly in this direction. Their present condition, then, is that of an almost exclusively manufacturing and commercial association, placed in the midst of a new and boundless country, which their principal object is to explore for purposes of profit. This is the characteristic which most distinguishes the American people from all others at the present time.

All those quiet virtues which tend to give a regular movement to the community, and to encourage business, will therefore be held in peculiar honor by that people, and to neglect those virtues will be to incur public contempt. All the more turbulent virtues, which often dazzle, but more frequently disturb society, will, on the contrary, occupy a subordinate rank in the estimation of this same people; they may be neglected without forfeiting the esteem of the community; to acquire them would perhaps be to run a risk of losing it.

The Americans make a no less arbitrary classification of men's vices. There are certain propensities which appear censurable to the general reason and the universal conscience of mankind, but which happen to agree with the peculiar and temporary wants of the American community: these propensities are lightly reproved, sometimes even encouraged; for instance, the love of wealth and the secondary propensities connected with it may be more particularly cited. To clear, to till, and to transform the vast uninhabited continent which is his domain, the American requires the daily support of an energetic passion; that passion can only be the love of wealth; the passion for wealth is therefore not reprobated in America, and, provided it does not go beyond the bounds assigned to it for public security, it is held in honor. The American lauds as a noble and praiseworthy ambition what our own forefathers, in the Middle Ages, stigmatized as servile cupidity, just as he treats as a blind and barbarous frenzy that ardor of conquest and martial temper which bore them to battle.

In the United States, fortunes are lost and regained without difficulty; the country is boundless, and its resources inexhaustible. The people have all the wants and cravings of a growing creature; and, whatever be their efforts, they are always surrounded by more than they can appropriate. It is not the ruin of a few individuals, which may be soon repaired, but the inactivity and sloth of the community at large, which would be fatal to such a people. Boldness of enterprise is the foremost cause of its rapid progress, its strength, and its greatness. Commercial business is there like a vast lottery, by which a small number of men continually lose, but the state is always a gainer; such a people ought therefore to encourage and do honor to boldness in commercial speculations. But any bold speculation risks the fortune of the speculator and of all those who put their trust in him. The Americans, who make a virtue of commercial temerity, have no right in any case to brand with disgrace those who practise it. Hence arises the strange indulgence which is shown to bankrupts in the United States; their honor does not suffer by such an accident. In this respect the Americans differ, not only from the nations of Europe, but from all the commercial nations of our time; and accordingly they resemble none of them in their position or their wants.

In America, all those vices which tend to impair the purity of morals, and to destroy the conjugal tie, are treated with a degree of severity which is unknown in the rest of the world. At first sight, this seems strangely at variance with the tolerance shown there on other subjects, and one is surprised to meet with a morality so relaxed and also so austere amongst the self-same people. But these things are less incoherent than they seem to be. Public opinion in the United States very gently represses that love of wealth which promotes the commercial greatness and the prosperity of the nation, and it especially condemns that laxity of morals which diverts the human mind from the pursuit of well-being, and disturbs the internal order of domestic life which is so necessary to success in business. To earn the esteem of their countrymen, the Americans are therefore constrained to adapt themselves to orderly habits; and it may be said in this sense that they make it a matter of honor to live chastely.

On one point, American honor accords with the notions of honor acknowledged in Europe; it places courage as the highest virtue, and treats it as the greatest of the moral necessities of man; but the notion of courage itself assumes a different aspect. In the United States, martial valor is but little prized; the courage which is best known and most esteemed is that which emboldens men to brave the dangers of the ocean, in order to arrive earlier in port,— to support the privations of the wilderness without complaint, and solitude more cruel than privations,—the courage which renders them almost insensible to the loss of a fortune laboriously acquired, and instantly prompts to fresh exertions to make another. Courage of this kind is peculiarly necessary to the maintenance and prosperity of the American communities, and it is held by them in peculiar honor and estimation; to betray a want of it is to incur certain disgrace.

I have yet another characteristic point which may serve

to place the idea of this chapter in stronger relief. In a democratic society like that of the United States, where fortunes are scanty and insecure, everybody works, and work opens a way to everything: this has changed the point of honor quite ronnd, and has turned it against idleness. I have sometimes met in America with young men of wealth, personally disinclined to all laborious exertion, but who had been compelled to embrace a profession. Their disposition and their fortune allowed them to remain without employment: public opinion forbade it, too imperiously to be disobeyed. In the European countries, on the contrary, where aristocracy is still struggling with the flood which overwhelms it, I have often seen men, constantly spurred on by their wants and desires, remain in idleness, in order not to lose the esteem of their equals; and I have known them submit to ennui and privations rather than to work. No one can fail to perceive that these opposite obligations are two different rules of conduct, both nevertheless originating in the notion of honor.

What our forefathers designated as honor absolutely was in reality only one of its forms; they gave a generic name to what was only a species. Honor, therefore, is to be found in democratic as well as in aristocratic ages, but it will not be difficult to show that it assumes a different aspect in the former. Not only are its injunctions different, but we shall shortly see that they are less numerous, less precise, and that its dictates are less rigorously obeyed.

The position of a caste is always much more peculiar than that of a people. Nothing is so exceptional in the world as a small community invariably composed of the same families, (as was, for instance, the aristocracy of the Middle Ages,) whose object is to concentrate and to retain, exclusively and hereditarily, education, wealth, and power amongst its own members. But the more exceptional the position of a community happens to be, the more numerous are its special wants, and the more extensive are its notions of honor corresponding to those wants.

The rules of honor will therefore always be less numerous amongst a people not divided into castes than amongst any other. If ever any nations are constituted in which it may even be difficult to find any peculiar classes of society, the notion of honor will be confined to a small number of precepts, which will be more and more in accordance with the moral laws adopted by the mass of mankind.

Thus the laws of honor will be less peculiar and less multifarious amongst a democratic people than in an aristocracy. They will also be more obscure; and this is a necessary consequence of what goes before; for as the distinguishing marks of honor are less numerous and less peculiar, it must often be difficult to distinguish them. To this other reasons may be added. Amongst the aristocratic nations of the Middle Ages, generation succeeded generation in vain; each family was like a never-dying, ever-stationary man, and the state of opinions was hardly more changeable than that of conditions. Every one then had the same objects always before his eyes, which he contemplated from the same point; his eyes gradually detected the smallest details, and his discernment could not fail to become in the end clear and accurate. Thus, not only had the men of feudal times very extraordinary opinions in matters of honor, but each of those opinions was present to their minds under a clear and precise form.

This can never be the case in America, where all men are in constant motion, and where society, transformed daily by its own operations, changes its opinions together with its wants. In such a country, men have glimpses of the rules of honor, but they seldom have time to fix attention upon them.

But even if society were motionless, it would still be difficult to determine the meaning which ought to be attached to the word honor. In the Middle Ages, as each class had its own honor, the same opinion was never received at the same time by a large number of men; and this rendered it possible to give it a determined and accurate form, which was the more easy, as all those by whom it was received, having a perfectly identical and most peculiar position, were naturally disposed to agree upon the points of a law which was made for themselves alone.

Thus the code of honor became a complete and detailed system, in which everything was anticipated and provided for beforehand, and a fixed and always palpable standard was applied to human actions. Amongst a democratic nation, like the Americans, in which ranks are confounded, and the whole of society forms one single mass, composed of elements which are all analogous though not entirely similar, it is impossible ever to agree beforehand on what shall or shall not be allowed by the laws of honor.

Amongst that people, indeed, some national wants exist, which give rise to opinions common to the whole nation on points of honor: but these opinions never occur at the same time, in the same manner, or with the same intensity, to the minds of the whole community; the law of honor exists, but it has no organs to promulgate it.

The confusion is far greater still in a democratic country like France, where the different classes of which the former fabric of society was composed, being brought together but not yet mingled, import day by day into each other's circles various and sometimes conflicting notions of honor, — where every man, at his own will and pleasure, forsakes one portion of his forefathers' creed, and retains another; so that, amidst so many arbitrary measures, no common rule can ever be established, and it is almost impossible to predict which actions will be held in honor and which will be thought disgraceful. Such times are wretched, but they are of short duration.

As honor, amongst democratic nations, is imperfectly defined, its influence is of course less powerful; for it is difficult to apply with certainty and firmness a law which is not distinctly known. Public opinion, the natural and supreme interpreter of the laws of honor, not clearly discerning to which side censure or approval ought to lean, can only pronounce a hesitating judgment. Sometimes the opinion of the public may contradict itself; more frequently it does not act, and lets things pass.

The weakness of the sense of honor in democracies also arises from several other causes. In aristocratic countries, the same notions of honor are always entertained by only a few persons, always limited in number, often separated from the rest of their fellow-citizens. Honor is easily mingled and identified in their minds with the idea of all that distinguishes their own position; it appears to them as the chief characteristic of their own rank; they apply its different rules with all the warmth of personal interest, and they feel (if I may use the expression) a passion for complying with its dictates.

This truth is extremely obvious in the old black-letter law-books on the subject of trial by battel. The nobles, in their disputes, were bound to use the lance and sword; whereas the villains amongst themselves used only sticks, "inasmuch as," to use the words of the old books, "villains have no honor." This did not mean, as it may be imagined at the present day, that these people were contemptible; but simply that their actions were not to be judged by the same rules which were applied to the actions of the aristocracy.

It is surprising, at first sight, that, when the sense of honor is most predominant, its injunctions are usually most strange; so that, the further it is removed from common reason, the better it is obeyed; whence it has sometimes been inferred that the laws of honor were strengthened by their own extravagance. The two things, indeed, originate from the same source, but the one is not derived from the other. Honor becomes fantastical in proportion to the peculiarity of the wants which it denotes, and the paucity of the men by whom those wants are felt; and it is because it denotes wants of this kind that its influence is great. Thus, the notion of honor is not the stronger for being fantastical, but it is fantastical and strong from the self-same cause.

Further, amongst aristocratic nations each rank is different, but all ranks are fixed; every man occupies a place in his own sphere which he cannot relinquish, and he lives there amidst other men who are bound by the same ties. Amongst these nations, no man can either hope or fear to escape being seen; no man is placed so low but that he has a stage of his own, and none can avoid censure or applause by his obscurity.

In democratic states, on the contrary, where all the members of the community are mingled in the same crowd and in constant agitation, public opinion has no hold on men; they disappear at every instant, and elude its power. Consequently, the dictates of honor will be there less imperious and less stringent; for honor acts solely for the public eye, — differing in this respect from mere virtue, which lives upon itself, contented with its own approval.

If the reader has distinctly apprehended all that goes before, he will understand that there is a close and necessary relation between the inequality of social conditions and what has here been styled honor, — a relation which, if I am not mistaken, had not before been clearly pointed out. I shall therefore make one more attempt to illustrate it satisfactorily.

Suppose a nation stands apart from the rest of mankind: independently of certain general wants inherent in the human race, it will also have wants and interests peculiar to itself: certain opinions in respect to censure or approbation forthwith arise in the community, which are peculiar to itself, and which are styled honor by the members of that community. Now suppose that in this same nation a caste arises, which, in its turn, stands apart from all the other classes, and contracts certain peculiar wants, which give rise in their turn to special opinions. The honor of this caste, composed of a medley of the peculiar notions of the nation, and the still more peculiar notions of the caste, will be as remote as it is possible to conceive from the simple and general opinions of men.

Having reached this extreme point of the argument, I now return.

When ranks are commingled and privileges abolished, the men of whom a nation is composed being once more equal and alike, their interests and wants become identical, and all the peculiar notions which each caste styled honor successively disappear: the notion of honor no longer proceeds from any other source than the wants peculiar to the nation at large, and it denotes the individual character of that nation to the world.

Lastly, if it were allowable to suppose that all the races of mankind should be commingled, and that all the nations of earth should ultimately come to have the same interests, the same wants, undistinguished from each other by any characteristic peculiarities, no conventional value whatever would then be attached to men's actions; they would all be regarded by all in the same light; the general necessities of mankind, revealed by conscience to every man, would become the common standard. The simple and general notions of right and wrong only would then be recognized in the world, to which, by a natural and necessary tie, the idea of censure or approbation would be attached.

Thus, to comprise all my meaning in a single proposition, the dissimilarities and inequalities of men gave rise to the notion of honor; that notion is weakened in proportion as these differences are obliterated, and with them it would disappear.

CHAPTER XIX.

WHY SO MANY AMBITIOUS MEN AND SO LITTLE LOFTY AMBITION ARE TO BE FOUND IN THE UNITED STATES.

THE first thing which strikes a traveller in the United States is the innumerable multitude of those who seek to emerge from their original condition; and the second is the rarity of lofty ambition to be observed in the midst of the universally ambitious stir of society. No Americans are devoid of a yearning desire to rise; but hardly any appear to entertain hopes of great magnitude, or to pursue very lofty aims. All are constantly seeking to acquire property, power, and reputation; few contemplate these things upon a great scale; and this is the more surprising, as nothing is to be discerned in the manners or laws of America to limit desire, or to prevent it from spreading its impulses in every direction. It seems difficult to attribute this singular state of things to the equality of social condition; for as soon as that same equality was established in France, the flight of ambition became unbounded. Nevertheless, I think that we may find the principal cause of this fact in the social condition and democratic manners of the Americans.

All revolutions enlarge the ambition of men: this is more peculiarly true of those revolutions which overthrow an aristocracy. When the former barriers which kept back the multitude from fame and power are suddenly thrown down, a violent and universal movement takes place towards that eminence so long coveted and at length to be enjoyed. In this first burst of triumph, nothing seems impossible to any one: not only are desires boundless, but the power of satisfying them seems almost boundless too. Amidst the general and sudden change of laws and customs, in this vast confusion of all men and all ordinances, the various members of the community rise and sink again with excessive rapidity, and power passes so quickly from hand to hand that none need despair of catching it in turn.

It must be recollected, moreover, that the people who destroy an aristocracy have lived under its laws; they have witnessed its splendor, and they have unconsciously imbibed the feelings and notions which it entertained. Thus, at the moment when an aristocracy is dissolved, its spirit still pervades the mass of the community, and its tendencies are retained long after it has been defeated. Ambition is therefore always extremely great as long as a democratic revolution lasts, and it will remain so for some time after the revolution is consummated.

The reminiscence of the extraordinary events which men have witnessed is not obliterated from their memory in a day. The passions which a revolution has roused do not disappear at its close. A sense of instability remains in the midst of re-established order; a notion of easy success survives the strange vicissitudes which gave it birth; desires still remain extremely enlarged, while the means of satisfying them are diminished day by day. The taste for large fortunes subsists, though large fortunes are rare; and on every side we trace the ravages of inordinate and unsuccessful ambition kindled in hearts which it consumes in secret and in vain.

At length, however, the last vestiges of the struggle are effaced; the remains of aristocracy completely disappear; the great events by which its fall was attended are forgotten; peace succeeds to war, and the sway of order is restored in the new realm; desires are again adapted to the means by which they may be fulfilled; the wants, the opinions, and the feelings of men cohere once more; the level of the community is permanently determined, and democratic society established.

A democratic nation, arrived at this permanent and regular state of things, will present a very different spectacle from that which we have just described; and we may readily conclude that, if ambition becomes great whilst the conditions of society are growing equal, it loses that quality when they have grown so.

As wealth is subdivided and knowledge diffused, no one is entirely destitute of education or of property; the privileges and disqualifications of caste being abolished, and men having shattered the bonds which once held them fixed, the notion of advancement suggests itself to every mind, the desire to rise swells in every heart, and all men want to mount above their station; ambition is the universal feeling.

But if the equality of conditions gives some resources to all the members of the community, it also prevents any of them from having resources of great extent, which necessarily circumscribes their desires within somewhat narrow limits. Thus, amongst democratic nations, ambition is ardent and continual, but its aim is not habitually lofty; and life is generally spent in eagerly coveting small objects which are within reach.

What chiefly diverts the men of democracies from lofty ambition is not the scantiness of their fortunes, but the vehemence of the exertions they daily make to improve them. They strain their faculties to the utmost to achieve paltry results, and this cannot fail speedily to limit their range of view, and to circumscribe their powers. They might be much poorer, and still be greater.

The small number of opulent citizens who are to be found amidst a democracy do not constitute an exception to this rule. A man who raises himself by degrees to wealth and power, contracts, in the course of this protracted labor, habits of prudence and restraint which he cannot afterwards shake off. A man cannot gradually enlarge his mind as he does his house.

The same observation is applicable to the sons of such a man: they are born, it is true, in a lofty position, but their parents were humble; they have grown up amidst feelings and notions which they cannot afterwards easily get rid of; and it may be presumed that they will inherit the propensities of their father, as well as his wealth.

It may happen, on the contrary, that the poorest scion of a powerful aristocracy may display vast ambition, because the traditional opinions of his race and the general spirit of his order still buoy him up for some time above his fortune.

Another thing which prevents the men of democratic periods from easily indulging in the pursuit of lofty objects, is the lapse of time which they foresee must take place before they can be ready to struggle for them. "It is a great advantage," says Pascal, "to be a man of quality, since it brings one man as forward at eighteen or twenty, as another man would be at fifty, which is a clear gain of thirty years." Those thirty years are commonly wanting to the ambitious characters of democracies. The principle of equality, which allows every man to arrive at everything, prevents all men from rapid advancement.

In a democratic society, as well as elsewhere, there are only a certain number of great fortunes to be made; and as the paths which lead to them are indiscriminately open to all, the progress of all must necessarily be slackened. As the candidates appear to be nearly alike, and as it is difficult to make a selection without infringing the principle of equality, which is the supreme law of democratic societies, the first idea which suggests itself is to make them all advance at the same rate, and submit to the same trials. Thus, in proportion as men become more alike, and the principle of equality is more peaceably and deeply infused into the institutions and manners of the country, the rules for advancement become more inflexible, advancement itself slower, the difficulty of arriving quickly at a certain height far greater. From hatred of privilege and from the embarrassment of choosing, all men are at last constrained, whatever may be their standard, to pass the same ordeal; all are indiscriminately subjected to a multitude of petty preliminary exercises, in which their youth is wasted and their imagination quenched, so that they despair of ever fully attaining what is held out to them; and when at length they are in a condition to perform any extraordinary acts, the taste for such things has forsaken them.

In China, where the equality of conditions is very great and very ancient, no man passes from one public office to another without undergoing a competitive trial. This probation occurs afresh at every stage of his career; and the notion is now so rooted in the manners of the people, that I remember to have read a Chinese novel in which the hero, after numberless crosses, succeeds at length in touching the heart of his mistress by taking honors. A lofty ambition breathes with difficulty in such an atmosphere.

The remark I apply to politics extends to everything: equality everywhere produces the same effects; where the laws of a country do not regulate and retard the advancement of men by positive enactment, competition attains the same end.

In a well-established democratic community, great and rapid elevation is therefore rare; it forms an exception to the common rule; and it is the singularity of such occurrences that makes men forget how rarely they happen.

Men living in democracies ultimately discover these things; they find out at last that the laws of their country open a boundless field of action before them, but that no one can hope to hasten across it. Between them and the final object of their desires they perceive a multitude of small intermediate impediments, which must be slowly surmounted: this prospect wearies and discourages their ambition at once. They therefore give up hopes so doubtful and remote, to search nearer to themselves for less lofty and more easy enjoyments. Their horizon is not bounded by the laws, but narrowed by themselves.

I have remarked that lofty ambitions are more rare in the ages of democracy than in times of aristocracy: I may add, that when, in spite of these natural obstacles, they do spring into existence, their character is different. In aristocracies, the career of ambition is often wide, but its boundaries are determined. In democracies, ambition commonly ranges in a narrower field, but, if once it gets beyond that, hardly any limits can be assigned to it. As men are individually weak, — as they live asunder, and in constant motion, — as precedents are of little authority, and laws but of short duration, — resistance to novelty is languid, and the fabric of society never appears perfectly erect or firmly consolidated. So that, when once an ambitious man has the power in his grasp, there is nothing he may not dare; and when it is gone from him, he meditates the overthrow of the state to regain it. This gives to great political ambition a character of revolutionary violence, which it seldom exhibits to an equal degree in aristocratic communities. The common aspect of democratic nations will present a great number of small and very rational objects of ambition, from amongst which a few ill-controlled desires of a larger growth will at intervals break out; but no such a thing as ambition, conceived and regulated on a vast scale, is to be met with there.

I have shown elsewhere by what secret influence the principle of equality makes the passion for physical gratification and the exclusive love of the present predominate in the human heart: these different propensities mingle with the sentiment of ambition, and tinge it, as it were, with their hues.

I believe that ambitious men in democracies are less engrossed than any others with the interests and the judgment of posterity; the present moment alone engages and absorbs them. They are more apt to complete a number of undertakings with rapidity, than to raise lasting monuments of their achievements; and they care much more for success than for fame. What they most ask of men is obedience, what they most covet is empire. Their manners have, in almost all cases, remained below their station; the consequence is, that they frequently carry very low tastes into their extraordinary fortunes, and that they seem to have acquired the supreme power only to minister to their coarse or paltry pleasures.

I think that, in our time, it is very necessary to purify, to regulate, and to proportion the feeling of ambition, but that it would be extremely dangerous to seek to impoverish and to repress it over much. We should attempt to lay down certain extreme limits, which it should never be allowed to outstep; but its range within those established limits should not be too much checked.

I confess that I apprehend much less for democratic society from the boldness than from the mediocrity of desires. What appears to me most to be dreaded is, that, in the midst of the small, incessant occupations of private life, ambition should lose its vigor and its greatness; that the passions of man should abate, but at the same time be lowered; so that the march of society should every day become more tranquil and less aspiring.

I think, then, that the leaders of modern society would be wrong to seek to lull the community by a state of too uniform and too peaceful happiness; and that it is well to expose it from time to time to matters of difficulty and danger, in order to raise ambition, and to give it a field of action.

Moralists are constantly complaining that the ruling vice of the present time is pride. This is true in one sense, for indeed every one thinks that he is better than his neighbor, or refuses to obey his superior; but it is extremely false in another, for the same man who cannot endure subordination or equality, has so contemptible an opinion of himself that he thinks he is born only to indulge in vulgar pleasures. He willingly takes up with low desires, without daring to embark in lofty enterprises, of which he scarcely dreams.

Thus, far from thinking that humility ought to be preached to our contemporaries, I would have endeavors made to give them a more enlarged idea of themselves and of their kind. Humility is unwholesome to them; what they most want is, in my opinion, pride. I would willingly exchange several of our small virtues for this one vice.

CHAPTER XX.

THE TRADE OF PLACE-HUNTING IN CERTAIN DEMOCRATIC COUNTRIES.

IN the United States, as soon as a man has acquired some education and pecuniary resources, he either endeavors to get rich by commerce or industry, or he buys land in the bush and turns pioneer. All that he asks of the state is, not to be disturbed in his toil, and to be secure of his earnings. Amongst most European nations, when a man begins to feel his strength and to extend his desires, the first thing that occurs to him is to get some public employment. These opposite effects, originating in the same cause, deserve our passing notice.

When public employments are few in number, ill-paid, and precarious, whilst the different kinds of business are numerous and lucrative, it is to business, and not to official duties, that the new and eager desires created by the principle of equality turn from every side. But if, whilst the ranks of society are becoming more equal, the education of the people remains incomplete, or their spirit the reverse of bold, — if commerce and industry, checked in their growth, afford only slow and arduous means of making a fortune, — the various members of the community, despairing of ameliorating their own condition, rush to the head of the state and demand its assistance. To relieve their own necessities at the cost of the public treasury appears to them the easiest and most open, if not the only, way of rising above a condition which no longer contents them; place-hunting becomes the most generally followed of all trades.

This must especially be the case in those great centralized monarchies, in which the number of paid offices is immense, and the tenure of them tolerably secure, so that no one despairs of obtaining a place, and of enjoying it as undisturbedly as an hereditary fortune.

I shall not remark that the universal and inordinate desire for place is a great social evil; that it destroys the spirit of independence in the citizen, and diffuses a venal and servile humor throughout the frame of society; that it stifles the manlier virtues: nor shall I be at the pains to demonstrate that this kind of traffic only creates an unproductive activity, which agitates the country without adding to its resources: all these things are obvious. But I would observe, that a government which encourages this tendency risks its own tranquillity, and places its very existence in great jeopardy.

I am aware that, at a time like our own, when the love and respect which formerly clung to authority are seen gradually to decline, it may appear necessary to those in power to lay a closer hold on every man by his own interest, and it may seem convenient to use his own passions to keep him in order and in silence; but this cannot be so long, and what may appear to be a source of strength for a certain time will assuredly become, in the end, a great cause of embarrassment and weakness.

Amongst democratic nations, as well as elsewhere, the number of official appointments has, in the end, some limits; but amongst those nations, the number of aspirants is unlimited; it perpetually increases, with a gradual and irresistible rise, in proportion as social conditions become more equal, and is only checked by the limits of the population.

Thus, when public employments afford the only outlet for ambition, the government necessarily meets with a permanent opposition at last; for it is tasked to satisfy with limited means unlimited desires. It is very certain that, of all people in the world, the most difficult to restrain and to manage are a people of office-hunters. Whatever endeavors are made by rulers, such a people can never be contented; and it is always to be apprehended that they will ultimately overturn the constitution of the country, and change the aspect of the state, for the sole purpose of making a clearance of places.

The sovereigns of the present age, who strive to fix upon themselves alone all those novel desires which are aroused by equality, and to satisfy them, will repent in the end, if I am not mistaken, that ever they embarked in this policy: they will one day discover that they have hazarded their own power by making it so necessary, and that the more safe and honest course would have been to teach their subjects the art of providing for themselves.

CHAPTER XXI.

WHY GREAT REVOLUTIONS WILL BECOME MORE RARE.

A PEOPLE who have existed for centuries under a system of castes and classes, can only arrive at a democratic state of society by passing through a long series of more or less critical transformations, accomplished by violent efforts, and after numerous vicissitudes; in the course of which, property, opinions, and power are rapidly transferred from one to another. Even after this great revolution is consummated, the revolutionary habits produced by it may long be traced, and it will be followed by deep commotion. As all this takes place at the very time when social conditions are becoming more equal, it is inferred that some concealed relation and secret tie exists between the principle of equality itself and revolution, insomuch that the one cannot exist without giving rise to the other.

On this point, reasoning may seem to lead to the same result as experience. Amongst a people whose ranks are nearly equal, no ostensible bond connects men together, or keeps them settled in their station. None of them have either a permanent right or power to command, none are forced by their condition to obey; but every man, finding himself possessed of some education and some resources, may choose his own path, and proceed apart from all his fellow-men. The same causes which make the members of the community independent of each other, continually impel them to new and restless desires, and constantly spur them onwards. It therefore seems natural that, in a democratic community, men, things, and opinions should be forever changing their form and place, and that democratic ages should be times of rapid and incessant transformation.

But is this really the case? Does the equality of social conditions habitually and permanently lead men to revolution? Does that state of society contain some perturbing principle, which prevents the community from ever subsiding into calm, and disposes the citizens to alter incessantly their laws, their principles, and their manners? I do not believe it; and as the subject is important, I beg for the reader's close attention.

Almost all the revolutions which have changed the aspect of nations have been made to consolidate or to destroy social inequality. Remove the secondary causes which have produced the great convulsions of the world, and you will almost always find the principle of inequality at the bottom. Either the poor have attempted to plunder the rich, or the rich to enslave the poor. If, then, a state of society can ever be founded in which every man shall have something to keep, and little to take from others, much will have been done for the peace of the world.

I am aware that, amongst a great democratic people, there will always be some members of the community in great poverty, and others in great opulence; but the poor, instead of forming the immense majority of the nation, as is always the case in aristocratic communities, are comparatively few in number, and the laws do not bind them together by the ties of irremediable and hereditary penury.

The wealthy, on their side, are few and powerless; they have no privileges which attract public observation; even their wealth, as it is no longer incorporated and bound up with the soil, is impalpable, and, as it were, invisible. As there is no longer a race of poor men, so there is no longer a race of rich men; the latter spring up daily from the multitude, and relapse into it again. Hence they do not form a distinct class, which may be easily marked out and plundered; and, moreover, as they are connected with the mass of their fellow-citizens by a thousand secret ties, the people cannot assail them without inflicting an injury upon themselves.

Between these two extremes of democratic communities stand an innumerable multitude of men almost alike, who, without being exactly either rich or poor, are possessed of sufficient property to desire the maintenance of order, yet not enough to excite envy. Such men are the natural enemies of violent commotions; their stillness keeps all beneath them and above them still, and secures the balance of the fabric of society.

Not, indeed, that even these men are contented with what they have gotten, or that they feel a natural abhorrence for a revolution in which they might share the spoil without sharing the calamity; on the contrary, they desire, with unexampled ardor, to get rich, but the difficulty is to know from whom riches can be taken. The same state of society which constantly prompts desires, restrains these desires within necessary limits; it gives men more liberty of changing, and less interest in change.

Not only are the men of democracies not naturally desirous of revolutions, but they are afraid of them. All revolutions more or less threaten the tenure of property: but most of those who live in democratic countries are possessed of property; not only are they possessed of property, but they live in the condition where men set the greatest store upon their property.

If we attentively consider each of the classes of which society is composed, it is easy to see that the passions created by property are keenest and most tenacious amongst the middle classes. The poor often care but little for what they possess, because they suffer much more from the want of what they have not, than they enjoy the little they have. The rich have many other passions besides that of riches to satisfy; and, besides, the long and arduous enjoyment of a great fortune sometimes makes them in the end insensible to its charms. But the men who have a competency, alike removed from opulence and from penury, attach an enormous value to their possessions. As they are still almost within the reach of poverty, they see its privations near at hand, and dread them; between poverty and themselves there is nothing but a scanty fortune, upon which they immediately fix their apprehensions and their hopes. Every day increases the interest they take in it, by the constant cares which it occasions; and they are the more attached to it by their continual exertions to increase the amount. The notion of surrendering the smallest part of it is insupportable to them, and they consider its total loss as the worst of misfortunes.

Now, these eager and apprehensive men of small property constitute the class which is constantly increased by the equality of conditions. Hence, in democratic communities, the majority of the people do not clearly see what they have to gain by a revolution, but they continually and in a thousand ways feel that they might lose by one.

I have shown, in another part of this work, that the equality of conditions naturally urges men to embark in commercial and industrial pursuits, and that it tends to increase and to distribute real property: I have also pointed out the means by which it inspires every man with an eager and constant desire to increase his welfare. Nothing is more opposed to revolutionary passions than these things. It may happen that the final result of a revolution is favorable to commerce and manufactures; but its first consequence will almost always be the ruin of manufactures and mercantile men, because it must always change at once the general principles of consumption, and temporarily upset the existing proportion between supply and demand.

I know of nothing more opposite to revolutionary manners than commercial manners. Commerce is naturally adverse to all the violent passions; it loves to temporize, takes delight in compromise, and studiously avoids irritation. It is patient, insinuating, flexible, and never has recourse to extreme measures until obliged by the most absolute necessity. Commerce renders men independent of each other, gives them a lofty notion of their personal importance, leads them to seek to conduct their own affairs, and teaches how to conduct them well; it therefore prepares men for freedom, but preserves them from revolutions.

In a revolution, the owners of personal property have more to fear than all others; for, on the one hand, their property is often easy to seize; and, on the other, it may totally disappear at any moment, — a subject of alarm to which the owners of real property are less exposed, since, although they may lose the income of their estates, they may hope to preserve the land itself through the greatest vicissitudes. Hence the former are much more alarmed at the symptoms of revolutionary commotion than the latter. Thus, nations are less disposed to make revolutions in proportion as personal property is augmented and distributed amongst them, and as the number of those possessing it is increased.

Moreover, whatever profession men may embrace, and whatever species of property they may possess, one characteristic is common to them all. No one is fully contented with his present fortune; all are perpetually striving, in a thousand ways, to improve it. Consider any one of them at any period of his life, and he will be found engaged with some new project for the purpose of increasing what he has; talk not to him of the interests and the rights of mankind, this small domestic concern absorbs for the time all his thoughts, and inclines him to defer political agitations to some other season. This not only prevents men from making revolutions, but deters men from desiring them.

Violent political passions have but little hold on those who have devoted all their faculties to the pursuit of their well-being. The ardor which they display in small matters calms their zeal for momentous undertakings.

From time to time, indeed, enterprising and ambitious men will arise in democratic communities, whose unbounded aspirations cannot be contented by following the beaten track. Such men like revolutions, and hail their approach; but they have great difficulty in bringing them about, unless extraordinary events come to their assistance. No man can struggle with advantage against the spirit of his age and country; and, however powerful he may be supposed to be, he will find it difficult to make his contemporaries share in feelings and opinions which are repugnant to all their feelings and desires.

It is a mistake to believe that, when once the equality of condition has become the old and uncontested state of society, and has imparted its characteristics to the manners of a nation, men will easily allow themselves to be thrust into perilous risks by an imprudent leader or a bold innovator. Not indeed that they will resist him openly, by well-contrived schemes, or even by a premeditated plan of resistance. They will not struggle energetically against him, — sometimes they will even applaud him; but they do not follow him. To his vehemence they secretly oppose their inertia, to his revolutionary tendencies their conservative interests, their homely tastes to his adventurous passions, their good sense to the flights of his genius, to his poetry their prose. With immense exertion he raises them for an instant, but they speedily escape from him, and fall back, as it were, by their own weight. He strains himself to rouse the indifferent and distracted multitude, and finds at last that he is reduced to impotence, not because he is conquered, but because he is alone.

I do not assert that men living in democratic communities are naturally stationary; I think, on the contrary, that a perpetual stir prevails in the bosom of those societies, and that rest is unknown there; but I think that men bestir themselves within certain limits, beyond which they hardly ever go. They are forever varying, altering, and restoring secondary matters; but they carefully abstain from touching what is fundamental. They love change, but they dread revolutions.

Although the Americans are constantly modifying or abrogating some of their laws, they by no means display revolutionary passions. It may be easily seen, from the promptitude with which they check and calm themselves when public excitement begins to grow alarming, and at the very moment when passions seem most roused, that they dread a revolution as the worst of misfortunes, and that every one of them is inwardly resolved to make great sacrifices to avoid such a catastrophe. In no country in the world is the love of property more active and more anxious than in the United States; nowhere does the majority display less inclination for those principles which threaten to alter, in whatever manner, the laws of property.

I have often remarked, that theories which are of a revolutionary nature, since they cannot be put in practice without a complete and sometimes a sudden change in the state of property and persons, are much less favorably viewed in the United States than in the great monarchical countries of Europe: if some men profess them, the bulk of the people reject them with instinctive abhorrence. I do not hesitate to say, that most of the maxims commonly called democratic in France would be proscribed by the democracy of the United States. This may easily be understood; in America, men have the opinions and passions of democracy; in Europe, we have still the passions and opinions of revolution.

If ever America undergoes great revolutions, they will

be brought about by the presence of the black race on the soil of the United States; that is to say, they will owe their origin, not to the equality, but to the inequality of condition.

When social conditions are equal, every man is apt to live apart, centred in himself and forgetful of the public. If the rulers of democratic nations were either to neglect to correct this fatal tendency, or to encourage it from a notion that it weans men from political passions and thus wards off revolutions, they might eventually produce the evil they seek to avoid, and a time might come when the inordinate passions of a few men, aided by the unintelligent selfishness or the pusillanimity of the greater number, would ultimately compel society to pass through strange vicissitudes. In democratic communities, revolutions are seldom desired except by a minority; but a minority may sometimes effect them.

I do not assert that democratic nations are secure from revolutions; I merely say that the state of society in those nations does not lead to revolutions, but rather wards them off. A democratic people left to itself will not easily embark in great hazards; it is only led to revolutions unawares; it may sometimes undergo them, but it does not make them: and I will add, that, when such a people has been allowed to acquire sufficient knowledge and experience, it will not suffer them to be made.

I am well aware that, in this respect, public institutions may themselves do much; they may encourage or repress the tendencies which originate in the state of society. I therefore do not maintain, I repeat, that a people is secure from revolutions simply because conditions are equal in the community; but I think that, whatever the institutions of such a people may be, great revolutions will always be far less violent and less frequent than is supposed; and I can easily discern a state of polity which, when combined with the principle of equality, would render society more stationary than it has ever been in our western part of the world.

The observations I have here made on events may also be applied in part to opinions. Two things are surprising in the United States, — the mutability of the greater part of human actions, and the singular stability of certain principles. Men are in constant motion; the mind of man appears almost unmoved. When once an opinion has spread over the country and struck root there, it would seem that no power on earth is strong enough to eradicate it. In the United States, general principles in religion, philosophy, morality, and even politics, do not vary, or at least are only modified by a hidden and often an imperceptible process: even the grossest prejudices are obliterated with incredible slowness, amidst the continual friction of men and things.

I hear it said that it is in the nature and the habits of democracies to be constantly changing their opinions and feelings. This may be true of small democratic nations, like those of the ancient world, in which the whole community could be assembled in a public place, and then excited at will by an orator. But I saw nothing of the kind amongst the great democratic people which dwells upon the opposite shores of the Atlantic Ocean. What struck me in the United States was, the difficulty of shaking the majority in an opinion once conceived, or of drawing it off from a leader once adopted. Neither speaking nor writing can accomplish it; nothing but experience will avail, and even experience must be repeated.

This is surprising at first sight, but a more attentive investigation explains the fact. I do not think that it is as easy as is supposed to uproot the prejudices of a democratic people, to change its belief, to supersede principles once established by new principles in religion, politics, and morals, — in a word, to make great and frequent changes in men's minds. Not that the human mind is there at rest, — it is in constant agitation; but it is engaged in infinitely varying the consequences of known principles, and in seeking for new consequences, rather than in seeking for new principles. Its motion is one of rapid circumvolution, rather than of straightforward impulse by rapid and direct effort; it extends its orbit by small continual and hasty movements, but it does not suddenly alter its position.

Men who are equal in rights, in education, in fortune, or, to comprise all in one word, in their social condition, have necessarily wants, habits, and tastes which are hardly dissimilar. As they look at objects under the same aspect, their minds naturally tend to similar conclusions; and, though each of them may deviate from his contemporaries and form opinions of his own, they will involuntarily and unconsciously concur in a certain number of received opinions. The more attentively I consider the effects of equality upon the mind, the more am I persuaded that the intellectual anarchy which we witness about us is not, as many men suppose, the natural state of democratic nations. I think it is rather to be regarded as an accident peculiar to their youth, and that it only breaks out at that period of transition when men have already snapped the former ties which bound them together, but are still amazingly different in origin, education, and manners; so that, having retained opinions, propensities, and tastes of great diversity, nothing any longer prevents men from avowing them openly. The leading opinions of men become similar in proportion as their conditions assimilate: such appears to me to be the general and permanent law; the rest is casual and transient.

I believe that it will rarely happen to any man, in a democratic community, suddenly to frame a system of notions very remote from that which his contemporaries have adopted; and if some such innovator appeared, I apprehend that he would have great difficulty in finding listeners, still more in finding believers. When the conditions of men are almost equal, they do not easily allow themselves to be persuaded by each other. As they all live in close intercourse, as they have learned the same things together, and as they lead the same life, they are not naturally disposed to take one of themselves for a guide, and to follow him implicitly. Men seldom take the opinion of their equal, or of a man like themselves, upon trust.

Not only is confidence in the superior attainments of certain individuals weakened amongst democratic nations, as I have elsewhere remarked, but the general notion of the intellectual superiority which any man whatsoever may acquire in relation to the rest of the community is soon overshadowed. As men grow more like each other, the doctrine of the equality of the intellect gradually infuses itself into their opinions; and it becomes more difficult for any innovator to acquire or to exert much influence over the minds of a people. In such communities, sudden intellectual revolutions will therefore be rare; for, if we read aright the history of the world, we shall find that great and rapid changes in human opinions have been produced far less by the force of reasoning than by the authority of a name.

Observe, too, that, as the men who live in democratic societies are not connected with each other by any tie, each of them must be convinced individually; whilst, in aristocratic society, it is enough to convince a few, the rest follow. If Luther had lived in an age of equality, and had not had princes and potentates for his audience, he would perhaps have found it more difficult to change the aspect of Europe.

Not, indeed, that the men of democracies are naturally strongly persuaded of the certainty of their opinions, or are unwavering in belief; they frequently entertain doubts which no one, in their eyes, can remove. It sometimes happens, at such times, that the human mind would willingly change its position; but as nothing urges or guides it forward, it oscillates to and fro without progressive motion.*

Even when the confidence of a democratic people has been won, it is still no easy matter to gain their attention. It is extremely difficult to obtain a hearing from men living in democracies, unless it be to speak to them of themselves. They do not attend to the things said to them, because they are always fully engrossed with the things they are doing. For, indeed, few men are idle in democratic nations; life is passed in the midst of noise and excitement, and men are so engaged in acting that little time remains to them for thinking. I would especially remark, that they are not only employed, but that they are passionately devoted to their employments. They are always in action, and each of their actions absorbs their faculties: the zeal which they display in business puts out the enthusiasm they might otherwise entertain for ideas.

I think that it is extremely difficult to excite the enthu-

* If I inquire what state of society is most favorable to the great revolutions of the mind, I find that it occurs somewhere between the complete equality of the whole community and the absolute separation of ranks. Under a system of castes, generations succeed each other without altering men's positions: some have nothing more, others nothing better, to hope for. The imagination slumbers amidst this universal silence and stillness, and the very idea of change fades from the human mind.

When ranks have been abolished and social conditions are almost equalized, all men are in ceaseless excitement, but each of them stands alone, independent and weak. This latter state of things is excessively different from the former one; yet it has one point of analogy, — great revolutions of the human mind seldom occur in it.

But between these two extremes of the history of nations is an intermediate period, — a period as glorious as it is agitated, — when the conditions of men are not sufficiently settled for the mind to be lulled in torpor, when they are sufficiently unequal for men to exercise a vast power on the minds of one another, and when some few may modify the convictions of all. It is at such times that great reformers start up, and new opinions suddenly change the face of the world.

siasm of a democratic people for any theory which has not a palpable, direct, and immediate connection with the daily occupations of life: therefore they will not easily forsake their old opinions; for it is enthusiasm which flings the minds of men out of the beaten track, and effects the great revolutions of the intellect, as well as the great revolutions of the political world.

Thus, democratic nations have neither time nor taste to go in search of novel opinions. Even when those they possess become doubtful, they still retain them, because it would take too much time and inquiry to change them; they retain them, not as certain, but as established.

There are yet other and more cogent reasons which prevent any great change from being easily effected in the principles of a democratic people. I have already adverted to them in the nineteenth chapter.

If the influence of individuals is weak and hardly perceptible amongst such a people, the power exercised by the mass upon the mind of each individual is extremely great, — I have already shown for what reasons. I would now observe, that it is wrong to suppose that this depends solely upon the form of government, and that the majority would lose its intellectual supremacy if it were to lose its political power.

In aristocracies, men have often much greatness and strength of their own: when they find themselves at variance with the greater number of their fellow-countrymen, they withdraw to their own circle, where they support and console themselves. Such is not the case in a democratic country; there, public favor seems as necessary as the air we breathe, and to live at variance with the multitude is, as it were, not to live. The multitude require no laws to coerce those who think not like themselves: public disapprobation is enough; a sense of their loneliness and impotence overtakes them and drives them to despair.

Whenever social conditions are equal, public opinion presses with enormous weight upon the minds of each individual; it surrounds, directs, and oppresses him; and this arises from the very constitution of society, much more than from its political laws. As men grow more alike, each man feels himself weaker in regard to all the rest; as he discerns nothing by which he is considerably raised above them, or distinguished from them, he mistrusts himself as soon as they assail him. Not only does he mistrust his strength, but he even doubts of his right; and he is very near acknowledging that he is in the wrong, when the greater number of his countrymen assert that he is so. The majority do not need to constrain him; they convince him. In whatever way, then, the powers of a democratic community may be organized and balanced, it will always be extremely difficult to believe what the bulk of the people reject, or to profess what they condemn.

This circumstance is extraordinarily favorable to the stability of opinions. When an opinion has taken root amongst a democratic people, and established itself in the minds of the bulk of the community, it afterwards subsists by itself and is maintained without effort, because no one attacks it. Those who at first rejected it as false, ultimately receive it as the general impression; and those who still dispute it in their hearts, conceal their dissent; they are careful not to engage in a dangerous and useless conflict.

It is true, that, when the majority of a democratic people change their opinions, they may suddenly and arbitrarily effect strange revolutions in men's minds; but their opinions do not change without much difficulty, and it is almost as difficult to show that they are changed.

Time, events, or the unaided individual action of the mind, will sometimes undermine or destroy an opinion, without any outward sign of the change. It has not been openly assailed, no conspiracy has been formed to make war on it, but its followers one by one noiselessly secede; day by day a few of them abandon it, until at last it is only professed by a minority. In this state it will still continue to prevail. As its enemies remain mute, or only interchange their thoughts by stealth, they are themselves unaware for a long period that a great revolution has actually been effected; and in this state of uncertainty they take no steps; they observe each other and are silent. The majority have ceased to believe what they believed before; but they still affect to believe, and this empty phantom of public opinion is strong enough to chill innovators, and to keep them silent and at a respectful distance.

We live at a time which has witnessed the most rapid changes of opinion in the minds of men; nevertheless it may be that the leading opinions of society will erelong be more settled than they have been for several centuries in our history: that time is not yet come, but it may perhaps be approaching. As I examine more closely the natural wants and tendencies of democratic nations, I grow persuaded that, if ever social equality is generally and permanently established in the world, great intellectual and political revolutions will become more difficult and less frequent than is supposed. Because the men of democracies appear always excited, uncertain, eager, changeable in their wills and in their positions, it is imagined that they are suddenly to abrogate their laws, to adopt new opinions, and to assume new manners. But if the principle of equality predisposes men to change, it also suggests to them certain interests and tastes which cannot be satisfied without a settled order of things; equality urges them on, but at the same time it holds them back; it spurs them, but fastens them to earth; it kindles their desires, but limits their powers.

This, however, is not perceived at first; the passions which tend to sever the citizens of a democracy are obvious enough; but the hidden force which restrains and unites them is not discernible at a glance.

Amidst the ruins which surround me, shall I dare to say that revolutions are not what I most fear for coming generations? If men continue to shut themselves more closely within the narrow circle of domestic interests, and to live upon that kind of excitement, it is to be apprehended that they may ultimately become inaccessible to those great and powerful public emotions which perturb nations, but which develop them and recruit them. When property becomes so fluctuating, and the love of property so restless and so ardent, I cannot but fear that men may arrive at such a state as to regard every new theory as a peril, every innovation as an irksome toil, every social improvement as a stepping-stone to revolution, and so refuse to move altogether for fear of being moved too far. I dread, and I confess it, lest they should at last so entirely give way to a cowardly love of present enjoyment, as to lose sight of the interests of their future selves and those of their descendants; and prefer to glide along the easy current of life, rather than to make, when it is necessary, a strong and sudden effort to a higher purpose.

It is believed by some that modern society will be ever changing its aspect; for myself, I fear that it will ultimately be too invariably fixed in the same institutions, the same prejudices, the same manners, so that mankind will be stopped and circumscribed; that the mind will swing backwards and forwards forever, without begetting fresh ideas; that man will waste his strength in bootless and solitary trifling; and, though in continual motion, that humanity will cease to advance.

CHAPTER XXII.

WHY DEMOCRATIC NATIONS ARE NATURALLY DESIROUS OF PEACE, AND DEMOCRATIC ARMIES OF WAR.

THE same interests, the same fears, the same passions, which deter democratic nations from revolutions, deter them also from war; the spirit of military glory and the spirit of revolution are weakened at the same time and by the same causes. The ever-increasing numbers of men of property who are lovers of peace, the growth of personal wealth which war so rapidly consumes, the mildness of manners, the gentleness of heart, those tendencies to pity which are produced by the equality of conditions, that coolness of understanding which renders men comparatively insensible to the violent and poetical excitement of arms, — all these causes concur to quench the military spirit. I think it may be admitted as a general and constant rule, that, amongst civilized nations, the warlike passions will become more rare and less intense in proportion as social conditions shall be more equal.

War is nevertheless an occurrence to which all nations are subject, democratic nations as well as others. Whatever taste they may have for peace, they must hold themselves in readiness to repel aggression, or, in other words, they must have an army. Fortune, which has conferred so many peculiar benefits upon the inhabitants of the United States, has placed them in the midst of a wilderness, where they have, so to speak, no neighbors: a few thousand soldiers are sufficient for their wants; but this is peculiar to America, not to democracy.

The equality of conditions, and the manners as well as the institutions resulting from it, do not exempt a democratic people from the necessity of standing armies, and their armies always exercise a powerful influence over their fate. It is therefore of singular importance to inquire what are the natural propensities of the men of whom these armies are composed.

Amongst aristocratic nations, especially amongst those in which birth is the only source of rank, the same inequality exists in the army as in the nation; the officer is noble, the soldier is a serf; the one is naturally called upon to command, the other to obey. In aristocratic armies, the private soldier's ambition is therefore circumscribed within very narrow limits. Nor has the ambition of the officer an unlimited range. An aristocratic body not only forms a part of the scale of ranks in the nation, but it contains a scale of ranks within itself: the members of whom it is composed are placed one above another, in a particular and unvarying manner. Thus, one man is born to the command of a regiment, another to that of a company; when once they have reached the utmost object of their hopes, they stop of their own accord, and remain contented with their lot.

There is, besides, a strong cause, which, in aristocracies, weakens the officer's desire of promotion. Amongst aristocratic nations, an officer, independently of his rank in the army, also occupies an elevated rank in society; the former is almost always, in his eyes, only an appendage to the latter. A nobleman who embraces the profession of arms follows it less from motives of ambition than from a sense of the duties imposed on him by his birth. He enters the army in order to find an honorable employment for the idle years of his youth, and to be able to bring back to his home and his peers some honorable recollections of military life; but his principal object is not to obtain by that profession either property, distinction, or power, for he possesses these advantages in his own right, and enjoys them without leaving his home.

In democratic armies, all the soldiers may become officers, which makes the desire of promotion general, and immeasurably extends the bounds of military ambition. The officer, on his part, sees nothing which naturally and necessarily stops him at one grade more than at another; and each grade has immense importance in his eyes, because his rank in society almost always depends on his rank in the army. Amongst democratic nations, it often happens that an officer has no property but his pay, and no distinction but that of military honors: consequently, as often as his duties change his fortune changes, and he becomes, as it were, a new man. What was only an appendage to his position in aristocratic armies, has thus become the main point, the basis of his whole condition.

Under the old French monarchy, officers were always called by their titles of nobility; they are now always called by the title of their military rank. This little change in the forms of language suffices to show that a great revolution has taken place in the constitution of society and in that of the army.

In democratic armies, the desire of advancement is almost universal: it is ardent, tenacious, perpetual; it is strengthened by all other desires, and only extinguished with life itself. But it is easy to see, that, of all armies in the world, those in which advancement must be slowest in time of peace are the armies of democratic countries. As the number of commissions is naturally limited, whilst the number of competitors is almost unlimited, and as the strict law of equality is over all alike, none can make rapid progress, — many can make no progress at all. Thus, the desire of advancement is greater, and the opportunities of advancement fewer there than elsewhere. All the ambitious spirits of a democratic army are consequently ardently desirous of war, because war makes vacancies, and warrants the violation of that law of seniority which is the sole privilege natural to democracy.

We thus arrive at this singular consequence, that, of all armies, those most ardently desirous of war are democratic armies, and of all nations, those most fond of peace are democratic nations; and what makes these facts still more extraordinary is, that these contrary effects are produced at the same time by the principle of equality.

All the members of the community, being alike, constantly harbor the wish and discover the possibility of changing their condition and improving their welfare: this makes them fond of peace, which is favorable to industry, and allows every man to pursue his own little undertakings to their completion. On the other hand, this same equality makes soldiers dream of fields of battle, by increasing the value of military honors in the eyes of those who follow the profession of arms, and by rendering those honors accessible to all. In either case, the inquietude of the heart is the same, the taste for enjoyment as insatiable, the ambition of success as great, — the means of gratifying it alone are different.

These opposite tendencies of the nation and the army expose democratic communities to great dangers. When a military spirit forsakes a people, the profession of arms immediately ceases to be held in honor, and military men fall to the lowest rank of the public servants: they are little esteemed, and no longer understood. The reverse of what takes place in aristocratic ages then occurs; the men who enter the army are no longer those of the highest, but of the lowest rank. Military ambition is only indulged when no other is possible. Hence arises a circle of cause and consequence from which it is difficult to escape: the best part of the nation shuns the military profession because that profession is not honored, and the profession is not honored because the best part of the nation has ceased to follow it.

It is then no matter of surprise that democratic armies are often restless, ill-tempered, and dissatisfied with their lot, although their physical condition is commonly far better, and their discipline less strict, than in other countries. The soldier feels that he occupies an inferior position, and his wounded pride either stimulates his taste for hostilities which would render his services necessary, or gives him a desire for revolution, during which he may hope to win by force of arms the political influence and personal importance now denied him.

The composition of democratic armies makes this last-mentioned danger much to be feared. In democratic communities, almost every man has some property to preserve; but democratic armies are generally led by men without property, most of whom have little to lose in civil broils. The bulk of the nation is naturally much more afraid of revolutions than in the ages of aristocracy, but the leaders of the army much less so.

Moreover, as amongst democratic nations (to repeat what I have just remarked) the wealthiest, best educated, and ablest men seldom adopt the military profession, the army, taken collectively, eventually forms a small nation by itself, where the mind is less enlarged, and habits are more rude, than in the nation at large. Now, this small uncivilized nation has arms in its possession, and alone knows how to use them; for, indeed, the pacific temper of the community increases the danger to which a democratic people is exposed from the military and turbulent spirit of the army. Nothing is so dangerous as an army amidst an unwarlike nation; the excessive love of the whole community for quiet continually puts the constitution at the mercy of the soldiery.

It may therefore be asserted, generally speaking, that, if democratic nations are naturally prone to peace from their interests and their propensities, they are constantly drawn to war and revolutions by their armies. Military revolutions, which are scarcely ever to be apprehended in aristocracies, are always to be dreaded amongst democratic nations. These perils must be reckoned amongst the most formidable which beset their future fate, and the attention of statesmen should be sedulously applied to find a remedy for the evil.

When a nation perceives that it is inwardly affected by the restless ambition of its army, the first thought which occurs is to give this inconvenient ambition an object by going to war. I do not wish to speak ill of war: war almost always enlarges the mind of a people, and raises their character. In some cases, it is the only check to the excessive growth of certain propensities which naturally spring out of the equality of conditions, and it must be considered as a necessary corrective to certain inveterate diseases to which democratic communities are liable.

War has great advantages, but we must not flatter ourselves that it can diminish the danger I have just pointed out. That peril is only suspended by it, to return more fiercely when the war is over; for armies are much more impatient of peace after having tasted military exploits. War could only be a remedy for a people who should always be athirst for military glory.

I foresee that all the military rulers who may rise up in great democratic nations will find it easier to conquer with their armies, than to make their armies live at peace after conquest. There are two things which a democratic people will always find very difficult, — to begin a war and to end it.

Again, if war has some peculiar advantages for democratic nations, on the other hand, it exposes them to certain dangers, which aristocracies have no cause to dread to an equal extent. I shall point out only two of these.

Although war gratifies the army, it embarrasses and often exasperates that countless multitude of men whose minor passions every day require peace in order to be satisfied. Thus there is some risk of its causing, under another form, the very disturbance it is intended to prevent.

No protracted war can fail to endanger the freedom of a democratic country. Not indeed that, after every victory, it is to be apprehended that the victorious generals will possess themselves by force of the supreme power, after the manner of Sylla and Cæsar: the danger is of another kind. War does not always give over democratic communities to military government, but it must invariably and immeasurably increase the powers of civil government; it must almost compulsorily concentrate the direction of all men and the management of all things in the hands of the administration. If it lead not to despotism by sudden violence, it prepares men for it more gently by their habits. All those who seek to destroy the liberties of a democratic nation ought to know that war is the surest and the shortest means to accomplish it. This is the first axiom of the science.

One remedy, which appears to be obvious when the ambition of soldiers and officers becomes the subject of alarm, is to augment the number of commissions to be distributed by increasing the army. This affords temporary relief, but it plunges the country into deeper difficulties at some future period. To increase the army may produce a lasting effect in an aristocratic community, because military ambition is there confined to one class of men, and the ambition of each individual stops, as it were, at a certain limit; so that it may be possible to satisfy all who feel its influence. But nothing is gained by increasing the army amongst a democratic people, because the number of aspirants always rises in exactly the same ratio as the army itself. Those whose claims have been satisfied by the creation of new commissions are instantly succeeded by a fresh multitude beyond all power of satisfaction; and even those who were but now satisfied soon begin to crave more advancement; for the same excitement prevails in the ranks of the army as in the civil classes of democratic society, and what men want is, not to reach a certain grade, but to have constant promotion. Though these wants may not be very vast, they are perpetually recurring. Thus a democratic nation, by augmenting its army, only allays for a time the ambition of the military profession, which soon becomes even more formidable, because the number of those who feel it is increased.

I am of opinion that a restless and turbulent spirit is an evil inherent in the very constitution of democratic armies, and beyond hope of cure. The legislators of democracies, must not expect to devise any military organization capable by its influence of calming and restraining the military profession: their efforts would exhaust their powers, before the object could be attained.

The remedy for the vices of the army is not to be found in the army itself, but in the country. Democratic nations are naturally afraid of disturbance and of despotism; the object is to turn these natural instincts into intelligent, deliberate, and lasting tastes. When men have at last learned to make a peaceful and profitable use of freedom, and have felt its blessings, — when they have conceived a manly love of order, and have freely submitted themselves to discipline, — these same men, if they follow the profession of arms, bring into it, unconsciously and almost against their will, these same habits and manners. The general spirit of the nation being infused into the spirit peculiar to the army, tempers the opinions and desires engendered by military life, or represses them by the mighty force of public opinion. Teach but the citizens to be educated, orderly, firm, and free, and the soldiers will be disciplined and obedient.

Any law which, in repressing the turbulent spirit of the army, should tend to diminish the spirit of freedom in the nation, and to overshadow the notion of law and right, would defeat its object: it would do much more to favor, than to defeat the establishment of military tyranny.

After all, and in spite of all precautions, a large army amidst a democratic people will always be a source of great danger; the most effectual means of diminishing that danger would be to reduce the army, but this is a remedy which all nations are not able to apply.

CHAPTER XXIII.

WHICH IS THE MOST WARLIKE AND MOST REVOLUTIONARY CLASS IN DEMOCRATIC ARMIES.

IT is of the essence of a democratic army to be very numerous in proportion to the people to which it belongs, as I shall hereafter show. On the other hand, men living in democratic times seldom choose a military life. Democratic nations are therefore soon led to give up the system of voluntary recruiting for that of compulsory enlistment. The necessity of their social condition compels them to resort to the latter means, and it may easily be foreseen that they will all eventually adopt it.

When military service is compulsory, the burden is indiscriminately and equally borne by the whole community. This is another necessary consequence of the social condition of these nations, and of their notions. The government may do almost whatever it pleases, provided it appeals to the whole community at once: it is the unequal distribution of the weight, not the weight itself, which commonly occasions resistance. But as military service is common to all the citizens, the evident consequence is, that each of them remains but for a few years on active duty. Thus it is in the nature of things that the soldier in democracies only passes through the army, whilst, among most aristocratic nations, the military profession is one which the soldier adopts, or which is imposed upon him, for life.

This has important consequences. Amongst the soldiers of a democratic army, some acquire a taste for military life; but the majority, being enlisted against their will, and ever ready to go back to their homes, do not consider themselves as seriously engaged in the military profession, and are always thinking of quitting it. Such men do not contract the wants, and only half partake in the passions, which that mode of life engenders. They adapt themselves to their military duties, but their minds are still attached to the interests and the duties which engaged them in civil life. They do not therefore imbibe the spirit of the army, or, rather, they infuse the spirit of the community at large into the army, and retain it there. Amongst democratic nations, the private soldiers remain most like civilians: upon them the habits of the nation have the firmest hold, and public opinion has most influence. It is through the private soldiers, especially, that it may be possible to infuse into a democratic army the love of freedom and the respect for rights, if these principles have once been successfully inculcated on the people at large. The reverse happens amongst aristocratic nations, where the soldiery have eventually nothing in common with their fellow-citizens, and where they live amongst them as strangers, and often as enemies.

In aristocratic armies, the officers are the conservative element, because the officers alone have retained a strict connection with civil society, and never forego their purpose of resuming their place in it sooner or later: in democratic armies, the private soldiers stand in this position, and from the same cause.

It often happens, on the contrary, that, in these same democratic armies, the officers contract tastes and wants wholly distinct from those of the nation, — a fact which may be thus accounted for. Amongst democratic nations, the man who becomes an officer severs all the ties which bound him to civil life; he leaves it forever, and no interest urges him to return to it. His true country is the army, since he owes all he has to the rank he has attained in it; he therefore follows the fortunes of the army, rises or sinks with it, and henceforward directs all his hopes to that quarter only. As the wants of an officer are distinct from those of the country, he may, perhaps, ardently desire war, or labor to bring about a revolution, at the very moment when the nation is most desirous of stability and peace.

There are, nevertheless, some causes which allay this restless and warlike spirit. Though ambition is universal and continual amongst democratic nations, we have seen that it is seldom great. A man who, being born in the lower classes of the community, has risen from the ranks to be an officer, has already taken a prodigious step. He has gained a footing in a sphere above that which he filled in civil life, and has acquired rights which most democratic nations will ever consider as inalienable.* He is willing to pause after so great an effort, and to enjoy what he has won. The fear of risking what he has already obtained damps the desire of acquiring what he has not got. Having conquered the first and greatest impediment which opposed his advancement, he resigns himself with less impatience to the slowness of his progress. His ambition will be more and more cooled in proportion as the increasing distinction of his rank teaches him that he has more to put in jeopardy. If I am not mistaken, the least warlike, and also the least revolutionary, part of a democratic army will always be its chief commanders.

But the remarks I have just made on officers and soldiers are not applicable to a numerous class which, in all armies, fills the intermediate space between them; I mean the class of non-commissioned officers. This class of non-

* The position of officers is indeed much more secure amongst democratic nations than elsewhere; the lower the personal standing of the man, the greater is the comparative importance of his military grade, and the more just and necessary is it that the enjoyment of that rank should be secured by the laws.

commissioned officers, which had never acted a part in history until the present century, is henceforward destined, I think, to play one of some importance. Like the officers, non-commissioned officers have broken, in their minds, all the ties which bound them to civil life; like the former, they devote themselves permanently to the service, and perhaps make it even more exclusively the object of all their desires; but non-commissioned officers are men who have not yet reached a firm and lofty post, at which they may pause and breathe more freely, ere they can attain further promotion.

By the very nature of his duties, which are invariable, a non-commissioned officer is doomed to lead an obscure, confined, comfortless, and precarious existence; as yet, he sees nothing of military life but its dangers; he knows nothing but its privations and its discipline, — more difficult to support than dangers: he suffers the more from his present miseries, from knowing that the constitution of society and of the army allow him to rise above them; he may, indeed, at any time, obtain his commission, and enter at once upon command, honors, independence, rights, and enjoyments. Not only does this object of his hopes appear to him of immense importance, but he is never sure of reaching it till it is actually his own; the grade he fills is by no means irrevocable; he is always entirely abandoned to the arbitrary pleasure of his commanding officer, for this is imperiously required by the necessity of discipline: a slight fault, a whim, may always deprive him in an instant of the fruits of many years of toil and endeavor; until he has reached the grade to which he aspires, he has accomplished nothing; not till he reaches that grade does his career seem to begin. A desperate ambition cannot fail to be kindled in a man thus incessantly goaded on by his youth, his wants, his passions, the spirit of his age, his hopes, and his fears.

Non-commissioned officers are therefore bent on war, — on war always, and at any cost; but if war be denied them, then they desire revolutions, to suspend the authority of established regulations, and to enable them, aided by the general confusion and the political passions of the time, to get rid of their superior officers, and to take their places. Nor is it impossible for them to bring about such a crisis, because their common origin and habits give them much influence over the soldiers, however different may be their passions and their desires.

It would be an error to suppose that these various characteristics of officers, non-commissioned officers, and men belong to any particular time or country; they will always occur at all times, and amongst all democratic nations. In every democratic army the non-commissioned officers will be the worst representatives of the pacific and orderly spirit of the country, and the private soldiers will be the best. The latter will carry with them into military life the strength or weakness of the manners of the nation; they will display a faithful reflection of the community: if that community is ignorant and weak, they will allow themselves to be drawn by their leaders into disturbances, either unconsciously or against their will; if it is enlightened and energetic, the community will itself keep them within the bounds of order.

CHAPTER XXIV.

CAUSES WHICH RENDER DEMOCRATIC ARMIES WEAKER THAN OTHER ARMIES AT THE OUTSET OF A CAMPAIGN, AND MORE FORMIDABLE IN PROTRACTED WARFARE.

ANY army is in danger of being conquered at the outset of a campaign, after a long peace; any army which has long been engaged in warfare has strong chances of victory: this truth is peculiarly applicable to democratic armies. In aristocracies, the military profession, being a privileged career, is held in honor even in time of peace. Men of great talents, great attainments, and great ambition embrace it; the army is in all respects on a level with the nation, and frequently above it.

We have seen, on the contrary, that, amongst a democratic people, the choicer minds of the nation are gradually drawn away from the military profession, to seek by other paths distinction, power, and especially wealth. After a long peace, — and in democratic times the periods of peace are long, — the army is always inferior to the country itself. In this state, it is called into active service; and, until war has altered it, there is danger for the country as well as for the army.

I have shown that, in democratic armies, and in time of peace, the rule of seniority is the supreme and inflexible law of promotion. This is a consequence, as I have before observed, not only of the constitution of these armies, but of the constitution of the people; and it will always occur.

Again, as amongst these nations, the officer derives his position in the country solely from his position in the army, and as he draws all the distinction and the competency he enjoys from the same source, he does not retire from his profession, or is not superannuated, till very near the close of life. The consequence of these two causes is, that, when a democratic people goes to war after a long interval of peace, all the leading officers of the army are old men. I speak not only of the generals, but of the non-commissioned officers, who have most of them been stationary, or have advanced only step by step. It may be remarked with surprise, that, in a democratic army, after a long peace, all the soldiers are mere boys, and all the superior officers in declining years; so that the former are wanting in experience, the latter in vigor. This is a leading cause of defeat, for the first condition of successful generalship is youth: I should not have ventured to say so, if the greatest captain of modern times had not made the observation.

These two causes do not act in the same manner upon aristocratic armies: as men are promoted in them by right of birth much more than by right of seniority, there are in all ranks a certain number of young men who bring to their profession all the early vigor of body and mind. Again, as the men who seek for military honors amongst an aristocratic people enjoy a settled position in civil society, they seldom continue in the army until old age overtakes them. After having devoted the most vigorous years of youth to the career of arms, they voluntarily retire, and spend at home the remainder of their maturer years.

A long peace not only fills democratic armies with elderly officers, but it also gives to all the officers habits both of body and mind which render them unfit for actual service. The man who has long lived amidst the calm and lukewarm atmosphere of democratic manners, can at first ill adapt himself to the harder toils and sterner duties of warfare; and if he has not absolutely lost the taste for arms, at least he has assumed a mode of life which unfits him for conquest.

Amongst aristocratic nations, the enjoyments of civil life exercise less influence on the manners of the army, because, amongst those nations, the aristocracy commands the army; and an aristocracy, however plunged in luxurious pleasures, has always many other passions besides that of its own well-being, and to satisfy those passions more thoroughly its well-being will be readily sacrificed.*

I have shown that, in democratic armies, in time of peace, promotion is extremely slow. The officers at first support this state of things with impatience; they grow excited, restless, exasperated; but in the end most of them make up their minds to it. Those who have the largest share of ambition and of resources quit the army; others, adapting their tastes and their desires to their scanty fortunes, ultimately look upon the military profession in a civil point of view. The quality they value most in it is the competency and security which attend it: their whole notion of the future rests upon the certainty of this little provision, and all they require is peaceably to enjoy it. Thus, not only does a long peace fill an army with old men, but it frequently imparts the views of old men to those who are still in the prime of life.

I have also shown that, amongst democratic nations, in time of peace, the military profession is held in little honor and practised with little spirit. This want of public favor is a heavy discouragement to the army; it weighs down the minds of the troops, and when war breaks out at last, they cannot immediately resume their spring and vigor. No similar cause of moral weakness exists in aristocratic armies: there, the officers are never lowered, either in their own eyes or in those of their countrymen; because, independently of their military greatness, they are personally great. But, even if the influence of peace operated on the

* See Appendix U.

two kinds of armies in the same manner, the results would still be different.

When the officers of an aristocratic army have lost their warlike spirit and the desire of raising themselves by service, they still retain a certain respect for the honor of their class, and an old habit of being foremost to set an example. But when the officers of a democratic army have no longer the love of war and the ambition of arms, nothing whatever remains to them.

I am therefore of opinion, that, when a democratic people engages in a war after a long peace, it incurs much more risk of defeat than any other nation; but it ought not easily to be cast down by its reverses, for the chances of success for such an army are increased by the duration of the war. When a war has at length, by its long continuance, roused the whole community from their peaceful occupations, and ruined their minor undertakings, the same passions which made them attach so much importance to the maintenance of peace will be turned to arms. War, after it has destroyed all modes of speculation, becomes itself the great and sole speculation, to which all the ardent and ambitious desires that equality engenders are exclusively directed. Hence it is, that the selfsame democratic nations which are so reluctant to engage in hostilities, sometimes perform prodigious achievements when once they have taken the field.

As the war attracts more and more of public attention, and is seen to create high reputations and great fortunes in a short space of time, the choicest spirits of the nation enter the military profession: all the enterprising, proud, and martial minds, no longer of the aristocracy solely, but of the whole country, are drawn in this direction. As the number of competitors for military honors is immense, and war drives every man to his proper level, great generals are always sure to spring up. A long war produces upon a democratic army the same effects that a revolution produces upon a people; it breaks through regulations, and allows extraordinary men to rise above the common level. Those officers whose bodies and minds have grown old in peace, are removed, or superannuated, or they die. In their stead, a host of young men are pressing on, whose frames are already hardened, whose desires are extended and inflamed by active service. They are bent on advancement at all hazards, and perpetual advancement; they are followed by others with the same passions and desires, and after these are others, yet unlimited by aught but the size of the army. The principle of equality opens the door of ambition to all, and death provides chances for ambition. Death is constantly thinning the ranks, making vacancies, closing and opening the career of arms.

There is, moreover, a secret connection between the military character and the character of democracies, which war brings to light. The men of democracies are naturally passionately eager to acquire what they covet, and to enjoy it on easy conditions. They for the most part worship chance, and are much less afraid of death than of difficulty. This is the spirit which they bring to commerce and manufactures; and this same spirit, carried with them to the field of battle, induces them willingly to expose their lives in order to secure in a moment the rewards of victory. No kind of greatness is more pleasing to the imagination of a democratic people than military greatness, — a greatness of vivid and sudden lustre, obtained without toil, by nothing but the risk of life.

Thus, whilst the interest and the tastes of the members of a democratic community divert them from war, their habits of mind fit them for carrying on war well: they soon make good soldiers, when they are aroused from their business and their enjoyments.

If peace is peculiarly hurtful to democratic armies, war

secures to them advantages which no other armies ever possess; and these advantages, however little felt at first, cannot fail in the end to give them the victory. An aristocratic nation, which, in a contest with a democratic people, does not succeed in ruining the latter at the outset of the war, always runs a great risk of being conquered by it.

CHAPTER XXV.

OF DISCIPLINE IN DEMOCRATIC ARMIES.

IT is a very common opinion, especially in aristocratic countries, that the great social equality which prevails in democracies ultimately renders the private soldier independent of the officer, and thus destroys the bond of discipline. This is a mistake, for there are two kinds of discipline, which it is important not to confound.

When the officer is noble and the soldier a serf, — one rich, the other poor, — the one educated and strong, the other ignorant and weak, — the strictest bond of obedience may easily be established between the two men. The soldier is broken in to military discipline, as it were, before he enters the army; or rather, military discipline is nothing but an enhancement of social servitude. In aristocratic armies, the soldier will soon become insensible to everything but the orders of his superior officers; he acts without reflection, triumphs without enthusiasm, and dies without complaint: in this state, he is no longer a man, but he is still a most formidable animal trained for war.

A democratic people must despair of ever obtaining from soldiers that blind, minute, submissive, and invariable obedience, which an aristocratic people may impose on them without difficulty. The state of society does not prepare them for it, and the nation might be in danger of losing its natural advantages, if it sought artificially to acquire advantages of this particular kind. Amongst democratic communities, military discipline ought not to attempt to annihilate the free action of the faculties; all that can be done by discipline is to direct it; the obedience thus inculcated is less exact, but it is more eager and more intelligent. It has its root in the will of him who obeys: it rests not only on his instinct, but on his reason; and consequently, it will often spontaneously become more strict as danger requires. The discipline of an aristocratic army is apt to be relaxed in war, because that discipline is founded upon habits, and war disturbs those habits. The discipline of a democratic army, on the contrary, is strengthened in sight of the enemy, because every soldier then clearly perceives that he must be silent and obedient in order to conquer.

The nations which have performed the greatest warlike achievements knew no other discipline than that which I speak of. Amongst the ancients, none were admitted into the armies but freemen and citizens, who differed but little from one another, and were accustomed to treat each other as equals. In this respect, it may be said that the armies of antiquity were democratic, although they came out of the bosom of aristocracy; the consequence was, that in those armies a sort of fraternal familiarity prevailed between the officers and the men. Plutarch's lives of great commanders furnish convincing instances of the fact: the soldiers were in the constant habit of freely addressing their general, and the general listened to and answered whatever the soldiers had to say; they were kept in order by language and by example, far more than by constraint or punishment; the general was as much their companion as their chief. I know not whether the soldiers of Greece and Rome ever carried the minutiæ of military discipline to the same degree of perfection as the Russians have done; but this did not prevent Alexander from conquering Asia,—and Rome, the world.

CHAPTER XXVI.

SOME CONSIDERATIONS ON WAR IN DEMOCRATIC COMMUNITIES.

WHEN the principle of equality is spreading, not only amongst a single nation, but amongst several neighboring nations at the same time, as is now the case in Europe, the inhabitants of these different countries, notwithstanding the dissimilarity of language, of customs, and of laws, still resemble each other in their equal dread of war and their common love of peace.* It is in vain that ambition or anger puts arms in the hands of princes; they are appeased in spite of themselves by a species of general apathy and good-will, which makes the sword drop from their grasp, and wars become more rare.

As the spread of equality, taking place in several countries at once, simultaneously impels their various inhabitants to follow manufactures and commerce, not only do their tastes become similar, but their interests are so mixed and entangled with one another, that no nation can inflict evils on other nations without those evils falling back upon itself; and all nations ultimately regard war as a calamity almost as severe to the conqueror as to the conquered.

Thus, on the one hand, it is extremely difficult in democratic times to draw nations into hostilities; but, on the

* It is scarcely necessary for me to observe, that the dread of war displayed by the nations of Europe is not attributable solely to the progress made by the principle of equality amongst them; independently of this permanent cause, several other accidental causes of great weight might be pointed out, and I may mention, before all the rest, the extreme lassitude which the wars of the Revolution and the Empire have left behind them.

other, it is almost impossible that any two of them should go to war without embroiling the rest. The interests of all are so interlaced, their opinions and their wants so much alike, that none can remain quiet when the others stir. Wars therefore become more rare, but when they break out, they spread over a larger field.

Neighboring democratic nations not only become alike in some respects, but they eventually grow to resemble each other in almost all.* This similitude of nations has consequences of great importance in relation to war.

* This is not only because these nations have the same social condition, but it arises from the very nature of that social condition, which leads men to imitate and identify themselves with each other.

When the members of a community are divided into castes and classes, they not only differ from one another, but they have no taste and no desire to be alike; on the contrary, every one endeavors, more and more, to keep his own opinions undisturbed, to retain his own peculiar habits, and to remain himself. The characteristics of individuals are very strongly marked.

When the state of society amongst a people is democratic, — that is to say, when there are no longer any castes or classes in the community, and all its members are nearly equal in education and in property, — the human mind follows the opposite direction. Men are much alike, and they are annoyed, as it were, by any deviation from that likeness: far from seeking to preserve their own distinguishing singularities, they endeavor to shake them off, in order to identify themselves with the general mass of the people, which is the sole representative of right and of might to their eyes. The characteristics of individuals are nearly obliterated.

In the ages of aristocracy, even those who are naturally alike strive to create imaginary differences between themselves: in the ages of democracy, even those who are not alike seek nothing more than to become so, and to copy each other, — so strongly is the mind of every man always carried away by the general impulse of mankind.

Something of the same kind may be observed between nations: two nations, having the same aristocratic social condition, might remain thoroughly distinct and extremely different, because the spirit of aristocracy is to retain strong individual characteristics; but if two neighboring nations have the same democratic social condition, they cannot fail to adopt similar opinions and manners, because the spirit of democracy tends to assimilate men to each other.

If I inquire why it is that the Helvetic Confederacy made the greatest and most powerful nations of Europe tremble in the fifteenth century, whilst, at the present day, the power of that country is exactly proportioned to its population, I perceive that the Swiss are become like all the surrounding communities, and those surrounding communities like the Swiss: so that, as numerical strength now forms the only difference between them, victory necessarily attends the largest army. Thus, one of the consequences of the democratic revolution which is going on in Europe is to make numerical strength preponderate on all fields of battle, and to constrain all small nations to incorporate themselves with large states, or at least to adopt the policy of the latter.

As numbers are the determining cause of victory, each people ought of course to strive by all the means in its power to bring the greatest possible number of men into the field. When it was possible to enlist a kind of troops superior to all others, such as the Swiss infantry or the French horse of the sixteenth century, it was not thought necessary to raise very large armies; but the case is altered when one soldier is as efficient as another.

The same cause which begets this new want also supplies means of satisfying it; for, as I have already observed, when men are all alike they are all weak, and the supreme power of the state is naturally much stronger amongst democratic nations than elsewhere. Hence, whilst these nations are desirous of enrolling the whole male population in the ranks of the army, they have the power of effecting this object: the consequence is, that, in democratic ages, armies seem to grow larger in proportion as the love of war declines.

In the same ages, too, the manner of carrying on war is likewise altered by the same causes. Machiavelli observes, in "The Prince," "that it is much more difficult to subdue a people who have a prince and his barons for their leaders, than a nation which is commanded by a prince and his slaves." To avoid offence, let us read "public functionaries" for "slaves," and this important truth will be strictly applicable to our own time.

A great aristocratic people cannot either conquer its neighbors or be conquered by them, without great difficulty. It cannot conquer them, because all its forces can never be collected and held together for a considerable period: it cannot be conquered, because an enemy meets at every step small centres of resistance, by which invasion is arrested. War against an aristocracy may be compared to war in a mountainous country, — the defeated party has constant opportunities of rallying its forces to make a stand in a new position.

Exactly the reverse occurs amongst democratic nations: they easily bring their whole disposable force into the field, and when the nation is wealthy and populous it soon becomes victorious; but if ever it is conquered, and its territory invaded, it has few resources at command; and if the enemy takes the capital, the nation is lost. This may very well be explained: as each member of the community is individually isolated and extremely powerless, no one of the whole body can either defend himself or present a rallying-point to others. Nothing is strong in a democratic country except the state; as the military strength of the state is destroyed by the destruction of the army, and its civil power paralyzed by the capture of the chief city, all that remains is only a multitude without strength or government, unable to resist the organized power by which it is assailed. I am aware that this danger may be lessened by the creation of local liberties, and consequently of local powers; but this remedy will always be insufficient. For after such a catastrophe, not only is the population unable to carry on hostilities, but it may be apprehended that they will not be inclined to attempt it.

According to the law of nations adopted in civilized countries, the object of war is, not to seize the property of private individuals, but simply to get possession of political power. The destruction of private property is only occasionally resorted to, for the purpose of attaining the latter object.

When an aristocratic country is invaded after the defeat of its army, the nobles, although they are at the same time the wealthiest members of the community, will continue to defend themselves individually rather than submit; for if the conqueror remained master of the country he would deprive them of their political power, to which they cling even more closely than to their property. They therefore prefer fighting to submission, which is to them the greatest of all misfortunes; and they readily carry the people along with them, because the people have long been used to follow and obey them, and besides have but little to risk in the war.

Amongst a nation in which equality of condition prevails, on the contrary, each citizen has but a slender share of political power, and often has no share at all: on the other hand, all are independent, and all have something to lose; so that they are much less afraid of being conquered, and much more afraid of war, than an aristocratic people. It will always be extremely difficult to decide a democratic population to take up arms when hostilities have reached its own territory. Hence the necessity of giving to such a people the rights and the political character which may impart to every citizen some of those interests that cause the nobles to act for the public welfare in aristocratic countries.

It should never be forgotten by the princes and other leaders of democratic nations, that nothing but the love and the habit of freedom can maintain an advantageous contest with the love and the habit of physical well-being.

I can conceive nothing better prepared for subjection, in case of defeat, than a democratic people without free institutions.

Formerly, it was customary to take the field with a small body of troops, to fight in small engagements, and to make long regular sieges: modern tactics consist in fighting decisive battles, and, as soon as a line of march is open before the army, in rushing upon the capital city, in order to terminate the war at a single blow. Napoleon, it is said, was the inventor of this new system; but the invention of such a system did not depend on any individual man, whoever he might be. The mode in which Napoleon carried on war was suggested to him by the state of society in his time; that mode was successful, because it was eminently adapted to that state of society, and because he was the first to employ it. Napoleon was the first commander who marched at the head of an army from capital to capital; but the road was opened for him by the ruin of feudal society. It may fairly be believed that, if that extraordinary man had been born three hundred years ago, he would not have derived the same results from his method of warfare, or, rather, that he would have had a different method.

I shall add but a few words on civil wars, for fear of exhausting the patience of the reader. Most of the remarks which I have made respecting foreign wars are applicable *a fortiori* to civil wars. Men living in democracies have not naturally the military spirit; they sometimes acquire it, when they have been dragged by compulsion to the field; but to rise in a body, and voluntarily to expose themselves to the horrors of war, and especially of civil war, is a course which the men of democracies are not apt to adopt. None but the most adventurous members of the community consent to run into such risks; the bulk of the population remain motionless.

But even if the population were inclined to act, considerable obstacles would stand in their way; for they can resort to no old and well-established influence which they are willing to obey, — no well-known leaders to rally the discontented, as well as to discipline and to lead them, — no political powers subordinate to the supreme power of the nation, which afford an effectual support to the resistance directed against the government.

In democratic countries, the moral power of the majority is immense, and the physical resources which it has at its command are out of all proportion to the physical resources which may be combined against it. Therefore, the party which occupies the seat of the majority, which speaks in its name and wields its power, triumphs instantaneously and irresistibly over all private resistance; it does not even give such opposition time to exist, but nips it in the bud.

Those who, in such nations, seek to effect a revolution by force of arms, have no other resource than suddenly to seize upon the whole engine of government as it stands, which can better be done by a single blow than by a war; for as soon as there is a regular war, the party which represents the state is always certain to conquer.

The only case in which a civil war could arise is, if the army should divide itself into two factions, the one raising the standard of rebellion, the other remaining true to its allegiance. An army constitutes a small community, very closely united together, endowed with great powers of vitality, and able to supply its own wants for some time. Such a war might be bloody, but it could not be long; for either the rebellious army would gain over the government by the sole display of its resources, or by its first victory, and then the war would be over; or the struggle would take place, and then that portion of the army which should not be supported by the organized powers of the state would speedily either disband itself, or be destroyed. It may therefore be admitted as a general truth, that, in ages of equality, civil wars will become much less frequent and less protracted.*

* It should be borne in mind that I speak here of sovereign and independent democratic nations, not of confederate democracies; in confederacies, as the preponderating power always resides, in spite of all political fictions, in the state governments, and not in the federal government, civil wars are, in fact, nothing but foreign wars in disguise.

FOURTH BOOK.

INFLUENCE OF DEMOCRATIC IDEAS AND FEELINGS ON POLITICAL SOCIETY.

I SHOULD imperfectly fulfil the purpose of this book, if, after having shown what ideas and feelings are suggested by the principle of equality, I did not point out, ere I conclude, the general influence which these same ideas and feelings may exercise upon the government of human societies. To succeed in this object, I shall frequently have to retrace my steps; but I trust the reader will not refuse to follow me through paths already known to him, which may lead to some new truth.

CHAPTER I.

EQUALITY NATURALLY GIVES MEN A TASTE FOR FREE INSTITUTIONS.

THE principle of equality, which makes men independent of each other, gives them a habit and a taste for following, in their private actions, no other guide than their own will. This complete independence, which they constantly enjoy in regard to their equals and in the intercourse of private life, tends to make them look upon all authority with a jealous eye, and speedily suggests to them the notion and the love of political freedom. Men living at such times have a natural bias to free institutions. Take any one of them at a venture, and search if you can his most deep-seated instincts; and you will find that, of all governments, he will soonest conceive and most highly value that government whose head he has himself elected, and whose administration he may control.

Of all the political effects produced by the equality of conditions, this love of independence is the first to strike the observing, and to alarm the timid; nor can it be said that their alarm is wholly misplaced, for anarchy has a more formidable aspect in democratic countries than elsewhere. As the citizens have no direct influence on each other, as soon as the supreme power of the nation fails, which kept them all in their several stations, it would seem that disorder must instantly reach its utmost pitch, and that, every man drawing aside in a different direction, the fabric of society must at once crumble away.

I am persuaded, however, that anarchy is not the principal evil which democratic ages have to fear, but the least. For the principle of equality begets two tendencies: the one leads men straight to independence, and may suddenly drive them into anarchy; the other conducts them by a longer, more secret, but more certain road, to servitude. Nations readily discern the former tendency, and are prepared to resist it; they are led away by the latter, without perceiving its drift; hence it is peculiarly important to point it out.

For myself, I am so far from urging it as a reproach to the principle of equality that it renders men intractable, that this very circumstance principally calls forth my approbation. I admire to see how it deposits in the mind and heart of man the dim conception and instinctive love of political independence, thus preparing the remedy for the evil which it produces: it is on this very account that I am attached to it.

CHAPTER II.

THAT THE OPINIONS OF DEMOCRATIC NATIONS ABOUT GOVERNMENT ARE NATURALLY FAVORABLE TO THE CONCENTRATION OF POWER.

THE notion of secondary powers, placed between the sovereign and his subjects, occurred naturally to the imagination of aristocratic nations, because those communities contained individuals or families raised above the common level, and apparently destined to command by their birth, their education, and their wealth. This same notion is naturally wanting in the minds of men in democratic ages, for converse reasons; it can only be introduced artificially, it can only be kept there with difficulty; whereas they conceive, as it were without thinking upon the subject, the notion of a single and central power, which governs the whole community by its direct influence. Moreover, in politics as well as in philosophy and in religion, the intellect of democratic nations is peculiarly open to simple and general notions. Complicated systems are repugnant to it, and its favorite conception is that of a great nation composed of citizens all formed upon one pattern, and all governed by a single power.

The very next notion to that of a single and central power, which presents itself to the minds of men in the ages of equality, is the notion of uniformity of legislation. As every man sees that he differs but little from those about him, he cannot understand why a rule which is applicable to one man should not be equally applicable to all others. Hence the slightest privileges are repugnant to his reason; the faintest dissimilarities in the political institutions of the same people offend him, and uniformity of legislation appears to him to be the first condition of good government.

I find, on the contrary, that this notion of a uniform rule, equally binding on all the members of the community, was almost unknown to the human mind in aristocratic ages; it was either never broached, or it was rejected.

These contrary tendencies of opinion ultimately turn on both sides to such blind instincts and ungovernable habits, that they still direct the actions of men, in spite of particular exceptions. Notwithstanding the immense variety of conditions in the Middle Ages, a certain number of persons existed at that period in precisely similar circumstances; but this did not prevent the laws then in force from assigning to each of them distinct duties and different rights. On the contrary, at the present time, all the powers of government are exerted to impose the same customs and the same laws on populations which have as yet but few points of resemblance.

As the conditions of men become equal amongst a people, individuals seem of less, and society of greater importance; or rather, every citizen, being assimilated to all the rest, is lost in the crowd, and nothing stands conspicuous but the great and imposing image of the people at large. This naturally gives the men of democratic periods a lofty opinion of the privileges of society, and a very humble notion of the rights of individuals; they are ready to admit that the interests of the former are everything, and those of the latter nothing. They are willing to acknowledge that the power which represents the community has far more information and wisdom than any of the members of that community; and that it is the duty, as well as the right, of that power, to guide as well as govern each private citizen.

If we closely scrutinize our contemporaries, and penetrate to the root of their political opinions, we shall detect some of the notions which I have just pointed out, and we shall perhaps be surprised to find so much accordance between men who are so often at variance.

The Americans hold, that, in every state, the supreme power ought to emanate from the people; but when once that power is constituted, they can conceive, as it were, no limits to it, and they are ready to admit that it has the right to do whatever it pleases. They have not the slightest notion of peculiar privileges granted to cities, families, or persons: their minds appear never to have foreseen that it might be possible not to apply with strict uniformity the same laws to every part of the state, and to all its inhabitants.

These same opinions are more and more diffused in Europe; they even insinuate themselves amongst those nations which most vehemently reject the principle of the sovereignty of the people. Such nations assign a different origin to the supreme power, but they ascribe to that power the same characteristics. Amongst them all, the idea of intermediate powers is weakened and obliterated; the idea of rights inherent in certain individuals is rapidly disappearing from the minds of men; the idea of the omnipotence and sole authority of society at large rises to fill its place. These ideas take root and spread in proportion as social conditions become more equal, and men more alike; they are produced by equality, and in turn they hasten the progress of equality.

In France, where the revolution of which I am speaking has gone further than in any other European country, these opinions have got complete hold of the public mind. If we listen attentively to the language of the various parties in France, we shall find that there is not one which has not adopted them. Most of these parties censure the conduct of the government, but they all hold that the government ought perpetually to act and interfere in everything that is done. Even those which are most at variance are nevertheless agreed upon this head. The unity, the ubiquity, the omnipotence of the supreme power, and the uniformity of its rules, constitute the principal characteristics of all the political systems which have been put forward in our age. They recur even in the wildest visions of political regeneration: the human mind pursues them in its dreams.

If these notions spontaneously arise in the minds of private individuals, they suggest themselves still more forcibly to the minds of princes. Whilst the ancient fabric of European society is altered and dissolved, sovereigns acquire new conceptions of their opportunities and their duties; they learn for the first time that the central power which they represent may and ought to administer, by its own agency and on a uniform plan, all the concerns of the whole community. This opinion, which, I will venture to say, was never conceived before our time by the monarchs of Europe, now sinks deeply into the minds of kings, and abides there amidst all the agitation of more unsettled thoughts.

Our contemporaries are therefore much less divided than is commonly supposed; they are constantly disputing as to the hands in which supremacy is to be vested, but they readily agree upon the duties and the rights of that supremacy. The notion they all form of government is that of a sole, simple, providential, and creative power.

All secondary opinions in politics are unsettled; this one remains fixed, invariable, and consistent. It is adopted by statesmen and political philosophers; it is eagerly laid hold of by the multitude; those who govern and those who are governed agree to pursue it with equal ardor; it is the earliest notion of their minds, it seems innate. It originates, therefore, in no caprice of the human intellect, but it is a necessary condition of the present state of mankind.

CHAPTER III.

THAT THE SENTIMENTS OF DEMOCRATIC NATIONS ACCORD WITH THEIR OPINIONS IN LEADING THEM TO CONCENTRATE POLITICAL POWER.

IF it be true that, in ages of equality, men readily adopt the notion of a great central power, it cannot be doubted, on the other hand, that their habits and sentiments predispose them to recognize such a power, and to give it their support. This may be demonstrated in a few words, as the greater part of the reasons to which the fact may be attributed have been previously stated.*

As the men who inhabit democratic countries have no superiors, no inferiors, and no habitual or necessary partners in their undertakings, they readily fall back upon themselves, and consider themselves as beings apart. I had occasion to point this out at considerable length in treating of individualism. Hence such men can never, without an effort, tear themselves from their private affairs to engage in public business; their natural bias leads them to abandon the latter to the sole visible and permanent representative of the interests of the community, that is to say, to the state. Not only are they naturally wanting in a taste for public business, but they have frequently no time to attend to it. Private life in democratic times is so busy, so excited, so full of wishes and of work, that hardly any energy or leisure remains to each individual for public life. I am the last man to contend that these propensities are unconquerable, since my chief object in writing this book has

* See Appendix V.

been to combat them. I only maintain that, at the present day, a secret power is fostering them in the human heart, and that, if they are not checked, they will wholly overgrow it.

I have also had occasion to show how the increasing love of well-being and the fluctuating character of property cause democratic nations to dread all violent disturbances. The love of public tranquillity is frequently the only passion which these nations retain, and it becomes more active and powerful amongst them in proportion as all other passions droop and die. This naturally disposes the members of the community constantly to give or to surrender additional rights to the central power, which alone seems to be interested in defending them by the same means that it uses to defend itself.

As in periods of equality, no man is compelled to lend his assistance to his fellow-men, and none has any right to expect much support from them, every one is at once independent and powerless. These two conditions, which must never be either separately considered or confounded together, inspire the citizen of a democratic country with very contrary propensities. His independence fills him with self-reliance and pride amongst his equals; his debility makes him feel from time to time the want of some outward assistance, which he cannot expect from any of them, because they are all impotent and unsympathizing. In this predicament, he naturally turns his eyes to that imposing power which alone rises above the level of universal depression. Of that power his wants and especially his desires continually remind him, until he ultimately views it as the sole and necessary support of his own weakness.*

* In democratic communities, nothing but the central power has any stability in its position or any permanence in its undertakings. All the members of society are in ceaseless stir and transformation. Now it is in the nature of all governments to seek constantly to enlarge their sphere of

This may more completely explain what frequently takes place in democratic countries, where the very men who are so impatient of superiors patiently submit to a master, exhibiting at once their pride and their servility.

The hatred which men bear to privilege increases in proportion as privileges become fewer and less considerable, so that democratic passions would seem to burn most fiercely just when they have least fuel. I have already given the reason of this phenomenon. When all conditions are unequal, no inequality is so great as to offend the eye; whereas the slightest dissimilarity is odious in the midst of general uniformity: the more complete this uniformity is, the more insupportable does the sight of such a difference become. Hence it is natural that the love of equality should constantly increase together with equality itself, and that it should grow by what it feeds on.

action; hence it is almost impossible that such a government should not ultimately succeed, because it acts with a fixed principle and a constant will, upon men whose position, whose notions, and whose desires are in continual vacillation.

It frequently happens that the members of the community promote the influence of the central power without intending it. Democratic ages are periods of experiment, innovation, and adventure. At such times, there are always a multitude of men engaged in difficult or novel undertakings, which they follow alone, without caring for their fellow-men. Such persons may be ready to admit, as a general principle, that the public authority ought not to interfere in private concerns; but, by an exception to that rule, each of them craves its assistance in the particular concern on which he is engaged, and seeks to draw upon the influence of the government for his own benefit, though he would restrict it on all other occasions. If a large number of men apply this particular exception to a great variety of different purposes, the sphere of the central power extends itself insensibly in all directions, although each of them wishes it to be circumscribed.

Thus a democratic government increases its power simply by the fact of its permanence. Time is on its side; every incident befriends it; the passions of individuals unconsciously promote it; and it may be asserted, that, the older a democratic community is, the more centralized will its government become.

This never-dying, ever-kindling hatred, which sets a democratic people against the smallest privileges, is peculiarly favorable to the gradual concentration of all political rights in the hands of the representative of the state alone. The sovereign, being necessarily and incontestably above all the citizens, excites not their envy, and each of them thinks that he strips his equals of the prerogative which he concedes to the crown. The man of a democratic age is extremely reluctant to obey his neighbor who is his equal; he refuses to acknowledge superior ability in such a person; he mistrusts his justice, and is jealous of his power; he fears and he contemns him; and he loves continually to remind him of the common dependence in which both of them stand to the same master.

Every central power, which follows its natural tendencies, courts and encourages the principle of equality; for equality singularly facilitates, extends, and secures the influence of a central power.

In like manner, it may be said that every central government worships uniformity: uniformity relieves it from inquiry into an infinity of details, which must be attended to if rules have to be adapted to different men, instead of indiscriminately subjecting all men to the same rule: thus the government likes what the citizens like, and naturally hates what they hate. These common sentiments, which, in democratic nations, constantly unite the sovereign and every member of the community in one and the same conviction, establish a secret and lasting sympathy between them. The faults of the government are pardoned for the sake of its tastes; public confidence is only reluctantly withdrawn in the midst even of its excesses and its errors; and it is restored at the first call. Democratic nations often hate those in whose hands the central power is vested; but they always love that power itself.

Thus, by two separate paths, I have reached the same

conclusion. I have shown that the principle of equality suggests to men the notion of a sole, uniform, and strong government: I have now shown that the principle of equality imparts to them a taste for it. To governments of this kind the nations of our age are therefore tending. They are drawn thither by the natural inclination of mind and heart; and in order to reach that result, it is enough that they do not check themselves in their course.

I am of opinion, that, in the democratic ages which are opening upon us, individual independence and local liberties will ever be the products of art; that centralization will be the natural government.*

* See Appendix W.

CHAPTER IV.

OF CERTAIN PECULIAR AND ACCIDENTAL CAUSES, WHICH EITHER LEAD A PEOPLE TO COMPLETE THE CENTRALIZATION OF GOVERNMENT, OR WHICH DIVERT THEM FROM IT.

IF all democratic nations are instinctively led to the centralization of government, they tend to this result in an unequal manner. This depends on the particular circumstances which may promote or prevent the natural consequences of that state of society, — circumstances which are exceedingly numerous, but of which I shall mention only a few.

Amongst men who have lived free long before they became equal, the tendencies derived from free institutions combat, to a certain extent, the propensities superinduced by the principle of equality; and although the central power may increase its privileges amongst such a people, the private members of such a community will never entirely forfeit their independence. But when the equality of conditions grows up amongst a people who have never known, or have long ceased to know, what freedom is, (and such is the case upon the continent of Europe,) as the former habits of the nation are suddenly combined, by some sort of natural attraction, with the new habits and principles engendered by the state of society, all powers seem spontaneously to rush to the centre. These powers accumulate there with astonishing rapidity, and the state instantly attains the utmost limits of its strength, whilst private persons allow themselves to sink as suddenly to the lowest degree of weakness.

The English who emigrated three hundred years ago to found a democratic commonwealth on the shores of the New World had all learned to take a part in public affairs in their mother country; they were conversant with trial by jury; they were accustomed to liberty of speech and of the press, — to personal freedom, to the notion of rights and the practice of asserting them. They carried with them to America these free institutions and manly customs, and these institutions preserved them against the encroachments of the state. Thus, amongst the Americans, it is freedom which is old, — equality is of comparatively modern date. The reverse is occurring in Europe, where equality, introduced by absolute power and under the rule of kings, was already infused into the habits of nations long before freedom had entered into their thoughts.

I have said that, amongst democratic nations, the notion of government naturally presents itself to the mind under the form of a sole and central power, and that the notion of intermediate powers is not familiar to them. This is peculiarly applicable to the democratic nations which have witnessed the triumph of the principle of equality by means of a violent revolution. As the classes which managed local affairs have been suddenly swept away by the storm, and as the confused mass which remains has as yet neither the organization nor the habits which fit it to assume the administration of these affairs, the state alone seems capable of taking upon itself all the details of government, and centralization becomes, as it were, the unavoidable state of the country.

Napoleon deserves neither praise nor censure for having centred in his own hands almost all the administrative power of France; for, after the abrupt disappearance of the nobility and the higher rank of the middle classes, these powers devolved on him of course: it would have been almost as difficult for him to reject as to assume them.

But a similar necessity has never been felt by the Americans, who, having passed through no revolution, and having governed themselves from the first, never had to call upon the state to act for a time as their guardian. Thus, the progress of centralization amongst a democratic people depends not only on the progress of equality, but on the manner in which this equality has been established.

At the commencement of a great democratic revolution, when hostilities have but just broken out between the different classes of society, the people endeavor to centralize the public administration in the hands of the government, in order to wrest the management of local affairs from the aristocracy. Towards the close of such a revolution, on the contrary, it is usually the conquered aristocracy who endeavor to make over the management of all affairs to the state, because such an aristocracy dread the tyranny of a people who have become their equal, and not unfrequently their master. Thus, it is not always the same class of the community which strives to increase the prerogative of the government; but as long as the democratic revolution lasts, there is always one class in the nation, powerful in numbers or in wealth, who are induced, by peculiar passions or interests, to centralize the public administration, independently of that hatred of being governed by one's neighbor which is a general and permanent feeling amongst democratic nations.

It may be remarked, that, at the present day, the lower orders in England are striving with all their might to destroy local independence, and to transfer the administration from all the points of the circumference to the centre; whereas the higher classes are endeavoring to retain this administration within its ancient boundaries. I venture to predict that a time will come when the very reverse will happen.

These observations explain why the supreme power is

always stronger, and private individuals weaker, amongst a democratic people, who have passed through a long and arduous struggle to reach a state of equality, than amongst a democratic community in which the citizens have been equal from the first. The example of the Americans completely demonstrates the fact. The inhabitants of the United States were never divided by any privileges; they have never known the mutual relation of master and inferior; and as they neither dread nor hate each other, they have never known the necessity of calling in the supreme power to manage their affairs. The lot of the Americans is singular: they have derived from the aristocracy of England the notion of private rights and the taste for local freedom; and they have been able to retain both, because they have had no aristocracy to combat.

If education enables men at all times to defend their independence, this is most especially true in democratic times. When all men are alike, it is easy to found a sole and all-powerful government by the aid of mere instinct. But men require much intelligence, knowledge, and art to organize and to maintain secondary powers under similar circumstances, and to create, amidst the independence and individual weakness of the citizens, such free associations as may be able to struggle against tyranny without destroying public order.

Hence the concentration of power and the subjection of individuals will increase amongst democratic nations, not only in the same proportion as their equality, but in the same proportion as their ignorance. It is true that, in ages of imperfect civilization, the government is frequently as wanting in the knowledge required to impose a despotism upon the people, as the people are wanting in the knowledge required to shake it off; but the effect is not the same on both sides. However rude a democratic people may be, the central power which rules them is never completely devoid of cultivation, because it readily draws to its own uses what little cultivation is to be found in the country, and, if necessary, may seek assistance elsewhere. Hence, amongst a nation which is ignorant as well as democratic, an amazing difference cannot fail speedily to arise between the intellectual capacity of the ruler and that of each of his subjects. This completes the easy concentration of all power in his hands: the administrative function of the state is perpetually extended, because the state alone is competent to administer the affairs of the country.

Aristocratic nations, however unenlightened they may be, never afford the same spectacle, because, in them, instruction is nearly equally diffused between the monarch and the leading members of the community.

The Pacha who now rules in Egypt found the population of that country composed of men exceedingly ignorant and equal, and he has borrowed the science and ability of Europe to govern that people. As the personal attainments of the sovereign are thus combined with the ignorance and democratic weakness of his subjects, the utmost centralization has been established without impediment, and the Pacha has made the country his manufactory, and the inhabitants his workmen.

I think that extreme centralization of government ultimately enervates society, and thus, after a length of time, weakens the government itself; but I do not deny that a centralized social power may be able to execute great undertakings with facility in a given time and on a particular point. This is more especially true of war, in which success depends much more on the means of transferring all the resources of a nation to one single point, than on the extent of those resources. Hence it is chiefly in war that nations desire, and frequently need, to increase the powers of the central government. All men of military genius are fond of centralization, which increases their strength; and all men of centralizing genius are fond of war, which compels nations to combine all their powers in the hands of the government. Thus, the democratic tendency which leads men unceasingly to multiply the privileges of the state, and to circumscribe the rights of private persons, is much more rapid and constant amongst those democratic nations which are exposed by their position to great and frequent wars, than amongst all others.

I have shown how the dread of disturbance and the love of well-being insensibly lead democratic nations to increase the functions of central government, as the only power which appears to be intrinsically sufficiently strong, enlightened, and secure to protect them from anarchy. I would now add, that all the particular circumstances which tend to make the state of a democratic community agitated and precarious, enhance this general propensity, and lead private persons more and more to sacrifice their rights to their tranquillity.

A people are therefore never so disposed to increase the functions of central government as at the close of a long and bloody revolution, which, after having wrested property from the hands of its former possessors, has shaken all belief, and filled the nation with fierce hatreds, conflicting interests, and contending factions. The love of public tranquillity becomes at such times an indiscriminate passion, and the members of the community are apt to conceive a most inordinate devotion to order.

I have already examined several of the incidents which may concur to promote the centralization of power, but the principal cause still remains to be noticed. The foremost of the incidental causes which may draw the management of all affairs into the hands of the ruler in democratic countries, is the origin of that ruler himself, and his own propensities. Men who live in the ages of equality are naturally fond of central power, and are willing to extend its privileges; but if it happens that this same power faithfully represents their own interests, and exactly copies their own inclinations, the confidence they place in it knows no bounds, and they think that whatever they bestow upon it is bestowed upon themselves.

The attraction of administrative powers to the centre will always be less easy and less rapid under the reign of kings who are still in some way connected with the old aristocratic order, than under new princes, the children of their own achievements, whose birth, prejudices, propensities, and habits appear to bind them indissolubly to the cause of equality. I do not mean that princes of aristocratic origin who live in democratic ages do not attempt to centralize; I believe they apply themselves as diligently as any others to that object. For them, the sole advantages of equality lie in that direction; but their opportunities are less great, because the community, instead of volunteering compliance with their desires, frequently obey them with reluctance. In democratic communities, the rule is, that centralization must increase in proportion as the sovereign is less aristocratic.

When an ancient race of kings stands at the head of an aristocracy, as the natural prejudices of the sovereign perfectly accord with the natural prejudices of the nobility, the vices inherent in aristocratic communities have a free course, and meet with no corrective. The reverse is the case when the scion of a feudal stock is placed at the head of a democratic people. The sovereign is constantly led, by his education, his habits, and his associations, to adopt sentiments suggested by the inequality of conditions, and the people tend as constantly, by their social condition, to those manners which are engendered by equality. At such times, it often happens that the citizens seek to control the central power far less as a tyrannical than as an aristocratical power, and that they persist in the firm defence of their independence, not only because they would remain free, but especially because they are determined to remain equal.

A revolution which overthrows an ancient regal family in order to place new men at the head of a democratic people may temporarily weaken the central power; but, however anarchical such a revolution may appear at first, we need not hesitate to predict that its final and certain consequence will be to extend and to secure the prerogatives of that power.

The foremost, or indeed the sole condition, which is required in order to succeed in centralizing the supreme power in a democratic community, is to love equality, or to get men to believe you love it. Thus, the science of despotism, which was once so complex, is simplified, and reduced, as it were, to a single principle.

CHAPTER V.

THAT AMONGST THE EUROPEAN NATIONS OF OUR TIME THE SOVEREIGN POWER IS INCREASING, ALTHOUGH THE SOVEREIGNS ARE LESS STABLE.

ON reflecting upon what has already been said, the reader will be startled and alarmed to find that in Europe everything seems to conduce to the indefinite extension of the prerogatives of government, and to render every day private independence more weak, more subordinate, and more precarious.

The democratic nations of Europe have all the general and permanent tendencies which urge the Americans to the centralization of government, and they are moreover exposed to a number of secondary and incidental causes with which the Americans are unacquainted. It would seem as if every step they make towards equality brings them nearer to despotism.

And, indeed, if we do but cast our looks around, we shall be convinced that such is the fact. During the aristocratic ages which preceded the present time, the sovereigns of Europe had been deprived of, or had relinquished, many of the rights inherent in their power. Not a hundred years ago, amongst the greater part of European nations, numerous private persons and corporations were sufficiently independent to administer justice, to raise and maintain troops, to levy taxes, and frequently even to make or interpret the law. The state has everywhere resumed to itself alone these natural attributes of sovereign power; in all matters of government, the state tolerates no intermediate agent between itself and the people, and it directs them by itself in general affairs. I am far from blaming this concentration of power, — I simply point it out.

At the same period a great number of secondary powers existed in Europe, which represented local interests and administered local affairs. Most of these local authorities have already disappeared; all are speedily tending to disappear, or to fall into the most complete dependence. From one end of Europe to the other the privileges of the nobility, the liberties of cities, and the powers of provincial bodies are either destroyed or are upon the verge of destruction.

Europe has endured, in the course of the last half-century, many revolutions and counter revolutions, which have agitated it in opposite directions; but all these perturbations resemble each other in one respect, — they have all shaken or destroyed the secondary powers of government. The local privileges which the French did not abolish in the countries they conquered, have finally succumbed to the policy of the princes who conquered the French. Those princes rejected all the innovations of the French Revolution except centralization: that is the only principle they consented to receive from such a source.

My object is to remark, that all these various rights, which have been successively wrested, in our time, from classes, corporations, and individuals, have not served to raise new secondary powers on a more democratic basis, but have uniformly been concentrated in the hands of the sovereign. Everywhere the state acquires more and more direct control over the humblest members of the community, and a more exclusive power of governing each of them in his smallest concerns.*

* This gradual weakening of individuals in relation to society at large may be traced in a thousand things. I shall select from amongst these examples one derived from the law of wills.

In aristocracies, it is common to profess the greatest reverence for the last

Almost all the charitable establishments of Europe were formerly in the hands of private persons or of corporations; they are now almost all dependent on the supreme government, and in many countries are actually administered by that power. The state almost exclusively undertakes to supply bread to the hungry, assistance and shelter to the sick, work to the idle, and to act as the sole reliever of all kinds of misery.

Education, as well as charity, is become in most countries, at the present day, a national concern. The state receives, and often takes, the child from the arms of the mother, to hand it over to official agents: the state undertakes to train the heart and to instruct the mind of each generation. Uniformity prevails in the courses of public instruction as in everything else; diversity, as well as freedom, are disappearing day by day.

Nor do I hesitate to affirm, that, amongst almost all the Christian nations of our days, Catholic as well as Protestant, religion is in danger of falling into the hands of the government. Not that rulers are over-jealous of the right of settling points of doctrine, but they get more and more hold upon the will of those by whom doctrines are expounded; they deprive the clergy of their property, and pay them by salaries; they divert to their own use the influence of the priesthood, they make them their own minis-

testamentary dispositions of a man; this feeling sometimes even became superstitious amongst the elder nations of Europe: the power of the state, far from interfering with the caprices of a dying man, gave full force to the very least of them, and insured to him a perpetual power.

When all living men are enfeebled, the will of the dead is less respected; it is circumscribed within a narrow range, beyond which it is annulled or checked by the supreme power of the laws. In the Middle Ages, testamentary power had, so to speak, no limits: amongst the French, at the present day, a man cannot distribute his fortune amongst his children without the interference of the state; after having domineered over a whole life, the law insists upon regulating the very last act of it.

ters, — often their own servants, — and by this alliance with religion they reach the inner depths of the soul of man.*

But this is as yet only one side of the picture. The authority of government has not only spread, as we have just seen, throughout the sphere of all existing powers, till that sphere can no longer contain it, but it goes further, and invades the domain heretofore reserved to private independence. A multitude of actions, which were formerly entirely beyond the control of the public administration, have been subjected to that control in our time, and the number of them is constantly increasing.

Amongst aristocratic nations, the supreme government usually contented itself with managing and superintending the community in whatever directly and ostensibly concerned the national honor; but in all other respects, the people were left to work out their own free will. Amongst these nations, the government often seemed to forget that there is a point at which the faults and the sufferings of private persons involved the general prosperity, and that to prevent the ruin of a private individual must sometimes be a matter of public importance.

The democratic nations of our time lean to the opposite extreme. It is evident that most of our rulers will not content themselves with governing the people collectively; it would seem as if they thought themselves responsible for the actions and private condition of their subjects, — as if they had undertaken to guide and to instruct each of them in the various incidents of life, and to secure their happiness quite independently of their own consent. On the

* In proportion as the duties of the central power are augmented, the number of public officers by whom that power is represented must increase also. They form a nation in each nation; and as they share the stability of the government, they more and more fill up the place of an aristocracy.

In almost every part of Europe, the government rules in two ways; it rules one portion of the community by the fear which they entertain of its agents, and the other by the hope they have of becoming its agents.

other hand, private individuals grow more and more apt to look upon the supreme power in the same light; they invoke its assistance in all their necessities, and they fix their eyes upon the administration as their mentor or their guide.

I assert that there is no country in Europe in which the public administration has not become, not only more centralized, but more inquisitive and more minute: it everywhere interferes in private concerns more than it did; it regulates more undertakings, and undertakings of a lesser kind; and it gains a firmer footing every day about, above, and around all private persons, to assist, to advise, and to coerce them.

Formerly, a sovereign lived upon the income of his lands, or the revenue of his taxes; this is no longer the case now that his wants have increased as well as his power. Under the same circumstances which formerly compelled a prince to put on a new tax, he now has recourse to a loan. Thus the state gradually becomes the debtor of most of the wealthier members of the community, and centralizes the largest amounts of capital in its own hands.

Small capital is drawn into its keeping by another method. As men are intermingled and conditions become more equal, the poor have more resources, more education, and more desires; they conceive the notion of bettering their condition, and this teaches them to save. These savings are daily producing an infinite number of small capitals, the slow and gradual produce of labor, which are always increasing. But the greater part of this money would be unproductive, if it remained scattered in the hands of its owners. This circumstance has given rise to a philanthropic institution, which will soon become, if I am not mistaken, one of our most important political institutions. Some charitable persons conceived the notion of collecting the savings of the poor and placing them out at interest. In some countries, these benevolent associations are still completely distinct from the state; but in almost all, they manifestly tend to identify themselves with the government; and in some of them, the government has superseded them, taking upon itself the enormous task of centralizing in one place, and putting out at interest, on its own responsibility, the daily savings of many millions of the working classes.

Thus the state draws to itself the wealth of the rich by loans, and has the poor man's mite at its disposal in the savings banks. The wealth of the country is perpetually flowing around the government, and passing through its hands; the accumulation increases in the same proportion as the equality of conditions; for in a democratic country, the state alone inspires private individuals with confidence, because the state alone appears to be endowed with strength and durability.*

Thus the sovereign does not confine himself to the management of the public treasury; he interferes in private money matters; he is the superior, and often the master, of all the members of the community; and, in addition to this, he assumes the part of their steward and paymaster.

The central power not only fulfils of itself the whole of the duties formerly discharged by various authorities, — extending those duties, and surpassing those authorities, — but it performs them with more alertness, strength, and independence than it displayed before. All the governments of Europe have, in our time, singularly improved the science of administration: they do more things, and they do everything with more order, more celerity, and at

* On the one hand, the taste for worldly welfare is perpetually increasing; and, on the other, the government gets more and more complete possession of the sources of that welfare.

Thus men are following two separate roads to servitude; the taste for their own welfare withholds them from taking a part in the government, and their love of that welfare places them in closer dependence upon those who govern.

less expense; they seem to be constantly enriched by all the experience of which they have stripped private persons. From day to day, the princes of Europe hold their subordinate officers under stricter control, and invent new methods for guiding them more closely, and inspecting them with less trouble. Not content with managing everything by their agents, they undertake to manage the conduct of their agents in everything: so that the public administration not only depends upon one and the same power, but it is more and more confined to one spot and concentrated in the same hands. The government centralizes its agency whilst it increases its prerogative; — hence a twofold increase of strength.

In examining the ancient constitution of the judicial power, amongst most European nations, two things strike the mind, — the independence of that power, and the extent of its functions. Not only did the courts of justice decide almost all differences between private persons, but in very many cases they acted as arbiters between private persons and the state.

I do not here allude to the political and administrative functions which courts of judicature had in some countries usurped, but to the judicial duties common to them all. In most of the countries of Europe, there were, and there still are, many private rights, connected for the most part with the general right of property, which stood under the protection of the courts of justice, and which the state could not violate without their sanction. It was this semi-political power which mainly distinguished the European courts of judicature from all others; for all nations have had judges, but all have not invested their judges with the same privileges.

Upon examining what is now occurring amongst the democratic nations of Europe which are called free, as well as amongst the others, it will be observed that new and more dependent courts are everywhere springing up by the side of the old ones, for the express purpose of deciding, by an extraordinary jurisdiction, such litigated matters as may arise between the government and private persons. The elder judicial power retains its independence, but its jurisdiction is narrowed ; and there is a growing tendency to reduce it to be exclusively the arbiter between private interests.

The number of these special courts of justice is continually increasing, and their functions increase likewise. Thus, the government is more and more absolved from the necessity of subjecting its policy and its rights to the sanction of another power. As judges cannot be dispensed with, at least the state is to select them, and always to hold them under its control ; so that between the government and private individuals they place the effigy of justice rather than justice itself. The state is not satisfied with drawing all concerns to itself, but it acquires an ever-increasing power of deciding on them all, without restriction and without appeal.*

There exists amongst the modern nations of Europe one great cause, independent of all those which have already been pointed out, which perpetually contributes to extend the agency or to strengthen the prerogative of the supreme power, though it has not been sufficiently attended to: I mean the growth of manufactures, which is fostered by the progress of social equality. Manufacturers generally collect a multitude of men on the same spot, amongst whom new and complex relations spring up. These men are exposed

* A strange sophism has been uttered on this head in France. When a suit arises between the government and a private person, it is not to be tried before an ordinary judge, — in order, they say, not to mix the administrative and the judicial powers ; as if it were not to mix those powers, and to mix them in the most dangerous and oppressive manner, to invest the government with the office of judging and administering at the same time.

by their calling to great and sudden alternations of plenty and want, during which public tranquillity is endangered. It may also happen that these employments sacrifice the health, and even the life, of those who gain by them, or of those who live by them. Thus, the manufacturing classes require more regulation, superintendence, and restraint than the other classes of society, and it is natural that the powers of government should increase in the same proportion as those classes.

This is a truth of general application; what follows more especially concerns the nations of Europe. In the centuries which preceded that in which we live, the aristocracy was in possession of the soil, and was competent to defend it: landed property was therefore surrounded by ample securities, and its possessors enjoyed great independence. This gave rise to laws and customs which have been perpetuated, notwithstanding the subdivision of lands and the ruin of the nobility; and, at the present time, land-owners and agriculturists are still those amongst the community who most easily escape from the control of the supreme power.

In these same aristocratic ages, in which all the sources of our history are to be traced, personal property was of small importance, and those who possessed it were despised and weak: the manufacturing class formed an exception in the midst of those aristocratic communities; as it had no certain patronage, it was not outwardly protected, and was often unable to protect itself. Hence a habit sprang up of considering manufacturing property as something of a peculiar nature, not entitled to the same deference, and not worthy of the same securities, as property in general; and manufacturers were looked upon as a small class in the social hierarchy, whose independence was of small importance, and who might with propriety be abandoned to the disciplinary passions of princes. On glancing over the codes of the Middle Ages, one is surprised to see, in those periods of personal independence, with what incessant royal regulations manufactures were hampered, even in their smallest details: on this point, centralization was as active and as minute as it can ever be.

Since that time, a great revolution has taken place in the world; manufacturing property, which was then only in the germ, has spread till it covers Europe: the manufacturing class has been multiplied and enriched by the remnants of all other ranks: it has grown, and is still perpetually growing, in number, in importance, in wealth. Almost all those who do not belong to it are connected with it at least on some one point: after having been an exception in society, it threatens to become the chief, if not the only class; nevertheless, the notions and political habits created by it of old still continue. These notions and habits remain unchanged, because they are old, and also because they happen to be in perfect accordance with the new notions and general habits of our contemporaries.

Manufacturing property, then, does not extend its rights in the same ratio as its importance. The manufacturing classes do not become less dependent, whilst they become more numerous; but, on the contrary, it would seem as if despotism lurked within them, and naturally grew with their growth.*

* I shall quote a few facts in corroboration of this remark.

Mines are the natural sources of manufacturing wealth: as manufactures have grown up in Europe, as the produce of mines has become of more general importance, and good mining more difficult from the subdivision of property which is a consequence of the equality of conditions, most governments have asserted a right of owning the soil in which the mines lie, and of inspecting the works, which has never been the case with any other kind of property.

Thus, mines, which were private property, liable to the same obligations and sheltered by the same guaranties as all other landed property, have fallen under the control of the state. The state either works them or farms them; the owners of them are mere tenants, deriving their rights from the

As a nation becomes more engaged in manufactures, the want of roads, canals, harbors, and other works of a semi-public nature, which facilitate the acquisition of wealth, is more strongly felt; and as a nation becomes more democratic, private individuals are less able, and the state more able, to execute works of such magnitude. I do not hesitate to assert, that the manifest tendency of all governments at the present time is to take upon themselves alone the execution of these undertakings, by which means they daily hold in closer dependence the population which they govern.

On the other hand, in proportion as the power of a state increases, and its necessities are augmented, the state consumption of manufactured produce is always growing larger; and these commodities are generally made in the arsenals or establishments of the government. Thus, in every kingdom, the ruler becomes the principal manufacturer: he collects and retains in his service a vast number of engineers, architects, mechanics, and handicraftsmen.

Not only is he the principal manufacturer, but he tends more and more to become the chief, or rather the master, of all other manufacturers. As private persons become powerless by becoming more equal, they can effect nothing in manufactures without combination; but the government naturally seeks to place these combinations under its own control.

state; and, moreover, the state almost everywhere claims the power of directing their operations: it lays down rules, enforces the adoption of particular methods, subjects the mining adventurers to constant superintendence, and, if refractory, they are ousted by a government court of justice, and the government transfers their contract to other hands; so that the government not only possesses the mines, but has all the adventurers in its power. Nevertheless, as manufactures increase, the working of old mines increases also; new ones are opened; the mining population extends and grows up; day by day, governments augment their subterranean dominions, and people them with their agents.

It must be admitted that these collective beings, which are called companies, are stronger and more formidable than a private individual can ever be, and that they have less of the responsibility of their own actions; whence it seems reasonable that they should not be allowed to retain so great an independence of the supreme government as might be conceded to a private individual.

Rulers are the more apt to follow this line of policy, as their own inclinations invite them to it. Amongst democratic nations it is only by association that the resistance of the people to the government can ever display itself: hence the latter always looks with ill-favor on those associations which are not in its own power; and it is well worthy of remark, that, amongst democratic nations, the people themselves often entertain against these very associations a secret feeling of fear and jealousy, which prevents the citizens from defending the institutions of which they stand so much in need. The power and the duration of these small private bodies, in the midst of the weakness and instability of the whole community, astonish and alarm the people; and the free use which each association makes of its natural powers is almost regarded as a dangerous privilege. All the associations which spring up in our age are, moreover, new corporate powers, whose rights have not been sanctioned by time; they come into existence at a time when the notion of private rights is weak, and when the power of government is unbounded; hence it is not surprising that they lose their freedom at their birth.

Amongst all European nations there are some kinds of associations or companies which cannot be formed until the state has examined their by-laws and authorized their existence. In several others, attempts are made to extend this rule to all associations; the consequences of such a policy, if it were successful, may easily be foreseen.

If once the sovereign had a general right of authorizing

associations of all kinds upon certain conditions, he would not be long without claiming the right of superintending and managing them, in order to prevent them from departing from the rules laid down by himself. In this manner, the state, after having reduced all who are desirous of forming associations into dependence, would proceed to reduce into the same condition all who belong to associations already formed, — that is to say, almost all the men who are now in existence.

Governments thus appropriate to themselves and convert to their own purposes the greater part of this new power which manufacturing interests have in our time brought into the world. Manufactures govern us, they govern manufactures.

I attach so much importance to all that I have just been saying, that I am tormented by the fear of having impaired my meaning in seeking to render it more clear. If the reader thinks that the examples I have adduced to support my observations are insufficient or ill-chosen, — if he imagines that I have anywhere exaggerated the encroachments of the supreme power, and, on the other hand, that I have underrated the extent of the sphere which still remains open to the exertions of individual independence, — I entreat him to lay down the book for a moment, and to turn his mind to reflect upon the subjects I have attempted to explain. Let him attentively examine what is taking place in France and in other countries, let him inquire of those about him, let him search himself, and I am much mistaken if he does not arrive, without my guidance, and by other paths, at the point to which I have sought to lead him.

He will perceive that, for the last half-century, centralization has everywhere been growing up in a thousand different ways. Wars, revolutions, conquests, have served to promote it; all men have labored to increase it. In the course of the same period, during which men have succeeded each other with singular rapidity at the head of affairs, their notions, interests, and passions have been infinitely diversified; but all have, by some means or other, sought to centralize. This instinctive centralization has been the only settled point amidst the extreme mutability of their lives and their thoughts.

If the reader, after having investigated these details of human affairs, will seek to survey the wide prospect as a whole, he will be struck by the result. On the one hand, the most settled dynasties shaken or overthrown; the people everywhere escaping by violence from the sway of their laws, — abolishing or limiting the authority of their rulers or their princes; the nations which are not in open revolution restless at least, and excited, — all of them animated by the same spirit of revolt: and, on the other hand, at this very period of anarchy, and amongst these untract able nations, the incessant increase of the prerogative of the supreme government, becoming more centralized, more adventurous, more absolute, more extensive, — the people perpetually falling under the control of the public administration, — led insensibly to surrender to it some further portion of their individual independence, till the very men who from time to time upset a throne and trample on a race of kings, bend more and more obsequiously to the slightest dictate of a clerk. Thus, two contrary revolutions appear, in our days, to be going on; the one continually weakening the supreme power, the other as continually strengthening it: at no other period in our history has it appeared so weak or so strong.

But, upon a more attentive examination of the state of the world, it appears that these two revolutions are intimately connected together, that they originate in the same source, and that, after having followed a separate course, they lead men at last to the same result.

I may venture once more to repeat what I have already said or implied in several parts of this book: great care must be taken not to confound the principle of equality itself with the revolution which finally establishes that principle in the social condition and the laws of a nation: here lies the reason of almost all the phenomena which occasion our astonishment.

All the old political powers of Europe, the greatest as well as the least, were founded in ages of aristocracy, and they more or less represented or defended the principles of inequality and of privilege. To make the novel wants and interests which the growing principle of equality introduced preponderate in government, our contemporaries had to overturn or to coerce the established powers. This led men to make revolutions, and breathed into many of them that fierce love of disturbance and independence, which all revolutions, whatever be their object, always engender.

I do not believe that there is a single country in Europe in which the progress of equality has not been preceded or followed by some violent changes in the state of property and persons; and almost all these changes have been attended with much anarchy and license, because they have been made by the least civilized portion of the nation against that which is most civilized.

Hence proceeded the twofold contrary tendencies which I have just pointed out. As long as the democratic revolution was glowing with heat, the men who were bent upon the destruction of old aristocratic powers hostile to that revolution displayed a strong spirit of independence; but as the victory of the principle of equality became more complete, they gradually surrendered themselves to the propensities natural to that condition of equality, and they strengthened and centralized their governments. They had sought to be free in order to make themselves equal;

but in proportion as equality was more established by the aid of freedom, freedom itself was thereby rendered of more difficult attainment.

These two states of a nation have sometimes been contemporaneous: the last generation in France showed how a people might organize a stupendous tyranny in the community, at the very time when they were baffling the authority of the nobility and braving the power of all kings, — at once teaching the world the way to win freedom, and the way to lose it.

In our days, men see that constituted powers are crumbling down on every side, — they see all ancient authority dying out, all ancient barriers tottering to their fall, and the judgment of the wisest is troubled at the sight: they attend only to the amazing revolution which is taking place before their eyes, and they imagine that mankind is about to fall into perpetual anarchy: if they looked to the final consequences of this revolution, their fears would perhaps assume a different shape. For myself, I confess that I put no trust in the spirit of freedom which appears to animate my contemporaries. I see well enough that the nations of this age are turbulent, but I do not clearly perceive that they are liberal; and I fear lest, at the close of those perturbations which rock the base of thrones, the dominion of sovereigns may prove more powerful than it ever was before.

CHAPTER VI.

WHAT SORT OF DESPOTISM DEMOCRATIC NATIONS HAVE TO FEAR.

I HAD remarked during my stay in the United States, that a democratic state of society, similar to that of the Americans, might offer singular facilities for the establishment of despotism; and I perceived, upon my return to Europe, how much use had already been made, by most of our rulers, of the notions, the sentiments, and the wants created by this same social condition, for the purpose of extending the circle of their power. This led me to think that the nations of Christendom would perhaps eventually undergo some oppression like that which hung over several of the nations of the ancient world.

A more accurate examination of the subject, and five years of further meditation, have not diminished my fears, but have changed the object of them.

No sovereign ever lived in former ages so absolute or so powerful as to undertake to administer by his own agency, and without the assistance of intermediate powers, all the parts of a great empire: none ever attempted to subject all his subjects indiscriminately to strict uniformity of regulation, and personally to tutor and direct every member of the community. The notion of such an undertaking never occurred to the human mind; and if any man had conceived it, the want of information, the imperfection of the administrative system, and, above all, the natural obstacles caused by the inequality of conditions, would speedily have checked the execution of so vast a design.

When the Roman Emperors were at the height of their power, the different nations of the empire still preserved manners and customs of great diversity; although they were subject to the same monarch, most of the provinces were separately administered; they abounded in powerful and active municipalities; and although the whole government of the empire was centred in the hands of the Emperor alone, and he always remained, in case of need, the supreme arbiter in all matters, yet the details of social life and private occupations lay for the most part beyond his control. The Emperors possessed, it is true, an immense and unchecked power, which allowed them to gratify all their whimsical tastes, and to employ for that purpose the whole strength of the state. They frequently abused that power arbitrarily to deprive their subjects of property or of life: their tyranny was extremely onerous to the few, but it did not reach the many; it was fixed to some few main objects, and neglected the rest; it was violent, but its range was limited.

It would seem that, if despotism were to be established amongst the democratic nations of our days, it might assume a different character; it would be more extensive and more mild; it would degrade men without tormenting them. I do not question, that, in an age of instruction and equality like our own, sovereigns might more easily succeed in collecting all political power into their own hands, and might interfere more habitually and decidedly with the circle of private interests, than any sovereign of antiquity could ever do. But this same principle of equality which facilitates despotism, tempers its rigor. We have seen how the manners of society become more humane and gentle, in proportion as men become more equal and alike. When no member of the community has much power or much wealth, tyranny is, as it were, without opportunities and a field of action. As all fortunes are scanty, the passions of men are naturally circumscribed, their imagination limited, their pleasures simple. This universal moderation moderates the sovereign himself, and checks within certain limits the inordinate stretch of his desires.

Independently of these reasons, drawn from the nature of the state of society itself, I might add many others arising from causes beyond my subject; but I shall keep within the limits I have laid down.

Democratic governments may become violent, and even cruel, at certain periods of extreme effervescence or of great danger; but these crises will be rare and brief. When I consider the petty passions of our contemporaries, the mildness of their manners, the extent of their education, the purity of their religion, the gentleness of their morality, their regular and industrious habits, and the restraint which they almost all observe in their vices no less than in their virtues, I have no fear that they will meet with tyrants in their rulers, but rather with guardians.*

I think, then, that the species of oppression by which democratic nations are menaced is unlike anything which ever before existed in the world: our contemporaries will find no prototype of it in their memories. I seek in vain for an expression which will accurately convey the whole of the idea I have formed of it; the old words despotism and tyranny are inappropriate: the thing itself is new, and since I cannot name, I must attempt to define it.

I seek to trace the novel features under which despotism may appear in the world. The first thing that strikes the observation is an innumerable multitude of men, all equal and alike, incessantly endeavoring to procure the petty and paltry pleasures with which they glut their lives. Each of them, living apart, is as a stranger to the fate of all the rest,—his children and his private friends constitute to him the whole of mankind; as for the rest of his fellow-

* See Appendix X.

citizens, he is close to them, but he sees them not;—he touches them, but he feels them not; he exists but in himself and for himself alone; and if his kindred still remain to him, he may be said at any rate to have lost his country.

Above this race of men stands an immense and tutelary power, which takes upon itself alone to secure their gratifications, and to watch over their fate. That power is absolute, minute, regular, provident, and mild. It would be like the authority of a parent, if, like that authority, its object was to prepare men for manhood; but it seeks, on the contrary, to keep them in perpetual childhood: it is well content that the people should rejoice, provided they think of nothing but rejoicing. For their happiness such a government willingly labors, but it chooses to be the sole agent and the only arbiter of that happiness; it provides for their security, foresees and supplies their necessities, facilitates their pleasures, manages their principal concerns, directs their industry, regulates the descent of property, and subdivides their inheritances: what remains, but to spare them all the care of thinking and all the trouble of living?

Thus, it every day renders the exercise of the free agency of man less useful and less frequent; it circumscribes the will within a narrower range, and gradually robs a man of all the uses of himself. The principle of equality has prepared men for these things; it has predisposed men to endure them, and oftentimes to look on them as benefits.

After having thus successively taken each member of the community in its powerful grasp, and fashioned him at will, the supreme power then extends its arm over the whole community. It covers the surface of society with a network of small complicated rules, minute and uniform, through which the most original minds and the most energetic characters cannot penetrate, to rise above the crowd.

The will of man is not shattered, but softened, bent, and guided; men are seldom forced by it to act, but they are constantly restrained from acting: such a power does not destroy, but it prevents existence; it does not tyrannize, but it compresses, enervates, extinguishes, and stupefies a people, till each nation is reduced to be nothing better than a flock of timid and industrious animals, of which the government is the shepherd.

I have always thought that servitude of the regular, quiet, and gentle kind which I have just described might be combined more easily than is commonly believed with some of the outward forms of freedom, and that it might even establish itself under the wing of the sovereignty of the people.

Our contemporaries are constantly excited by two conflicting passions; they want to be led, and they wish to remain free: as they cannot destroy either the one or the other of these contrary propensities, they strive to satisfy them both at once. They devise a sole, tutelary, and all-powerful form of government, but elected by the people. They combine the principle of centralization and that of popular sovereignty; this gives them a respite: they console themselves for being in tutelage by the reflection that they have chosen their own guardians. Every man allows himself to be put in leading-strings, because he sees that it is not a person or a class of persons, but the people at large, who hold the end of his chain.

By this system, the people shake off their state of dependence just long enough to select their master, and then relapse into it again. A great many persons at the present day are quite contented with this sort of compromise between administrative despotism and the sovereignty of the people; and they think they have done enough for the protection of individual freedom when they have surrendered it to the power of the nation at large. This does not satisfy me: the nature of him I am to obey signifies less to me than the fact of extorted obedience.

I do not, however, deny that a constitution of this kind appears to me to be infinitely preferable to one which, after having concentrated all the powers of government, should vest them in the hands of an irresponsible person or body of persons. Of all the forms which democratic despotism could assume, the latter would assuredly be the worst.

When the sovereign is elective, or narrowly watched by a legislature which is really elective and independent, the oppression which he exercises over individuals is sometimes greater, but it is always less degrading; because every man, when he is oppressed and disarmed, may still imagine that, whilst he yields obedience, it is to himself he yields it, and that it is to one of his own inclinations that all the rest give way. In like manner, I can understand that, when the sovereign represents the nation, and is dependent upon the people, the rights and the power of which every citizen is deprived not only serve the head of the state, but the state itself; and that private persons derive some return from the sacrifice of their independence which they have made to the public. To create a representation of the people in every centralized country is, therefore, to diminish the evil which extreme centralization may produce, but not to get rid of it.

I admit that, by this means, room is left for the intervention of individuals in the more important affairs; but it is not the less suppressed in the smaller and more private ones. It must not be forgotten that it is especially dangerous to enslave men in the minor details of life. For my own part, I should be inclined to think freedom less necessary in great things than in little ones, if it were possible to be secure of the one without possessing the other.

Subjection in minor affairs breaks out every day, and is felt by the whole community indiscriminately. It does not drive men to resistance, but it crosses them at every turn, till they are led to surrender the exercise of their own will. Thus their spirit is gradually broken and their character enervated; whereas that obedience which is exacted on a few important but rare occasions, only exhibits servitude at certain intervals, and throws the burden of it upon a small number of men. It is in vain to summon a people, who have been rendered so dependent on the central power, to choose from time to time the representatives of that power; this rare and brief exercise of their free choice, however important it may be, will not prevent them from gradually losing the faculties of thinking, feeling, and acting for themselves, and thus gradually falling below the level of humanity.*

I add, that they will soon become incapable of exercising the great and only privilege which remains to them. The democratic nations which have introduced freedom into their political constitution, at the very time when they were augmenting the despotism of their administrative constitution, have been led into strange paradoxes. To manage those minor affairs in which good sense is all that is wanted, — the people are held to be unequal to the task; but when the government of the country is at stake, the people are invested with immense powers; they are alternately made the playthings of their ruler, and his masters, — more than kings, and less than men. After having exhausted all the different modes of election, without finding one to suit their purpose, they are still amazed, and still bent on seeking further; as if the evil they remark did not originate in the constitution of the country, far more than in that of the electoral body.

It is, indeed, difficult to conceive how men who have entirely given up the habit of self-government should succeed in making a proper choice of those by whom they are

* See Appendix Y.

to be governed; and no one will ever believe that a liberal, wise, and energetic government can spring from the suffrages of a subservient people.

A constitution which should be republican in its head, and ultra-monarchical in all its other parts, has ever appeared to me to be a short-lived monster. The vices of rulers and the inaptitude of the people would speedily bring about its ruin; and the nation, weary of its representatives and of itself, would create freer institutions, or soon return to stretch itself at the feet of a single master.

CHAPTER VII.

CONTINUATION OF THE PRECEDING CHAPTERS.

I BELIEVE that it is easier to establish an absolute and despotic government amongst a people in which the conditions of society are equal, than amongst any other; and I think that, if such a government were once established amongst such a people, it would not only oppress men, but would eventually strip each of them of several of the highest qualities of humanity. Despotism, therefore, appears to me peculiarly to be dreaded in democratic times. I should have loved freedom, I believe, at all times, but in the time in which we live I am ready to worship it.

On the other hand, I am persuaded that all who shall attempt, in the ages upon which we are entering, to base freedom upon aristocratic privilege, will fail; that all who shall attempt to draw and to retain authority within a single class, will fail. At the present day, no ruler is skilful or strong enough to found a despotism by re-establishing permanent distinctions of rank amongst his subjects: no legislator is wise or powerful enough to preserve free institutions, if he does not take equality for his first principle and his watchword. All of our contemporaries who would establish or secure the independence and the dignity of their fellow-men, must show themselves the friends of equality; and the only worthy means of showing themselves as such is to be so: upon this depends the success of their holy enterprise. Thus, the question is not how to reconstruct aristocratic society, but how to make liberty proceed out of that democratic state of society in which God has placed us.

These two truths appear to me simple, clear, and fertile in consequences; and they naturally lead me to consider what kind of free government can be established amongst a people in which social conditions are equal.

It results, from the very constitution of democratic nations and from their necessities, that the power of government amongst them must be more uniform, more centralized, more extensive, more searching, and more efficient than in other countries. Society at large is naturally stronger and more active, the individual more subordinate and weak; the former does more, the latter less; and this is inevitably the case.

It is not, therefore, to be expected that the range of private independence will ever be as extensive in democratic as in aristocratic countries;—nor is this to be desired; for, amongst aristocratic nations, the mass is often sacrificed to the individual, and the prosperity of the greater number to the greatness of the few. It is both necessary and desirable that the government of a democratic people should be active and powerful: and our object should not be to render it weak or indolent, but solely to prevent it from abusing its aptitude and its strength.

The circumstance which most contributed to secure the independence of private persons in aristocratic ages was, that the supreme power did not affect to take upon itself alone the government and administration of the community; those functions were necessarily partially left to the members of the aristocracy: so that, as the supreme power was always divided, it never weighed with its whole weight and in the same manner on each individual.

Not only did the government not perform everything by its immediate agency; but, as most of the agents who discharged its duties derived their power, not from the state, but from the circumstance of their birth, they were not perpetually under its control. The government could not make or unmake them in an instant, at pleasure, or bend them in strict uniformity to its slightest caprice; — this was an additional guaranty of private independence.

I readily admit that recourse cannot be had to the same means at the present time; but I discover certain democratic expedients which may be substituted for them. Instead of vesting in the government alone all the administrative powers of which corporations and nobles have been deprived, a portion of them may be intrusted to secondary public bodies temporarily composed of private citizens: thus the liberty of private persons will be more secure, and their equality will not be diminished.

The Americans, who care less for words than the French, still designate by the name of County the largest of their administrative districts; but the duties of the count or lord-lieutenant are in part performed by a provincial assembly.

At a period of equality like our own, it would be unjust and unreasonable to institute hereditary officers; but there is nothing to prevent us from substituting elective public officers to a certain extent. Election is a democratic expedient, which insures the independence of the public officer in relation to the government as much as hereditary rank can insure it amongst aristocratic nations, and even more so.

Aristocratic countries abound in wealthy and influential persons who are competent to provide for themselves, and who cannot be easily or secretly oppressed: such persons restrain a government within general habits of moderation and reserve. I am well aware that democratic countries contain no such persons naturally; but something analogous to them may be created by artificial means. I firmly believe that an aristocracy cannot again be founded in the world; but I think that private citizens, by combining together, may constitute bodies of great wealth, influence, and strength, corresponding to the persons of an aristocracy. By this means, many of the greatest political advantages of aristocracy would be obtained, without its injustice or its dangers. An association for political, commercial, or manufacturing purposes, or even for those of science and literature, is a powerful and enlightened member of the community, which cannot be disposed of at pleasure, or oppressed without remonstrance; and which, by defending its own rights against the encroachments of the government, saves the common liberties of the country.

In periods of aristocracy, every man is always bound so closely to many of his fellow-citizens that he cannot be assailed without their coming to his assistance. In ages of equality, every man naturally stands alone; he has no hereditary friends whose co-operation he may demand; no class upon whose sympathy he may rely: he is easily got rid of, and he is trampled on with impunity. At the present time, an oppressed member of the community has therefore only one method of self-defence, — he may appeal to the whole nation; and if the whole nation is deaf to his complaint, he may appeal to mankind: the only means he has of making this appeal is by the press. Thus, the liberty of the press is infinitely more valuable amongst democratic nations than amongst all others; it is the only cure for the evils which equality may produce. Equality sets men apart and weakens them; but the press places a powerful weapon within every man's reach, which the weakest and loneliest of them all may use. Equality deprives a man of the support of his connections; but the press enables him to summon all his fellow-countrymen and all his fellow-men to his assistance. Printing has accelerated the progress of equality, and it is also one of its best correctives.

I think that men living in aristocracies may, strictly speaking, do without the liberty of the press: but such is not the case with those who live in democratic countries. To protect their personal independence I trust not to great political assemblies, to parliamentary privilege, or to the assertion of popular sovereignty. All these things may, to a certain extent, be reconciled with personal servitude. But that servitude cannot be complete if the press is free: the press is the chief democratic instrument of freedom.

Something analogous may be said of the judicial power. It is a part of the essence of judicial power to attend to private interests, and to fix itself with predilection on minute objects submitted to its observation: another essential quality of judicial power is never to volunteer its assistance to the oppressed, but always to be at the disposal of the humblest of those who solicit it; their complaint, however feeble they may themselves be, will force itself upon the ear of justice and claim redress, for this is inherent in the very constitution of courts of justice.

A power of this kind is therefore peculiarly adapted to the wants of freedom, at a time when the eye and finger of the government are constantly intruding into the minutest details of human actions, and when private persons are at once too weak to protect themselves, and too much isolated for them to reckon upon the assistance of their fellows. The strength of the courts of law has ever been the greatest security which can be offered to personal independence; but this is more especially the case in democratic ages: private rights and interests are in constant danger, if the judicial power does not grow more extensive and more strong to keep pace with the growing equality of conditions.

Equality awakens in men several propensities extremely dangerous to freedom, to which the attention of the legislator ought constantly to be directed. I shall only remind the reader of the most important amongst them.

Men living in democratic ages do not readily comprehend the utility of forms: they feel an instinctive contempt for them, — I have elsewhere shown for what reasons. Forms excite their contempt, and often their hatred; as they commonly aspire to none but easy and present gratifications, they rush onwards to the object of their desires, and the slightest delay exasperates them. This same temper, carried with them into political life, renders them hostile to forms, which perpetually retard or arrest them in some of their projects.

Yet this objection, which the men of democracies make to forms, is the very thing which renders forms so useful to freedom; for their chief merit is to serve as a barrier between the strong and the weak, the ruler and the people, to retard the one, and give the other time to look about him. Forms become more necessary in proportion as the government becomes more active and more powerful, whilst private persons are becoming more indolent and more feeble. Thus democratic nations naturally stand more in need of forms than other nations, and they naturally respect them less. This deserves most serious attention.

Nothing is more pitiful than the arrogant disdain of most of our contemporaries for questions of form; for the smallest questions of form have acquired in our time an importance which they never had before: many of the greatest interests of mankind depend upon them. I think, that, if the statesmen of aristocratic ages could sometimes contemn forms with impunity, and frequently rise above them, the statesmen to whom the government of nations is now confided ought to treat the very least among them with respect, and not neglect them without imperious necessity. In aristocracies, the observance of forms was superstitious; amongst us, they ought to be kept up with a deliberate and enlightened deference.

Another tendency, which is extremely natural to democratic nations and extremely dangerous, is that which leads them to despise and undervalue the rights of private persons. The attachment which men feel to a right, and the respect which they display for it, is generally proportioned to its importance, or to the length of time during which they have enjoyed it. The rights of private persons amongst democratic nations are commonly of small importance, of recent growth, and extremely precarious; the consequence is, that they are often sacrificed without regret, and almost always violated without remorse.

But it happens that, at the same period and amongst the same nations in which men conceive a natural contempt for the rights of private persons, the rights of society at large are naturally extended and consolidated: in other words, men become less attached to private rights just when it is most necessary to retain and defend what little remains of them. It is therefore most especially in the present democratic times, that the true friends of the liberty and the greatness of man ought constantly to be on the alert, to prevent the power of government from lightly sacrificing the private rights of individuals to the general execution of its designs. At such times, no citizen is so obscure that it is not very dangerous to allow him to be oppressed; no private rights are so unimportant that they can be surrendered with impunity to the caprices of a government. The reason is plain: — if the private right of an individual is violated at a time when the human mind is fully impressed with the importance and the sanctity of such rights, the injury done is confined to the individual whose right is infringed; but to violate such a right at the present day is deeply to corrupt the manners of the nation, and to put the whole community in jeopardy, because the very notion of this kind of right constantly tends amongst us to be impaired and lost.

There are certain habits, certain notions, and certain vices which are peculiar to a state of revolution, and which a protracted revolution cannot fail to create and to propagate, whatever be, in other respects, its character, its purpose, and the scene on which it takes place. When any nation has, within a short space of time, repeatedly varied its rulers, its opinions, and its laws, the men of whom it is composed eventually contract a taste for change, and grow accustomed to see all changes effected by sudden violence. Thus they naturally conceive a contempt for forms which daily prove ineffectual; and they do not support, without impatience, the dominion of rules which they have so often seen infringed.

As the ordinary notions of equity and morality no longer suffice to explain and justify all the innovations daily begotten by a revolution, the principle of public utility is called in, the doctrine of political necessity is conjured up, and men accustom themselves to sacrifice private interests without scruple, and to trample on the rights of individuals in order more speedily to accomplish any public purpose.

These habits and notions, which I shall call revolutionary, because all revolutions produce them, occur in aristocracies just as much as amongst democratic nations; but amongst the former they are often less powerful and always less lasting, because there they meet with habits, notions, defects, and impediments, which counteract them: they consequently disappear as soon as the revolution is terminated, and the nation reverts to its former political courses. This is not always the case in democratic countries, in which it is ever to be feared that revolutionary tendencies, becoming more gentle and more regular, without entirely disappearing from society, will be gradually transformed into habits of subjection to the administrative authority of the government. I know of no countries in which revolutions are more dangerous than in democratic countries; because, independently of the accidental and transient evils which must always attend them, they may always create some evils which are permanent and unending.

I believe that there are such things as justifiable resistance and legitimate rebellion: I do not therefore assert, as an absolute proposition, that the men of democratic ages ought never to make revolutions; but I think that they have especial reason to hesitate before they embark in them, and that it is far better to endure many grievances in their present condition, than to have recourse to so perilous a remedy.

I shall conclude by one general idea, which comprises not only all the particular ideas which have been expressed in the present chapter, but also most of those which it is the object of this book to treat of. In the ages of aristocracy which preceded our own, there were private persons of great power, and a social authority of extreme weakness.. The outline of society itself was not easily discernible, and constantly confounded with the different powers by which the community was ruled. The principal efforts of the men of those times were required to strengthen, aggrandize, and secure the supreme power; and, on the other hand, to circumscribe individual independence within narrower limits, and to subject private interests to the interests of the public. Other perils and other cares await the men of our age. Amongst the greater part of modern nations, the government, whatever may be its origin, its constitution, or its name, has become almost omnipotent, and private persons are falling, more and more, into the lowest stage of weakness and dependence.

In olden society, everything was different; unity and uniformity were nowhere to be met with. In modern society, everything threatens to become so much alike, that the peculiar characteristics of each individual will soon be entirely lost in the general aspect of the world. Our forefathers were ever prone to make an improper use of the notion that private rights ought to be respected; and we are naturally prone, on the other hand, to exaggerate the idea that the interest of a private individual ought always to bend to the interest of the many.

The political world is metamorphosed: new remedies must henceforth be sought for new disorders. To lay down extensive but distinct and settled limits to the action of the government; to confer certain rights on private persons, and to secure to them the undisputed enjoyment of those rights; to enable individual man to maintain whatever independence, strength, and original power he still possesses; to raise him by the side of society at large, and uphold him in that position, — these appear to me the main objects of legislators in the ages upon which we are now entering.

It would seem as if the rulers of our time sought only to use men in order to make things great; I wish that they would try a little more to make great men; that they would set less value on the work, and more upon the workman; that they would never forget that a nation cannot long remain strong when every man belonging to it is individually weak; and that no form or combination of social polity has yet been devised to make an energetic people out of a community of pusillanimous and enfeebled citizens.

I trace amongst our contemporaries two contrary notions which are equally injurious. One set of men can perceive nothing in the principle of equality but the anarchical tendencies which it engenders: they dread their own free agency, they fear themselves. Other thinkers, less numerous but more enlightened, take a different view: beside that track which starts from the principle of equality to terminate in anarchy, they have at last discovered the road which seems to lead men to inevitable servitude. They shape their souls beforehand to this necessary condition; and, despairing of remaining free, they already do obeisance in their hearts to the master who is soon to appear. The former abandon freedom because they think it dangerous; the latter, because they hold it to be impossible.

If I had entertained the latter conviction, I should not

have written this book, but I should have confined myself to deploring in secret the destiny of mankind. I have sought to point out the dangers to which the principle of equality exposes the independence of man, because I firmly believe that these dangers are the most formidable, as well as the least foreseen, of all those which futurity holds in store; but I do not think that they are insurmountable.

The men who live in the democratic ages upon which we are entering have naturally a taste for independence; they are naturally impatient of regulation, and they are wearied by the permanence even of the condition they themselves prefer. They are fond of power; but they are prone to despise and hate those who wield it, and they easily elude its grasp by their own mobility and insignificance.

These propensities will always manifest themselves, because they originate in the groundwork of society, which will undergo no change: for a long time they will prevent the establishment of any despotism, and they will furnish fresh weapons to each succeeding generation which shall struggle in favor of the liberty of mankind. Let us, then, look forward to the future with that salutary fear which makes men keep watch and ward for freedom, not with that faint and idle terror which depresses and enervates the heart.

CHAPTER VIII.

GENERAL SURVEY OF THE SUBJECT.

BEFORE closing forever the subject that I have now discussed, I would fain take a parting survey of all the different characteristics of modern society, and appreciate at last the general influence to be exercised by the principle of equality upon the fate of mankind; but I am stopped by the difficulty of the task, and, in presence of so great a theme, my sight is troubled, and my reason fails.

The society of the modern world, which I have sought to delineate, and which I seek to judge, has but just come into existence. Time has not yet shaped it into perfect form; the great revolution by which it has been created is not yet over; and, amidst the occurrences of our time, it is almost impossible to discern what will pass away with the revolution itself, and what will survive its close. The world which is rising into existence is still half encumbered by the remains of the world which is waning into decay; and, amidst the vast perplexity of human affairs, none can say how much of ancient institutions and former manners will remain, or how much will completely disappear.

Although the revolution which is taking place in the social condition, the laws, the opinions, and the feelings of men is still very far from being terminated, yet its results already admit of no comparison with anything that the world has ever before witnessed. I go back from age to age up to the remotest antiquity, but I find no parallel to what is occurring before my eyes: as the past has ceased to throw its light upon the future, the mind of man wanders in obscurity.

Nevertheless, in the midst of a prospect so wide, so novel, and so confused, some of the more prominent characteristics may already be discerned and pointed out. The good things and the evils of life are more equally distributed in the world: great wealth tends to disappear, the number of small fortunes to increase; desires and gratifications are multiplied, but extraordinary prosperity and irremediable penury are alike unknown. The sentiment of ambition is universal, but the scope of ambition is seldom vast. Each individual stands apart in solitary weakness; but society at large is active, provident, and powerful: the performances of private persons are insignificant, those of the state immense.

There is little energy of character, but manners are mild, and laws humane. If there be few instances of exalted heroism or of virtues of the highest, brightest, and purest temper, men's habits are regular, violence is rare, and cruelty almost unknown. Human existence becomes longer, and property more secure: life is not adorned with brilliant trophies, but it is extremely easy and tranquil. Few pleasures are either very refined or very coarse; and highly polished manners are as uncommon as great brutality of tastes. Neither men of great learning, nor extremely ignorant communities, are to be met with; genius becomes more rare, information more diffused. The human mind is impelled by the small efforts of all mankind combined together, not by the strenuous activity of a few men. There is less perfection, but more abundance, in all the productions of the arts. The ties of race, of rank, and of country are relaxed; the great bond of humanity is strengthened.

If I endeavor to find out the most general and most prominent of all these different characteristics, I perceive that what is taking place in men's fortunes manifests itself under a thousand other forms. Almost all extremes are softened or blunted: all that was most prominent is superseded by some middle term, at once less lofty and less low, less brilliant and less obscure, than what before existed in the world.

When I survey this countless multitude of beings, shaped in each other's likeness, amidst whom nothing rises and nothing falls, the sight of such universal uniformity saddens and chills me, and I am tempted to regret that state of society which has ceased to be. When the world was full of men of great importance and extreme insignificance, of great wealth and extreme poverty, of great learning and extreme ignorance, I turned aside from the latter to fix my observation on the former alone, who gratified my sympathies. But I admit that this gratification arose from my own weakness: it is because I am unable to see at once all that is around me, that I am allowed thus to select and separate the objects of my predilection from among so many others. Such is not the case with that Almighty and Eternal Being, whose gaze necessarily includes the whole of created things, and who surveys distinctly, though at once, mankind and man.

We may naturally believe that it is not the singular prosperity of the few, but the greater well-being of all, which is most pleasing in the sight of the Creator and Preserver of men. What appears to me to be man's decline is, to His eye, advancement; what afflicts me is acceptable to Him. A state of equality is perhaps less elevated, but it is more just: and its justice constitutes its greatness and its beauty. I would strive, then, to raise myself to this point of the Divine contemplation, and thence to view and to judge the concerns of men.

No man, upon the earth, can as yet affirm, absolutely and generally, that the new state of the world is better than its former one; but it is already easy to perceive that this state is different. Some vices and some virtues were so inherent in the constitution of an aristocratic nation, and are so opposite to the character of a modern people, that they can never be infused into it; some good tendencies and some bad propensities which were unknown to the former, are natural to the latter; some ideas suggest themselves spontaneously to the imagination of the one, which are utterly repugnant to the mind of the other. They are like two distinct orders of human beings, each of which has its own merits and defects, its own advantages and its own evils. Care must therefore be taken not to judge the state of society which is now coming into existence, by notions derived from a state of society which no longer exists; for, as these states of society are exceedingly different in their structure, they cannot be submitted to a just or fair comparison. It would be scarcely more reasonable to require of our contemporaries the peculiar virtues which originated in the social condition of their forefathers, since that social condition is itself fallen, and has drawn into one promiscuous ruin the good and evil which belonged to it.

But as yet these things are imperfectly understood. I find that a great number of my contemporaries undertake to make a selection from amongst the institutions, the opinions, and the ideas which originated in the aristocratic constitution of society as it was: a portion of these elements they would willingly relinquish, but they would keep the remainder and transplant them into their new world. I apprehend that such men are wasting their time and their strength in virtuous but unprofitable efforts. The object is, not to retain the peculiar advantages which the inequality of conditions bestows upon mankind, but to secure the new benefits which equality may supply. We have not to seek to make ourselves like our progenitors, but to strive to work out that species of greatness and happiness which is our own.

For myself, who now look back from this extreme limit

of my task, and discover from afar, but at once, the various objects which have attracted my more attentive investigation upon my way, I am full of apprehensions and of hopes. I perceive mighty dangers which it is possible to ward off, — mighty evils which may be avoided or alleviated; and I cling with a firmer hold to the belief, that, for democratic nations to be virtuous and prosperous, they require but to will it.

I am aware that many of my contemporaries maintain that nations are never their own masters here below, and that they necessarily obey some insurmountable and unintelligent power, arising from anterior events, from their race, or from the soil and climate of their country. Such principles are false and cowardly; such principles can never produce aught but feeble men and pusillanimous nations. Providence has not created mankind entirely independent or entirely free. It is true, that around every man a fatal circle is traced, beyond which he cannot pass; but within the wide verge of that circle he is powerful and free: as it is with man, so with communities. The nations of our time cannot prevent the conditions of men from becoming equal; but it depends upon themselves whether the principle of equality is to lead them to servitude or freedom, to knowledge or barbarism, to prosperity or wretchedness.

APPENDIX.

Appendix A. — Vol. I. p. 22.

FOR information concerning all the countries of the West which have not yet been visited by Europeans, consult the account of two expeditions undertaken at the expense of Congress by Major Long. This traveller particularly mentions, on the subject of the great American desert, that a line may be drawn nearly parallel to the 20th degree of longitude (meridian of Washington, 97° of Greenwich), beginning from the Red River, and ending at the River Platte. From this imaginary line to the Rocky Mountains, which bound the valley of the Mississippi on the west, lie immense plains, which are generally covered with sand incapable of cultivation, or scattered over with masses of granite. In summer, these plains are destitute of water, and nothing is to be seen on them but herds of buffaloes and wild horses. Some hordes of Indians are also found there, but in no great numbers.

Major Long was told that, in travelling northwards from the River Platte, you find the same desert lying constantly on the left; but he was unable to ascertain the truth of this report. (Long's Expedition, Vol. II. p. 361.)

However worthy of confidence may be the narrative of Major Long, it must be remembered that he only passed through the country of which he speaks, without deviating widely from the line which he had traced out for his journey.

Appendix B. — Vol. I. p. 24.

SOUTH America, in the regions between the tropics, produces an incredible profusion of climbing plants, of which the Flora of the Antilles alone furnishes forty different species.

Among the most graceful of these shrubs is the Passion-flower, which, according to Descourtiz, climbs trees by means of the tendrils with which it is provided, and forms moving bowers of rich and elegant festoons, decorated with blue and purple flowers, and fragrant with perfume. (Vol. I. p. 265.)

The *Mimosa scandens* (*Acacia à grandes gousses*) is a creeper of enormous and rapid growth, which climbs from tree to tree, and sometimes covers more than half a league. (Vol. III. p. 227.)

Appendix C. — Vol. I. p. 26.

THE languages which are spoken by the Indians of America, from the Pole to Cape Horn, are said to be all formed upon the same model, and subject to the same grammatical rules; whence it may fairly be concluded that all the Indian nations sprang from the same stock.

Each tribe of the American continent speaks a different dialect; but the number of languages, properly so called, is very small, — a fact which tends to prove that the nations of the New World had not a very remote origin.

Moreover, the languages of America have a great degree of regularity, from which it seems probable that the tribes which employ them had not undergone any great revolutions, or been incorporated, voluntarily or by constraint, with foreign nations; for it is generally the union of several languages into one which produces grammatical irregularities.

It is not long since the American languages, especially those of the North, first attracted the serious attention of philologists, when the discovery was made, that this idiom of a barbarous people was the product of a complicated system of ideas and very learned combinations. These languages were found to be very rich, and great pains had been taken at their formation to render them agreeable to the ear.

The grammatical system of the Americans differs from all others in several points, but especially in the following: —

Some nations of Europe, amongst others the Germans, have the power of combining at pleasure different expressions, and thus giving a complex sense to certain words. The Indians have given a most surprising extension to this power, so as to connect a great number of ideas with a single term. This will be easily understood with the help of an example quoted by Mr. Duponceau, in the Memoirs of the Philosophical Society of America.

"A Delaware woman playing with a cat or a young dog," says this writer, "is heard to pronounce the word *kuligatschis*, which is thus composed: *k* is the sign of the second person, and signifies 'thou' or 'thy'; *uli* is a part of the word *wulit*, which signifies 'beautiful,' 'pretty'; *gat* is another fragment of the word *wichgat*, which means 'paw'; and, lastly, *schis* is a diminutive giving the idea of smallness. Thus, in one word, the Indian woman has expressed, 'Thy pretty little paw.'"

Take another example of the felicity with which the savages of America have composed their words. A young man, in the Delaware tongue, is called *pilapé*. This word is formed from *pilsit*, chaste, innocent; and *lenapé*, man; — viz. man in his purity and innocence.

This facility of combining words is most remarkable in the strange formation of their verbs. The most complex action is often expressed by a single verb, which serves to convey all the shades of an idea by the modification of its construction.

Those who may wish to examine more in detail this subject, which I have only glanced at superficially, should read, —

1. The correspondence of Mr. Duponceau and the Rev. Mr. Heckewelder relative to the Indian languages, found in the first volume of the Memoirs of the Philosophical Society of America, published at Philadelphia, 1819.

2. The grammar of the Delaware or Lenape language by

Geiberger, and the Preface of Mr. Duponceau. All these are in the same collection, Vol. III.

3. An excellent account of these works, which is at the end of the sixth volume of the American Encyclopædia.

Appendix D. — Vol. I. p. 28.

SEE, in Charlevoix, Vol. I. p. 235, the history of the first war which the French inhabitants of Canada carried on, in 1610, against the Iroquois. The latter, armed with bows and arrows, offered a desperate resistance to the French and their allies. Charlevoix is not a great painter, yet he exhibits clearly enough in this narrative the contrast between the European manners and those of savages, as well as the different sense which the two races had of honor.

When the French, says he, seized upon the beaver-skins which covered the Indians who had fallen, the Hurons, their allies, were greatly offended at this proceeding; but they set to work in their usual manner, inflicting horrid cruelties upon the prisoners, and devouring one of those who had been killed, which made the Frenchmen shudder. Thus the barbarians prided themselves upon a disinterestedness which they were surprised at not finding in our nation, and could not understand that there was less to reprehend in stripping dead bodies than in devouring their flesh like wild beasts.

Charlevoix, in another place (Vol. I. p. 230), thus describes the first torture of which Champlain was an eyewitness, and the return of the Hurons into their own village.

"Having proceeded about eight leagues," says he, "our allies halted; and having singled out one of their captives, they reproached him with all the cruelties which he had practised upon the warriors of their nation who had fallen into his hands, and told him that he might expect to be treated in like manner, adding, that, if he had any spirit, he would prove it by singing. He immediately chanted forth his death-song, and then his war-song, and all the songs he knew, but in a very mournful strain," says Champlain, who was not then aware that all savage music has a melancholy character. The tortures which succeeded, accompanied by all the horrors which we shall mention hereafter, terrified the French, who made every effort to put a stop to them, but in vain. The following night, one of the Hurons having dreamt that they were pursued, the retreat was changed to a real flight, and the savages never stopped until they were out of the reach of danger.

"The moment they perceived the cabins of their own village, they cut themselves long sticks, to which they fastened the scalps which had fallen to their share, and carried them in triumph. At this sight, the women swam to the canoes, where they received the bloody scalps from the hands of their husbands, and tied them round their necks."

The warriors offered one of these horrible trophies to Champlain; they also presented him with some bows and arrows, — the only spoils of the Iroquois which they had ventured to seize, — entreating him to show them to the King of France.

Champlain lived a whole winter quite alone among these barbarians, without being under any alarm for his person or property.

Appendix E. — Vol. I. p. 48.

ALTHOUGH the puritanical strictness which presided over the establishment of the English colonies in America is now much relaxed, remarkable traces of it are still found in their habits and laws. In 1792, at the very time when the Anti-christian republic of France began its ephemeral existence, the legislative body of Massachusetts promulgated the following law, to compel the citizens to observe the Sabbath. We give the preamble and a few articles of this law, which is worthy of the reader's attention.

"Whereas," says the legislator, "the observation of the Sunday is an affair of public interest; inasmuch as it produces a necessary suspension of labor, leads men to reflect upon the duties of life and the errors to which human nature is liable, and provides for the public and private worship of God, the Creator and Governor of the universe, and for the performance of such acts of charity as are the ornament and comfort of Christian societies: —

"Whereas irreligious or light-minded persons, forgetting the duties which the Sabbath imposes, and the benefits which these duties confer on society, are known to profane its sanctity, by following their pleasures or their affairs; this way of acting being contrary to their own interest as Christians, and calculated to annoy those who do not follow their example; being also of great injury to society at large, by spreading a taste for dissipation and dissolute manners;

"Be it enacted and ordained by the Governor, Council, and Representatives convened in General Court of Assembly, that all and every person and persons shall on that day carefully apply themselves to the duties of religion and piety, that no tradesman or laborer shall exercise his ordinary calling, and that no game or recreation shall be used on the Lord's day, upon pain of forfeiting ten shillings.

"That no one shall travel on that day, or any part thereof, under pain of forfeiting twenty shillings; that no vessel shall leave a harbor of the colony; that no person shall keep outside the meeting-house during the time of public worship, or profane the time by playing or talking, on penalty of five shillings." (Law of the 8th March, 1792; *General Laws of Massachusetts*, Vol. I. p. 410.)

On the 11th of March, 1797, a new law increased the amount of fines, half of which was to be given to the informer. (Same collection, Vol. I. p. 525.)

On the 16th of February, 1816, a new law confirmed these same measures. (Same collection, Vol. II. p. 405.)

Similar enactments exist in the laws of the State of New York, revised in 1827 and 1828. (See *Revised Statutes*, Part I. chapter 20, p. 675.) In these it is declared that no one is allowed on the Sabbath to sport, to fish, to play at games, or to frequent houses where liquor is sold. No one can travel, except in case of necessity.

And this is not the only trace which the religious strictness and austere manners of the first emigrants have left behind them in the American laws.

In the Revised Statutes of the State of New York, Vol. I. p. 662, is the following clause: —

"Whoever shall win or lose in the space of twenty-four hours, by gaming or betting, the sum of twenty-five dollars, shall be found guilty of a misdemeanor, and, upon conviction, shall be condemned to pay a fine equal to at least five times the value of the sum lost or won; which shall be paid to the inspector of the poor of the township. He that loses twenty-five dollars or more may bring an action to recover them; and if he neglects to do so, the inspector of the poor may prosecute the winner, and oblige him to pay into the poor's box both the sum he has gained and three times as much besides."

The laws we quote from are of recent date; but they are unintelligible without going back to the very origin of the Colonies. I have no doubt that, in our days, the penal part of these laws is very rarely applied. Laws preserve their inflexibility long after the manners of a nation have yielded to the influence of time. It is still true, however, that nothing strikes a foreigner on his arrival in America more forcibly than the regard paid to the Sabbath.

There is one, in particular, of the large American cities, in which all social movements begin to be suspended even on Saturday evening. You traverse its streets at the hour when you expect men in the middle of life to be engaged in business, and young people in pleasure; and you meet with solitude and silence. Not only have all ceased to work, but they appear to have ceased to exist. Neither the movements of industry are heard, nor the accents of joy, nor even the confused murmur which arises from the midst of a great city. Chains are hung across the streets in the neighborhood of the churches; the half-closed shutters of the houses scarcely admit a ray of sun into the dwellings of the citizens. Now and then you perceive a solitary individual, who glides silently along the deserted streets and lanes.

But on Monday, at early dawn, the rolling of carriages, the noise of hammers, the cries of the population, begin to make themselves heard again. The city is awake. An eager crowd hastens towards the resort of commerce and industry; everything around you bespeaks motion, bustle, hurry. A feverish activity succeeds to the lethargic stupor of yesterday; you might almost suppose that they had but one day to acquire wealth and to enjoy it.

Appendix F. — Vol. I. p. 55.

IT is unnecessary to say, that, in the chapter which has just been read, I have not pretended to give a history of America. My only object has been to enable the reader to appreciate the influence which the opinions and manners of the first emigrants had exercised upon the fate of the different colonies, and of the Union in general. I have therefore cited only a few detached fragments.

I do not know whether I am deceived, but it appears to me that, by pursuing the path which I have merely pointed out, it would be easy to present such pictures of the American republics as would not be unworthy the attention of the public, and could not fail to suggest to the statesman matter for reflection. Not being able to devote myself to this labor, I am anxious to render it easy to others; and, for this purpose, I subjoin a short catalogue and analysis of the works which seem to me the most important to consult.*

At the head of the general documents which it would be advantageous to examine, I place the work entitled *An Historical Collection of State Papers, and other authentic Documents, intended as Materials for a History of the United States of America;*

* As this catalogue, though novel and interesting for many readers in France, contains little that is new or important for persons in this country, and has also in great part been superseded by later publications, I have considerably abridged it. — Am. Ed.

by Ebenezer Hasard. The first volume of this compilation, which was printed at Philadelphia in 1792, contains a literal copy of all the charters granted by the Crown of England to the emigrants, as well as the principal acts of the colonial governments, during the commencement of their existence. The second volume is almost entirely devoted to the acts of the Confederation of 1643. This federal compact, which was entered into by the Colonies of New England with the view of resisting the Indians, was the first instance of union afforded by the Anglo-Americans.

Each colony has, besides, its own historic monuments, some of which are extremely curious; beginning with Virginia, the State which was first peopled. The earliest historian of Virginia was its founder, Captain John Smith. Captain Smith has left us an octavo volume, entitled *The generall Historie of Virginia and New England, by Captain John Smith, sometymes Governor in those Countryes, and Admirall of New England; printed at London in* 1627. The work is adorned with curious maps and engravings of the time when it appeared; the narrative extends from the year 1584 to 1626.

The second historian to consult is Beverley, who commences his narrative with the year 1585, and ends it with 1700. The first part of his book contains historical documents, properly so called, relative to the infancy of the Colony. The second affords a most curious picture of the state of the Indians at this remote period. The third conveys very clear ideas concerning the manners, social condition, laws, and political customs of the Virginians in the author's lifetime.

I saw in America another work which ought to be consulted, entitled *The History of Virginia, by William Stith.* This book affords some curious details, but I thought it long and diffuse.

The most ancient, as well as the best document to be consulted on the history of Carolina, is a work in small quarto, entitled *The History of Carolina, by John Lawson, printed at London in* 1718. This work contains, in the first part, a journey of discovery in the west of Carolina; the account of which, given in the form of a journal, is in general confused and superficial; but it contains a very striking description of the mortality caused among the savages of that time both by the small-pox and the immoderate use of brandy; with a curious picture of the corruption of manners prevalent amongst them, which was increased by the presence of Europeans. The second part of Lawson's book is taken up with a description of the physical condition of Carolina and its productions.

From the southern I pass at once to the northern extremity of the United States, as the intermediate space was not peopled till a later period.

I would first mention a very curious compilation, entitled *Collections of the Massachusetts Historical Society, printed for the first time at Boston in* 1792, *and reprinted in* 1806. This Collection, which is continued to the present day, contains a great number of very valuable documents relating to the history of the different States of New England. Among them are letters which have never been published, and authentic pieces which had been buried in provincial archives. The whole work of Gookin, concerning the Indians, is inserted there.

I have mentioned several times, in the chapter to which this note relates, the work of Nathaniel Morton, entitled *New England's Memorial;* sufficiently, perhaps, to prove that it deserves the attention of those who would be conversant with the history of New England.

The most valuable and important authority which exists upon the history of New England is the work of the Rev. Cotton Mather, entitled *Magnalia Christi Americana, or the Ecclesiastical History of New England,* 1620–1698, 2 vols. 8vo, *reprinted at Hartford, United States, in* 1820. The author divided his work into seven books. The first presents the history of the events which prepared and brought about the establishment of New England. The second contains the lives of the first governors and chief magistrates who presided over the country. The third is devoted to the lives and labors of the evangelical ministers who, during the same period, had the care of souls. In the fourth, the author relates the institution and progress of the University of Cambridge (Massachusetts). In the fifth, he describes the principles and the discipline of the Church of New England. The sixth is taken up in retracing certain facts, which, in the opinion of Mather, prove the merciful interposition of

Providence in behalf of the inhabitants of New England. Lastly, in the seventh, the author gives an account of the heresies and the troubles to which the Church of New England was exposed. Cotton Mather was an evangelical minister, who was born at Boston, and passed his life there. His narratives are distinguished by the same ardor and religious zeal which led to the foundation of the colonies of New England. Traces of bad taste often occur in his manner of writing; but he interests, because he is full of enthusiasm. He is often intolerant, still oftener credulous, but he never betrays an intention to deceive.

When he declares the principles of the Church of New England with respect to morals, Mather inveighs with violence against the custom of drinking healths at table, which he denounces as a pagan and abominable practice. He proscribes with the same rigor all ornaments for the hair used by the female sex, as well as their custom of having the arms and neck uncovered. In another part of his work, he relates several instances of witchcraft which had alarmed New England. It is plain that the visible action of the Devil in the affairs of this world appeared to him an incontestable and evident fact.

In passing from the general documents relative to the history of New England to those which describe the several States comprised within its limits, I ought first to notice *The History of the Colony of Massachusetts, by Thomas Hutchinson, Lieutenant-Governor of the Massachusetts Province*, 2 vols. 8vo. The History by Hutchinson, which I have several times quoted in the chapter to which this note relates, commences in the year 1628, and ends in 1750. Throughout the work there is a striking air of truth and the greatest simplicity of style: it is full of minute details.

The best History to consult concerning Connecticut is that of Benjamin Trumbull, entitled *A Complete History of Connecticut, Civil and Ecclesiastical*, 1630–1764, 2 vols. 8vo, *printed in* 1818, *at New Haven.* This History contains a clear and calm account of all the events which happened in Connecticut during the period given in the title. The author drew from the best sources, and his narrative bears the stamp of truth.

The History of New Hampshire, by Jeremy Belknap, is a work held in merited estimation. It was printed at Boston in 1792, in 2 vols. 8vo. The third chapter of the first volume is particularly worthy of attention for the valuable details it affords on the political and religious principles of the Puritans, on the causes of their emigration, and on their laws. The reader of Belknap will find in his work more general ideas, and more strength of thought, than are to be met with in the American historians even to the present day.

Among the Central States which deserve our attention for their remote origin, New York and Pennsylvania are the foremost. The best History we have of the former is entitled, *A History of New York, by William Smith, printed at London in* 1757. Smith gives us important details of the wars between the French and English in America. His is the best acccount of the famous confederation of the Iroquois.

With respect to Pennsylvania, I cannot do better than point out the work of Proud, entitled the *History of Pennsylvania, from the original Institution and Settlement of that Province, under the first Proprietor and Governor, William Penn, in* 1681, *till after the Year* 1742, *by Robert Proud,* 2 vols. 8vo, *printed at Philadelphia in* 1797. This work is deserving of the especial attention of the reader; it contains a mass of curious documents concerning Penn, the doctrine of the Quakers, and the character, manners, and customs of the first inhabitants of Pennsylvania.

I need not add, that among the most important documents relating to this State are the works of Penn himself, and those of Franklin.

Appendix G. — Vol. I. p. 63.

WE read in Jefferson's Memoirs as follows: —

"At the time of the first settlement of the English in Virginia, when land was to be had for little or nothing, some provident persons having obtained large grants of it, and being desirous of maintaining the splendor of their families, entailed their property upon their descendants. The transmission of these estates from generation to generation, to men who bore the same name, had the effect of raising up a distinct class of families, who, possessing by law the privilege of perpetuating their wealth, formed by these means a sort of patrician order, distinguished by the grandeur and luxury of their establishments. From this order it was that the King usually chose his councillors of state."

In the United States, the principal provisions of English law respecting inheritance have been universally rejected. "The first rule that we follow," says Chancellor Kent, "touching inheritance, is the following: — If a man dies intestate, his property goes to his heirs in a direct line. If he has but one heir or heiress, he or she succeeds to the whole. If there are several heirs of the same degree, they divide the inheritance equally amongst them, without distinction of sex."

This rule was prescribed for the first time in the State of New York, by a statute of the 23d of February, 1786. At the present day, this law holds good throughout the whole of the United States, with the exception of the State of Vermont, where the male heir inherits a double portion. (Kent's *Commentaries*, Vol. IV. p. 370.) Chancellor Kent, in the same work, Vol. IV. pp. 1 – 22, gives an historical account of American legislation on the subject of entail: by this we learn that, previous to the Revolution, the Colonies followed the English law of entail. Estates tail were abolished in Virginia in 1776, on motion of Mr. Jefferson. They were suppressed in New York in 1786, and have since been abolished in North Carolina, Kentucky, Tennessee, Georgia, and Missouri. In Vermont, Indiana, Illinois, South Carolina, and Louisiana, entail was never introduced. Those States which thought proper to preserve the English law of entail, modified it in such a way as to deprive it of its most aristocratic tendencies. "Our general principles on the subject of government," says Kent, "tend to favor the free circulation of property."

It cannot fail to strike the French reader who studies the law of inheritance, that on these questions the French legislation is infinitely more democratic even than the American.

The American law makes an equal division of the father's property, but only in the case of his will not being known; "for every man," says the law, "in the State of New York, has entire liberty, power, and authority to dispose of his property by will, to leave it entire, or divided in favor of any persons he chooses as his heirs, provided he do not leave it to a political body or any corporation." The French law obliges the testator to divide his property equally, or nearly so, among his heirs.

Most of the American republics still admit of entails, under certain restrictions; but the French law prohibits entail in all cases.

If the social condition of the Americans is more democratic than that of the French, the laws of the latter are the more democratic of the two. This may be explained more easily than at first appears to be possible. In France, democracy is still occupied in the work of destruction; in America, it reigns quietly over the ruins it has made.

Appendix H. — Vol. I. p. 71.

SUMMARY OF THE QUALIFICATIONS OF VOTERS IN THE UNITED STATES.*

ALL the States agree in granting the right of voting at the age of twenty-one. In all of them, it is necessary to have resided for a certain time in the district where the vote is given. This period varies from three months to two years.

As to the qualification, — in the State of Massachusetts, it is

* I retain this note only as a curious illustration of the rapid progress of democracy in the United States, which, in the thirty years since this book was written, has swept away nearly every one of the limitations of the right of suffrage that are here enumerated by M. de Tocqueville. Generally it may be said, that, to be a voter now in any of the States, it is only necessary to be twenty-one years of age, to have resided a short time in the district where the vote is given, and to have paid a tax which may not amount to more than one or two dollars. Several of the States do not require even this payment of a tax. — Am. Ed.

necessary to have an income of three pounds sterling, or a capital of sixty pounds.

In Rhode Island, a man must possess landed property to the amount of 133 dollars.

In Connecticut, he must have a property which gives an income of seventeen dollars. A year of service in the militia also gives the elective privilege.

In New Jersey, an elector must have a property of fifty pounds a year.

In South Carolina and Maryland, the elector must possess fifty acres of land.

In Tennessee, he must possess some property.

In the States of Mississippi, Ohio, Georgia, Virginia, Pennsylvania, Delaware, New York, the only necessary qualification for voting is that of paying the taxes; and in most of the States, to serve in the militia is equivalent to the payment of taxes.

In Maine and New Hampshire, any man can vote who is not on the pauper list.

Lastly, in the States of Missouri, Alabama, Illinois, Louisiana, Indiana, Kentucky, and Vermont, the conditions of voting have no reference to the property of the elector.

I believe there is no other State beside that of North Carolina in which different conditions are applied to voting for the Senate and electing the House of Representatives. The electors of the former, in this case, should possess in property fifty acres of land; to vote for the latter, nothing more is required than to pay taxes.

Appendix I. — Vol. I. p. 119.

THE small number of custom-house officers employed in the United States, and the great extent of the coast, render smuggling very easy; notwithstanding, it is less practised than elsewhere, because everybody endeavors to repress it. In America, there is no police for the prevention of fires, and such accidents are more frequent than in Europe; but, in general, they are more speedily extinguished, because the surrounding population is prompt to lend assistance.

Appendix K. — Vol. I. p. 121.

IT is incorrect to say that centralization was produced by the French Revolution: the Revolution brought it to perfection, but did not create it. The mania for centralization and government regulations dates from the period when jurists began to take a share in the government, in the time of Philippe-le-Bel; ever since this period, they have been on the increase. In the year 1775, M. de Malesherbes, speaking in the name of the *Cour des Aides*, said to Louis XIV.: —

"Every corporation and every community of citizens retained the right of administering its own affairs, — a right which not only forms part of the primitive constitution of the kingdom, but has a still higher origin; for it is the right of nature and of reason. Nevertheless, your subjects, Sire, have been deprived of it; and we do not fear to say that, in this respect, your government has fallen into puerile extremes. From the time when powerful ministers made it a political principle to prevent the convocation of a national assembly, one consequence has succeeded another, until the deliberations of the inhabitants of a village are declared null if they have not been authorized by the Intendant. Of course, if the community has an expensive undertaking to carry through, it must remain under the control of the sub-delegate of the Intendant, and, consequently, follow the plan he proposes, employ his favorite workmen, pay them according to his pleasure; and if an action at law is deemed necessary, the Intendant's permission must be obtained. The cause must be pleaded before this first tribunal, previous to its being carried into a public court; and if the opinion of the Intendant is opposed to that of the inhabitants, or if their adversary enjoys his favor, the community is deprived of the power of defending its rights. Such are the means, Sire, which have been exerted to extinguish the municipal spirit in France, and to stifle, if possible, the opinions of the citizens. The nation may be said to lie under an interdict, and to be in wardship under guardians."

What could be said more to the purpose at the present day, when the Revolution has achieved what are called *its victories* in centralization?

In 1789, Jefferson wrote from Paris to one of his friends: "There is no country where the mania for over-governing has taken deeper root than in France, or been the source of greater mischief." Letter to Madison, 28th August, 1789.

The fact is, that, for several centuries, the central power of France has done everything it could to extend central administration; it has acknowledged no other limits than its own strength. The central power to which the Revolution gave birth made more rapid advances than any of its predecessors, because it was stronger and wiser than they had been. Louis XIV. committed the welfare of the municipal communities to the caprice of an Intendant; Napoleon left them to that of the Minister. The same principle governed both, though its consequences were more or less remote.

APPENDIX L. — Vol. I. p. 126.

THIS immutability of the Constitution in France is a necessary consequence of the laws.

To begin with the most important of all the laws, — that which decides the order of succession to the throne; what can be more immutable in its principle than a political order founded upon the natural succession of father to son? In 1814, Louis XVIII. established the perpetual law of hereditary succession in favor of his own family. Those who regulated the consequences of the Revolution of 1830 followed his example; they merely established the perpetuity of the law in favor of another family. In this respect, they imitated the Chancellor Maupeou, who, when he erected the new Parliament upon the ruins of the old, took care to declare in the same ordinance, that the rights of the new magistrates should be as inalienable as those of their predecessors had been.

The laws of 1830, like those of 1814, point out no way of changing the Constitution; and it is evident that the ordinary means of legislation are insufficient for this purpose. As the King, the Peers, and the Deputies, all derive their authority from the Constitution, these three powers united cannot alter a law by virtue of which alone they govern. Out of the Constitution, they are nothing: where, then, could they take their stand to effect a change in its provisions? The alternative is clear: either their efforts are powerless against the Charter, which continues to exist in spite of them, in which case they only reign in the name of the Charter; or, they succeed in changing the Charter, and then the law by which they existed being annulled, they themselves cease to exist. By destroying the Charter, they destroy themselves.

This is much more evident in the laws of 1830 than in those of 1814. In 1814, the royal prerogative took its stand above and beyond the Constitution; but in 1830, it was avowedly created by, and dependent on, the Constitution.

A part, therefore, of the French Constitution is immutable, because it is united to the destiny of a family; and the body of the Constitution is equally immutable, because there appear to be no legal means of changing it.

These remarks are not applicable to England. That country having no written Constitution, who can tell when its Constitution is changed?

Appendix M. — Vol. I. p. 126.

THE most esteemed authors who have written upon the English Constitution agree with each other in establishing the omnipotence of Parliament.

Delolme says, "It is a fundamental principle with the English lawyers, that Parliament can do everything except making a woman a man, or a man a woman."

Blackstone expresses himself more in detail, if not more energetically, than Delolme, in the following terms: —

"The power and jurisdiction of Parliament, says Sir Edward Coke (4 Inst. 36), is so transcendent and absolute, that it cannot be confined, either for causes or persons, within any bounds. And of this high Court, he adds, may truly be said, '*Si antiquitatem spectes, est vetustissima; si dignitatem, est honoratissima; si jurisdictionem, est capacissima.*' It hath sovereign and uncontrollable authority in the making, confirming, enlarging, restraining, abrogating, repealing, reviving, and expounding of laws, concerning matters of all possible denominations; ecclesiastical or temporal; civil, military, maritime, or criminal; this being the place where that absolute despotic power which must, in all governments, reside somewhere, is intrusted by the Constitution of these kingdoms. All mischiefs and grievances, operations and remedies, that transcend the ordinary course of the laws, are within the reach of this extraordinary tribunal. It can regulate or new-model the succession to the Crown; as was done in the reign of Henry VIII. and William III. It can alter the established religion of the land; as was done in a variety of instances in the reigns of King Henry VIII. and his three children. It can *change and create afresh even the Constitution of the kingdom*, and of parliaments themselves; as was done by the Act of Union and the several statutes for triennial and septennial elections. It can, in short, do everything that is not naturally impossible to be done; and, therefore, some have not scrupled to call its power, by a figure rather too bold, the omnipotence of Parliament."

APPENDIX N. — Vol. I. p. 139.

THERE is no question upon which the American Constitutions agree more fully than upon that of political jurisdiction. All the Constitutions which take cognizance of this matter give to the

House of Representatives the exclusive right of impeachment; excepting only the Constitution of North Carolina, which grants the same privilege to grand juries. (Article 23.)

Almost all the Constitutions give to the Senate, or to the legislative body which occupies its place, the exclusive right of trying the impeachment and pronouncing judgment.

The only punishments which the political tribunals can inflict are removal from office, and the interdiction of public functions for the future. The Constitution of Virginia alone enables them to inflict any kind of punishment.

The crimes which are subject to political jurisdiction are, — in the Federal Constitution (Section 4, Art. 1); in that of Indiana (Art. 3, paragraphs 23 and 24); of New York (Art. 5); of Delaware (Art. 5), — high treason, bribery, and other high crimes or misdemeanors.

In the Constitution of Massachusetts (Chap. 1, Section 2); that of North Carolina (Art. 23); of Virginia (p. 252), — misconduct and maladministration.

In the Constitution of New Hampshire (p. 105), corruption, intrigue, and maladministration.

In Vermont (Chap. 2, Art. 24), maladministration.

In South Carolina (Art. 5); Kentucky (Art. 5); Tennessee (Art. 4); Ohio (Art. 1, §§ 23, 24); Louisiana (Art. 5); Mississippi (Art. 5); Alabama (Art. 6); Pennsylvania (Art. 4), — crimes committed in the performance of official duties.

In the States of Illinois, Georgia, Maine, and Connecticut, no particular offences are specified.

Appendix O. — Vol. I. p. 218.

IT is true that the powers of Europe may carry on maritime wars against the Union; but there is always greater facility and less danger in supporting a maritime than a continental war. Maritime warfare only requires one species of effort. A commercial people which consents to furnish its government with the necessary funds, is sure to possess a fleet. And it is far easier to induce a nation to part with its money, almost unconsciously, than to reconcile it to sacrifices of men and personal efforts. Moreover, defeat by sea rarely compromises the existence or independence of the people which endures it.

As for continental wars, it is evident that the nations of Europe cannot be formidable in this way to the American Union. It would be very difficult to transport and maintain in America more than 25,000 soldiers, — an army which may be considered to represent a nation of about 2,000,000 of men. The most populous nation of Europe, contending in this way against the Union, is in the position of a nation of 2,000,000 of inhabitants at war with one of 12,000,000. Add to this, that America has all its resources within reach, whilst the European is at 4,000 miles distance from his; and that the immensity of the American continent would of itself present an insurmountable obstacle to its conquest.

Appendix P. — Vol. I. p. 239.

THE first American journal appeared in April, 1704, and was published at Boston. See *Collections of the Historical Society of Massachusetts*, Vol. VI. p. 66.

It would be a mistake to suppose that the periodical press has always been entirely free in the American Colonies: an attempt was made to establish something like a censorship and preliminary security. Consult the Legislative Documents of Massachusetts for the 14th of January, 1722.

The Committee appointed by the General Assembly (the legislative body of the Province), for the purpose of examining an affair relative to a paper entitled "The New England Courant," expresses its opinion that "the tendency of the said journal is to turn religion into derision, and bring it into contempt; that it mentions the sacred writers in a profane and irreligious manner; that it puts malicious interpretations upon the conduct of the ministers of the Gospel; and that the government of His Majesty is insulted, and the peace and tranquillity of the Province disturbed, by the said journal. The Committee is consequently of opinion that the printer and publisher, James Franklin, should be forbidden to print and publish the said journal or any other work in future, without having previously submitted it to the Secretary of the Province; and that the justices of the peace for the county of Suffolk should be commissioned to require bail of the said James Franklin for his good conduct during the ensuing year."

The suggestion of the Committee was adopted, and passed into a law; but the effect was null, for the journal eluded the prohibition by putting the name of Benjamin Franklin, instead of James Franklin, at the bottom of its columns, and this manœuvre was supported by public opinion.

Appendix Q. — Vol. I. p. 362.

THE Federal Constitution has introduced the jury into the tribunals of the Union, just as the States had introduced it into their own several courts; but as it has not established any fixed rules for the choice of jurors, the Federal Courts select them from the ordinary jury-list which each State makes for itself. The laws of the States must therefore be examined for the theory of the formation of juries.

In order thoroughly to understand American principles with respect to the formation of juries, I examined the laws of States at a distance from one another, and the following observations were the result of my inquiries.

In America, all the citizens who exercise the elective franchise have the right of serving upon a jury. The great State of New York, however, has made a slight difference between the two privileges, but in a spirit quite contrary to that of the laws of France; for in the State of New York there are fewer persons eligible as jurymen than there are electors. It may be said, in general, that the right of forming part of a jury, like the right of electing representatives, is open to all the citizens; the exercise of this right, however, is not put indiscriminately into any hands.

Every year, a body of town or county magistrates — called *selectmen* in New England, *supervisors* in New York, *trustees* in Ohio, and *sheriffs of the parish* in Louisiana — choose for each county a certain number of citizens who have the right of serving as jurymen, and who are supposed to be capable of doing so. These magistrates, being themselves elective, excite no distrust; their powers, like those of most republican magistrates, are very extensive and very arbitrary, and they frequently make use of them, especially in New England, to remove unworthy or incompetent jurymen.

The names of the jurymen thus chosen are transmitted to the County Court; and the jury who have to decide any affair are drawn by lot from the whole list of names.

The Americans have endeavored in every way to make the common people eligible to the jury, and to render the service as little onerous as possible. The jurors being very numerous, each one's turn does not come round oftener than once in three years. The sessions are held in the chief town of every county, and the jury are indemnified for their attendance either by the State or the parties concerned. They receive in general a dollar per day, besides their travelling expenses. In America, the being placed upon the jury is looked upon as a burden, but it is a burden which is very supportable.

Appendix R. — Vol. I. p. 366.

If we attentively examine the constitution of the jury in civil proceedings in England, we shall readily perceive that the jurors are under the immediate control of the judge. It is true that the verdict of the jury, in civil as well as in criminal cases, comprises the questions of fact and of law in the same reply. Thus, a house is claimed by Peter as having been purchased by him; this is the fact to be decided. The defendant puts in a plea of incompetency on the part of the vendor: this is the legal question to be resolved. The jury simply says that the house shall be delivered to Peter, and thus decides both the questions of fact and of law.

But, according to the practice of the English courts, the opinion of the jury is not held to be infallible in civil, as it is in criminal cases. If the judge thinks that their verdict has made a wrong application of the law, he may refuse to receive it, and send back the jury to deliberate over again. Even if the judge allows the verdict to pass without observation, the case is not yet finally determined; there are still many modes of arresting judgment. The principal one consists in asking the court to set aside the verdict, and order a new trial before another jury. It is true that such a request is seldom granted, and never more than twice; yet I have actually known this to happen. See Blackstone's *Commentaries.*

Appendix S. — Vol. II. p. 248.

I FIND in my travelling-journal a passage which may serve to convey a more complete notion of the trials to which the women of America, who consent to follow their husbands into the wilds, are often subjected. This description has nothing to recommend it but its perfect truth.

"From time to time, we come to fresh clearings; all these places are alike: I shall describe the one at which we halted to-night, since it will serve me for a picture of all the others.

"The bell which the pioneers hang round the necks of their cattle, in order to find them again in the woods, announced from afar our approach to a clearing; and we soon afterwards heard the stroke of the axe, hewing down the trees of the forest. As we came nearer, traces of destruction marked the presence of civilized man: the road was strewn with cut boughs; trunks of trees, half consumed by fire, or mutilated by the axe, were still standing in the track. We proceeded till we reached a wood in which all the trees seemed to have been suddenly struck dead; in the middle of summer, their boughs were as leafless as in winter; and, upon closer examination, we found that a deep circle had been cut through the bark, which, by stopping the circulation of the sap, soon kills the tree. We were informed that this is commonly the first thing a pioneer does; as he cannot, in the first year, cut down all the trees which cover his new domain, he sows Indian corn under their branches, and puts the trees to death in order to prevent them from injuring his crop. Beyond this field, at present imperfectly traced out, — the first work of civilization in the desert, — we suddenly came upon the cabin of its owner, situated in the centre of a plot of ground more carefully cultivated than the rest, but where man was still waging unequal warfare with the forest; there the trees were cut down, but their roots were not removed, and the trunks still encumbered the ground which they so recently shaded. Around these dry blocks, wheat, suckers of trees, and plants of every kind, grow and intertwine in all the luxuriance of wild, untutored Nature. Amidst this vigorous and various vegetation stands the house of the pioneer, or, as they call it, the *log-house*. Like the ground about it, this rustic dwelling bore marks of recent and hasty labor: its length seemed not to exceed thirty feet, its height fifteen; the walls as well as the roof were formed of rough trunks of trees, between which a little moss and clay had been inserted to keep out the cold and rain.

"As night was coming on, we determined to ask the master of the log-house for a lodging. At the sound of our footsteps, the children who were playing amongst the scattered branches sprang up, and ran towards the house, as if they were frightened at the sight of man; whilst two large dogs, almost wild, with ears erect and outstretched nose, came growling out of their hut, to cover the retreat of their young masters. The pioneer himself made his appearance at the door of his dwelling; he looked at us with a rapid and inquisitive glance, made a sign to the dogs to go into the house, and set them the example, without betraying either curiosity or apprehension at our arrival.

"We entered the log-house: the inside is quite unlike that of the cottages of the peasantry of Europe: it contains more that is superfluous, less that is necessary. A single window with a muslin blind; on a hearth of trodden clay an immense fire, which lights the whole interior; above the hearth, a good rifle, a deer's skin, and plumes of eagles' feathers; on the right hand of the chimney, a map of the United States, raised and shaken by the wind through the crannies in the wall; near the map, upon a shelf formed of a roughly hewn plank, a few volumes of books, — a Bible, the six first books of Milton, and two of Shakespeare's plays; along the wall, trunks instead of closets; in the centre of the room, a rude table, with legs of green wood with the bark still upon them, looking as if they grew out of the ground on which they stood; but on this table a teapot of British ware, silver spoons, cracked tea-cups, and some newspapers.

"The master of this dwelling has the angular features and lank limbs peculiar to the native of New England. It is evident that this man was not born in the solitude in which we have found him: his physical constitution suffices to show that his earlier years were spent in the midst of civilized society, and that he belongs to that restless, calculating, and adventurous race of men, who do with the utmost coolness things only to be accounted for by the ardor of passion, and who endure the life of savages for a time, in order to conquer and civilize the backwoods.

"When the pioneer perceived that we were crossing his threshold, he came to meet us and shake hands, as is their custom; but his face was quite unmoved; he opened the conversation by inquiring what was going on in the world; and when his curiosity was satisfied, he held his peace, as if he were tired of the noise and importunity of mankind. When we questioned him in our turn, he gave us all the information we asked; he then attended sedulously, but without eagerness, to our wants. Whilst he was engaged in providing thus kindly for us, how came it that, in spite of ourselves, we felt our gratitude die upon our lips? It is, that our host, whilst he performs the duties of hospitality, seems to be obeying an irksome necessity of his condition: he treats it as a duty imposed upon him by his situation, not as a pleasure.

"By the side of the hearth sits a woman with a baby on her lap; she nods to us without disturbing herself. Like the pioneer, this woman is in the prime of life; her appearance seems superior to her condition, and her apparel even betrays a lingering taste for dress; but her delicate limbs appear shrunken, her features are drawn in, her eye is mild and melancholy; her whole physiognomy bears marks of religious resignation, a deep quiet of all passions, and some sort of natural and tranquil firmness, ready to meet all the ills of life without fearing and without braving them.

"Her children cluster about her, full of health, turbulence, and energy: they are true children of the wilderness; their mother watches them from time to time with mingled melancholy and joy: to look at their strength and her languor, one might imagine that the life she has given them has exhausted her own, and still she regrets not what they have cost her.

"The house inhabited by these emigrants has no internal partition or loft. In the one chamber of which it consists the whole family is gathered for the night. The dwelling is itself a little world, — an ark of civilization amidst an ocean of foliage: a hundred steps beyond it the primeval forest spreads its shades, and solitude resumes its sway."

Appendix T. — Vol. II. p. 276.

SETTING aside all those who do not think at all, and those who dare not say what they think, the immense majority of the Americans will still be found to appear satisfied with their political institutions; and I believe they really are so. I look upon this state of public opinion as an indication, but not as a proof, of the absolute excellence of American laws. National pride, the gratification of certain ruling passions by the law, a concourse of circumstances, defects which escape notice, and, more than all the rest, the influence of a majority which shuts the mouth of all cavillers, may long perpetuate the delusions of a people as well as those of a man.

Look at England throughout the eighteenth century. No nation was ever more prodigal of self-applause, no people were ever better satisfied with themselves; then, every part of their constitution was right, — everything, even to its most obvious defects, was irreproachable. At the present day, a vast number of Englishmen seem to be occupied only in proving that this constitution was faulty in a thousand respects. Which was right? — the English people of the last century, or the English people of the present day?

The same thing occurred in France. It is certain that, during the reign of Louis XIV., the great bulk of the nation was devotedly attached to the form of government which then governed the community. It is a vast error to suppose that there was anything degraded in the character of the French of that age. There might be some sort of servitude in France at that time, but assuredly there was no servile spirit among the people. The writers of that age felt a species of genuine enthusiasm in raising the power of their king over all other authority; and there was no peasant so obscure in his hovel as not to take a pride in the glory of his sovereign, and to die cheerfully with the cry "Vive le Roi!" upon his lips. These same forms of loyalty have now become odious to the French people. Which are wrong? — the French of the age of Louis XIV., or their descendants of the present day?

Our judgment of the laws of a people, then, must not be founded exclusively upon its inclinations, since those inclinations change from age to age; but upon more elevated principles and a more general experience. The love which a people may show for its laws proves only this, that we should not be in a hurry to change them.

Appendix U. — Vol. II. p. 340.

IN the chapter to which this note relates I have pointed out one source of danger; I am now about to point out another, more rare indeed, but more formidable if it were ever to appear.

If the love of physical gratification and the taste for well-being, which are naturally suggested to men by a state of equality, were to possess the mind of a democratic people, and to fill it completely, the manners of the nation would become so totally opposed to military pursuits, that perhaps even the army would eventually acquire a love of peace, in spite of the peculiar interest which leads it to desire war. Living in a state of general relaxation, the troops would ultimately think it better to rise without efforts, by the slow but commodious advancement of a peace establishment, than to purchase more rapid promotion at the cost of all the toils and privations of the field. With these feelings, they would take up arms without enthusiasm, and use them without energy; they would allow themselves to be led to meet the foe, instead of marching to attack him.

It must not be supposed that this pacific state of the army would render it adverse to revolutions; for revolutions, and especially military revolutions, which are generally very rapid, are attended indeed with great dangers, but not with protracted toil; they gratify ambition at less cost than war; life only is at stake, and the men of democracies care less for their lives than for their comfort.

Nothing is more dangerous for the freedom and the tranquillity of a people than an army afraid of war, because, as such an army no longer seeks to maintain its importance and its influence on the field of battle, it seeks to assert them elsewhere. Thus it might happen, that the men of whom a democratic army consists should lose the interests of citizens without acquiring the virtues of soldiers; and that the army should cease to be fit for war without ceasing to be turbulent. I shall here repeat what I have said in the text: the remedy for these dangers is not to be found in the army, but in the country; a democratic people which has preserved the manliness of its character will never be at a loss for military prowess in its soldiers.

Appendix V. — Vol. II. p. 360.

MEN place the greatness of their idea of unity in the means, God in the ends; hence this idea of greatness, as men conceive it, leads us to infinite littleness. To compel all men to follow the same course towards the same object, is a human conception; to introduce infinite variety of action, but so combined that all these acts lead in a thousand different ways to the accomplishment of one great design, is a conception of the Deity.

The human idea of unity is almost always barren; the Divine idea is infinitely fruitful. Men think they manifest their greatness by simplifying the means they use; but it is the purpose of God which is simple, — his means are infinitely varied.

Appendix W. — Vol. II. p. 364.

A DEMOCRATIC people is not only led by its own taste to centralize its government, but the passions of all the men by whom it is governed constantly urge it in the same direction. It may easily be foreseen that almost all the able and ambitious members of a democratic community will labor unceasingly to extend the powers of government, because they all hope at some time or other to wield those powers. It would be a waste of time to attempt to prove to them that extreme centralization may be injurious to the state, since they are centralizing it for their own benefit. Amongst the public men of democracies, there are hardly any but men of great disinterestedness or extreme mediocrity who seek to oppose the centralization of government: the former are scarce, the latter powerless.

Appendix X. — Vol. II. p. 391.

I HAVE often asked myself what would happen if, amidst the relaxation of democratic manners, and as a consequence of the restless spirit of the army, a military government were ever to be founded amongst any of the nations of our times. I think that such a government would not differ much from the outline I have drawn in the chapter to which this note belongs, and that it would retain none of the fierce characteristics of a military oligarchy. I am persuaded that, in such a case, a sort of fusion would take place between the habits of official men and those of the military service. The administration would assume something of a military character, and the army some of the usages of the civil administration. The result would be a regular, clear, exact, and absolute system of government; the people would become the reflection of the army, and the community be drilled like a garrison.

Appendix Y. — Vol. II. p. 395.

IT cannot be absolutely or generally affirmed that the greatest danger of the present age is license or tyranny, anarchy or despotism. Both are equally to be feared; and the one may as easily proceed as the other from the self-same cause, namely, that *general apathy*, which is the consequence of what I have termed *individualism:* it is because this apathy exists, that the executive government, having mustered a few troops, is able to commit acts of oppression one day; and the next day, a party which has mustered some thirty men in its ranks can also commit acts of oppression. Neither the one nor the other can found anything to last; and the causes which enable them to succeed easily prevent them from succeeding long: they rise because nothing opposes them, and they sink because nothing supports them. The proper object, therefore, of our most strenuous resistance, is far less either anarchy or despotism, than that apathy which may almost indifferently beget either the one or the other.

DEMOCRACY IN SWITZERLAND.

A REPORT MADE TO THE ACADEMY OF THE MORAL AND POLITICAL SCIENCES IN 1847, BY M. DE TOCQUEVILLE.

M. CHERBULIEZ, Professor of Law in the University of Geneva, has published a work upon the political institutions and manners of his countrymen, entitled "Democracy in Switzerland," and has presented a copy of this book to the Academy of the Moral Sciences. I have thought that the importance of the subject treated by him required a special examination of his work; and I have undertaken it, believing that such an examination might be useful.

My intention is, to take my stand entirely beyond the range of the prejudices of the passing hour, as it is proper to do in this assembly, to pass in silence over present occurrences which do not concern us, and to regard, in Switzerland, not so much what the political society is now doing, as this society itself, the laws which constitute it, their origin, their tendencies, and their character. I hope that the picture, though thus limited, will yet be worthy of interest. What is now passing in Switzerland * is not an isolated fact; it is but one step in the general movement which is overturning the whole edifice of the old institu-

* The author here alludes to the warlike agitation which then pervaded Switzerland, consequent upon the proceedings of the Sonderbund, or League of the Seven Cantons. — AM. ED.

tions of Europe. The spectacle has some grandeur, then, though the theatre is a small one; above all, it has a singular originality. The democratic revolution which is now agitating the world has nowhere appeared under circumstances at once so strange and so complicated. One people, composed of several races, speaking different languages, professing various beliefs, many opposing sects, two equally established and privileged churches, all political questions now turning upon religious disputes, then all theological controversies ending in political movements, and, finally, two communities, the one very old and the other very young, but indissolubly united in spite of the difference in their ages, — such is the spectacle which we now behold in Switzerland. To make a faithful picture of it, I think we should take a higher point of view than our author has chosen. M. Cherbuliez declares in his Preface, and I believe the assertion is a very sincere one, that he has aimed at strict impartiality. He even fears that the completely impartial character of his work has made the treatment of the subject somewhat monotonous. This apprehension is certainly unfounded. In fact, the author wishes to be impartial, but has not succeeded in his wish. His book manifests learning, clear-sightedness, real talent, and unmistakable good faith, which shines forth even in the midst of passionate judgments. The very quality in which it is most deficient is impartiality. We find in it much intellect, and very little liberty of intellect.

What forms of political association does the author prefer? At first, it seems difficult to tell. He approves, to a certain extent, the conduct of the most zealous Catholics in Switzerland; yet he is a decided opponent of Catholicism, and even wishes to prohibit by law the Catholic religion from extending into districts where it is not already established. On the other hand, he is a determined adversary of the various Protestant sects. Opposed to the government of the people, he also dislikes the dominion of the nobility. In religion, a Protestant church controlled by the state; in politics, a state governed by an aristocracy among the citizens, — such is the ideal which our author contemplates. This was the condition of Geneva before its latest revolution.

But if we cannot always clearly perceive what it is that he prefers, it is easy to see what he thoroughly dislikes. What he hates is democracy. Wounded in his opinions, in his friendships, perhaps in his interests, by the democratic revolution which he describes, he never speaks of it but as an adversary. Democracy is attacked by him, not only in some of its consequences, but even in its principle. He is blind to its good qualities and implacable to its faults. Among the evils which may result from it, he does not distinguish those which are radical and permanent from those which are accidental and transitory, — what must be borne with because inevitable, from what is within our power and capable of amendment. Perhaps the subject could not but be viewed in this manner by a man as deeply concerned as M. Cherbuliez has been in the agitations of his country. This we must be permitted to regret. We shall see, in the course of this analysis, that Swiss democracy has great need to be enlightened upon the imperfection of its laws. But to do this to any good purpose, the first condition is, not to be a hater of democracy.

"Democracy in Switzerland" is the title that M. Cherbuliez has given to his work. This would lead one to believe that, in his opinion, Switzerland is a country in which we can study the theory of democracy, and where democratic institutions are exhibited as they really are, or in their natural state. This opinion I hold to be the chief source of almost all the errors of his book. In fact, Switzerland has been for fifteen years in a revolutionary state. Democracy there is not so much a regular form of government, as a weapon which is habitually used to destroy, and sometimes to defend, the old forms of society. We find there the particular phenomena resulting from the revolutionary state in the democratic period in which our lot is cast, but not democracy itself in its permanent and tranquil aspect. Whoever does not have this fact as a point of departure constantly present to his mind, will have great difficulty in understanding Swiss institutions as they now appear; for my own part, I should find it almost impossible to explain my judgment of what is, without saying how I understand what has been.

There is a very common mistake as to the condition of Switzerland at the time of the outbreak of the French Revolution. As the Swiss had then been living for a long time under a republican form of government, it was easy to imagine that they were much nearer than the other nations of Continental Europe to the institutions which constitute, and the spirit which animates, modern liberty. But this is the very opposite of the truth.

Although the independence of the Swiss was born from an insurrection against the aristocracy, the governments which were then established soon borrowed from aristocracy its customs, its laws, and even its opinions and inclinations. Liberty presented itself to them only under the form of privilege, and the idea of a universal and preexistent right of all men to be free, was as foreign to their apprehension as it could be to that of the princes of the house of Austria whom they had vanquished. All the powers of government, therefore, were drawn without delay into the hands of small, close aristocracies perpetuating themselves, and were retained there. In the north, these aristocracies assumed a commercial or manufacturing character; in the south, they had a military organization. But in both cases, they were equally narrow and exclusive. In most of the Cantons, three fourths of the inhabitants were excluded from any participation whatever, direct or indirect, in the administration of the country; and moreover, each Canton had subjects, or communities existing entirely under their control.

These small societies, to which a great convulsion had given rise, soon became so firmly established that no movement could take place in them. The aristocracy, finding themselves neither urged forward by the people nor controlled by a king, held society there immovable under the old garb of the Middle Ages. Switzerland remained closed against modern ideas of freedom, long after the progress of the age had introduced them into the most monarchical nations of Europe.

The principle of separating legislative, executive, and judicial powers was admitted by all publicists; but it was not applied in Switzerland. The liberty of the press, which existed, practically at least, in several absolute monarchies on the Continent, had no existence there either *de facto* or *de jure;* the power of forming political associations there was neither acknowledged nor exercised; and even liberty of speech, for the Swiss, was restrained within very narrow limits. The equality of burdens, towards which all enlightened governments were tending, was as unknown to them as the equality of rights. Industry there labored under many fetters; personal liberty there had no legal guaranty. Religious liberty, which was beginning to penetrate even into the most orthodox states, had not yet dawned upon Switzerland. Dissenting churches were entirely prohibited in several Cantons, and loaded with restraints in all. Differences of religious profession were almost everywhere punished by political disfranchisement.

Switzerland was still in this condition in 1798, when the French Revolution by force of arms broke into its territory. There it overturned for a time the old institutions, but put nothing fixed and durable in their place. Some years afterwards, Napoleon, who by the Act of Mediation rescued the Swiss from anarchy, gave them the principle of equality indeed, but not constitutional liberty; the political system which he imposed upon them was so constructed that public life was paralyzed. The government, exercised in the name of the people, but placed far above them, was surrendered entirely into the hands of the executive power.

A few years later, when the Act of Mediation was thrown down together with its author, the Swiss did not gain liberty by the change, but only lost equality. Everywhere the old aristocracies resumed the reins of government, and brought again into force the exclusive and superannuated principles which had prevailed before the revolution. M. Cherbuliez truly says, that things then returned nearly to the same position where they were in 1798. The allied monarchs have been wrongly accused of imposing this restoration upon Switzerland by force. It was done with their consent, but not by their agency. The truth is, that the Swiss, like the other nations on the Continent, were carried away by that short-lived but universal reaction which then suddenly re-established the old institutions of society throughout Europe; and as, in their case, the restoration was not effected by the monarchs, whose interests after all are separate from those of the old privileged classes, but by those privileged classes themselves, it was there more complete, more blind, and more obstinate, than in the other portions of Europe. It did not appear tyrannical, but it was very exclusive. A legislative power entirely under the control of the executive authority; the latter vested exclusively in the hands of an aristocracy by birth; the middle classes shut out of the government entirely; and the whole people deprived of political life altogether; — such was the picture presented in almost every part of Switzerland down to 1830. It was then that the new era of democracy first opened upon the Swiss people.

The object of this brief exposition has been, to cause two things to be clearly understood. The first is, that Switzerland is the country where the revolution was more thorough, and the restoration which followed it more complete, than in any other part of Europe; so that, institutions foreign or hostile to the new demands of the age having there preserved or recovered a strong hold, the tendency to a new revolution must also have been greater there than elsewhere. The second is, that in the greater part of Switzerland, the people, down to our own day, have never had even the smallest share in the government; that the judicial forms which are the safeguards of civil liberty, the liberty of association, the liberty of speech, the liberty of the press, the liberty of religious belief, have also always been, I might almost say, more unknown to the great majority of the citizens of these republics, than they could have been, at the same period, to the subjects of most monarchies.

These are the facts which M. Cherbuliez often loses sight of, but which ought to be unceasingly present to our minds in the careful examination which we are now to make of the institutions which Switzerland has established.

All the world knows that, in Switzerland, the sovereignty is divided into parts; on the one hand is the Federal power, and on the other, the governments of the Cantons. M. Cherbuliez begins with the consideration of what is taking place in the Cantons; and he is right, for in them is the real government of the community. I shall follow him in this respect, and shall first consider the constitutions of the Cantons. All these constitutions, at present, are democratic; but democracy does not show itself in all of them under the same features. In a majority of the Cantons, the exercise of power has been delegated to assemblies which represent the people; in the others, the people have reserved this power to themselves. They form themselves into one body, and thus constitute the government. The former are denominated by our author *representative democracies;* the latter he calls *pure democracies.*

I shall take the liberty not to follow the author in the very interesting examination which he has made of pure democracies; and this for several reasons. Although the Cantons which live under a pure democracy have played a great part in history, and may still play a considerable one in politics, a study of them would be rather curious than useful. Pure democracy is a fact almost unique in the modern world, and very rare even in Switzerland, where only a thirteenth part of the population are governed in this manner. Moreover, it is a transitory form. It is not sufficiently known that, even in the Swiss Cantons, where the people have the best preserved the exercise of power, a representative body still exists, upon whom devolves in part the business of government. Now it is easy to see, in studying the recent history of Switzerland, that the affairs which are managed by the whole people are gradually diminishing, while, on the other hand, those which are directed by their representatives are every day increasing in number and variety. Thus the principle of pure democracy is losing ground which the opposite system gains. The one insensibly becomes the exception, the other the rule.

Besides, the pure democracies of Switzerland belong to another age; they can teach us nothing in regard either to the present or the future. Although we are obliged, in order to designate them, to make use of a term borrowed from modern science, they live only in the past. Every age has its dominant spirit, which nothing is able to resist.

If principles should be introduced under its reign which are foreign or hostile to it, very soon it infuses itself into them, and if it cannot shut out their action altogether, it appropriates them and assimilates them to itself. The Middle Ages succeeded at last in shaping democratic liberty itself into an aristocratic form. In the midst of the most republican laws, by the side of universal suffrage itself, were placed religious dogmas, opinions, sentiments, customs, associations, families, which kept the real power beyond the action of the people. The petty governments of the Swiss Cantons must be regarded as the last, though the respectable, relics of an age which has passed away.

On the contrary, the representative democracies of Switzerland are the true progeny of the spirit of modern times. All of them are founded on the ruins of a preceding aristocratic state of society; all emanate from the single principle of the sovereignty of the people; all have made almost the same application of it in their laws. We shall see that these laws are very imperfect, and this fact alone would suffice to indicate, in the silence of history, that democracy, and even liberty, in Switzerland, have neither age nor experience in their favor.

It is first to be observed that, even in the representative democracies of Switzerland, the people have kept in their own hands the direct exercise of a portion of their power. In some Cantons, after the principal laws have received the assent of the legislature, they must still be submitted to the approval or disapproval of the people. Hence, in these special cases, the representative degenerates into the pure form of democracy. In almost all the Cantons, the people must be consulted from time to time, usually at short intervals, to know whether they wish to modify or to maintain the constitution. All the laws are thus made to waver at once, and at frequently recurring periods.

All legislative authority which the people have not retained in their own hands is confided to a single assembly, which acts in their name and under their observation. In no Canton is the legislature divided into two branches, everywhere it consists of a single body; not only its movements are not delayed by the necessity of coming to an agreement with another assembly, but its wishes do not find even the hinderance of a prolonged deliberation. The discussion of the general laws is subject to certain formalities, which require time; but the most important resolutions, under the name of decrees, may be proposed, discussed, and enacted in a moment. The decrees cause the secondary laws to be as unforeseen, as rapid, and as irresistible in their operation, as the passions of a multitude.

Outside of the legislature, there is no resisting power. The separation, and, above all, the relative independence, of the legislative, administrative, and judicial authorities have never been established. In none of the Cantons are the representatives of the executive power chosen directly by the people; it is the legislature that elects them. The executive power, consequently, has no strength which is peculiar to it; it is only the creature, and it may be only the servile agent, of another power. To this cause of weakness several others are added. Nowhere is the executive power delegated to a single person. It is vested in a small assembly, where its responsibility is divided and its action debilitated. Moreover, several of the prerogatives which properly belong to executive authority are taken away. It exercises no veto, or only an insignificant one, on the enactment of laws. It has not the pardoning power, it does not appoint its own agents, and cannot deprive them of office. It may even be said that it has no agents, as it is generally obliged to make use only of the municipal magistrates.

But, above all, it is through the bad constitution and bad

materials of the judicial power that the Swiss democracy suffers. M. Cherbuliez remarks this defect, but does not place stress enough upon it in my opinion. He does not seem perfectly to understand, that it is the judicial power in democracies which is destined to be at the same time a barrier and a safeguard for the power of the people.

The independence of the judiciary is a modern idea. The Middle Ages had never thought of such a thing, or, at most, had formed only a very obscure conception of it. It may be said, that, in all the nations of Europe, executive and judicial functions were at first joined together; even in France, where, by a happy exception, the administration of justice had at an early period a very vigorous separate existence, we are still able to affirm that the division of the two powers remained very incomplete. It was not, it is true, the administration which retained judicial power in its own hands, but it was the judiciary which exercised in part administrative functions. Switzerland, on the other hand, of all the countries of Europe, has most completely confounded judicial with political authority, making the former one of the attributes of the latter. It may be said that the very idea which we have of the judiciary, that free impartial power which is interposed between all interests and all authorities, in order to enforce upon all a respect for the law, has never been present to the minds of the Swiss, and, even at the present day, is but very imperfectly understood by them.

The new constitutions have undoubtedly given to the legal tribunals a more distinct place than that which they occupied in the old division of power, but not a more independent position. The inferior judges are elected by the people, and subject to a re-election. The supreme court of each Canton is appointed, not by the executive, but by the legislative power, and thus its members have no security against the daily caprices of the majority. Not only do the people, or the assembly which represents the people, choose the judges, but no restraint is imposed upon their choice. In general, no qualifications are required. The judge, moreover, a simple executor of the law, has no right to inquire whether this law is conformable to the constitution. In truth, it is the majority itself which judges, employing the judiciary only as its organ. In Switzerland, too, the judicial authority, even if it had received from the law the independence and the rights which are essential to it, would still find great difficulty in exercising its functions, for it is a power resting upon tradition and opinion, and needing to be fortified by judicial ideas and manners.

I could easily expose the defects which are found in the institutions that I have just described, and prove that they all tend to render the government of the people irregular in its action, precipitate in its resolutions, and tyrannical in its acts. But this would carry me too far. I shall confine myself to bringing out the contrast between these laws and those which have been established in a democratic society which is older, more peaceable, and more prosperous. M. Cherbuliez thinks that the imperfect institutions which the Swiss Cantons possess are the only ones which are natural to a democracy, or are even compatible with it. The comparison which I am about to make will prove the contrary, and will show how it has been possible elsewhere, aided by more experience, more art, and greater wisdom, to deduce different results from the principle of the sovereignty of the people. I shall take for an example the State of New York, which alone contains as many inhabitants as the whole of Switzerland.

In the State of New York, as in the Swiss Cantons, the principle of government is the sovereignty of the people, exercised through universal suffrage. But the people there exercise their authority only for a single day, in the choice of their delegates. In no case do they habitually keep in their own hands any portion whatever of the legislative, executive, or judicial authority. They make choice of those who are to govern in their name, and then abdicate their power till the next election.

Although the laws are subject to change, their foundation is fixed. The idea has never been entertained of subjecting the constitution, as in Switzerland, to successive and periodical revisions, which, as they come round or are looked forward to, keep the community in constant suspense. When a new want is felt, the legislature decide that a modification of the constitution has become necessary, and the following legislature effects it.

Although the legislative authority cannot, any more than in Switzerland, shake off the directing power of public opinion, it is so constituted as to resist its caprices. No proposition can become a law till it has been subjected to examination by two legislative bodies. These two portions of the legislature are chosen in the same manner and composed of the same elements; both emanate equally from the people, but do not represent the people exactly in the same manner; the office of the one is to follow the daily impressions, that of the other to obey the habitual instincts and permanent inclinations, of the community.

In New York, the division of the powers of government exists not only in appearance, but in reality. The executive authority is exercised, not by a number of persons, but by one man, who alone is responsible for it, and exercises with decision and firmness its rights and prerogatives. Chosen by the people, he is not, as in Switzerland, the creature and the agent of the legislature; he stands beside it as its equal, representing equally, though in a different sphere, the sovereign in whose name they both act. He draws his strength from the same source whence they derive theirs. He has not only the name of the executive power, but he exercises its natural and legitimate prerogatives. He is the commander-in-chief of the military force, and appoints its principal officers; he nominates several of the higher functionaries of the State; he exercises the right of pardon; the veto which he can oppose to the decisions of the legislature, though not absolute, is still efficacious. Though the Governor of the State of New York is undoubtedly much less powerful than a constitutional king in Europe, at least he is infinitely more so than a petty Council in Switzerland.

But it is especially in the organization of the judicial power that the difference becomes striking.

The judge, although he emanates from the people and is dependent upon them, is still a power to which the people themselves are subject. The judiciary there occupies this exceptional position in respect to its origin, its permanence, its competency, and especially in relation to public manners and public opinion.

The members of the higher tribunals are not chosen, as in Switzerland, by the legislature, a collective power which is often passionate, sometimes blind, and always irresponsible, but by the Governor of the State.* The legal magistrate, when once inducted into office, is regarded as irremovable. No litigation can be determined, no penalty inflicted, except by his agency. Not only does he interpret the law, it may even be said that he judges it. When the legislators, drawn by the manœuvres of contending factions, depart from the spirit or the letter of the constitution, the legal tribunals bring them back to it by refusing to apply their enactments; so that, if the judge cannot compel the people to preserve their constitution, he obliges them, at

* Unfortunately, since M. de Tocqueville wrote, the constitution of the New York judiciary in this respect has been altered. The judges are now elected directly by the people, and only for a limited period of years. This is a change pregnant with disastrous results, though as yet these are but imperfectly developed. — AM. ED.

least, to respect it so long as it exists. He does not guide, but he restrains and keeps within certain bounds, the action of the community. The judiciary, which hardly exists in Switzerland, is the true moderator of the American democracy.

Now let us examine this constitution, even in its smallest details, and we shall not find in it an atom of aristocracy; — nothing that resembles a class or a privilege, but everywhere the same rights, one spirit animating all the institutions, and no conflicting tendencies; the principle of democracy pervades and governs all things. And yet these governments, so completely democratic, have a far more solid foundation, a more peaceable aspect, and much more regular movements, than the democratic governments of Switzerland.

It is allowable to say, that this comes in part from the difference of the laws. The laws of the State of New York, which I have just described, are so contrived as to balance and remedy the natural defects of democracy, while the Swiss institutions which I have portrayed seem made for the very purpose of enhancing them. Here they restrain the people, there they incite them. In America, the fear was lest they should be tyrannical; while in Switzerland, the only desire seems to have been to render them irresistible.

I would not exaggerate the influence which the mechanism of the laws may exert upon the destiny of a nation. I know that there are other causes, more general and more deeply-seated, to which must chiefly be attributed the great events of this world. But it cannot be denied that the institutions of government have a certain virtue which is peculiar to them, and that, in themselves alone, they contribute largely to the prosperity or the misery of society.

If, instead of absolutely condemning almost all the laws of his country, M. Cherbuliez had pointed out wherein they are faulty, and how they might be improved without altering the principle on which they rest, he would have written a book more worthy of posterity, and more useful to his contemporaries.

After showing how democracy works in the Cantons, the author inquires into the influence which it exerts upon the Confederacy itself. Before following him in this direction, it is necessary to do what he has left undone, and clearly indicate what the Federal government is, how it is organized in theory and in fact, and how it operates.

It will be proper to ask, in the first place, if the legislators of the Swiss Confederation wished to make a federal constitution, or only to establish a league; in other words, if they intended to sacrifice a portion of the sovereignty of the Cantons, or not to alienate any part of it. When it is considered that the Cantons are forbidden to exercise several rights which are inherent in sovereignty, and that these are permanently conceded to the Federal government, and especially if we reflect that they have determined the will of the majority to be the law upon the questions thus surrendered to their government, it cannot be doubted that the legislators of the Swiss Confederation desired to establish a true federal constitution, and not a simple league. But it must be confessed that they have concerted measures very ill for success in this undertaking. I do not hesitate to avow my own opinion, that the Federal constitution of Switzerland is the most imperfect of all the institutions of this sort which have hitherto appeared in the world. One would think, on reading it, that we had gone back quite to the Middle Ages, and we cannot be too much astonished to learn, that this confused and imperfect work is the product of an age so well informed and so rich in experience as our own.*

* It must not be forgotten that all this was written in 1847, and before the reaction from the Revolution of 1848 had brought about a reform of the old Federal compact.

It is often alleged, and not without reason, that the Compact restricted altogether too much the rights of the Confederation; that it left outside of the action of the Federal government certain objects, essentially national in character, which it would naturally belong to the Diet to regulate, — such, for example, as the administration of the post-office and the mails, the regulation of weights and measures, and the coining of money; and the weakness of the Federal power has been attributed to the small number of functions which have been confided to its management.

It is very true, that the Compact has denied to the Federal authority several of the powers which naturally, and even necessarily, belong to this government. But it is not here that we are to look for the true cause of the weakness of this authority, since the rights which the Compact has given it would suffice, if it could use them, soon to acquire all those which are now wanting.

The Diet can collect troops, levy money, declare war, make peace, conclude treaties of commerce, and appoint ambassadors. The constitutions of the Cantons, and the great principles of equality before the law, are placed under its protection; which would enable it, in case of need, to interfere in all local affairs. Duties upon imports, tolls upon roads, &c., are regulated by the Diet, so that it is authorized to direct or control the great public works. Finally, the fourth article of the Compact says, *the Diet takes all measures necessary for the security of Switzerland, both at home and abroad*, — which gives it the power of doing anything.

The strongest federal governments have not had greater prerogatives; and, far from thinking that the powers of the central government in Switzerland are too restricted, I am inclined to believe that their limits are not carefully enough determined.

How comes it, then, that, with such great privileges, the

government of the Confederation usually has so little power? The reason is a very simple one: it is because the Compact has not furnished the means of accomplishing what has actually been granted to it, namely, the right to say that certain things ought to be done. Never was a government more completely reduced to inaction and impotence through the imperfection of its organs.

It belongs to the essence of a federal government to act, not in the name of the people, but in the name of the states of which the confederation is composed. If it were otherwise, the constitution would immediately cease to be federal. Hence it results, among other necessary and inevitable consequences, that federal governments are habitually less daring in their resolutions, and slower in their movements, than others.

Most legislators of confederations have endeavored, by the aid of more or less ingenious contrivances, into an examination of which I do not wish to enter, to correct in part this natural vice of the federal system. The Swiss have rendered it vastly more obvious than anywhere else, through the special forms which they have adopted. In their case, not merely do the members of the Diet act only in the name of the different Cantons which they represent, but, generally speaking, they do not take any resolution which has not been foreseen or approved by these Cantons. Hardly anything is left to their free will; every one of them believes himself bound by an imperative mandate imposed beforehand; so that the Diet is a deliberative assembly, where, to say the truth, there is nothing left for deliberation, and where the members speak, not before those who are to adopt the resolution, but before those who have only the right of carrying it into effect. The Diet is a government which determines nothing of itself, but only realizes what twenty-two other governments have separately determined, — a government which, whatever be the nature of events, can decide nothing, foresee nothing, provide for nothing. No combination could be imagined which would be better fitted to increase the natural inactivity of the Federal government, or to change its weakness into a sort of senile incapacity.

There are yet many other causes which, independently of the vices inherent in all federal constitutions, explain the habitual impotence of the government of the Swiss Confederation.

Not only has the Confederation a weak government, but it may be said that it has no government of its own. The constitution, in this respect, is without a parallel in the world. At its head are rulers who do not represent the Confederation. The members of the Directory, who constitute the executive authority of Switzerland, are not chosen by the Diet, still less by the Helvetic people; it is a government of chance, which the Confederation borrows every two years from Berne, from Zurich, or from Lucerne. This Directory, chosen by the inhabitants of a Canton to direct the affairs of a Canton, becomes, in addition to its main function, the head and the arm of the whole country. Certainly, this may pass for one of the greatest political curiosities which the history of human laws affords. The results of such an arrangement are always deplorable, and often very extraordinary. For example, nothing could be more strange than what happened in 1839. That year the Diet was sitting at Zurich, and the Confederation had for its governing body the Directory of the state of Zurich. A revolution took place in the Canton of Zurich, where a popular insurrection overturned the constituted authorities. The Diet immediately found itself without a President, and the federal life remained suspended, till it pleased the Canton to institute for itself other laws and other rulers. The people of Zurich, by changing their local administration, had decapitated Switzerland without wishing it.

Even if the Confederation had an executive authority of its own, its government would still be powerless to compel obedience, from the want of any direct and immediate action upon the citizens. This cause of weakness is more fertile in itself alone than all the others put together; but in order that it may be well understood, we must do more than merely indicate it.

A federal government may have a very limited sphere of action, and yet be strong. If, in this narrow sphere, it can act of itself, without intervention, as ordinary governments do in the unlimited sphere in which they move; if it has its own functionaries, who address themselves directly to every citizen, its own tribunals, who compel every citizen to submit to its laws, — it easily obtains obedience, because it has never anything to fear but the resistance of individuals, and as all obstacles which are raised against it terminate in lawsuits.

On the other hand, a federal government may have a very large field of action, and yet possess only a very weak and very precarious authority, if, instead of addressing itself individually to the citizens, it is obliged to have recourse to the provincial governments; for if these resist, the federal power immediately finds itself at variance, not so much with a subject, as with a rival, from whom it can obtain redress only by war.

The strength of a federal government, then, consists much less in the extent of the powers conferred upon it, than in the greater or less ability which it has of exercising them through its own agents. It is always strong when it can command the citizens; it is always weak when it can issue its commands only to the local governments. The history of confederations affords examples of both systems. But in no confederation that I know of has the central authority been so entirely deprived of all means of action upon the citizens, as in Switzerland. There is not, so to speak, one of its powers which the Federal government there can exercise of itself; there are no functionaries who are entirely dependent upon it, no tribunals which represent exclusively its sovereignty. One would say it was a being to whom some power had given life, but had deprived it of any organs.

Such is the Federal constitution as it is determined by the Compact. Now let us consider, in a few words, with the author of the book which we are analyzing, what influence is exercised upon it by democracy. It cannot be denied, that the democratic revolutions which have successively changed almost all the constitutions of the Cantons during the last fifteen years, have had a great influence also upon the Federal government; but this influence has been exercised in two entirely opposite directions. It is very necessary to have a complete view of this double phenomenon.

The effect of the democratic revolutions which have taken place in the several Cantons has been, to give to the local authorities more activity and more power. The new governments created by these revolutions, resting upon the people and incited by them, found in themselves, all at once, greater strength and a higher idea of their strength, than could be manifested by the governments which they had overturned. And as a similar renovation was not accomplished at the same time in the Federal government, the result which ought to have been expected, and which actually followed, was, that the latter found itself weaker, in comparison with the former, than it had previously been. Provincial pride, the instinct of local independence, impatience of any control in the internal affairs of each Canton, jealousy of a central and supreme authority, are all feelings which have waxed stronger since the establishment of democracy; and from this point of view, it may be said, that democracy has weakened the already feeble power of the

Confederation, and has rendered its daily and habitual task more laborious and more difficult.

But in other respects, it has given it an energy, and, so to speak, an existence, which it never before possessed.

The establishment of democratic institutions in Switzerland has brought about two things entirely new. Every Canton formerly had its separate interests and separate inclinations. The accession of democracy has divided all the Swiss, to whatever Cantons they belonged, into two parties, the one favorable to democratic principles, the other opposed to them. It has created common interests and common passions, which have felt the need, in order to satisfy themselves, of a general and common power, which should extend at the same time over the whole country. The Federal government thus obtained, for the first time, a great aid which it has always wanted; it has been able to rest upon a party; — a source of strength which is dangerous, but indispensable in free countries, where, without it, the government can hardly do anything.

At the same time that democracy divided Switzerland into two parties, it arrayed Switzerland in one of the great parties which divide the world; it created for it a foreign policy; as it gave the country natural allies, it also created for it necessary enemies; it caused the nation to feel the absolute necessity of a government, in order to cultivate and restrain the former, to guard against and repel the latter. It caused a local public spirit to give place to a national public spirit.

Such are the direct effects by which democracy fortified the national government. The indirect influence which it has exercised, and will exercise, in the long run, is not less important. The opposition and the difficulties which a federal government meets with are greater and more various in proportion as the confederate communities are more dissimilar in their institutions, their sentiments, their usages, and their opinions. Similarity of interests is even less important than that resemblance of the laws, the opinions, and the social condition of the people, which makes the task of the government of the American Union so easy. It may even be said, that the strange weakness of the old Federal government in Switzerland was principally due to the prodigious difference and singular opposition which existed between the characters, the opinions, and the laws of the various communities which it had to govern. To keep under the same direction, and to embrace within the same political system, people who are naturally so far apart and so unlike each other, was a most laborious undertaking. A government far better constituted and more skilfully organized would not have succeeded in such an endeavor. The effect of the democratic revolution which is taking place in Switzerland is, to cause certain institutions, certain maxims of government, certain similar ideas, to prevail successively in all the Cantons. If the democratic revolution enhances in the Cantons their spirit of independence of the central power, on the other hand it facilitates the action of that power; it takes away, in a great degree, the causes of opposition, and, without giving the Cantonal governments any stronger desire to obey the Federal government, it makes obedience to its commands infinitely easier.

We ought to study with great care the two contrary effects which I have described, in order to understand the present state, and to foresee the impending condition, of the country. It is by paying attention to only one of these two tendencies, that some have been induced to believe, that the accession of democracy in the governments of the Cantons will produce, as its immediate result, an easy extension of the legislative sphere of the Federal government, and will concentrate in its hands the ordinary direction of local affairs; in a word, that it will modify the whole economy of the Compact by increasing the centralization of affairs. For my own part, I am convinced that, for a long time, such a revolution will meet with far more obstacles than is generally imagined. The present governments of the Cantons will show no more inclination than their predecessors for a revolution of this sort, and they will do all they can to prevent its accomplishment.

And yet I believe that, in spite of this opposition, the Federal government is destined, in the long run, to acquire greater power. In this respect, laws will not favor it so much as other circumstances. It will not, perhaps, very visibly increase its prerogatives, but it will make a different and more frequent use of them. It will become greater in fact, it will remain the same in theory; its power will be developed rather by the interpretation, than by the alteration, of the Compact; and its authority will preponderate over all others, before it has become capable of governing Switzerland.

It may also be foreseen, that the very persons who, up to the present time, have been the most opposed to the regular extension of the Federal authority, will soon be induced to favor it, either to escape the intermittent pressure of a power so ill-organized, or to protect themselves against the heavier and more imminent tyranny of the local governments.

But it is certain that, for the future, whatever modifications may be made in the letter of the Compact, the Federal constitution of Switzerland is thoroughly and irrevocably changed. The Confederation has changed its nature. It has become a new thing in Europe; an energetic policy has succeeded to its former one of inertness and neutrality; its existence, from being purely municipal, has become national, — an existence which is grander, but more laborious, more agitated, and more uncertain.

SPEECH OF M. DE TOCQUEVILLE

IN THE CHAMBER OF DEPUTIES, JANUARY 27, 1848, IN THE DEBATE ON THE PROPOSED ANSWER TO AN ADDRESS FROM THE THRONE.*

MY intention, gentlemen, is not to continue the particular discussion which has been begun. I think the subject will be taken up again to better advantage when we come to consider the bill for the regulation of prisons. My object in taking the floor is a more general one.

The fourth paragraph of the Address, which is now under discussion, naturally invites the Chamber to take a general view of our whole internal policy, and especially of that aspect of our home politics which has been pointed out, and made the subject of an amendment, by my honorable friend, M. Billault. It is this portion of the discussion on the Address which I wish to bring before the Chamber.

I may be deceived, gentlemen, but it seems to me that

* In the advertisement prefixed to the twelfth edition of this work, the author thought himself entitled to say, that the Revolution of 1848 had not taken him by surprise. Our readers will thank us, then, for inserting here, as a proof of this assertion, a report of the speech made by him in the Chamber of Deputies just one month before the fearful outbreak of the Revolution of 1848. In this remarkable speech, with great precision and truly prophetic forecast, qualities for which he was indebted to the thorough study that he had made of modern democracy, the great publicist foretold, not only the imminence of the Revolution, but the social and economical, rather than political, character which it was at once to manifest. — *Note by the French publisher.*

the present state of things, the present state of opinion, the present state of people's minds in France, is such as to create alarm and distress. For my own part, I sincerely declare that, for the first time for fifteen years, I feel a special dread of the future; and what proves to me that I am right, is that I am not alone in this impression. I believe I may appeal to all who hear me, and all will answer, that, in the districts which they represent, a similar impression exists; that a peculiar uneasiness, an undefined dread, pervades the minds of men; that, for the first time perhaps for sixteen years, the sentiment, the instinct, of instability, that sentiment which is the precursor of revolutions, which often announces and sometimes produces them, that this sentiment exists in the country to a very grave degree.

If I perfectly understood what was said the other day in conclusion by the Minister of Finance, the Cabinet themselves admit the reality of the impression of which I speak; but he attributes it to certain special causes, to certain recent accidental events in political life which have agitated the minds of men, and to words which have roused their passions.

Gentlemen, by attributing the admitted evil to the causes thus indicated, I fear that they impute it not to the disease itself, but only to its symptoms. For my own part, I am convinced that the malady is not there; it is more general and more deeply seated. This disease, which must be cured, cost what it may, and which, believe me, will sweep us all away, — understand me! all, if we do not beware, — is the present condition of the public mind and of public morals. Here lies the complaint; it is to this point that I wish to draw your attention. I believe that the public morals, the public mind, are in a dangerous condition; and I believe, too, that the government have contributed, and contributed in the gravest manner, to increase the danger. This is what has made me rise to speak.

Gentlemen, when I attentively consider the class who govern, the class who have political rights, and then turn to those who are governed, I am troubled and appalled by what I see in both. And, to speak first of those whom I have called the class who govern, — (observe that I use these words in their most general acceptation, — I speak not merely of the middle classes, but of all citizens, in whatever position they may be, who possess and exercise political rights,) — I say, then, that I am troubled and appalled by what is manifest in the governing class. What I see there, gentlemen, I can express in a word. Public morals are degraded there, — they are already deeply degraded; they are degraded there more and more every day; common opinions, sentiments, and ideas are there giving place every day, more and more, to individual interests, private aims, and motives borrowed from private life and private ambition.

I do not intend to compel the Chamber to expatiate any more than is necessary upon these sad details; I will only address myself to my opponents themselves, to my fellow-members of the ministerial majority. I entreat them to make for their own use a sort of statistical review of the electoral colleges which have made them their deputies in this place. Let them form a first class of those who have voted for them, not from political opinions, but from sentiments of private friendship or good neighborhood. In a second class let them put those who vote for them, not from any motive of public or common interest, but for purely local purposes. To this second category let them finally add a third, consisting of those who vote for them from motives of exclusively private interest; and I ask them if those who remain are very numerous, — I ask them if those who vote from disinterested public sentiment, led by opinion or public feeling, if these form the majority of the voters who have conferred upon them the office of Deputy. I am sure that they must answer in the negative. I will venture also to ask of them, if, to their certain knowledge, for five years, ten years, fifteen years, the number of those who vote for them from motives of personal and private interest has not been continually increasing, and the number of those who vote from political opinion continually decreasing. Finally, let them say if, around them, under their own eyes, there has not been establishing itself, by degrees, in public opinion a kind of singular toleration for the facts of which I speak; if, by degrees, a kind of low and vulgar morality is not created, according to which the man who possesses political rights owes it to himself, owes it to his children, to his wife, to his relations, to make a personal use of these rights to further their interests; and if this is not gradually rising to be considered as a sort of duty on the part of a father of a family, — if this new morality, unknown in the grander periods of our history, unknown at the beginning of our Revolution, is not developing itself more and more, and every day gaining possession of the minds of men. I ask them this.

Now, what does all this amount to, except a continuous and profound degradation, a depravation more and more complete of the public morals?

And if, turning from public to private life, I consider what is passing, — if I pay attention to all that you have witnessed, especially during the last year, to all those notorious scandals, all those crimes, all those misdemeanors, all those offences, all those extraordinary vices, which every circumstance has seemed to bring to light in all quarters, and which every judicial investigation reveals, — if I attend to all this, have I not cause to be appalled? Am I not entitled to say, that not only our public, but our private morals, are becoming more and more depraved?

And observe that I do not say this from a moralist's point of view, but that I speak from a political motive. Do you know what is the general, efficient, deeply-seated cause, why private morals are degraded? It is because public morals have first become depraved. It is because pure morality does not govern the principal actions of life, that it does not descend to the smaller ones. It is because private interest has taken the place of disinterested sentiment in public action, that selfishness has become the law in private life.

It has been said that there are two sorts of morality, the one for politics, and the other for private life. Certainly, if what is passing around us really is what I see it to be, never was the falsity of such an assertion proved in a more striking and unhappy manner than in our own day. Yes, I believe that a change is taking place in our private morals of such a nature as to trouble and alarm all good citizens, and that this change proceeds in great part from what is coming to pass in our public morals. (*Marks of dissent.*)

Well, gentlemen, if you will not believe me on this point, you will at least believe the general impression of Europe. I think I am as well informed as any person in this Chamber of what is said and published about us in other parts of Europe; and I assure you, in the sincerity of my heart, that I am not only saddened, but profoundly distressed, at what I hear and read every day; I am distressed when I see the advantage which is taken against us from the facts of which I speak, the exaggerated consequences that are deduced from them against the whole nation, against the entire national character. I am distressed when I see how much the power of France is gradually weakened in the world; I am distressed when I see that not only the moral power of France, but the power of her principles, her ideas, and her sentiments, is enfeebled.

France was the first to throw into the world, amid the thunders of her first Revolution, dogmas which have subsequently become the regenerating principles of all modern societies. This has been her glory; it is the most precious portion of her history. Now it is these very principles which our example at the present day is depriving of force. The application which we seem to make of them in our own case leads the world to doubt their truth. Europe, which is watching us, begins to ask if we were right or wrong; she asks if it is true, what we have so often affirmed, that we are leading the nations of the world towards a happier and more prosperous future, or whether we are not dragging them down after us into moral degradation and ruin. This, gentlemen, is what is causing me most grief in the spectacle which we are offering to the world. It not only injures us, but it injures our principles, it injures our cause, it injures this intellectual country to which, for my own part, as a Frenchman, I am more attached than to the material and physical country which is before our eyes.

Gentlemen, if the spectacle which we are offering produces such an effect when seen from afar, when viewed from the confines of Europe, what effect do you think it is producing in France itself, upon those classes who have no political rights, and who, from the midst of the political inaction to which they are condemned by our laws, behold us alone acting upon the grand theatre on which we are placed? What do you think is the effect produced on them by such a spectacle?

For my own part, I am appalled by it. Some say there is no danger, because there is no insurrection; they say that, as there is no material disorder on the surface of society, revolution is still far distant.

Gentlemen, allow me to tell you that I think you are deceived. Undoubtedly the disorder does not yet appear in overt acts, but it has sunk deeply into the minds of the people. Look at what is passing among the working classes, though at present, I own, they are tranquil. It is true that they are not agitated by political passions properly so called, as much as they formerly were; but do you not see that the agitation among them is no longer political, but social? Do you not see that there are gradually diffused among them opinions and ideas, which do not tend merely to overturn such and such laws, this or that ministry, this or that government even, but to subvert society itself, and to shake the very foundations on which it now rests? Do you not know what they are every day talking about? Do you not hear them incessantly declare, that all who are above them are incapable and unworthy to govern,—that the present distribution of wealth is unjust, and that property does not rest upon any equitable basis? And do you not believe that, when such opinions have taken root, when they are almost universally diffused, when they have penetrated deeply into the minds of the multitude, they must bring about sooner or later—I know not when, I know not how—but they must bring about sooner or later the most fearful revolutions?

This, gentlemen, is my profound conviction. I believe we are at the present moment slumbering upon a volcano. (*Murmurs.*) I am thoroughly convinced of it.

Now, permit me to inquire before you, in a few words, but with truth and perfect sincerity, who are the true authors, the principal authors, of the evil which I have just endeavored to describe.

I know very well that evils such as I have just spoken of do not all flow, perhaps do not even principally flow, from the action of governments. I know very well that the long revolutions, which have so often heaved and shaken the ground of this country, must have left a singular instability in the minds of men. I know very well that, in the passions and excitements of party, certain secondary but considerable causes may be found, which may serve to explain the deplorable phenomenon which I have just made known to you; but I have too high an idea of the part which the power of government plays in this world's affairs, not to be convinced that, when a great evil is produced in society,—a great political evil, a great moral evil,—the government is largely responsible for it.

What has the government done, then, to produce the evil which I have just described to you? What has it done to bring about this deeply seated disorder, first in public, and then in private morals? How has it contributed to this result?

I believe it can be said, without wounding anybody, that the government has again, especially during these latter years, seized upon larger rights, a greater influence, more considerable and more various prerogatives, than it had possessed at any other epoch. It has become infinitely greater than could ever have been imagined, not only by those who gave, but by those who received, it in 1830. It may be affirmed, on the other hand, that the principle of liberty has been less developed than any one could then have expected. I pass no judgment on the fact itself; I look only at its consequences. If a result so singular and so unexpected, so strange a turn of human affairs, has baffled some bad passions, some guilty hopes, do you not believe that, on witnessing it, many noble sentiments, many disinterested aspirations, have become extinct,—that there has followed from it, in many honest hearts, an abandonment of all political hopes as illusions, and a real depression of soul?

But it is especially the manner in which this result has been produced, the underhand, and, up to a certain point, the surreptitious manner in which this end has been obtained, which has given a fatal blow to the public morality.

It is by seizing again upon the old prerogatives which were supposed to have been abolished by the Revolution of July, by reviving old powers which seemed to have been annulled, by restoring to vigor old laws which people thought had been abrogated, by applying new laws to purposes for which they were not enacted, — it is by all these underhand means, by this skilful and patient management, that the government has at last obtained more power, more activity and influence, than it ever before possessed in France.

This, gentlemen, is what the government has done, and particularly what the present ministry have done. And think you that this manner, which I have just called underhand and surreptitious, of recovering power by degrees, of taking it as it were by surprise, by using other means than those which the constitution had granted, — think you that this strange spectacle of adroitness and skilful management, held up before the world for several years, on so vast a theatre, to a whole nation which is looking on, — think you that this spectacle has been such as to improve the public morals?

For my own part, I am profoundly convinced of the contrary. I would not attribute to my opponents dishonorable motives which they have not entertained; I will admit, if you wish, that, in making use of the means which I censure, they thought they were submitting to a necessary evil, — that the magnitude of the end concealed from them the danger and the immorality of the means. I am willing to believe all this; but does this make the means any the less dangerous? They believe that the revolution which has taken place during the last fifteen years in the powers of government was necessary; — be it so! that they have not made it to promote their own interests; — I am willing to believe it! But it is not the less true that they have effected it by means which the public morality disavows; it is not the less true that they have effected it by taking men, not by their honest side, but by their bad side, — by their passions, by their weakness, by their interests, often by their vices. Hence it is, that, while having perhaps an honest purpose, they have done things which were not honest. And in order to do these things, it was necessary to call to their side, to honor with their favor, to introduce into their daily company, men who desired from the power that was confided to them only the gross satisfaction of their private interests; they have thus granted a sort of premium to immorality and vice.

I will cite but one example to show what I mean; it is that of the minister, whose name I do not remember, who was called to be a member of the Cabinet, although all France, as well as his colleagues, knew already that he was unworthy to sit there; who left the Cabinet, because this unworthiness became too notorious, and was then placed — where? On the highest bench of the legal tribunals, whence he was soon obliged to descend to take his stand at the bar as a criminal under prosecution.

As for me, gentlemen, I do not regard this as an isolated fact; I consider it as the symptom of a general malady, the most striking example of a whole scheme of policy; by walking in the ways which you had chosen, you had need of such men.

But it is especially through the abuse of government influence, to which the Minister of Foreign Affairs has had recourse, that the moral evil of which I was speaking has been diffused and generalized, and has pervaded the country. It is here that you have acted, directly and without intervention, upon public morality, no longer by examples, but by acts. I do not wish in this respect to place the ministers in a worse position than they really occupy; I know well that they have been exposed to an immense temptation; I know well, that at no time, in no country, has a government ever been exposed to a similar one, — that nowhere has power had in its hands so many means of corruption, nowhere had before it a political class so limited in number, and standing so much in want of many things, that the facility of acting upon it by corruption appeared greater, or the desire of so acting upon it more irresistible. I admit, then, that it is not by a premeditated desire of acting upon men through their private interests only, as if this were the single chord in their hearts which could be made to vibrate, that the ministry have done this great evil; I know well that they have been hurried down an inclined plane, on which it was very difficult to hold their ground; I know all that. The only thing that I reproach them with is, that of having placed themselves there, of having put themselves in a position where, in order to govern, they found it necessary to appeal, not to opinions, to sentiments, to general ideas, but to private interests. Once embarked in this boat, I hold it for certain that, whatever might have been their wishes, whatever their desire to turn back, a fatality urged them, and must have urged them, constantly farther and farther on, to every position which they have since occupied. But one thing was wanting for this result, — that they should continue to live. Just as soon as they reached the point where I just now placed them, it was only necessary to exist eight years, in order to do all which we have seen that they have done, in order not only to use all the immoral means of government of which I have just spoken, but to exhaust them.

It was this fatality which first made them increase beyond bounds the number of offices; which then, when these failed them, induced them to divide, and, so to speak, to break up into fractions, in order to have a larger number, if not the offices, at least the emoluments, as has been done in all the bureaux of the Department of Finance. It was this same necessity which, when, in spite of this management, places and salaries were again wanted, caused them, as we saw the other day in Petit's case, to create vacancies artificially, and by underhand means, in places which had been already filled.

The Minister of Foreign Affairs has told us many times, that the opposition was unjust in its attacks, and that the accusations it had directed against him were violent, unfounded, and false. But I put the question to him directly, has the opposition ever, in its worst moments, accused him of what has this day been proved? The opposition has certainly uttered grave reproaches, — excessive reproaches, perhaps, but I know not; — but it has never accused him of doing what he has recently himself confessed that he had done.

And for my own part, I declare that not only have I never accused the Minister of Foreign Affairs of these things, but never had I even suspected him of them. Never, never would I have believed, on hearing him support from this place, with a marvellous command of language, the claims of morality in politics, — on hearing him hold such language, which made me, in spite of my opposition, proud of my country, — assuredly I would never have believed that what has happened was possible; I should have believed that I was wanting not only to him, but still more to myself, if I had supposed what was nevertheless the truth. Shall I believe, as was said the other day, that, when the Minister of Foreign Affairs held this fine and noble language, he was not saying what he thought? As for me, I will not go so far; I believe that the instinct, the taste, of the Minister was to act differently from what he has done. But he has been pushed on, drawn away in spite of himself, deprived of his own will, so to speak, by that sort of political and ministerial fatality which he has imposed upon himself, and which I just now portrayed.

He asked the other day, what there was so grave in the fact which he called a petty fact. What there is so grave in it is that it should be imputed to you,—that it should be you, you, of all the politicians perhaps in this Chamber, who by your language had given the least cause to think that you had committed acts of this sort,—that it is you who should be convicted of it.

And if this act, if this spectacle is of a nature to make a profound and painful impression, a deplorable one for morality in general, what impression do you not suppose it will make upon the particular morality of the agents of government? There is a comparison which appeared singularly striking to me, as soon as I became acquainted with the facts.

Three years ago, a functionary of the Minister of Foreign Affairs, a high functionary, differed in political opinion from the Minister upon one point. He did not express his dissent in an obtrusive manner, but he silently voted. The Minister of Foreign Affairs declared that it was impossible for him to live in the official company of a man who did not think precisely as he did; he dismisses him, or, to speak plainly, he expels him from office.

And now, behold another agent, placed not so high in the scale, but nearer to the person of the Minister of Foreign Affairs, commits the acts which you know of. At first, the Minister of Foreign Affairs did not deny that he was acquainted with them; he has since denied it; I admit for a moment that he was ignorant of them. But if he can deny any knowledge of these facts when they occurred, at least he cannot deny that they did take place, and that he now knows them; they are certain. Here there is no longer question concerning a difference of political opinion between you and this agent; the question relates to a moral disagreement, to what most intimately concerns the heart and conscience of man; it is not only the Minister who is here compromised, observe it well, it is the man. You, who have not been able to allow a difference of political opinion more or less important between you and an honorable man who had only voted against you, you find no blame — nay, more, you find recompense — for the functionary who, even if he has not carried out your own thought, has unworthily compromised you, has certainly placed you in the most serious and painful position in which you have ever been since you first entered political life. You retain this functionary, — much more, you recompense, you honor him.

What do you wish people should think of it? How do you suppose they can refrain from drawing one of these two conclusions: — either that you have a singular partiality for this class of differences of opinion, or that you are no longer free to punish them? I defy you, in spite of the immense talent which I acknowledge you to possess, I defy you to escape from this alternative. If the man of whom I speak has really acted in spite of you, why do you keep him near you? If you keep him near you, if you reward him, if you refuse to censure him, even in the lightest degree, we must necessarily draw the conclusion that I have just mentioned.

But let us admit that I am mistaken concerning the causes of the great evil of which I was speaking; let us admit, for a moment, that, in fact, the government in general and the cabinet in particular are in no wise responsible for it. The evil itself, gentlemen, is it any the less immense? Do we not owe it to our country, to ourselves, to make the most energetic and persevering efforts to overcome it? I was just now telling you that this evil would bring about, sooner or later, — I know not how, I know not whence it will come, — but, sooner or later, it will produce a most serious revolution in the country. Be sure of it.

When I begin to inquire what was the real efficient cause, which, at various times, at different epochs, among different nations, has brought about the ruin of the classes which held the government, I find indeed this or that event, this or that man, this or that accident or superficial cause; but believe me, the real cause, the efficient cause, which has made men lose power, is that they had become unworthy to hold it.

Consider, gentlemen, the old French monarchy; it was stronger than you are, stronger by its origin; it was supported better than you are by ancient usages, by ancestral manners, by venerable creeds; it was stronger than you are, and yet it was prostrated in the dust. And why did it fall? Think you that it was the action of this or that man, the deficit in the finances, the oath in the tennis-court, Lafayette, Mirabeau? No, gentlemen. There was a more real and deeply-seated cause, and this cause was, that the class which then formed the government, through its indifference, its selfishness, and its vices, had become unable and unworthy to govern. This was the true cause.

Oh! if it is right to have our minds engrossed by patriotic solicitude at all times, how much more incumbent is it upon us to be thus anxious at the present hour! Are you not aware, by a sort of instinctive intuition that you cannot analyze, but which is certain, that the ground is heaving anew in Europe? Do you not feel that the air is already stirred by the coming gust of a revolution? This movement in the air, one knows not what produces it, or whence it comes, or what it will sweep away; but is it at such a moment that you remain passive spectators of what it is not too strong a phrase to call the degradation of the public morals?

I speak without bitterness; I speak even, as I believe, without party spirit; I am attacking men against whom I have no personal animosity; but I am obliged to tell the country what is my profound and settled conviction. My profound and settled conviction is, that the public morals are becoming corrupt, and that this public corruption will bring upon you, in a short time, perhaps at an hour which is already at hand, a new revolution. Does the life of kings hang by a thread which is thicker or more difficult to break than that of other men? Do you know what may happen in France within a year, within a month, perhaps within a day. You know not; but what you do know is, that the tempest is on the horizon, that it is mounting over your heads. Will you allow it to burst upon you unawares?

Gentlemen, I beg you not to do so; I do not demand, I entreat; I would willingly bend my knees before you, so real and serious do I hold the danger to be, so truly do I believe that pointing it out is not having recourse to an empty rhetorical form. Yes, the danger is great! Guard against it, whilst there is yet time; avert the calamity by energetic measures; attack not merely its symptoms, but the malady itself.

Changes in our system of laws have been mentioned. I am much inclined to believe that these changes are not only useful, but necessary; thus, I believe in the utility of electoral reform, in the urgency of parliamentary reform. But, gentlemen, I am not foolish enough not to know, that it is not laws alone which shape the destiny of nations. No, it is not the mechanism of the laws which produces the great events of this world; that which regulates events is the spirit of the government. Keep the laws, if you will; although I believe it will be very wrong in you to do so, yet keep them; retain even the men, if that pleases you, and, for my own part, I will offer no opposition to your doing so; but for God's sake, change the spirit of the government, for I repeat it, that spirit is leading you to destruction.

BIOGRAPHICAL NOTICE OF DE TOCQUEVILLE.

THE family of Clerel, from which M. de Tocqueville was descended, belongs to the nobility of France, and has been established for centuries in that peninsula, forming the modern department of La Manche, which projects from the coast of Normandy into the English Channel, and has Cherbourg at its extremity. Here they possessed with seignorial rights the village and lands of Tocqueville, whence they derived their territorial designation. The title of Count, formally bestowed by Louis XVIII. on the father of Alexis, was only the acknowledgment of an ancient distinction. The chateau that formed the family residence consisted at first of a huge stone tower, now of great antiquity, which was enlarged in the seventeenth century by appending to it a quadrangle, that served both for the residence of the family and for farm buildings. An old "feudal weathercock" surmounted the great tower; and a large dove-cot, now tenantless, still marks the ancient right of the lord of the manor to keep his pigeons at the expense of his peasantry. "A stain over the door indicates the spot from which the Revolution of '93 tore the escutcheon of the family."

Count de Tocqueville, the father of Alexis, came into possession of this estate at an early age, and married Mademoiselle de Rosambo, a granddaughter of the celebrated M. de Malesherbes. This marriage took place in 1793, shortly after the execution of Louis XVI. had caused M. de Malesherbes to retire to his country-seat, at which place the wedding was celebrated. Only six months afterwards, the illustrious old man himself, — for so he is entitled to be called after his courageous defence of his king, — and his whole family, consisting of his daughter, his granddaughter, Madame de Chateaubriand, and her husband, a brother of the celebrated statesman and author, were seized and sent as prisoners to Paris; where, on the 22d of April, 1794, they were all guillotined together. Count de Tocqueville and his wife were arrested at about the same time; but after remaining a long time in prison, they were at length liberated by the fall of Robespierre. They then returned to his family mansion, and as they never emigrated, they were allowed to retain their estate, where they lived in dignified seclusion most of the time till the restoration of the Bourbons. Then the Count reaped some reward for his consistent and uncompromising conduct and opinions as an ardent royalist, being appointed successively Prefect at Metz, at Amiens, and at Versailles, and finally created a peer of France. Late in life, stimulated perhaps by the success of his son, the Count became an author, and achieved no small distinction, his "Philosophical History of the Reign of Louis XV." being one of the most valuable productions of the modern school of French historians.

These particulars respecting the parentage and family of De Tocqueville are interesting, as they show what were the influences under which he received his early training, and which undoubtedly colored his sentiments and opinions throughout life. He was, so to speak, born and bred an aristocrat and a loyalist, and as such he witnessed with mournful but dignified composure the rapid and overwhelming development of democracy in his day, which he knew full well would finally sweep away every vestige of those distinctions which had constituted the local grandeur of his house. What others would merely have brooded over as a misfortune, became to him an object of philosophical study; and, far from seeking to limit or repress, he sought only to direct and chasten, that irresistible growth of opinion and march of public affairs which are so swiftly levelling all inequalities of condition, and establishing the principle of the sovereignty of the people as the sole element in the government of this world's affairs. He came to America in order to study the phenomenon where it had existed the longest, and had been most freely developed under favorable circumstances. In the Introduction to his work, he says: "The whole book has been written under the impression of a kind of religious terror, produced in the author's mind by the view of that irresistible revolution which has advanced for centuries in spite of every obstacle, and which is still advancing in the midst of the ruins it has caused." This personal interest in his subject was unquestionably one great cause of the ardor and the success with which he studied and analyzed it; and this interest, as we have seen, arose from the circumstances of his birth and the position and history of his family.

Alexis Charles Henri Clerel de Tocqueville, the third son of his parents, was born at Paris, whither the family had gone upon a visit, on the 29th of July, 1805. While yet an infant, he was carried home to Tocqueville in a pannier slung across a horse, with his nurse on a pillion, the facilities for travelling in those days, in districts at any considerable distance from the capital, being of a very primitive character. He does not seem to have received a very regular or finished education, being trained chiefly at home, under the instruction of an Abbé Lesueur, to whom he was much attached, and afterwards at the College of Metz, where he began his classical studies while his father was Prefect of that city. There he did not acquire any distinction in the classics, but paid great attention to writing French prose, and in 1822 gained the first prize in rhetoric. But the most effective education which he had was an unconscious one under the quiet influences of home, where the counsels and example of his parents formed his manners, and developed in him a nice sense of honor and strong religious sentiment and conviction. On his father's death, in 1856, he wrote to one of his intimate friends, "If I am worth anything, I owe it above all to my education, to those examples of uprightness, simplicity, and honor which I found about me in coming into the world and as I advanced in life. I owe my parents much more than mere existence."

Having determined to enter the legal profession, he completed the study of law at Paris in 1826, and then set out upon a tour through Italy and Sicily, accompanied by his next elder brother, the Baron Edward de Tocqueville. A small portion of the copious memoranda which he made during this journey has been published in his Memoirs; it relates to the island of Sicily and its inhabitants, and is chiefly curious as showing how the philosophical bent of his mind turned, even in early manhood, to observation of the social and intellectual state of a people, as affected by their laws and political institutions.

From this delightful experience of Italian travel he was recalled by a letter from home, in April, 1827, announcing that he had been appointed *Juge Auditeur*, a sort of deputy or assistant prosecuting officer, attached to the lower courts at Versailles, of which town his father was then Prefect. It was the first round on the ladder of advancement in the legal magistracy, the higher steps remaining to be taken according as self-achieved distinction or interest with the ministry might in time secure his promotion. The office was one which might be held nearly as a sinecure, or to which the incumbent could cause regular duties to be attached. De Tocqueville was industrious and ambitious, and therefore solicited and obtained active employment. He soon displayed solid rather than brilliant talents, which, with his grave manner of speaking, caused more than one of the presiding judges to foretell his high advancement in the profession. But the strong tendency to generalization which he even then betrayed, and his aversion to technicalities and details, rendered it doubtful in the minds of some of his friends whether this prophecy would hold good. Among his colleagues at the bar he found M. Gustave de Beaumont, with whom he soon contracted a close intimacy, that continued throughout life. With this congenial associate, whatever time could be rescued from judicial labors was soon devoted to more attractive studies than that of the law, especially to those connected with general history and politics. Already the young friends aspired to become philosophical statesmen and to guide the helm of state.

These studies and day-dreams were soon broken by an untoward event for De Tocqueville, — the Revolution of 1830. All his philosophy had not overcome his early predilections as a legitimist, and only with great reluctance did he give in his adhesion to the new dynasty. The event contributed further to wean him from his profession, as he could no longer count upon his father's influence at court to facilitate his promotion. "Every day he became more and more convinced that France, in irresistibly drifting into democracy, was also drifting into its perils. He determined to visit the only great country in which those dangers have been conquered, and where perfect equality reigns side by side with liberty. He communicated his scheme to his late colleague at Versailles, then *Substitut du Procureur du Roi* in Paris, who was charmed with the proposal. Obstacles, however, stood in their way: as magistrates they both required leave of absence, and a legitimate cause for obtaining it. At that time, as is always the case immediately after a revolution, all innovation was held in honor, and a reform of real but of secondary importance (that of the prisons) attracted public attention. A penitentiary system, which had proved successful in the United States, was talked of. The two young magistrates presented to the then Minister of the Interior, the Comte de Montalivet, a paper in which, after setting forth the question, they offered to study it on the spot, if they might be sent on an official mission. It was granted to them; and the Minister of Justice having consented, the two friends set out with a leave obtained in due form. It has often been said that this mission was the cause of Alexis de Tocqueville's expedition. It was in truth only the pretext. His real and long premeditated object was to study the customs and institutions of American society."

Having arrived at New York on the 10th of May, 1831, De Tocqueville devoted about a year to travelling in the United States, to observations connected with the subject of his formal mission, and to other inquiries of a more general nature, which were to furnish the material for the great work which he was now meditating. While journeying in the depth of a severe winter through our Southwestern States, he was exposed to unaccustomed privations and hardships, which operated hardly on a constitution originally slender, and probably laid the seeds of a malady which was ultimately to prove fatal. Returning to Europe in the spring of 1832, his attention was necessarily first directed to the preparation of a report to the Minister of the Interior on the subject of his mission. This work, the joint composition of his friend and himself, soon appeared under the title of "The Penitentiary System in the United States, and its Application in France," and had good success. It passed through three editions, was translated both into German and English, and has shaped much of the subsequent legislation of France upon the subject.

Even before this report was completed, De Tocqueville had quitted the legal profession forever. De Beaumont, having refused to speak on an occasion when the official part which he had to play appeared to him discreditable, was summarily dismissed from office; and his friend resented this procedure so highly, that he immediately sent in his own resignation. He was probably glad of an opportunity to break off all connection with a government for which he had never entertained either sympathy or respect, to quit at the same time a profession which he had always disliked, and to give his whole time and effort to the preparation of the work on which his thoughts had so long been deeply engaged. The two years from 1832 to 1834, which were probably the happiest of his life, were devoted to the composition of the First Part, which, after being rejected by one publisher and accepted only with great reluctance by another, appeared in January, 1835. Even if it had not been successful, the labor bestowed upon it would have been its own exceeding great reward. Secluding himself during these two years from society, spending the daytime, in order to avoid interruption, in a lodging the secret of which was known to very few of his friends, sustained by the flattering dreams which always visit a young author and by the attachment which he had already formed to the lady whom he was soon to marry, he gave himself up to the intoxication which generally attends the continuous creative action of mind. The success of the work was great, but it was no more than he had anticipated.

"Since Montesquieu, there has been nothing like it," said Royer-Collard; and on a subsequent occasion, M. de Barante added, "Twenty years later, we repeat the same judgment." It has passed through fourteen editions at Paris, and has been translated into nearly all the languages of modern Europe. In 1836, the French Institute adjudged to its author the Monthyon prize, which is given annually for the work of the highest moral utility that has been produced during the year; and in this case, to mark a special distinction, the prize was increased from 6,000 francs, its usual amount, to 8,000. A year later, De Tocqueville was chosen a member of the Academy of the Moral and Political Sciences; and in 1841, he became one of the forty members of the French Academy, the highest literary honor that a Frenchman can attain. This last distinction was well deserved, for considered only as a specimen of refined and idiomatic French prose, evincing a careful study of the inimitable style of Pascal, but betraying also an imitation of the curt and sententious manner of Montesquieu, the book is fairly entitled to take rank as a classic in the literature of France. In respect to doctrine, it was welcomed both by the friends and opponents of democracy; by the former, because it points out so clearly the rapid development and future universal dominion of democratic principles; by the latter, because it shows with equal clearness the dangers incident to this progress, and the ease with which such dominion degenerates into a tyranny even more hateful than the despotism of one man. Perhaps the greatest merit of the author consists in the resolute impartiality with which he looks at the subject on all its sides, and shows that the welfare of a nation under democratic rule can be maintained only on condition of such a union of general intelligence and religious faith with submissiveness to constitutional restraint, as is rarely exemplified in the history of mankind.

In the same year in which his book became so generally popular, he married Miss Mary Motley, an English lady without fortune, but who united those qualities of character and intellect which rendered her, during an unbroken union of twenty-five years, his best companion, counsellor, and friend. He often remarked that his marriage, though censured by those prudent friends who look only to the contribution which a wife is first able to make to her husband's pecuniary or social position in the world, had proved to be the most sensible action of his life. About the same time, he visited England, whither his literary renown had preceded him, and where he consequently received a cordial welcome into the best circles of literary and aristocratic society. The character of De Tocqueville's mind, in several respects, approached more nearly to the English than the French standard of excellence; and he soon contracted an intimate friendship with many eminent Englishmen, on frequent intercourse with whom depended much of the happiness of his subsequent career. His personal qualities, indeed, were such as to make him an object of strong attachment to all his friends. An Englishman who knew him well says of him, that "the extreme delicacy of his physical organization, the fastidious refinement of his tastes, and the charm of his manners, made him the very type of a high-bred gentleman."

His mother died shortly after his return to France, and then, through a family arrangement with his two older brothers, he obtained possession of the paternal estate at Tocqueville, and made it his permanent residence. The old chateau was in bad repair, — "full of associations and ruins," says his French biographer; but the country around is rich and pleasant, and the upper part of the building commands a magnificent view of the sea-coast and the English Channel. Here De Tocqueville devoted himself to the management of the estate, for which his knowledge of agriculture did not very well qualify him, to the preparation of the Second Part of his work, and to cultivating that acquaintance with his country neighbors, on which he was to depend for election to the Chamber of Deputies, and thus for an introduction to political life. To this object his ambition was now directed; he longed for an opportunity to carry out in practice some of the theoretical views which he had so nobly developed; and perhaps his success in abstract speculation made him over-estimate his fitness for the practical management of affairs.

The Second Part of his work, which treats of the influence of democracy upon the action of mind, and upon feelings and manners, was published in 1840, and its success was decided, though not so brilliant and general as that of its predecessor. The subject, of course, had now less of novelty to recommend it, and the treatment of it, though even more elaborate in thought and expression than the First Part, abounded too much in abstract speculation and acute philosophical analysis for the taste of ordinary readers. The year before it was published, its author offered himself as a candidate to his own district for election to the Chamber of Deputies. His relative, Count Molé, then Prime Minister of France, gave orders, without consultation with him, that all the influence of the government should be exerted in his favor. Fearful lest he should be thus committed to a support of the ministerial policy, De Tocqueville wrote back with some haughtiness to decline the proffered aid. The Minister replied with considerable spirit, but with politeness and good sense, remarking that he had not intended to impose any obligation, that isolation is not independence, that the party of government were acting together, not from interested motives, but from sincere conviction, in defence of the institutions of the country, and that their assistance, as it was not desired, should be promptly withdrawn. The candidacy of De Tocqueville, thus deprived of government aid, proved unsuccessful; his neighbors could not be made to believe that, although he belonged by birth and social position to the nobility, he did not share the feelings and the prejudices of his order, but was really the friend and the expounder of democracy. The popular opinion respecting him was well expressed by his opponent, a retired manufacturer, who cried out lustily, "Beware! He is going to bring back his aristocratic pigeons into their old dove-cot." Two years afterwards, when his temper and principles had come to be better understood in the neighborhood, he was elected by a triumphant majority to the Chamber, and he continued to represent his district thoughout his parliamentary career.

That career lasted only twelve years, up to December, 1851, when Louis Napoleon's *coup d'état* destroyed the constitutional liberties of France, and De Tocqueville, unwilling to take an oath of fidelity to one whom he regarded as a usurper, retired altogether to private life. Up to February, 1848, he was a member of the opposition, and contended strongly, though without personal animosity, against Guizot's ministry; after the Revolution, he joined the party of the moderate republicans, who, with Cavaignac for a leader, strove gallantly, though with only faint hopes of success, against the mad schemes of the radicals on the one hand, and the intriguing ambition of the future Emperor on the other. But it must be owned that his mind was of too fine a texture, his principles too pure and unwavering, and his disposition for abstract thought and analytical investigation too strongly marked, to allow him to succeed in the strife of parties or the tournaments of parliamentary debate. He commanded the confidence of his friends and the respect of his opponents; but he was not put forward into the front rank in battle, nor elevated to the chief seat in council. The best portions of his parliamentary labors were his reports on the abolition of colonial slavery, on prison reform, and on the administration of Algeria, a country which he had twice visited, and whose affairs he thoroughly understood. When the new Republic was settling into a calm, he became a member of the Committee appointed to frame a new Constitution for France, and endeavored in vain to induce his colleagues to adopt the principle of a division of the legislature into two houses. Louis Napoleon understood his value arising from his weight of character, and endeavored to secure his aid by offering him considerable attention. But the bribe of a usurper was coldly declined. After dining with the President on one occasion at the Elysée, De Tocqueville remarked on leaving, "I have been dining with a man who believes in his own hereditary right to the crown as firmly as Charles X. himself."

"One chance remained to avert the final catastrophe. It was possible that the President might still be content to accept a constitutional position; to govern by responsible ministers, who hoped to effect a revision of the constitution by legal means. At any rate, to abandon or to oppose him was to compel him to resort to an immediate *coup d'état*. On this principle, M. Odilon Barrot and the leading liberals formed an administration on the 2d June, 1849, in which M. de Tocqueville took the important office of Minister of Foreign Affairs. It would be inappropriate here to enter upon the political transactions in which he was engaged. As he said, on quitting his office four months later,—'I have contributed to maintain order on the 13th of June, to preserve the general peace, to improve the relations of France and England. These are recollections which give some value to my passage through affairs. I need hardly say anything to you of the cause which led to the fall of the Cabinet. The President chooses to govern alone, and to have mere agents and creatures in his ministers. Perhaps he is right. I don't examine that question, but we were not the men to serve him on these terms.'"

After leaving the ministry, as his health was considerably impaired, he went to Italy, and spent the winter at Sorrento, engaged in his literary undertakings. On his return, he took little share in the proceedings of the

Assembly, except to draw up the celebrated Report on the Revision of the Constitution, which was presented on the 8th of July, 1851. It was the ablest of his parliamentary productions, and the presentation of it may be regarded as the closing act of his political life.

Yet he was present in the struggle, if it can be called one, of the 2d of December, 1851, and, in company with about 230 other representatives, signed a paper deposing the President from all authority, and requiring the High Court of Justice to proceed to judgment against him and his accomplices. It was a bootless proceeding, except for the purpose of putting on record the protest of the legislature; for Louis Napoleon immediately arrested the whole party, and the High Court of Justice too, and sent them to prison, whence most of them were released after only two days' confinement. De Tocqueville drew up a temperate narrative of the proceeding, which he published in *The Times* newspaper, England being then the only country in Europe where such a document could be printed with impunity. Then, with a sad heart, he went back to his residence in the country, to give the few years of life which remained to intercourse with his friends, to the care of his estate, and to one other literary effort in which he was deeply interested.

This project, as originally conceived, was that of a new history of the first French Revolution, with especial reference to the causes which had produced it in the preceding state of the country and the government. It was not to be so much a narrative of events, as a philosophical inquiry into the nature of the circumstances which precede and originate great changes in the constitution of society. Perhaps it would have been better if he had acted earlier upon the conviction which he expressed in January, 1851, in a letter to a friend. "It has occurred to me a hundred times," he says, "that, if I am to leave any traces of my passage through the world, it will be far more by my writings than by my actions." His subject required much research, not only in the great public libraries of the state, but among the archives of the old provincial administrations, especially in that of Tours; and to facilitate these researches, as well as to benefit his health, he resided for some months in 1854 at St. Cyr, near Tours. The next year, he visited Germany, and learned the language of the country, that he might be able to consult original documents in German. The first part of his work was published in 1856, entitled *L'Ancien Régime et la Revolution*, and was received with decided tokens of general approbation. It was translated into several languages, and commended in all the leading journals of Europe. Yet it was only a fragment, as the whole work would probably have filled three volumes. Two chapters only of the second volume were found at his death in so finished a state as to warrant their publication in his "Memoirs and Correspondence." The manuscript preparations for the remainder of the work were very extensive, but not in a state fit for presentation to the public.

Among his other unfinished works was one of considerable length, on the "Establishment of the English in India." His pen was always active, but he was chary of publication, except of a work which might aid some important object, or add to its author's fame; he could not tolerate bookmaking. Hence, though he left a great amount of manuscript, it is probable that only a small portion of it will ever see the light. One important fragment of contemporary history, however, will probably appear as soon as the French government can tolerate it, and delicacy to surviving individuals will permit; it is entitled "Souvenirs," and relates chiefly to public affairs in France in 1848-49. Some very interesting portions of his correspondence, also, are as yet kept back, as their appearance might irritate the government or wound the feelings of persons in private life.

The health of De Tocqueville had never been robust, and ever after 1850, at least, when he was compelled to spend the winter at Sorrento, he was affected by pulmonary disease, though it appears to have escaped the observation both of himself and his medical attendants. But in the summer of 1858 he broke a bloodvessel, and showed other unequivocal symptoms of the fatal malady. In the autumn, as his strength had rapidly declined, his physicians required him to go to the South of France for the winter. Though very reluctant to leave home, he prepared to obey; and having made large provision of books, manuscripts, and other materials for the completion of his work, he set out for Cannes, where he arrived early in November, 1858. He was accompanied by his wife and his brothers, and was visited in Provençe by several of his friends. With others he kept up a frequent correspondence, and even labored at times upon his work during the winter, though it was evident to every eye but his own that he was sinking fast. Christian faith, which had always governed his convictions and regulated his life, supported him in his last moments. Having received the sacraments according to the rites of that Church to which he was strongly attached, he died on the 16th of April, 1859, at the age of fifty-four. In conformity with his own request, his remains were carried to Tocqueville, and in the village cemetery there a plain wooden cross marks his grave.

THE END.

Cambridge: Stereotyped and Printed by Welch, Bigelow, & Co.

www.ingramcontent.com/pod-product-compliance
Lightning Source LLC
LaVergne TN
LVHW021316110826
845150LV00003B/587

* 9 7 8 1 4 2 5 5 5 7 7 3 7 *